LLEWELLYN'S NEW

A to Z

HOROSCOPE
MAKER AND
INTERPRETER

The Classic Text Revised & Expanded by
STEPHANIE JEAN CLEMENT, PH.D.
& MARYLEE BYTHERIVER

LLEWELLYN GEORGE

Llewellyn Publications
St. Paul, Minnesota U.S.A.

Llewellyn's New A to Z Horoscope Maker and Interpreter © 1981 by Llewellyn George, © 2003 by Llewellyn Worldwide, Ltd.

Fourteenth Edition (revised) 2003
Second Printing 2004

First Edition 1910

Cover design by the Llewellyn art department
Interior illustrations by the Llewellyn art department

Chart wheels were produced by the Kepler program by permission of Cosmic Patterns Software, Inc. (www.AstroSoftware.com)

ISBN 0-7387-0322-2
Library of Congress Cataloging-in-Publication Data (pending)

Llewellyn Publications
A Division of Llewellyn Worldwide, Ltd.
P.O. Box 64383, Dept. 0-7387-0322-2
St. Paul, MN 55164-0383, U.S.A.
www.llewellyn.com

 Printed in the United States of America on recycled paper

Dedication

To students of the useful arts and sciences and lovers of truth: to assist further research into the laws of nature, as interpreted by astrology, for the benefit of all beings.

And

To astrology teachers everywhere, who instruct and support their students to learn this ancient science and art of astrology.

Contents

Figures:

Tables:

FOREWORD

Llewellyn George was born on August 17, 1876, at 4:18 A.M. in Swansea, Wales. He grew up in Chicago, where he graduated from the Chicago School of Electricity in 1898. Though he was largely self-educated in the fields of philosophy and astrology, he did complete a course at the Sweltmer Institute of Suggestive Therapeutics in Nevada, Missouri.

After graduation, George moved to Portland, Oregon, and began to study astrology under Professor W. H. Chaney. At that time there was a growing interest in all metaphysical subjects among advanced thinkers in the U.S. and England.

In 1906 George published the first issue of *The Moon Sign Book*, which has been in continuous publication ever since. This annual almanac was as unique then as it is now, giving accurate, practical information on using the Moon's cycles in gardening and other daily activities.

In 1910 George published his major work, the *A to Z Horoscope Maker and Delineator,* from which this present volume stems. At that time there were very few good astrology books in English. Except for translations of historical manuscripts, Alan Leo's works were the only quality textbooks available.

As astrology gained respectability and prestige during George's long career, he became increasingly optimistic and sought every opportunity to popularize and publicize astrology. He wrote in the early 1940s, "Astrology is making rapid strides forward. The time has arrived for the masses as a whole to take an interest in the subject seriously and practically. Astrology has a grander, nobler, greater mission now than ever before in history."

Llewellyn George died in 1954 at the age of seventy-seven. His ideas continue to be relevant today. He, perhaps more than any other astrologer in the twentieth century, is credited with reestablishing astrology as a valid and workable system and removing the connotations of charlatanry and superstition from the astrologer's trade.

Many years ago Llewellyn George wrote:

> *By conscious cooperation with natural law indicated by the solar system, conditions are created which provide opportunities for us to rise above the common illusions of life by spiritual interpretation and finer reactions.*
>
> *If from these pages the reader gains but a small part of the pleasure and practical benefit the author has derived from the study of astrology, I will feel well repaid for thus presenting the results of investigation and practice which have extended over many years.*

INTRODUCTION

The word *astrology* derives from two Greek words: *astra*, a star, and *logos*, logic or reason. The study of astrology uses logic and reason to understand our relationship to the larger universe.

At one time no distinction was made between astronomy and astrology—all who studied the subject were called astrologers. Astronomy in contemporary times focuses on the purely objective study of the heavens, while astrology uses those objective observations to delve into the profound relationships of all parts of creation.

The advent of astrological computing programs has made the study of the mathematics less essential than it once was. Still, understanding the theory of chart construction is a valuable study, and the calculation portions of this book have been retained. They are found together in an appendix, along with sample pages from the ephemeris and table of houses, to illustrate the process of casting a chart.

The bulk of the book reflects the original work of Llewellyn George. His in-depth approach to horoscope delineation includes a level of detail seldom found in other astrological writings. His interpretations of the planets in the signs, houses, and aspect combinations are very fine, and he distinguishes among natal, progressed, and transiting aspects as well.

A new section on contemporary astrology has been added. Some of the techniques found in this section are not new at all, but their applications are revitalized by the advent of computer programs. The student can now create charts in a matter of moments that once took many hours to create. The level of accuracy is assured, as long as the birth data is input correctly and the appropriate charts are selected.

Modern techniques include cosmobiology, the use of Transneptunian points, asteroids, and Chiron. These tools provide new visual perspectives in astrology, and add a transpersonal viewpoint to this ancient science and art.

My own study of astrology has spanned a period of thirty years. For me, the astrological model explains all significant facets of life: physical, mental, emotional, and spiritual. I do not consider astrology to be my religion. It is, however, a mechanism by which we can perceive the order in our lives. We have the capacity and the responsibility to determine how to use our gifts and talents to make our lives more productive and more spiritually satisfying.

One of my first astrology texts was the *A to Z Horoscope Maker and Delineator*. In editing this new revision, I have rediscovered concepts, and I have remembered ideas so much a part of my astrological work that I don't even consciously consider them when I do a chart. This single book is the best compilation of astrological lore in print. Use it to discover or expand your understanding of the ancient art and science of astrology.

Stephanie Jean Clement, Ph.D.
September, 2002

Part One

BASIC PRINCIPLES OF ASTROLOGY

THE SIGNS OF THE ZODIAC

The Zodiac is a circle of space in the sky, containing the orbits of the planets. It may be imagined as a belt of space in the heavens about 15 degrees wide in which the planets travel. It is also the Sun's apparent path called the ecliptic. The zodiacal circle is divided into twelve parts; each part contains 30 degrees of space, making a total of 360 degrees in the circle. The twelve divisions are known as the *signs of the Zodiac.*

Each zodiacal sign possesses a certain specific influence and quality of its own. The revolution of the earth around the Sun, complete in one year, causes the Sun to appear to travel through the Zodiac at the rate of one sign per month, or approximately through 1 degree per day, and its influence (according to sign and degree) determines not only the seasons but also the general nature and character of beings born at that time.

The various planets as they travel through the Zodiac also exert an influence according to their separate natures and in correspondence with the quality of each aspect that they may form, blended with the nature of the signs in which they are located. The luminaries (Sun and Moon) are classified as planets, for convenience (see *The Planets in the Signs* in part 2).

When erecting a chart or horoscope, we draw a circle and divide it into twelve spaces. These spaces, or *houses,* are numbered from one to twelve. The First House is the space that is located just below the eastern angle of the chart on the left-hand side. The Twelfth House is the space just *above* the eastern angle. The cusps are the dividing lines between these houses. The sign that is placed on the cusp of the First House—i.e., the line marking the eastern horizon—is called the *rising sign,* or *Ascendant.* In the chart in figure 2, you will find the degree and sign on each house cusp. Note that opposite cusps share the same degree.

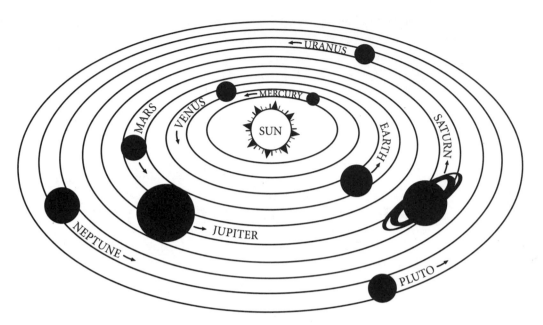

Figure 1: The Solar System

To an ordinary observer, the earth appears to be stationary and the signs of the Zodiac seem to revolve around it from east to west. This appearance is due to the rotation of the earth from west to east. This causes a new degree of the Zodiac to appear to ascend above the eastern horizon every four minutes, a complete sign every two hours, and the whole twelve signs of the Zodiac in twenty-four hours. The First House is *always* the space just under the eastern horizon, regardless of which sign might be passing over that cusp.

Astrological researchers are very particular as to the time of a birth, in order to determine exactly what degree and sign were on the eastern horizon at that time.

"Each star has its own glory," quotes the Bible. Astrologers have determined that each of the twelve signs has its own distinctive qualities that are bestowed upon individuals according to their birthday. In fact, during the long ages in which some of the brightest minds of the world have given attention to the influence of the signs of the Zodiac, they have found that each of the 360 degrees, constituting the zodiacal circle, has a specific influence. The meanings resonate with individuals who have planets in those degrees.

At the moment of birth, one of the twelve signs of the Zodiac and 1 degree out of the 30 degrees constituting that particular sign are ascending on the eastern horizon, and these largely determine the personality and characteristics of that individual.

It is obvious that as the earth turns 1 degree in four minutes, 30 degrees (or one sign) will appear and pass up over the horizon every two hours; while during the twenty-four hours of one day all the signs and degrees will have passed the horizon. Consequently, it would seem that during the day there would be twelve types (signs) of characters, with thirty variations (degrees) in each sign type. By this is seen one reason why humans differ, instead of being all alike, when born on the same day. To accentuate this dissimilarity among those closely related in point of time (but disassociated in point of space), we have also to consider such elements as race, caste, and hereditary strain.

However, we are mainly concerned with potent astrological influences. If the earth's rotation on its axis were the only factor involved, we would have the comparatively limited number of 360 characters representing 360 zodiacal degrees differentiated (in groups of thirty) by the twelve signs. But in reality this number is augmented by the fact that during rotation on its axis in one day, the earth is also transiting 1 degree along its orbit, thereby each day giving a new variety to the types and the 360 variations of those born in that rotation. This variety multiplies for approximately thirty days during which time the earth will have traversed 30 degrees in orbit and will then enter the next sign of the Zodiac, to repeat the daily variations with a different lot of individuals under a new month-sign. The orbit transit from one sign to another determines the type of individuality, while, as before stated, the rotation on axis determines the type of personality. Thus, people born in the same Sun sign inherently possess similar individualities, but the date of the month and the time of day both operate to provide different personalities.

Astrologically, the individuality is designated by the apparent zodiacal position of the Sun; and personality is designated by the ascending degree and sign, due to the relative axial position of the earth as indicated from any certain latitude.

Individuality may be considered to be the inherent qualities, tendencies, and latent powers or those inner qualities by which the individual knows himself.

Personality may be regarded as the style or nature of expression that outwardly characterizes the person; that which distinguishes him and identifies him to others.

It has been said by esoteric students that your ascending sign in this birth was your Sun sign in the preceding incarnation; what is your Sun sign now will be your ascending sign in the next life. If your Sun sign and your Ascendant are now the same, you are repeating that sign because you failed to complete it properly or fully in your previous incarnation.

To this great variety of differences manifested in human beings, other astrological factors must be reckoned. Here are a few of those that make a considerable difference: the Sun either above or below the horizon at the moment of birth; the Moon above or below; the Moon's distance from the Ascendant; the location and position of the other planets by sign and house; the latitude and longitude of the place of birth, etc. All these factors act to produce the innumerable specimens of humanity.

Ascendant: Axial Rotation of the Earth Determines Personality

Every four minutes: a new ascending degree.

Every two hours: a new zodiacal sign.

Every twenty-four hours: twelve signs or 360°.

360 variations per day (axial) multiplied by 365 days per year (orbital) equals 131,400 variations of personality yearly.

Sun Sign: Orbital Revolutions of the Earth Determine Individuality

Each day: approximately 1 degree of the Zodiac.

Each month: one sign, giving the Sun the appearance of passing through one sign each month.

One year: twelve signs or 360°.

360 variations of individuality yearly.

Adding the variations produced by these earth movements, we have a total of 131,760 astrological types.

You may learn a great deal about anyone just by studying his or her Sun sign. You may acquire additional information by studying his or her Ascendant. You may learn still more about that person when you read the influence of the planets as they were located in the different signs at the time of birth. The house positions of the planets at the time of birth will provide further revelations.

Fate versus Free Will

The progressive student will do well to remember that destiny properly means "whatever is possible unto us," and fate means "the outward circumstances which appear in our pathway, to be manipulated and eventually overcome through effort and understanding." He who would slay dragons must first learn their habits. To overcome fate you must first know your fate. Astrology points the way to that desirable information.

Astrology is not a doctrine of fatalism. It provides us with an inventory of the working materials with which we were endowed at birth in the form of tendencies, mental capacity, physical endowments, and abilities; but how you use or neglect to use the tools remains within your own jurisdiction. "Wisdom puts an end to pain." Through astrology, you learn to improve your workmanship on the wheel of life and consequently to improve your fate by complying consciously with nature's laws instead of violating them.

Earth-Centered Astrology

This system of astrology is known as the modernized Arabian system, the oldest known system, but revised and adapted to present times and people. Corresponding to and harmonizing with astronomy, it is necessarily *geocentric* in its methods (*geo*, meaning "earth," and *centric*, meaning "center"). In other words, we use the earth as a center of influence and observation.

As it is difficult to perceive the movement of the earth in its orbit at the rate of 1,102.8 miles per minute, and as the apparent movement of the Sun seems so real, for simplicity and convenience these two bodies are transposed; that is, the earth is put in the center and the Sun is seen to transit the earth's path. Thus, modern astrology uses a geocentric instead of heliocentric system.

The earth is a planet whose orbit lies between that of Venus and Mars. It has an axial rotation complete in twenty-four hours, producing diurnal and nocturnal phenomena. This rotation from west to east gives the appearance of the Sun, Moon, and stars rising in the east and setting in the west, while actually the reverse is true. They in reality proceed in the direction of the order of the signs, from Aries to Taurus, etc. The earth's passage through the Zodiac, in which it revolves around the Sun in approximately 365¼ days, causes the Sun to appear to be transiting through the signs opposite to those through which the earth courses, hence the expressions *Sun in Aries, Sun in Taurus,* etc. When the Sun seems to be in Aries between March 21 and April 19, the earth is in the opposite sign, Libra, but the astrological influence and position are designated as Sun in Aries.

Placing the earth in the center of the chart also makes it easy to visualize how the signs appear to ascend on the eastern horizon and descend on the western horizon, as the earth turns on its axis.

The Chart Illustrated

The chart shown in figure 2 illustrates the position that the houses always maintain in a horoscope, as well as the direction in which the signs and planets appear to move, as already mentioned. It is a conventional type of astrological diagram of the heavens (Zodiac) at a certain date, time, and place.

The outer circle shows degrees of the signs that are crossing over the dividing cusps of the houses. The houses are the twelve segments or spaces in which the planets' place can be recorded, and are numbered one through twelve.

As the birthday was between August 23 and September 22, the Sun is in the zodiacal sign Virgo, so the Sun sign for this chart is Virgo.

At the time of day for this chart, the zodiacal sign Libra was on the Ascendant, of which 14 degrees was ascending or crossing the First House cusp. Each sign has 30° (a measurement of longitude). Table 1 shows how degrees of longitude make up the full circle of the Zodiac.

60 seconds (") make 1 minute (')

60 minutes (') make 1 degree (°)

30 degrees (°) make 1 sign

12 signs (or 360°) make a complete circle—the Zodiac

Table 1: Longitude

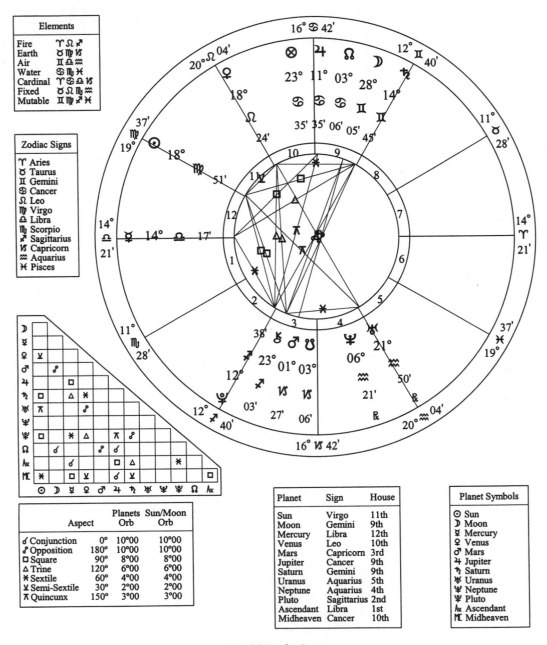

Elements

Fire	♈ ♌ ♐
Earth	♉ ♍ ♑
Air	♊ ♎ ♒
Water	♋ ♏ ♓
Cardinal	♈ ♋ ♎ ♑
Fixed	♉ ♌ ♏ ♒
Mutable	♊ ♍ ♐ ♓

Zodiac Signs

♈	Aries
♉	Taurus
♊	Gemini
♋	Cancer
♌	Leo
♍	Virgo
♎	Libra
♏	Scorpio
♐	Sagittarius
♑	Capricorn
♒	Aquarius
♓	Pisces

Aspect		Planets Orb	Sun/Moon Orb
☌ Conjunction	0°	10°00	10°00
☍ Opposition	180°	10°00	10°00
□ Square	90°	8°00	8°00
△ Trine	120°	6°00	6°00
✶ Sextile	60°	4°00	4°00
⚺ Semi-Sextile	30°	2°00	2°00
⊼ Quincunx	150°	3°00	3°00

Planet	Sign	House
Sun	Virgo	11th
Moon	Gemini	9th
Mercury	Libra	12th
Venus	Leo	10th
Mars	Capricorn	3rd
Jupiter	Cancer	9th
Saturn	Gemini	9th
Uranus	Aquarius	5th
Neptune	Aquarius	4th
Pluto	Sagittarius	2nd
Ascendant	Libra	1st
Midheaven	Cancer	10th

Planet Symbols

☉	Sun
☽	Moon
☿	Mercury
♀	Venus
♂	Mars
♃	Jupiter
♄	Saturn
♅	Uranus
♆	Neptune
♇	Pluto
Aᴄ	Ascendant
♍	Midheaven

World Trade Center

September 11, 2001 / New York, NY / 8:46 A.M. EST

Placidus Houses

Figure 2: The Chart Illustrated

♈	Aries	♎	Libra
♉	Taurus	♏	Scorpio
♊	Gemini	♐	Sagittarius
♋	Cancer	♑	Capricorn
♌	Leo	♒	Aquarius
♍	Virgo	♓	Pisces

Table 2: The Signs

Note: When placed in a chart, the signs of the Zodiac always come opposite to each other as shown here. Learn them in that order. In figure 2, note how the signs are placed on opposite cusps as shown in this table.

Practice making the symbols until you can make them very quickly and read them without referring to the text. Learn which signs are opposite each other. Also memorize thoroughly the names of the signs with their planetary rulers. Remember that a planet is a heavenly body, a sign is a space in the Zodiac, and a house is a section of a chart.

The Planetary Rulers

There is a corresponding vibration, a harmonious interchange as it were, between certain zodiacal signs and certain planets. To each sign is therefore assigned a planet which is that its *ruler*. Venus and Mercury each rule two signs. Memorize table 3, which contains the planetary rulerships.

♂ Mars rules ♈ Aries

♀ Venus rules ♉ Taurus and ♎ Libra

☿ Mercury rules ♊ Gemini and ♍ Virgo

☽ Moon rules ♋ Cancer

☉ Sun rules ♌ Leo

♇ Pluto rules ♏ Scorpio

♃ Jupiter rules ♐ Sagittarius

♄ Saturn rules ♑ Capricorn

♅ Uranus rules ♒ Aquarius

♆ Neptune rules ♓ Pisces

Table 3: The Signs and Their Planetary Rulers

Zones of the Human Body Ruled by the Zodiacal Signs

- Aries rules the head and face.
- Taurus rules the neck, throat, and ears.
- Gemini rules the hands, arms, shoulders, collarbone, lungs, and nervous system.
- Cancer rules the breasts and stomach.
- Leo rules the heart, sides, and the upper portion of the back.
- Virgo rules the solar plexus and the bowels.
- Libra rules the kidneys, veins, loins, ovaries, and the lower back.
- Scorpio rules the bladder and the sex organs.
- Sagittarius rules the liver, hips, and thighs.
- Capricorn rules the knees.
- Aquarius rules the calves and ankles.
- Pisces rules the feet.

Triplicity, or Trigon

The zodiacal signs are divided into four groups called *triplicities* (groups of three), representing the four elements: fire, earth, air, and water. These manifest in humanity as four specific temperaments.

The Fire Triplicity: Aries, Leo, Sagittarius

The fire triplicity is represented by the choleric or hot temperament, exhibiting a rash, feverish, easily excited, or impulsive nature, with inflammatory and bilious affections, and sudden illness, which is generally acute but usually of short duration.

The fiery signs represent the vital spirit, the bodily heat with its elements of combustion, all of which incline to activity: political, military, and speculative interests.

To this triplicity of fire and spirit belong the little nature spirits called Salamanders.

The Earth Triplicity: Taurus, Virgo, Capricorn

The earth triplicity is represented by the phlegmatic or nervous temperament, more especially noticed through Virgo and Capricorn, exhibiting alert, restless, worried, agitated, neurasthenic characteristics, with disposition to rheumatism and chronic disorders. The earthly signs represent the physical or temporal states, all of which produce artistic, imaginative, studious, and organizing tendencies.

"Little folk of the hills and vales," or Gnomes, as they are usually called, have an especial affinity for the triplicity of earth.

The Air Triplicity: Gemini, Libra, Aquarius

The air triplicity is represented by the sanguine temperament, exhibiting active circulation, plump body, good complexion, genial nature, cheerful anticipation, good fellowship, and general dexterity. The air signs are said to represent the relative or connective conditions both within and without the body. For instance, Gemini rules the nervous system, which connects the entire body and even neighbors, with whom the native is associated. This trigon expresses as active, scientific, and industrial. It has a tendency toward illnesses arising from exhaustion or overexertion.

In this airy family we find another relative not ordinarily included in that category—Sylphs.

The Water Triplicity: Cancer, Scorpio, Pisces

The water triplicity is represented by the melancholic or lymphatic temperament, exhibiting as languid, anemic, pallid, weak-pulsed, lack of red corpuscles in the blood, and deficient vascular action. The watery trigon represents the mutational and propagative conditions. This triplicity is known for being emotional, plastic, and contemplative.

Sprites of the waters, the Undines, find their best expression through the watery signs.

Quadrature, or Mode

The zodiacal signs are also divided into three groups called *quadratures,* representing cardinal, fixed, and mutable signs.

The Cardinal (or Movable) Signs: Aries, Cancer, Libra, Capricorn

The cardinal signs may be likened to the cardinal points of a compass: Aries, east; Libra, west; Cancer, north; Capricorn, south. These signs are called cardinal signs because they are the first signs in each season: Aries, spring; Cancer, summer; Libra, fall; Capricorn, winter. These changes of season are due to the Sun's apparent change of declination or, in reality, to the obliquity of the earth according to its location in its orbit.

Persons born during the time of cardinal signs are said to be versatile, adaptable, and readily capable of adjusting themselves to changing conditions as they occur.

The Fixed Signs: Taurus, Leo, Scorpio, Aquarius

The fixed signs may be likened to the middle of the season, there being three signs to every season. If the cardinal signs bring us into a change of season, then the fixed signs see us firmly centered or set in those seasons.

Those born in fixed signs are more set in their ways and more fixed in their views than those born in cardinal or mutable signs. They are likely to have more continuity and be more difficult to move, change, or sway. They do not readily change their minds, and are not so quick to adjust and adapt themselves.

The Mutable (or Common or Flexed) Signs: Gemini, Virgo, Sagittarius, Pisces

Mutable signs are the third or last months of the four seasons. We have all become well acquainted with the season throughout the cardinal and fixed months, and in the mutable signs we finish up the duties that are common to the season and begin to prepare for the change in the next quarter.

Those born in mutable signs have more or less the attributes of both the cardinal and fixed signs and can adapt themselves to the natures of both those signs; consequently, to the natives of the other signs, those of mutable signs seem to be unstable.

Classifications

Fruitful signs: Cancer, Scorpio, Pisces.

Barren signs: Aries, Gemini, Leo, Virgo, Sagittarius, Aquarius.

Semifruitful signs: Taurus, Libra, Capricorn.

Masculine, or positive, signs: Aries, Gemini, Leo, Libra, Sagittarius, Aquarius.

Feminine, or negative, signs: Taurus, Cancer, Virgo, Scorpio, Capricorn, Pisces.

Northern signs: Aries, Taurus, Gemini, Cancer, Leo, Virgo; signs in which the Sun has north declination from March 21 to September 23.

Southern signs: Libra, Scorpio, Sagittarius, Capricorn, Aquarius, Pisces; signs in which the Sun has south declination from September 24 to March 20.

Signs of short ascension: Capricorn, Aquarius, Pisces, Aries, Taurus, Gemini; these are signs that take less than two hours to rise over the horizon. Note that for places in the Southern Hemisphere, the signs of long and short ascension must be reversed.

Signs of long ascension: Cancer, Leo, Virgo, Libra, Scorpio, Sagittarius; these signs take longer to ascend over the horizon.

Bicorporeal, or double-bodied, signs: Gemini, Pisces, and the first half of Sagittarius; each sign is pictured as having two distinct parts: Gemini, the twins; Sagittarius, the horse and the archer; Pisces, the two fishes. They incline toward duality.

Equinoctial signs: Aries, Libra. These signs begin on the spring equinox, March 21, and the autumnal equinox, September 23.

Tropical signs: Cancer, Capricorn. The points in the ecliptic in which the Sun is farthest from the equator occur on June 22, the beginning of Cancer, at the Tropic of Cancer; and on December 22, the beginning of Capricorn, at the Tropic of Capricorn.

Human signs: Gemini, Virgo, Aquarius, and the first part of Sagittarius.

Bestial signs: Aries, Taurus, Leo, Capricorn, and the last half of Sagittarius.

Signs of voice: Gemini, Virgo, Libra, Sagittarius, and Aquarius.

Mute signs: Cancer, Scorpio, Pisces.

Decans

A decan, or decanate, consists of 10 degrees or one-third of a sign, hence there are three decans in each sign and thirty-six in the Zodiac. While a planet rules its sign as a whole and especially the first decan, the other two divisions of a sign each express a subinfluence of the planets that rule the remaining signs of the same triplicity. The most common method of assigning planets to decans uses planets that rule the signs of the same element. To illustrate: for Aries, Mars rules the whole sign and the first decan; the Sun, because it rules the next sign of the fire triplicity, Leo, rules the second decan; and Jupiter, because it rules the next sign of the fire triplicity, Sagittarius, rules the third decan.

The use of decans in natal astrology is applicable principally to the ascending sign. By noting which decan is on the First House cusp, we get an idea of what particular part of the sign the native is expressing. The planet ruling the decan ascending should be given attention along with the other planets that are the rulers in the horoscope.

Signs	0°–10°	11°–20°	21°–30°
Aries	Mars	Sun	Jupiter
Taurus	Venus	Mercury	Saturn
Gemini	Mercury	Venus	Uranus
Cancer	Moon	Pluto	Neptune
Leo	Sun	Jupiter	Mars
Virgo	Mercury	Saturn	Venus
Libra	Venus	Uranus	Mercury
Scorpio	Pluto	Neptune	Moon
Sagittarius	Jupiter	Mars	Sun
Capricorn	Saturn	Venus	Mercury
Aquarius	Uranus	Mercury	Venus
Pisces	Neptune	Moon	Pluto

Table 4: The Decans

THE PLANETS

Astrologers use ten of the heavenly bodies because of their size, proximity, and influence on the earth and on its human, animal, vegetable, and mineral kingdoms. In the proper order of their speed through the Zodiac, they are: ☽ the Moon, ☿ Mercury, ♀ Venus, ☉ the Sun, ♂ Mars, ♃ Jupiter, ♄ Saturn, ♅ Uranus, ♆ Neptune, and ♇ Pluto.

From our perspective on earth, it is simpler to imagine the earth as the center of observation and all planets revolving around it. In astronomy the Sun is the center of our solar system, and the earth actually revolves around the Sun in an orbit between Venus and Mars.

The Moon is a satellite of the earth and revolves about it. To an observer on the earth the Moon appears to be going through one sign after another, making the circuit in approximately twenty-eight days.

Nature of the Planets

The benefic planets are Jupiter and Venus; Jupiter is known as "the greater fortune" and Venus as "the lesser fortune." The influence of the Sun and Moon is also considered good.

Mars, Saturn, and Uranus are known as the malefics.

Mercury, Neptune, and Pluto are neutral planets—their influence is good when they are well aspected with other planets, but malefic when adversely aspected.

When you see words like "malefic," "adverse," "bad," "unfavorable," etc., bear in mind that such terms are used only for want of terminology that more fittingly describes planetary vibrations. All signs and all planets are good but our human reactions may be bad, according to our stage of development. As more people become astrologically educated, a new terminology will develop that will more definitely describe astrological influences. Later it will be shown that no planets are evil in nature, but our manifested responses may be judged as good or adverse.

The Moon

The Moon rules the domestic and maternal interests and represents the personality as shown outwardly. Personality is what we see of a person in physical appearance, word, act, etc., which distinguishes one person from another. If the Moon is well placed in the horoscope, the person exhibits a pleasing personality; vice versa if the Moon is not. Refer to what was said in the previous chapter about the sign ascending at the moment of birth and the personality.

The Moon is moist, cold, plastic, feminine, and fruitful. It governs the stomach and breasts and rules liquids and common commodities.

The Moon rules reproduction, the domestic and maternal instinct, growth of plant life, and publicity.

Mercury

Mercury is related to or rules the mind, objective sight, perception, and expression and has dominion over communications, travel, barter, and trade.

Mercury is neutral, convertible, cold, and moist. It governs the nervous system and intellectual perception. It rules handwriting, study, literature, and journalism.

Mercury rules sight, imitation, and the power to learn and convey to others what has been learned.

Venus

Venus rules the affections (love), the sense of touch, art, pleasure, toiletries, and luxury.

Venus is feminine, passive, warm, moist, fruitful, and benefic. It rules the throat and veins, and inclines to the finer attributes of the mind as expressed through the arts and crafts, grace, beauty, adornment, refined amusement, sympathy, and compassion. It is called the "lesser fortune." Venus rules conjugality, love, music, coquetry, entertainment, and sociability.

The Sun

The Sun rules character, individuality (that which we are), power and authority, the "top man."

The Sun is hot, dry, masculine, inflammatory, and electric. It also governs the sides, back, and heart. It signifies influence and high office.

The Sun rules the hope, courage, magnanimity, and the aspirations. It represents rulership and honor.

Mars

Mars rules energy, force, action, muscle, enterprise, initiative, contention, desire, the sense of taste, and accidents.

Mars is hot, dry, masculine, inflammatory, and malefic. It governs the head, face, and muscular system. It signifies strength and activity.

Mars rules volition, work, conquest, the desires, construction, and destruction.

Jupiter

Jupiter rules benevolence, expansion, optimism, and confidence in the meaning and purpose of life.

Jupiter is hot, moist, moderate, and temperate. It governs the blood, liver, and thighs. It rules reason and judgment. Being a benefic, its tendency is toward opulence and success and is called the "greater fortune."

Jupiter rules promotion, growth, joviality, reasoning, calculation, and philosophy.

Saturn

Saturn rules solidification, discrimination, reserve, delay, sorrow, and the sense of hearing.

Saturn is cold, hard, earthly, masculine, and malefic. It governs the bones generally, and the knees and spleen particularly. It is grave, cautious, and binding.

Saturn rules form and organization. It is contractile, cohesive, adhesive, cooling, and sustaining.

Uranus

Uranus rules inner sight (clairvoyance), intuition, surprise, adventure, ingenuity, originality, and invention.

Uranus is cold, dry, airy, positive, electromagnetic, occult, extreme, spasmodic, and precipitate. It governs the aura and intuitive perception and rules invention, investigation, reforms, revolution, and rebellion.

Neptune

Neptune rules feeling without physical contact (psychometry), psychics, and perversion.

Neptune is cold, moist, neutral, convertible, negative, and neurotic. It governs spirit perception and mediumship. It rules secret, mysterious, questionable, and obscure matters, as well as idealism and aesthetic art.

Neptune rules the psychic faculty, the sea, serums, narcotics, and mystery.

Pluto

Pluto is concerned with the underworld, poison, death, and other such murky matters. It has affinity with interests related to rejuvenation, regeneration, transformation, metamorphosis, the spirit world, materializations, and astral projection. It is concerned with the subconscious mind and the conscience, metabolism, and assimilation. Also chemistry, alchemy, refining processes, poisonous fumes, lethal drugs, counterirritants like liniments and capsicum, and possibly volatile oils and vapors used for energy and power.

Pluto rules the conscience, that inner prompter that helps us judge right from wrong. It also rules subconscious activities and stern, incorruptible judges.

A distinction should be made between the different ways in which signs and planets express their energy. The signs correspond to parts of the body and, by analogy, parts of the psyche. The twelve signs together represent the sum total of physical and psychological functioning. Their expression is moderated by the placement of the planets and their rulerships over the signs. Thus, a planet channels, interferes with, intensifies, concretizes, or affects in some way, according to the nature of that planet, the sign it is in, and the sign where it has rulership.

Octaves

Venus and Neptune

Venus, ruler of the signs Taurus and Libra, calls forth a response from the finer attributes of the being, inclining to beauty, harmony, sociability, gaiety, and popular music. It gives appreciation or ability for art and for producing beautiful music. Neptune is termed the higher octave of Venus. It reveres beauty in its broader, deeper, or universal aspect, in contradistinction to personal appearances. Venus may be said to represent the cultivated musician; Neptune the inspired. Venus rules the sense of touch or feeling; Neptune rules the psychometric faculty. Venus and Neptune are natural complements. Venus is exalted in Neptune's sign, Pisces.

Mercury and Uranus

Mercury is the ruler of the mental signs, Gemini and Virgo. Mercury rules ordinary mental processes through which one acquires knowledge by observation, perception, reading, writing, speaking, and listening.

Uranus is termed a higher octave of Mercury. It rules a mental sign, Aquarius. It governs that phase of the mind that is not dependent upon the ordinary perceptive processes. Mercury represents knowledge we acquire through present conditions; Uranus represents accumulated wisdom gained through previous experiences manifesting as intuition. Mercury is the learner; Uranus is the knower. Mercury rules sight; Uranus rules clairvoyance.

Mars and Pluto

Mars, ruler of Aries, is concerned with physical and sexual energy. It rules the physical body, health, and energy that is directed outward.

Pluto is a higher octave of Mars. Pluto is concerned with energy that is directed inward for spiritual growth. Mars represents destruction and violence; Pluto represents the rebirth that follows death, and the transformative process that should accompany the violent destruction of old, irrelevant life phases.

Planets and Occupations

The commercial world is divided into ten general divisions, each ruled by a planet in the following order:

The Moon: Food and food service, hotel management, longshoremen, night work.

Mercury: Schools, intellectual affairs, and publishing.

Venus: Entertainment, art, and social functions.

The Sun: Government employment.

Mars: Manufacturing, building, and munitions.

Jupiter: Religious, legal and financial affairs.

Saturn: Mining, farming, and cement work.

Uranus: Railroads, aerial and electric industries.

Neptune: Oil and fishing industries.

Pluto: Waste recycling and research work.

Each division is subject to ten subdivisions, which in turn are ruled by the ten planets. Take the oil industry for example: the first division is ruled by Neptune itself and the first impression is that this industry is a vast, intricate, complicated scheme whereby the people represented by every other planet down the scale are frequently deceived and robbed and the power to do this is gained through secret intrigues, lobbying interests, and other underhand and out-of-sight methods. This represents Neptune's unfavorable influence; more correctly speaking, a gross interpretation or manifestation of its influence.

The second division of the industry under consideration is ruled by Uranus, the enlightener (oil is used for light and power). This planet governs the transportation facilities connected therewith. The next division is ruled by Saturn and represents the oil well diggers, drillers, pipe men, etc. Jupiter represents the numerous legal departments, the financiers and cashiers. Mars represents the agents, contractors, and the construction departments. The Sun governs the various directors and high officials.

Venus, being the octave of Neptune, expresses some of the latter's subtleness by extending and maintaining the influence and prosperity of the industry through social intercourse at banquets and other such functions given for the purpose of influencing various dignitaries in power to gain the desired ends. Venus therefore rules the social and entertaining elements connected with the enterprise. Mercury rules the clerical forces, the advertising and the press agents that it maintains. The Moon rules the teamsters and other common employees and also the masses who buy and consume the product. Pluto represents the research of new products and the exploration of new oil deposits.

Beyond Good and Evil

There are no *evil* planets. Certain planetary configurations produce changes in the constituents of the human body. These changes develop into tendencies that may be classed as subnormal or abnormal, amounting to specific disorders, as in the case we mentioned before of the affliction to Saturn. Of themselves no planets are evil. When a planet arrives at a point in the Zodiac where its angular relation with another planet focuses the aspect on the earth, and when certain people who are responsive to it find it unpleasant or disruptive, it is commonly termed evil, adverse, or malign. In the course of time, as planetary vibrations are better understood, a more correct and appropriate terminology will develop.

Take the case of Saturn, a planet that has been much maligned. Saturn is often called a "malefic," yet the truth is that its vibrations are identified with contraction, cohesion, and stability. What would industry do if things did not properly set or contract? What would chemistry do if things did not properly cohere and adhere? What would the business world do if there were no stability, no regular foundation principles on which to establish trade? These are the attributes of Saturn.

By the same premise, Jupiter is not benefic, although it is generally termed fortunate. Its vibrations are identified with those things that please and gratify. Its vibrations direct the operation of growth, expansion, and increase.

In the realm of physical sensation it is easy to see how the vibrations of Saturn became associated with the word "malign." Its cooling, contracting, retarding, suppressing tendencies and its tissue destroying or catabolic actions lead to anxiety, apprehension, nervousness, or fearfulness of impending evil.

On the other hand, Jupiter is associated with the sensations of joviality, pleasure, generosity, relaxation, satisfaction, and contentment. Its anabolic action of tissue building promotes the attitude of safety, security, protection, and plenty, or the state of being fortunate.

A noted scientist once said, "Life is a constant internal adjustment to external environment." This is a statement nowhere so much appreciated as by astrologers. The "internal adjustments" mentioned are largely influenced and directed by planetary vibrations, which in turn give rise to urges, tendencies, attitudes, feelings, and thoughts. The quality and intensity of thought cause our actions; actions develop environment. Hence, planetary influences are intimately associated with our feelings, thoughts, and acts. So realistic is our expression of our reaction to planetary vibrations that an observant astrologer, while listening to your words and noting your actions, can tell just which planetary influence you are expressing at that time; that is, whether it is Saturn, Jupiter, or otherwise.

Outside the world of sensation we take a different view of the action of planetary vibrations. Here we see the activity of Jupiter in the shepherd protecting his flocks, the banker guarding funds, the merchant plying foreign trade, the dean directing the extension of knowledge, and the physician healing ills.

In Saturn's activities we see the forest denuded of its trees to furnish lumber, the surface of the earth scarred by mining, the decay of husks after the harvest, and the storms of winter renewing and replenishing the substance of the soil in preparation for the next season's planting.

So we perceive nature in operation in the activities of the planets. "There is no evil, but thinking makes it so"—thinking, *not the planets!* The catabolic action of Saturn in destroying worn-out cells is vitally important in view of the fact that Jupiter is constantly engaged in the anabolic action of cell building. Without Saturn this would soon promote plethora, while without Jupiter to rebuild, Saturn would soon cause devastation. In making observations we quickly realize that the planets are neither good nor evil. All the planets are expressing nature; we are continually reacting to their influences, and it is through knowledge of astrology that we can best learn to react in a finer, nobler manner.

The Lunar Effect

It is now an established scientific fact that the Moon is a principal factor in the ebb and flow of the tides, just as the ancient astrologers taught long ago. In relation to this idea of lunar rulership of water, a remarkable simile presents itself in that seven-tenths of the earth is covered by water while the human body is also seven-tenths fluid. The fluid chemicals of the body are much more finely composed and much more tenuous than the salty waters of the sea, hence they are infinitely more susceptible to lunar influence. Lunar vibrations cause the earth to expand and contract as if taking two great breaths daily, producing the tides. Lunar aspects with other planets cause subtle changes to occur in the human body, affecting it according to the nature and significance of those aspects.

The Symbolism of the Planets

Symbolism may be called a common language. By this is meant that certain concrete forms are employed to represent abstract ideas, which, presented to the view of one versed in the form, convey to the mind of that person a definite idea, though the spoken words for that idea will differ according to the language used. Thus the symbols for the planets used in astrology relate certain ideas about the nature of the planets.

Essentially the symbols for all the planets contain one or more of three elements: the *circle,* which denotes spirit, the *cross,* which denotes matter, and the *half-circle,* which denotes the intellectual aspect of the soul or mind.

Mercury ☿

Let us begin with the planet Mercury. Here we find the cross, the circle, and also the half-circle, showing that Mercury represents body, soul, and spirit, the threefold division of man. Hence we may deduce the fact that Mercury is preeminently the planet dealing with man, the thinker. It is spirit and matter with added faculty of mind. Those who have given any study to astrology know that Mercury represents the mind, or rather the inner understanding. Mercury is the connecting link that runs through the consciousness of man all the way from matter to the highest spirit. It is the link between spirit and matter, hence we see all three symbols joined together to represent the type of energy sent out from that planetary center.

Mars ♂

In Mars, from the symbol of the circle and the cross, we see a different form of energy working throughout nature, entering into the composition of the material and emotional bodies but not the mental, as we see no semicircle in connection with this planetary symbol, but the cross placed above the circle showing that the Mars force works almost entirely with material conditions. Its work is to energize that side of nature that, at the present time, obscures the spiritual. For instance, the Mars force is predominant in the animal kingdom and in the merely animal man, and is not directly connected with mind but with sensation. Its work with man is to spur him to action. Knowledge then comes as the result of his activities.

Venus ♀

After man has grown into a thinking and reasoning being and has begun to refine this wonderful Mars energy, we have what is called the reversing of the spheres of our being. In the symbol of Venus with the circle above the cross, the explosive and blustering energy of Mars has become the rhythmical and harmonious force of Venus. Venus brings beauty, sweetness, and love, and, while it does not directly work with the mentality of man, modifies the type of mind we express. For instance, if Venus and Mercury are conjoined, the result will be a beautiful and harmonious expression either in speaking or writing; it will be rhythmical and poetic. An overabundance of Mars force energizing a man would make him a warrior by choice; the same amount of force of the Venus type would present us with an actor or a dancer, someone who would express rhythm of motion and beauty. While the force of Mars energizing in working man would make him a blacksmith, the same amount of Venus force would make him an artistic craftsman. We see in the Venus symbol the circle above the cross, showing that the Venus force works with the spiritual side of man and deals directly with the appreciation of beauty by the human soul.

Saturn ♄

In Saturn we have only the cross and half-circle, showing its relation of matter to the mind in connection with matter. It has been said by some astrologers that we do not touch the higher side of Saturn, that "we do not reach Saturn above his belt." In other words, humanity at the present time can only respond to a limited range of the Saturn vibration. Saturn's special work in nature is to crystallize, to make stable. A harmonious aspect to the planet Mercury would tend to make the mind more material, to make it one-pointed and more stable, so that the ego can get better control of it and turn it to detailed study. We must always keep in mind that our relation to Saturn is purely material. If it touches our consciousness, it is only to materialize It.

Jupiter ♃

Just the opposite is the force that emanates from the lordly planet Jupiter. Here we find the mind or the half-circle placed above the cross, revealing to us the fact that though mind and matter are still conjoined, the mind is above the purely material side of the man's nature and can expand into the plane of pure reason, for Jupiter is expansive in nature and his work is to unfold, to throw from the center outward, just as it is the nature of Saturn to draw from the circumference to the center. The type of mind dominated by Jupiter would be broad, comprehensive, and benevolent. An overabundance of the Jupiter force would cause the mind to be too general to apply itself to detailed work; it would ever be dealing in glittering generalities, while the same amount of Saturn force energizing the mind would make it painfully detailed. Jupiter deals more with the etheric than with the physical brain, for it holds within itself the higher powers of the soul to a far greater degree than can be manifested through the physical brain today.

Uranus ♅

In the symbol of Uranus we find a combination of the Mars and Moon symbols, as the half-circle is on each side of the cross and circle. This shows that while spirit is still working through material conditions, it is completely controlled by mind. Not only is the symbol of the intellectual aspect of the soul (the semicircle) on one side of the cross, but also on both sides, showing the working of the higher and lower mind as one. When two or more forces work together, they produce a new force or property that was not possessed (or expressed) by either of the constituents working singly. Hence we find that Uranus strikes a new note that directly affects the superconsciousness in man. It is the great synthesizer, and we might say that it gathers up the various aspects of intelligence symbolized by all the planets and weaves them into a synthetic whole. From that comes the fully individualized man, the complete man, the master.

Neptune ♆

The symbol of Neptune, shown as a trident, indicates that it is more directly related to the threefold spirit in man and only those who have entered into a greater spiritual consciousness can come directly under its subtle and intangible influence. Negatively, this manifests mainly as psychic disturbances, which, acting through the emotional nature, produce strange physical disorders that are difficult to diagnose and even more difficult to overcome. At the same time its influence produces genius of an exceptional nature.

Pluto ♇

Various symbols have been proposed for the newest planet, Pluto. This version seems to have come into general usage and is used throughout this text. This symbol places the circle of spirit above both the crescent of intellect and the cross of form. The symbol for Pluto is given as ♇ in some sources.

Planetary Rulership, Detriment, Exaltation, and Fall

You have learned that certain signs and planets are closely related in nature and in the manner of their influence. Because of this harmonious relationship, certain planets are said to rule the signs in which they best express their natural qualities. The sign is said to be the "domicile" or "home" of the given planet. For instance, Venus is better able to express its refined, artistic, lovable characteristics when posited in the signs Libra, Taurus, or Pisces than if in Aries, Scorpio, or Virgo; just as people can better express the highest and noblest qualities of their nature in an environment of understanding and love than in one of strife and discord.

As the planets are constantly transiting through the Zodiac, they are often found in signs they do not rule. In some signs a planet may be quite powerful, while in others it will be weak or debilitated. It is necessary to understand the dignities of planets in order to determine the *strength of the ruling planets in a chart.* The home or ruling sign is the strongest position for a planet. The sign of its exaltation is the next in power. A planet in exaltation is like a guest in the sign—gracious in expressing its best qualities. When in the sign of its detriment, a planet tends to act inappropriately, possibly in a belligerent or emotional manner. In the sign of its fall, the planet is weak, like a second grader suddenly thrust into a high school class.

It should be understood that the planet itself does not thus become strong or weak, but that our responses to its influence are stronger or weaker.

Home Sign and Detriment

A planet is said to be in its *detriment* when located in the sign opposite to the one that it rules. For example, Mars rules Aries, and therefore Mars is in its detriment when located in the opposite sign, which is Libra.

As you have already learned which signs the planets rule, it is now necessary to remember that their detriments are in the signs opposite to the signs they govern.

Mars rules Aries and is in its detriment in Libra.

Venus rules Taurus and is in its detriment in Scorpio.

Mercury rules Gemini and is in its detriment in Sagittarius.

The Moon rules Cancer and is in its detriment in Capricorn.

The Sun rules Leo and is in its detriment in Aquarius.

Mercury rules Virgo and is in its detriment in Pisces.

Venus rules Libra and is in its detriment In Aries.

Pluto rules Scorpio and is in its detriment in Taurus.

Jupiter rules Sagittarius and is in its detriment in Gemini.

Saturn rules Capricorn and is in its detriment in Cancer.

Uranus rules Aquarius and is in its detriment in Leo.

Neptune rules Pisces and is in its detriment in Virgo.

The Moon's Nodes

The Moon's Nodes are not planets but points in the heavens where the Moon crosses the ecliptic from north latitude to south latitude and vice versa. They are commonly known as the *Dragon's Head* and the *Dragon's Tail*. The North Node (☊) is considered benefic and the South Node (☋) is considered malefic.

Exaltation and Fall

Classical astrologers determined the signs of exaltation and fall by considering planetary polarities, and also be considering the time of year when planets were strongest, aside from the signs they rule.

A planet's fall is the sign opposite its exaltation. Mars is exalted in the sign Capricorn; its fall is in the sign opposite, which is Cancer.

The following table shows the exaltation of the planets; their fall will always be in the sign opposite to the exaltation. Because ancient astrologers did not know about Uranus, Neptune, and Pluto, the dignity of these planets were not established until modern times, and may seem arbitrary.

The Sun is exalted in Aries and is in its fall in Libra.

The Moon is exalted in Taurus and is in its fall in Scorpio.

The North Node is exalted in Gemini and is in its fall in Sagittarius.

Jupiter is exalted in Cancer and is in its fall in Capricorn.

Neptune is exalted in Leo and is in its fall in Aquarius. (Some astrologers reverse these.)

Mercury is exalted in Virgo and is in its fall in Pisces.

Saturn is exalted in Libra and is in its fall in Aries.

Uranus is exalted in Scorpio and is in its fall in Taurus.

The South Node is exalted in Sagittarius and is in its fall in Gemini.

Mars is exalted in Capricorn and is in its fall in Cancer.

Venus is exalted in Pisces and in its fall in Virgo.

Pluto is exalted in either Leo or Aries, and falls in either Aquarius or Libra.

Dignities and Debilities

Table 5 shows the dignity and debility of the planets in the zodiacal signs. It also indicates the exaltation degrees—that is, the degrees where the dignity or debility is strongest.

Note: Some astrologers believe Neptune to be exalted in Cancer and in its fall in Capricorn.

Planet	Home	Detriment	Exaltation	Fall
Sun	Leo	Aquarius	19° Aries	19° Libra
Moon	Cancer	Capricorn	3° Taurus	3° Scorpio
Mercury	Gemini	Sagittarius	15° Virgo	15° Pisces
	Virgo	Pisces		
Venus	Taurus	Scorpio	27° Pisces	27° Virgo
	Libra	Aries		
Mars	Aries	Libra	28° Capricorn	28° Cancer
Jupiter	Sagittarius	Gemini	15° Cancer	15° Capricorn
Saturn	Capricorn	Cancer	21° Libra	21° Aries
Uranus	Aquarius	Leo	Scorpio	Taurus
Neptune	Pisces	Virgo	Aquarius	Leo
Pluto	Scorpio	Taurus	Leo	Aquarius
North Node			3° Gemini	3° Sagittarius
South Node			3° Sagittarius	3° Gemini

Table 5: Dignities and Debilities

Critical Degrees

These sensitive or critical degrees were given considerable importance by the ancients. A planet's strength or power in the horoscope is believed to be increased when in any of these degrees or within a 3° orb of the critical degree. A planet dignified by sign or house or strongly aspected receives still greater power, and one weakly placed or poorly aspected receives help from such location. Students may wish to observe these critical degree influences in horoscopes, as well as in horary charts and planets by transit over them.

Hylegical Degrees

The Sun or Moon is *hyleg*, or "the giver of life," if posited between 5° above to 25° below the Ascendant; 5° below to 25° above the cusp of the Seventh House; or between 5° below the cusp of the Ninth House to 25° below the cusp of the Eleventh House. If neither the Sun nor the Moon is in one of these places, then the ascending sign and degree are hyleg. When the hyleg is afflicted by directions, there is danger to life and health.

Sign	Degree		
Aries	0°	13°	26°
Taurus	9°	21°	
Gemini	4°	17°	
Cancer	0°	13°	26°
Leo	9°	21°	
Virgo	4°	17°	
Libra	0°	13°	26°
Scorpio	9°	21°	
Sagittarius	4°	17°	
Capricorn	0°	13°	26°
Aquarius	9°	21°	
Pisces	4°	17°	

Table 6: Critical Degrees

Delineations

When a planet is at home (in its own sign), exalted, dignified by position in the chart (in angles or being the planet most elevated or nearest the Midheaven), or well aspected by beneficent planets, it manifests its highest qualities; that is, the native is inclined to react wisely or favorably.

When a planet is out of dignity and debilitated by unfavorable sign position or aspects, especially by malefic planets, the lower side of its nature is more likely to be prominently manifested.

If a planet should receive a good aspect from a benefic and an adverse aspect from a malefic, the planet in question will manifest both sides of its nature—the higher and the lower—when influenced by directions and transits and in accordance with the nature of such aspects.

The following delineations will be helpful in understanding the principal expressions of each planet when dignified by sign, house position, or good aspects as compared with their expressions when ill dignified, that is, debilitated by sign, house position, or adverse aspects.

Moon

Dignified: Reflective, receptive, pliable, variable, refined, domestic, public, maternal, productive, adaptable.

Debilitated: Frivolous, passive, weak, conceited, common, nonsensical, personal, childish, changeable, loony.

Mercury

Dignified: Perceptive, observant, intellectual, accomplished, clever, skillful, vigilant, adroit, fluent, lucid, expeditious, studious, concentrative, possessed of good mental ability and memory.

Debilitated: Careless, profuse, indecisive, imitative, shiftless, desultory, embarrassed, nervous, rambling, unpoised, uninformed, forgetful, diffusive, shrewd, crafty, artful, untruthful.

Venus

Dignified: Affectionate, harmonious, chaste, sympathetic, contented, cheerful, graceful, humane, compassionate, refined, companionable, artistic.

Debilitated: Immodest, disorderly, lewd, emotional, indolent, loud, untidy, thoughtless, gaudy, extravagant, excessive love of pleasure and ease.

Sun

Dignified: Ambitious, honorable, lofty, dignified, loyal, faithful, distinguished, gallant.

Debilitated: Disdainful, proud, domineering, despotic, arrogant, authoritative, haughty.

Mars

Dignified: Courageous, venturesome, strong, daring, aggressive, energetic, active, fearless, constructive, passionate.

Debilitated: Bold, contemptuous, violent, irritable, coarse, audacious, forceful, impulsive, impatient, combative, destructive, sensual.

Jupiter

Dignified: Benevolent, philanthropic, generous, truthful, honest, moral, sincere, charitable, reasonable, compassionate, impartial.

Debilitated: Prodigal, wasteful, extravagant, pretentious, improvident, dissipated, hypocritical, thriftless, unjust, dishonest, artificial, despotic.

Saturn

Dignified: Prudent, contemplative, cautious, responsible, precise, persistent, persevering, industrious, provident, patient, economical, reserved, serious, resolute, considerate, mathematical, temperate, chaste, executive.

Debilitated: Skeptical, melancholic, deceitful, incompetent, exacting, avaricious, perverse, indifferent, laborious, impotent, repining, acquisitive, secretive, suspicious, fearful, slow, callous, lewd, pessimistic, unreliable.

Uranus

Dignified: Original, inventive, ingenious, progressive, reformative, intuitive, socially talented, metaphysical, unique, unconventional, clairvoyant, magnetic, premonitory, constructive.

Debilitated: Abnormal, fantastic, extreme, roving, eccentric, abrupt, repellent, erratic, grotesque, precipitate, premature, destructive, radical.

Neptune

Dignified: Psychic, inspirational, idealistic, psychometric, impressionable, mystical, spirit-perceptive, poetical, musical.

Debilitated: Vague, emotional, indulgent, supersensitive, deceptive, dreamy, vacillating, scheming, obsessed.

Pluto

Dignified: Conscientious, purifying, regenerative, liberating, just, incorruptible.

Debilitated: Suspicious, destructive, decaying, vicious, sorrowful, suffering, deadly, violent.

Ruling Planets

The planet that rules the rising sign in a horoscope at the moment of birth is called the *significator,* and its power and influence, according to the sign in which it may be located, is very important. Its tendencies according to the house in which it is posited, along with the indications as shown by the aspects it may bear with other planets, must be thoroughly considered, as well as its own inherent nature, i.e., good, evil, positive, neutral, etc. (Instructions on how to find the rising sign in a horoscope are found in Appendix 1.)

The features outlined in the following paragraphs are guides to the determining the strength of a planet. By this you will realize the necessity of knowing the nature of planets and their rulerships and the nature of the houses of a horoscope.

Planets other than the significator that have a ruling influence in a chart are:

1. Any planet within 12° above the rising degree (cusp of the First House) or within 20° below the First House cusp.

2. The planet ruling the sign in which the Sun is located at birth. This is called the *planetary ruler.*

3. The planet in the closest number of degrees of any aspect to the Sun. This is not necessarily the planet closest to the Sun.

4. The planet most elevated (nearest the Midheaven) in a map.

5. The Sun, Moon, and Mercury are always considered co-rulers. When reading a horoscope, pay strict attention to the rulers and co-rulers; take note of their position by zodiacal sign and houses and their aspects.

Aside from the significator, ruling planet, and the co-rulers, the strength of a planet may be determined as follows:

A planet is at its best when located in its own home sign, as Saturn in Capricorn, or Mercury in Gemini or Virgo. The next best is when it is located in the sign of its exaltation, as Sun in Aries, or Moon in Taurus. It is not so strong when in the sign of its detriment, as Venus in Scorpio or Aries. It is most weakly located when in the sign of its fall, as Mars in Cancer, or Jupiter in Capricorn.

When a planet isn't in its home sign, exaltation, detriment, or fall, its strength is judged according to its position by house in the horoscope, whether angular, succedent, or cadent. If angular, its strength is the same as though in home or exalted sign; if in a succedent house, it is the same as though in sign of detriment; if in a cadent house, it is the same as though in sign of fall.

The qualities of a planet are accentuated by the aspects it receives from other planets. Jupiter, for instance, in its own sign, angular, and well aspected, may bring the native great good fortune whenever well aspected by favorable directions or transits. But if in its fall, cadent, or adversely aspected, it has little or no power for good and the native may suffer lack of favorable opportunities at needed times, and also discredit or loss.

THE HOUSES

Just as we divide the ecliptic into twelve signs beginning with 0° Aries, so we divide the horoscope into twelve "houses" beginning with the Ascendant, the point that was on the eastern horizon when the native was born. While the expression of the twelve signs is all-pervasive across the planet, that of the Ascendant and houses is personal to the native. If we think of the signs as relating to the inherent psychic and physical anatomy, and the planets as functional modifiers of this pattern, then the houses will represent the outward environment and avenue of expression for this energy pattern. Thus, Saturn in Leo will represent a contracted heart, physically and psychologically, while a placement in the Third House will indicate that it is in the area of communication that the energy expresses itself, through one's own difficulty in communicating with others, and through difficulty in communicating with the native. An afflicted planet as Scorpio will indicate retention or poisoning by waste products. If it falls in the Fourth House, it may indicate faulty plumbing or food at home; in the Sixth House, poor eating habits.

The twelve houses reflect the meanings of the twelve signs. The First House is like Aries, the Second like Taurus, etc. The houses are grouped into three categories reflecting the three *quadratures*. These are *angular, succedent,* and *cadent* (analogous to cardinal, fixed, and mutable).

An *angular house* is a house situated on an angle. The angles are the four main points of the chart: the Ascendant, Descendant, Midheaven, and *Imum Coeli* (IC). (The *Imum Coeli* is also referred to as the *Nadir*.) The importance of these points is discussed later. Planets located in angular houses are traditionally held to be strengthened by this positioning, or "accidentally dignified." The angular houses are the First House, the Fourth House, the Seventh House, and the Tenth House, corresponding to the cardinal signs.

Succedent houses follow after angular houses; a planet placed therein is neither strengthened nor weakened. The succedent houses are the Second House, the Fifth House, the Eighth House, and the Eleventh House, corresponding to the fixed signs.

Cadent houses follow succedent houses. Planets located therein are traditionally held to be weakened, or "accidentally debilitated," except for the natural rulers of the cadent houses: Mercury of the Third House and the Sixth House, Jupiter of the Ninth House, and Neptune of the Twelfth House. The cadent houses are the Third House, the Sixth House, the Ninth House, and the Twelfth House. These correspond to the mutable signs.

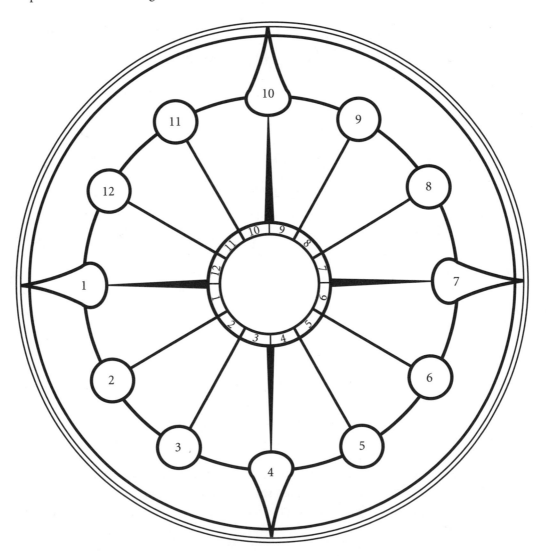

Figure 3: The Houses

The First House: Angular

Personality, natural disposition and tendencies, self-interest, and worldly outlook generally. The parts of the body represented are the head and face.

The Second House: Succedent

Financial affairs, monetary prospects, gain or loss. Also self-esteem and self-worth. Represents the throat and ears.

The Third House: Cadent

Brethren, short journeys, writings, studies, mental inclinations and ability. Denotes the shoulders, arms, hands, lungs, collarbones, and the nervous system.

The Fourth House: Angular

Father, home, environment, domestic affairs, and general condition at the close of life. The outlook regarding mines, lands, property. The result of undertakings. Rules the breasts, stomach, and digestive organs.

The Fifth House: Succedent

Children, love affairs, pleasurable emotions, and speculation. Rules the heart and back.

The Sixth House: Cadent

Sickness, servants, employees, service, work, food, hygiene, clothing, and small animals. Denotes the solar plexus and bowels.

The Seventh House: Angular

Unions, partnerships, marriage, contracts, lawsuits, open enemies, dealings with others and the public generally. Represents the kidneys, ovaries, and lower half of the back.

The Eighth House: Succedent

This house rules legacies, the money or goods of others, death and all matters connected with the dead and astral experiences. Also the financial affairs of the partner, being the Second House of the partner (the Seventh House). Rules the muscular system, bladder, and sex organs.

The Ninth House: Cadent

Long journeys, foreign countries, and places remote from birth, dreams, visions, psychic experiences, education, intuition and higher development, and scientific, philanthropic, philosophic, and spiritual tendencies. Partner's brother or sister, being the third house from the partner's own house (the Seventh House). Signifies the liver and thighs.

The Tenth House: Angular

Rules the profession, occupation, honor, fame, promotion, mother, employer, affairs of the country or government. Rules the knees.

The Eleventh House: Succedent

Friends, associations, hopes and wishes. Indicates the financial condition of the employer, being the second house from the employer's own house (the Tenth House). Rules the ankles.

The Twelfth House: Cadent

Unseen or unexpected troubles, restraint, limitations, exile, seclusion, secret sorrows, silent suffering, self-undoing, secret enemies, hospitals, large animals, occult or hidden side of life. Rules the feet.

> **Note:** Traditional astrologers assign the father to the Fourth House and the mother to the Tenth House. Some modern astrologers reverse this order while still others assign the parent of the same sex to the Fourth House and the parent of the opposite sex to the Tenth House. In actuality, it would appear that the parent who plays the emotional, nurturing, domestic role is represented by the Fourth House and the parent who fulfills the authoritarian, financially supportive role is ruled by the Tenth House.

THE ASPECTS

Measured from the center of the chart, there is an angle between every two planets in the horoscope that is measured in degrees. When the angle produces a significant interaction between two or more planets, they are said to be *in aspect*. The angles that give rise to the *major aspects* are produced by dividing a circle by units of two and three (just as the Zodiac is produced by such a division). These aspects are the conjunction (0°), the sextile (60°), the square (90°), the trine (120°), and the opposition (180°). In order for two planets to be in aspect to each other, they must be within a certain distance of the exact angle division. This is called the *orb* of the aspect and generally the planets must be within 5 to 12 degrees of a perfect aspect for the effect to be noticeable. For example, if Mars is at 19° Aquarius, and Mercury is at 21° Taurus, then the aspect is a square and the difference of 2° from the perfect angle is well within the allowable orb. The larger orbs are reserved for the Sun and Moon, and for conjunctions and oppositions. The smallest orbs are allowed for the *inner planets*—Mercury, Venus, and Mars—and the less powerful aspects.

Besides those aspects mentioned above, there is the semisextile (30°), the semisquare (45°), the sesquiquadrate (135°), and the quincunx (150°). These have traditionally been considered the *minor aspects,* but in recent times the quincunx (also called the *inconjunct*) has gained notoriety and has shown itself to be equal to any of the major aspects when it is properly understood. Two other important aspects are based not on the distance between two planets by angle, but on declination, or the number of degrees above or below the ecliptic. When two planets are the same distance above the ecliptic, they are said to be *parallel*. When they are the same distance on opposite sides of the ecliptic, they are *contraparallel*. The former is considered like a conjunction in effect, and the latter like an opposition.

Aspects are either considered "favorable" or "unfavorable" according to how harmoniously the planets function together. The favorable aspects are angle relationships based on division of a circle by three. The unfavorable aspects are based on division by two.

Of course, from a higher perspective, one cannot say that particular aspects are better or worse. It is merely a question of how these aspects are felt by the average person. It is said that if it were not for the "unfortunate" aspects, humanity would not have the urge to improve itself so strongly. Some astrologers consider the unfortunate aspects to be the only worthwhile ones to look at in a chart.

The conjunction occurs when planets come together. This produces a blending of planetary energies that is not, in itself, "unfavorable." Only when one of the outer planets (Uranus, Neptune, or Pluto) closely conjoins one of the "personal" planets (Mercury, Venus, Mars) or the Moon, do we get a difficult energy. This is because some otherwise personal aspect of life is conjoined with a very impersonal and extraordinary energy. For instance, when Mercury closely aspects Neptune, or Venus closely aspects Pluto, energy patterns are produced that resist the flow of everyday life.

Squares produce a "fight" between planets, with each one wanting to control or direct the behavior of the other. There is always a feeling that something is right and something else is wrong. The expression of each planet is in conflict with the other. The way to resolve this conflict is to accept each planetary force on its own ground as a valid statement in and of itself and to allow the conflict to continue, if necessary, but without taking sides.

Oppositions indicate a "stand-off" where it is impossible for two planets to function simultaneously. There is not a "fight" here, but an inability for the two to function at the same time. When one functions it forfeits the opportunity to work with the energy of the other. For example, if the Moon and Sun are in opposition, the conscious and unconscious forces oppose each other. When one acts, the other cannot contribute any of its own merits. The way to resolve this conflict is not to choose sides, but to allow each to express its own virtue, and also not to forget that the missing force is equally valid in its own field of action. This is considered an "unfavorable" aspect, though it does not produce the friction and tension of the square or quincunx.

Trines harmonize the functioning of different planets so that they "sympathize" with each other. When one is called forth to work, the other can aid it. This is particularly beneficial where the nature of the planets is otherwise antagonistic, but sometimes the effect is too mild to be consciously appreciated. We more often count our woes than our blessings.

Sextiles are based on a division of three and two, and indicate a sympathetic partnership between planets that may demand some conscious attunement in order to function. With trines, one rests on one's laurels, but with sextiles, one either uses the laurels or doesn't get any benefit from them.

The quincunx, or inconjunct, was long considered a minor aspect, but in recent years astrologers have come to consider it of substantial importance. Although the quincunx can be considered "unfortunate," it works in a way that is quite different from the square or opposition. The influence is more subtle, but often more powerful than other aspects. When a quincunx occurs between planets in a horoscope, the individual feels that the function of these two planets is somehow in opposition, yet requiring synthesis. The attempts of the particular individual to harmonize these forces produce a strain that is particularly distinctive. The individual is constantly attempting to unify these forces but never quite succeeds—sort of the Sisyphus syndrome. To the person and those in proximity, the effect is frustrating, grating, and abrasive, yet unless it is pointed out, the person is usually not conscious that the struggle is going on. He has made an assumption, on an unconscious level, that a certain action must take place. Often there is an inspirational quality to this assumption, a high ideal or a hope, but it is the nature of this aspect that this aspiration is based on an unconscious assumption that is presumptuous. The only solution to this problem is not to try harder at solving it consciously, but to leave it alone. There is a relationship between the quincunx and Virgo (150° from Aries) that teaches us that the native must bow his head in service to the two planets in aspect, and give up on a conscious solution to the situation. Virgo is the sign of service, and a true servant does not question the master.

Parallels of Declination

The parallel and contraparallel of declination have similar effects to the conjunction and opposition, respectively. When two planets form an aspect and also are parallel, the impact of the aspect is increased. The same is true for the contraparallel, except that this aspect takes on the tone of an opposition. In delineation, two planets forming an aspect that are also parallel or contraparallel will have more influence than aspecting planets that are not parallel or contraparallel.

Latitude

Latitude is a third consideration that some astrologers use to refine their delineations. Latitude describes the distance a planet is above or below the plane of the ecliptic. The measure of latitude from the ecliptic reflects the degree of latitude the planet has in its action. The smaller the degree of celestial latitude, the smaller the range of choices a person has when dealing with the energy of that planet. This consideration provides a third measurement of power or focus for each planet. In cases where aspects and parallels give contradictory indications, the more likely effects will come from planets at smaller degrees of latitude. This is especially true when the planet is at less than 1 degree of latitude.

Other Coordinate Systems

There are other coordinate systems, such as azimuth and altitude. Generally astrologers don't use these relationships for delineation. They are useful for other purposes, such as sighting stars. Azimuth is measured along the horizon, and altitude is the distance above the horizon.

How the Basic Principles of Astrology Work Together

The signs are the "organs" of our physical and psychological bodies. The angles and the houses show how we identify with the energy of the signs and planets, making them a part of ourselves (the Ascendant) or of our environment (the houses). The aspects show the interaction between the planets. The planets, by placement, channel the energy of the signs they occupy. By rulership they channel the energy of the signs they have affinity with. The horoscope reveals the physical and psychological body that the personality operates through. It shows how the personality relates to the environment surrounding it and to the spiritual elements that constitute its internal self, but not the spiritual character of that inner self per se. The components of astrology are based on the laws and truths of creation. They were placed by the Creator God in our environment to show the truths and laws of creation. We were placed in our environment to learn these things.

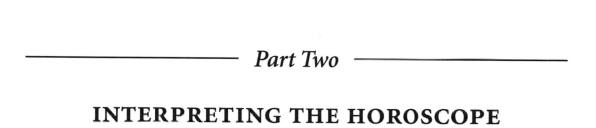

Part Two

INTERPRETING THE HOROSCOPE

INTRODUCTION TO
HOROSCOPE INTERPRETATION

It has been observed that many who learn to erect a horoscope are all at sea when it comes to delineating it. For that reason this chapter outlines the George Method of Horoscope Delineation used effectively for many years by Llewellyn George and his countless followers.

The secret of horoscope delineation lies in the preparation. That is, before you begin to delineate a chart, compile a *table of notes* for guidance. The more complete the memoranda, the simpler becomes the work of delineation. In the table make notes with each element to be featured. The orderly table of elements and the notes you make in connection with them, together with references to the horoscope delineations found in part 3 of this book, will enable you to modify or adjust the readings to suit the particular horoscope under consideration. Once more, let us impress upon the student the fact that the secret of success in delineation lies largely in the preparation.

Studying the Horoscope

Begin to study the chart by reading the influences of the Sun according to the zodiacal sign in which it is located.

Read the delineation of the influence of the ascending sign.

Read the influence of the Moon according to sign.

Read the influence of Mercury according to sign.

Read the influence of the significator and other co-rulers according to the signs in which they are located.

Read the aspects to the significator and to the co-rulers. Keep in mind whether or not the planets in question are in their home sign, exaltation, detriment, or fall, and regulate the delineations accordingly.

By this time you will have gained a fair idea of the power of each planet in the chart. Then proceed to read the planets according to their positions in the chart houses, being careful to adjust the delineations as conditions require. This will not be difficult when you are familiar with the nature of the planets, signs, aspects, and houses. Remember that no science or art can be mastered in a short time, but once the elements have been learned, their correct application brings accurate results. After the chart has been studied as just outlined, prepare to write a delineation.

Features of the Horoscope

The features are usually taken in this order:

Individuality	Marriage/Partnerships
Personality	Legacies
Finances	Death
Mentality	Voyages
Journeys	Education and the Higher Mind
Home Life	Occupation
Pleasure	Honors
Children	Friends
Health	Restrictions

To gather data for each feature, refer to part 3 of this book for the various delineations and make notes that relate to that feature.

House Cusps

The matter of house cusps cannot be confined to set rules, as the dividing line between houses is a mundane thing; in reality there aren't any dividing lines in the heavens. In fact, it should be treated as a psychological influence and has a close relation to the entire chart.

Cusps of Signs

When the Sun has reached 28° of a sign, its influence is mainly in the next sign. By way of example, if the Sun is in 28° Virgo, we use Mercury as the ruling planet, although the characteristics of Libra would be very noticeable in that person's make-up.

Physical Description

This is derived from the combined influences of the ascending sign; the planet ruling the Ascendant and the sign in which it is located, together with its principal aspects; and the planets that may be in the Ascendant. This combination is often difficult to delineate correctly. The average student may want to omit this delineation.

Individuality

Read the description of the sign occupied by the Sun. Read the house occupied by the Sun. Note which house the Sun rules in the chart and read its influence. Note which cusp Leo occupies, as the Sun is the planetary ruler of that particular house.

Make notes on the influence of the major aspects to the Sun.

Personality

Read the influence of the Ascendant.

Read the sign occupied by the ruler of the sign on the cusp of the First House.

Read the major aspects to that planet. If any planets are in the First House, read their influence by house and sign.

Read the influence of the Moon by sign, house, and principal aspects.

Note: In compiling notes you may at first experience difficulty defining individuality and personality. Remember that individuality, as indicated by the Sun sign, consists of inherent tendencies, capabilities, and abilities, or those inner qualities by which the individual knows himself. The personality may be considered as the outward expressions that characterize the person; that which distinguishes him or her and identifies him or her to others, as indicated by the Rising Sign.

Finances

Note which sign occupies the cusp of the Second House. Read its influence and that of its ruling planet by sign and house and their principal aspects.

Should any planet occupy the Second House, read its influence by the sign and house it occupies, then by the sign and house it rules in the chart.

Mentality

Note the sign that occupies the cusp of the Third House. Read its influence and that of its ruling planet by sign and house and their principal aspects.

Should any planet occupy the Third House, read its influence by the sign and house it occupies, and then by the sign and house it rules in the chart.

The mental rulers are the Sun, Moon, and Mercury, although all of the planets have an influence on the mind, especially the ruler of the Ascendant and the rulers of the Third and the Ninth Houses. Also consider Saturn and Uranus if they are in aspect to the mental rulers. Read their delineations according to the aspects they form. Uranus rules the intuition.

Journeys

Note which sign occupies the cusp of the Third House. Read its influence and that of its ruling planet by sign and house and their principal aspects. The Third House relates to short trips and short journeys.

Should any planet occupy the Third House, read its influence by the sign and house it occupies, then by the sign and house it rules in the chart.

Home Life

Note which sign occupies the cusp of the Fourth House. Read its influence and that of its ruling planet by sign and house and their principal aspects. The Fourth House relates to father, property, environment, and home life.

Should any planet occupy the Fourth House, read its influence by the sign and house it occupies, and then by the sign and house it rules in the chart.

Pleasures

Note which sign occupies the cusp of the Fifth House. Read its influence and that of its ruling planet by sign and house and their principal aspects. The Fifth House relates to pleasure, sports, speculation, and love affairs.

Should any planet occupy the Fifth House, read its influence by the sign and house it occupies, and then by the sign and house it rules in the chart.

Children

Note which sign occupies the cusp of the Fifth House. Read its influence and that of its ruling planet by sign and house and their principal aspects.

Should any planet occupy the Fifth House, read its influence by the sign and house it occupies, and then by the sign and house it rules in the chart.

The nature of the sign occupied by the Moon, and its aspects, are to be considered carefully in this question.

The Moon in Cancer, Scorpio, Pisces, or Taurus makes the native fruitful, and if in good aspect to Jupiter or Venus it usually gives a large family. The Moon angular (in the First, Fourth, Seventh, or Tenth House) increases the number of children. The Moon, Jupiter, or Venus in the Fifth or Eleventh House is a favorable testimony for children. The Sun in the Fifth House is a fruitful sign, and well aspected by the Moon or Venus is a testimony for producing many children or children of exceptional physical appearance.

Consider the Fifth and Eleventh Houses (the Eleventh House because it is the fifth one of the partner, counting the Seventh House as number one). Fruitful signs covering these cusps are favorable and increase the number of children.

A fruitful sign ascending or the Sun in a fruitful sign is favorable for children.

Barren signs on the cusps of the First, Fifth, or Eleventh House or the Sun in a barren sign, decrease fertility and lessen the chances of having offspring.

The Moon in Aries, Leo or Sagittarius, or afflicted by Uranus, Saturn, Mars, or the Sun also lessens the chances for having any children.

Uranus, Saturn, Mars, or the Sun in the Fifth or Eleventh House denies children or destroys them, according to the nature of the sign, the aspects, and the dignity of the planet.

Mercury and Neptune depend upon the aspects received and the nature of the sign occupied.

When the testimony is for children and the cusp of the Fifth House is covered by a feminine sign and its ruler a feminine planet, most of the children will be girls. When the sign and its ruler are masculine, most of the offspring will be boys.

The Fifth House shows the first child; the Seventh House the second child (because the Seventh is the third house from the Fifth, counting the Fifth as number one, and therefore indicates the sibling); the Ninth House the third child; the Eleventh House the fourth child; the First House the fifth child; the Third House the sixth child; the Fifth House the seventh child and so on around the circle. By children is meant not only those who live to be born and reared, but all conceptions.

If the Fifth House shows children and the Eleventh House denies them, or vice versa, some will live and some will die.

If a malefic planet influences the Seventh House, the second child may die, and so on. If the ruler of one of these houses is heavily afflicted, there is danger of losing that child.

Health

Note which sign occupies the cusp of the Sixth House. Read its influence and that of its ruling planet by sign and house and their principal aspects.

Should any planet occupy the Sixth House, read its influence by the sign and house it occupies, and then by the sign and house it rules in the chart.

For health, look to the Sun for a male, and to the Moon for a female.

The Sun in good aspect to the Moon, Mars, or Jupiter is favorable testimony for health and a strong constitution with an abundance of vitality, especially if the Sun is in the First House.

The Sun or Moon in the Sixth House is not good for health; Uranus there indicates peculiar and complex disorders, although there should be a chance of recovery by employing methods harmonizing with the nature of Uranus, such as electric, magnetic, of hypnotic treatments, etc.

Oriental positions of the planets signify short, sudden, sharp attacks of sickness, but occidental positions produce serious, lingering sickness and chronic diseases.

Note: The chart is divided into two halves: the western half, or *occidental* half, is that which begins at the Tenth House cusp, includes the Descendant, and ends with the Fourth House cusp. The *oriental* half, or eastern half, begins with the Fourth House cusp, includes the Ascendant, and ends at the Midheaven.

Remember to look to the Moon and its aspects when judging the health of a female. If the Moon is in adverse aspect to Venus, it weakens and deranges the constitution, and indicates annoying periodical sickness.

The particular physical ailments to which one is susceptible are judged by the Ascendant and by the signs occupied by the malefic planets, especially if any of them afflict the Sun or Moon; also judge by the sign that the Sun or Moon is in when so afflicted.

Marriage/Partnerships

Note which sign occupies the cusp of the Seventh House. Read its influence and that of its ruling planet by sign and house and their principal aspects.

Should any planet occupy the Seventh House, read its influence by the sign and house it occupies, and then by the sign and house it rules in the chart.

The Moon and Venus rule attractions in a male chart; the Sun and Mars in a female chart.

If the Moon and Venus (or the Sun and Mars in a female chart) are strong and free from affliction, especially by Saturn, the native has an early attraction.

The Sun or Moon in the Fifth or Seventh House and aspected to several planets causes an early attraction.

Fruitful signs on the cusps of the Fifth and Seventh Houses are favorable for an early union.

When Saturn afflicts the Sun or Moon, it delays marriage. Should these planets be weak and Saturn strong, and barren signs on the cusps of the First and Fifth Houses, the native is not likely to marry.

If the Sun or Moon applies to more than one aspect, it signifies more than one union; two aspects, two unions; three aspects, three unions; etc.

Astrology shows the union of affections regardless of whether the unions are made legal or not according to the laws of the land.

If the Sun or Moon is in Gemini, Sagittarius, or Pisces, more than one union is denoted.

If Saturn afflicts the Sun or Moon, death of the partner is signified, or coldness develops between them.

In a female chart, if the Sun is afflicted by Uranus, she is liable to go astray; Saturn afflicting the Sun, the husband is likely to be miserly, gloomy, crude, unfortunate, and somewhat sickly; Mars afflicting the Sun, the husband may be hot-tempered, coarse, and harsh; Venus afflicting the Sun, a passionate partner; the Moon afflicting the Sun, a changeable partner; Jupiter afflicting the Sun, a partner liable to financial losses.

In a male chart, when the Moon aspects Uranus, men cohabit with married women; if Venus aspects Uranus, they cohabit with single females. In either chart, male or female, if Uranus, Neptune, or Saturn is in either the First, Fifth, or Seventh House, seldom does the native lead an entirely chaste life.

Jupiter or Venus in the Seventh House gives domestic felicity and comfort; well aspected, gain by marriage.

The Sun or Moon in the Seventh House is favorable, but much depends upon the aspects and the dignity by sign.

The Moon (in a male chart) afflicted by Uranus, Saturn, or Mars indicates heavy misfortune for the wife through accident, sickness, or operation, and danger of her demise. In a female chart, the Sun afflicted in a like manner affects the husband.

Neptune in affliction with Venus indicates deception in courtship and marriage. Uranus in adverse aspect with Venus indicates mistrust, separation, and danger of scandals. Saturn in adverse aspect with Venus indicates delays, trouble, sorrow, and disappointment. Mars in adverse aspect with Venus indicates suspicion and irritability. Very little happiness, comfort, or prosperity is experienced if Uranus, Saturn, or Mars occupy the Seventh House (unless they are well dignified and aspected). If they are afflicted therein, the union will prove a very unfortunate event.

Legacies

Note which sign occupies the cusp of the Eighth House. Read its influence and that of its ruling planet by sign and house and their principal aspects. The Eighth House rules legacies, bequests, money received through insurance, and matters connected with the goods or property of the dead.

Should any planet occupy the Eighth House, read its influence by the sign and house it occupies, and then by the sign and house it rules in the chart.

Death

Note which sign occupies the cusp of the Eighth House. Read its influence and that of its ruling planet by sign and house and their principal aspects.

Should any planet occupy the Eighth House, read its influence by the sign and house it occupies, and then by the sign and house it rules in the chart.

The time or date of death is a difficult thing to ascertain definitively, and even if known it is seldom wise to announce it; but the kind of death is often signified by the Sun, Moon, ruler of the Ascendant, Sixth and Eighth Houses.

If these planets are afflicted by malefics in the oriental half of the chart, violent or sudden death is denoted.

Occidental planets and aspects point more to death by sickness.

The lights afflicted and the malefics elevated above them show violent death. The Sun or Moon in conjunction with Mars in the First, Sixth, Eighth, or Tenth House indicates sudden death, especially if Uranus or Saturn adds a testimony of affliction. Death usually occurs under a combination of aspects.

Neptune indicates a mysterious death by gas, drowning, drugs, or poisons. Uranus shows strange deaths, usually sudden and unexpected, through inventions, electricity, lightning, railroads, vehicles, explosions, travel, or suicide.

Saturn denotes colds, consumption, spleen disorder, and chronic diseases. Jupiter shows death by liver troubles, blood disorders, apoplexy, or inflammation of the lungs.

Mars indicates fevers, smallpox, bladder troubles, burst blood vessels, hemorrhage, miscarriage, abortion, difficult urination, cuts, burns, scalds, and wounds. Death is usually the result of a short, sudden attack of sickness.

The Sun shows heart troubles, fevers, or constitutional weakness.

Venus shows kidney or functional derangement.

Mercury indicates brain, nervous, or intestinal disorders.

The Moon inclines to stomach troubles, public death, by drowning, etc., according to the aspects.

It is generally a good policy not to attempt to tell people how or when they are likely to die.

Voyages

Note which sign occupies the cusp of the Ninth House. Read its influence and that of its ruling planet by sign and house and their principal aspects. The Ninth House relates to long journeys, voyages, foreign countries, foreign affairs, foreigners, and all places remote from that of birth regardless of whether actually under another flag. For example, to persons born in the United States, Alaska, or the Philippines would be foreign places. Judgment must be exercised on such questions as these, for circumstances alter cases. Distance does not make it a foreign affair, but circumstances, conditions, and new elements and activities do so.

Should any planet occupy the Ninth House, read its influence by the sign and house it occupies, and then by the sign and house it rules in the chart.

Education and the Higher Mind

Note the sign that occupies the cusp of the Ninth House. Read its influence and that of its ruling planet by sign and house and their principal aspects. The Ninth House relates to higher education, academic achievement, invention, and scientific attainments.

Should any planet occupy the Ninth House, read its influence by the sign and house it occupies, and then by the sign and house it rules in the chart.

Occupation

Note the signs that occupy the cusps of the Tenth House and the Sixth House. Read their influence and that of their ruling planets by sign and house and their principle aspects.

It is difficult to designate the exact occupation for several reasons. Some persons have no choice in the matter, their parents having decided their work for them, and they follow their parents' will, often in direct opposition to their own desires. In this respect the Tenth House may be regarded as designating the ideal or self-chosen occupation, and the Sixth House, work, service, and drudgery carried on under dislike, distaste, protest, or force of circumstances. On the other hand, many choose a line of work not because of any particular liking for it, but for monetary gain, thereby bringing their occupation largely under the rule of the Second House.

Any planet in the Tenth House will show in what direction the natural desires may lead, by blending the nature of the planet with the nature of the sign it occupies and the aspect that it may behold. The nature of the planet and the quality of its aspects will determine the benefits or difficulties of the occupation. It is necessary also to note the strongest planet in the nativity by house, sign, and aspect.

With most of the planets in the map below the earth, or weak, or mostly in mutable signs, the native should be in the employ of others. If above the earth, or strong, or well aspected, the native may be the employer of others. If the majority of planets are in air signs, a profession should be chosen, but if in the earth signs, a business would be best.

The Sun and its aspects are very important in this matter.

Mercury in conjunction with the Sun inclines to success in bookkeeping, accounting, clerking, secretarial work, and literary work.

Venus in good aspect to the Sun inclines to success as a jeweler, musician, artist, actor, photographer, etc.

The Sun in good aspect to Mars inclines to success in military affairs, work with iron and steel, dentist, barber, butcher, surgeon, chemist, or agent; in good aspect to Jupiter, inclines to success as a lawyer, clergyman, physician, banker, judge, or senator; in good aspect to Saturn, inclines to success in mining, agriculture, real estate, property, or lead, coal, or other minerals; in good aspect to Uranus, inclines to success in public or governmental positions or as an engineer, electrician, inventor, astrologer, or also as a reporter at a progressive paper; in good aspect to Neptune, inclines to success as a druggist, oil dealer, detective, speculator, or success in some occult, inspirational, or unusual pursuit.

The Moon in good aspect to the Sun inclines to success with the general public in liquids, common commodities, salesperson, cab driver, policeman, oysterman, laundryman, dairyman, milkman, sailor, fisherman, or traveler.

If many planets are in one sign, things signified by the sign and by the house they occupy will attract attention, but whether it will be fortunate or not depends upon the nature of the combination and the aspects.

The most success will come through things indicated by the planet best aspected and in connection with the sign and house it occupies in the chart.

With the Sun and Moon in good aspect, business and employment come readily and benefit through them; the adverse aspect of the Sun and Moon has a reverse effect.

With the Moon afflicting Saturn, there is likely loss in business through financial slumps and depression. When out of employment, the individual has a hard time getting started again.

The Sun and Moon in good aspect are very favorable for employment and business, denoting rapid advancement; the Sun afflicting Mars, disagreement with employers and danger of accidents.

Honors

Note the sign that occupies the cusp of the Tenth House. Read its influence and that of its ruling planet by sign and house and their principal aspects. The Tenth House rules honors, fame, and affairs of the country or government.

Should any planet occupy the Tenth House, read its influence by the sign and house it occupies, and then by the sign and house it rules in the chart.

Friends

Note the sign that occupies the cusp of the Eleventh House. Read its influence and that of its ruling planet by sign and house and their principal aspects. The Eleventh House rules friends and also hopes and wishes.

Should any planet occupy the Eleventh House, read its influence by the sign and house it occupies, and then by the sign and house it rules in the chart.

Restrictions

Note the sign that occupies the cusp of the Twelfth House. Read its influence and that of its ruling planet by sign and house and their principal aspects. The Twelfth House relates to unseen or unexpected troubles, secret enemies, secret sorrows, self-undoing, jails, hospitals, and the secret or occult side of life.

Should any planet occupy the Twelfth House, read its influence by the sign and house it occupies, and then by the sign and house it rules in the chart.

Some can read a chart more readily than others, but anyone who desires to do so can acquire the knack, on the same principle as acquiring musical ability; i.e., the elements having been learned, practice brings proficiency. The same rule applies to astrology inasmuch as the elements having been mastered, their correct application brings accurate results. After the system has been learned, the quickest way to further development and understanding along these lines is through casting and reading horoscopes.

Twins

Astrologers are often asked questions about twins. Why, for instance, if astrology is to be considered valid, do twins born at approximately the same time differ in appearance and character? One would expect identical twins to be identical in personality, and yet often they are not. The famous Siamese twins, Chang and Eng, had strikingly different personalities. One was a teetotaler and the other drank to excess, causing the premature death of both. Astrology can often provide clues to why twins are the way they are.

In studying this question, keep in mind that there are two kinds of twins: those who are genetically identical and those who are not identical (fraternal twins).

Let us consider a case that came under the observation of Llewellyn George, a very unusual case and one very difficult to explain satisfactorily except by means of astrology. Mr. George spent twenty years in the city where these twins were born and had the opportunity to observe their development from birth to maturity. The case surely proved interesting because, although born but four minutes apart, the boy and girl grew to manifest very dissimilar characteristics in addition to being quite different in appearance.

Llewellyn George was well acquainted with the prospective father and had urged him to secure the exact time of each birth. He said "each" birth because about six months previously, when there were indications of a family increase, the father asked about the matter and a horary chart made for the time of the query clearly indicated that his wife was pregnant; and because Mercury and Venus were in the same degree of Gemini in the Eleventh House, it was easy to predict twins, a boy and a girl: Mercury in Gemini, masculine, while Venus furnished the feminine indication. The Moon being in a position that designated months, the number of degrees and minutes required for it to make an aspect to the two planets told of the week in which the births would occur, a calculation that subsequently proved correct.

To those not versed in horoscopy, these correspondences seem astounding, but to the practitioner they are not unusual. The astrologer expects that the testimonies rendered by celestial phenomena will coincide exactly with the facts, events, or conditions.

The eventful day arrived. The clock time was carefully recorded for each birth, and after the proper adjustment was made between the standard clock time and mean time for that longitude, it was found that they were born just as the sign on the Ascendant was changing. The boy was born when the last degree of Virgo was ascending while the girl was born four minutes later with the beginning of Libra rising.

The planetary significator of the boy was Mercury, and that of the girl, Venus. In childhood the boy was shy and retiring; the girl enjoyed and readily made friendships. In youth the boy was quiet, studious, and frugal; the girl was sociable, dressy, and extravagant. He was dark and slender; she was fair and plump. The youth became a messenger, then a clerk, and then the owner of a grocery store. Note that Mercury indicates messengers and clerks, while Virgo indicates foodstuffs. The girl took music, a Venus occupation. In fact, they were just as different as could be, and as they should be, according to astrology, being born with different signs ascending, though only four minutes apart.

Another case that came under the observation of Llewellyn George was of twins who looked as alike as two peas. These two young men were the bane of their friends, with their practical jokes of substituting for each other. No one could tell which was which. They confided in Mr. George that one often went out with the other's girl just for a lark, until the young ladies were in despair and perplexity. Not only did they look alike but their habits were the same; they dressed alike, wore each other's clothes, had the same likes and dislikes, were ill at the same time, worked in the same store, and the women they were in love with were sisters.

With all these similar traits it would naturally be supposed that they were born at very nearly the same time. But strange to say, they were not. Yet astrology, better than anything else, logically accounts for the facts. They were born in the month of Gemini, symbolized by the Twins, and of that sign they were typical specimens as individuals. They were born one whole hour apart but at a time when the sign of Gemini was on the Ascendant at each birth.

Perhaps it might be argued that in large hospitals, where births are occurring every few minutes, children born nearly at the same time do not always resemble each other, although some have the same sign rising. In such instances it should be remembered that although born at the same place and at nearly the same time, conception took place at different times and at different places, with gestation in entirely different environments. Therefore the subject of twins must be considered further in relation to the prenatal epoch, heredity, environment, and other factors involving physiological and psychological principles. Even so, cases of "astrological twins" are well-known. The best example was recorded in Raphael's *Manual of Astrology* (London, 1828). This was the case of George the Third, king of England, and Samuel Hennings, an ironmonger. They were born at the same time and at almost the same location. Although born into entirely different social settings, their careers were parallel. When George the Third ascended to the throne in October 1760, Hennings went into business for himself as an ironmonger. Both were married on September 8, 1761, and both died at nearly the same time on January 28, 1820.

THE SIGNS

Aries

Classifications

Fire triplicity, cardinal quadrature. Hot, dry, masculine, positive. Short ascension, equinoctial, eastern. Inflammatory, choleric, sterile, violent, bestial, intemperate, mental-motive.

Planets

Ruler: Mars. **Detriment:** Venus, being a lustful sign. **Exaltation:** The Sun. **Fall:** Saturn.

General Description

Aries is the first sign, or head sign, of the Zodiac and is known to have an influence on the head and face. The Sun enters this sign on or around March 21 each year, constituting the vernal ingress. While it is in this eastern sign we celebrate Easter.

Symbols

Aries has been represented by the cock, denoting boastful or fighting qualities, but is more generally symbolized by the ram, being in nature rash, hardy, springy, lascivious, and combative. Aries represents the "gate of gold on the east," and is therefore called an oriental sign, denoting the beginning of right ascension (RA) or the oriental first Right Ascension Midheaven (RAM).

Biblical Correspondences

The Gospel says, "I have exalted thee, O Father," and in this sign the Sun is exalted, particularly in the nineteenth degree. In the New Testament it probably answers to Mark. **Archangel:** Malchidial. **Angel:** Sharhiel. **Apostle:** Matthias. **Tribe of Israel:** Gad. **Prophet:** Malachi.

Stellar Symbols

Stars in the Aries constellation are Shedar, Ruckbah, and Dat al Cursa. The first decan is Cassiopeia. Cetus, a monster constellation to the south of the ecliptic, represents the second decan. Perseus represents the third decan or constellation.

Anatomical Correspondences

Bones: Skull and face, except perhaps the nasal bones, which may be co-ruled by Scorpio. **Muscles:** The muscles used in eating, talking, smiling, and in making other expressions; the superficial muscles under the scalp; the deep muscles in the mouth; and the other muscles in the head. **Arteries:** Temporal and internal carotids (those carrying blood to the head). **Vein:** Cephalic (coming from the right arm).

Health

Morbid action is shown through various kinds of eruptive maladies affecting the head and face: pimples, ringworm, headaches, migraine, encephalitis, smallpox, and perhaps harelip. Worry, anxiety, excitement, or anger produce overstrain of the brain and tend to upset the general health. Aries people require plenty of rest and sleep, and peaceful and harmonious surroundings. They should partake freely of vegetables and brain food, avoiding stimulants and partaking lightly of meat. Herbs belonging to this sign are mustard, eyebright, bay, and others of a pungent nature.

Desirable Characteristics

Enterprising, action, ambition, courage, ardor, industry, generosity, pioneering, practicality, constructive, leadership.

Undesirable Characteristics

Belligerence, headstrong, excitability, audaciousness, impatience, irresolution, imprudence, insubordination, quarrelsomeness, foolhardiness, selfishness, disregard, jealousy.

Associations

Ash-Lesh (flaming star), Tuesday, Smith, Samael, Headen, Sang (herb), Taleh (sacrificial lamb), Ramah (exalted place), Rameses (the best in the land of Egypt), Ramadan (Muslim feast in spring), Benjamin, Rachael, Amroo.

Locations

Sandy, hilly, dry, or rather barren places; places where sheep are kept; lime or brick kilns, fireplaces, ceilings, plaster, tool houses, forges; prominent corner buildings facing east; east corner rooms.

Taurus

Classifications

Earth triplicity, fixed quadrature. Cold, moist, feminine, negative. Short ascension, eastern. Semi-fruitful, bestial, melancholy.

Planets

Ruler: Venus. **Detriment:** Mars, which is not at ease in the home of Venus. **Exaltation:** The Moon, particularly the third degree. **Fall:** Uranus.

General Description

Taurus is the second sign of the Zodiac, the Sun beginning its apparent yearly transit through it on or around April 20. It is the middle sign, or fixed sign, of the spring quarter.

Taurus suggests energy, reserve force, endurance, and stability. An energy devoted to stable things ensures a firm foundation and an enduring structure.

Symbols

Taurus is symbolized by a bull with unusual horns on its head and toes, appearing in a rage, crouched to rush forward with fierce energy; representing a stubborn and tenacious nature.

Taurus is one of the four fixed signs comprising the Cherubim. It was the original Bull, or Baal, of the Assyrian religious rites, sometimes referred to as "the Sacred Bull" or "the Golden Calf," emblematic of the period a few thousand years ago when the solar system was precessing through that constellation. Our May Day festival with its maypole and garlands are remnants of the ancient Egyptian festival celebrating the entrance of the Sun into Taurus.

Biblical Correspondences

Prophet: The Gospel apparently alludes to Haggai as the prophet. **Archangel:** Asmodeus. **Angel:** Araziel. **Disciple:** Thaddeus. **Tribe of Israel:** Ephraim in Hebraic mythology refers to the sign of Taurus.

Stellar Symbols

In the first decan of Taurus is the constellation Orion, to the south of the ecliptic but very beautiful. Rigel and Bellatrix are other stars that are also there. The second decan shows the constellation Eridanus. Auriga is the third constellation associated with this sign.

In Taurus are the Pleiades, a cluster of seven stars whose "sweet influences" are referred to with the band of Orion.

Anatomical Correspondences

This sign is said to include under its domain the neck, throat, ears, pharynx, Eustachian tubes, tonsils, upper portion of the esophagus, palate, thyroid gland, and vocal chords. **Bones:** Cervical vertebrae in the neck. **Muscles:** Those in the front and back of the neck enabling movement of the head. **Arteries:** External carotids and basilar artery. **Veins:** Jugulars in the neck and the veins of the thyroid gland.

Health

Morbid action manifests as sore throat, glandular swellings in the neck, croup, mumps, goiter, abscess, suffocation, strangulation, apoplexy. By reflex action from Leo and Scorpio the heart may be affected; also the excretory system, giving rise to hemorrhoids, fistulas, or bladder trouble.

Fattening foods should be used in moderation as this sign usually increases the appetite and tends to obesity and to fondness of ease. Moderate and regular exercise is essential in addition to moderation in food and drink. Because of failure to observe these essentials, rheumatism is prevalent among Taureans. Herbs belonging to this sign are ground ivy, deadly nightshade, and vervain.

Desirable Characteristics

Trustworthiness, steadfastness, perseverance, endurance, persistence, composure, self-reliance, constructive, practicality, humor, kindness, sympathy, magnetism, care, fearlessness.

Undesirable Characteristics

Stubbornness, domineering, exacting, obstructive, stolid, brusque, dogmatic, conceit, self-centeredness, covetous, lazy. It is said that their accusers are seldom forgiven and that they retain the memory of an injury for a long time.

Associations

This second sign is akin to the Second House with its relation to money, finances and movable effects of extrinsic value. Astarte, Ataur (Arabian name for Taurus), Mineves, Aleph, Reem (an animal resembling the bull but fiercer), Aurochs (similar to Reem), Unicorn Hunter, Capella (a star), Atlas.

Locations

Banks, cash boxes, money drawers, jewelry boxes; stables for cows, dairies; places where farming implements are kept or sold; pastures, feeding places; wheat or corn fields. In the house it represents the middle rooms or places in the middle of the block; also round things such as castors, rings, money, etc. Shoes, leather, purses; garlands, may poles, canes, altars, and all places where property or food are stored, e.g., refrigerators, cellars.

Gemini

Classifications

Air triplicity, mutable of flexed quadrature. Moist, masculine, positive. Short ascension, northern. Barren, sanguine, double-bodied, dual, human, violent.

Planets

Ruler: Mercury. **Detriment:** Jupiter. **Exaltation:** The Moon's North Node. **Fall:** The Moon's South Node.

General Description

The Sun enters this sign on or around May 21 and apparently transits through it by June 20. Gemini inclines to a tall, upright body, long arms and hands; feet short; a quick walker with swinging arms, open hands, fingers spread apart slightly; piercing eye, quick sight; keen mentality.

Symbols

Gemini is symbolized by the twins, the portals, a monkey. The monkey is associated with Gemini by the Chinese; they depict it as the Three Graces symbolized by the three little monkeys with hands over eyes, ears, and mouth. Gemini is also related by the Aryans or ancient Hindus to Buddha or Krishna. The twins are sometimes Castor and Pollux, Eros and Anteros, Gog and Magog, Romulus and Remus. Sometimes pictured as a man and woman walking hand in hand, perhaps Adam and Eve. In the Babylonian calendar they are the "Two Gods of the Door."

Biblical Correspondences

Gemini is biblically referred to as Cain and Abel, and as Simeon and Levi. **Archangel:** Ambriel. **Angel:** Sarayel. **Prophet:** Zachariah. **Disciple:** Simeon. **Tribe of Israel:** Manasseh.

Stellar Symbols

In the first decan south of the ecliptic is Lepus, "the hare." The stars in Sirius, "the great dog," which is the second decan, are Mirzam, "the ruler," Muliphen, "leader," Wasen, "shining," and Adhara, "glorious." The third decan also shows a wolf or dog (Canis Minor) somewhat smaller and behind the first one. Procyon and Al Gomeize, two prominent stars, are in this constellation.

Anatomical Correspondences

Gemini rules the nervous system by which all parts of the body are brought into communication, giving it sensation and flexibility. The process of respiration furnishes the two lungs with water from the air that normally bathes them and oxygen, which they pass into the blood. **Bones:** Upper ribs, collarbones, shoulder blades, and the bones in the upper arms, forearms, wrists, and hands. **Veins:** Those coming from the shoulders, arms, lungs, and rib cage. **Arteries:** Those carrying blood to the lungs, rib cage area, shoulders, and arms.

Health

Nervous disorders are liable through worry, anxiety, mental strain, restlessness, and excessive activity. The lungs, shoulders, arms, and hands are subject to afflictions and accidents. Tubercular tendencies or disorders of the respiratory organs may develop. Gemini indicates such disorders as asthma, bronchitis, pleurisy, and pneumonia.

This mentally motivated sign requires attention to proper breathing, light outdoor exercises, and walking with long, deliberate steps. The chest and lung area should be given protection and rubbing. Particular care should be given to the diet, cereals and nerve foods being essential.

Desirable Characteristics

Intelligence, expressiveness, eloquence, idealism, studiousness, inquiring mind, ambition, resourcefulness, dexterity, courage, tolerance, responsiveness, generosity, sympathy, temperance, liberalism.

Undesirable Characteristics

Restlessness, variation, verbosity, effusiveness, trickiness, shiftlessness, diffusion, diffidence, waywardness, improvidence, impulsiveness, exaggeration, theory, lack of concentration.

Associations

Thaumin (Hebrew name for Gemini meaning "united"), Anubis, Hermes, Messia, messenger, or wandering teacher.

The third sign of the Zodiac has things in common with the Third House in that they both indicate letters, communications, messengers, news, inquiries, information, rumors, newspapers, magazines, neighbors, relatives, short journeys, lecturing, debating, teaching, advertising, clerical work, reporting, story writing, merchandising, printing, education.

Locations

Where hay or straw are kept, granaries; coffers or chests with doors; pillared buildings, doorways, walls, wainscoting, upper back rooms, bookcases; hills and mountains of a barren nature; things made or sold in pairs such as salt and pepper shakers, etc.

Cancer

Classifications

Water triplicity, cardinal quadrature. Cold, moist, feminine, negative. Long ascension, solstitial, tropical, northern. Fruitful, maternal; domestic, mute, phlegmatic.

Planets

Ruler: The Moon. **Detriment:** Saturn. **Exaltation:** Jupiter, especially the fifteenth degree. **Fall:** Mars.

General Description

The Sun enters Cancer on or around June 21 and apparently transits through the sign by July 22. Reference to any ephemeris will show that the Sun apparently reaches its highest point or north declination (23° 27') and remains in it for three days, apparently standing still, after which it slowly starts, crablike, backward toward its south declination. The middle day of the three mentioned is therefore the longest day of the year.

Cancer is said to be receptive, transforming, metamorphic, and nurturing, but lacking in vitality.

Symbols

The crab represents possession and retention; it carries its house on its back. The symbol is drawn from the breasts, emblematic of motherhood, to nurture, cherish, to ripen, to carry, to bear. Although it has land-travel facilities, the crab is a creature born of water. The Egyptians represented this sign with the scarab.

Biblical Correspondences

In the Gospel, Issachar is likened to a strong ass that at one time was the symbol of Cancer. **Archangel:** Muriel. **Angel:** Pakiel. **Prophet:** It is said that Cancer refers to the prophet Amos. **Disciple:** John. **Tribe of Israel:** Issachar.

Stellar Symbols

Within the constellation Cancer is Praescpe, "the manger." The first decan is called Ursa Minor, or Little Bear. It contains the pole star. Ursa Major, or Great Bear (the big dipper), is the second decan. The third decan is Argo, "the heavenly ship," whose main star is Canopus.

Anatomical Correspondences

Cancer has dominion over that zone of the body containing the breasts, chest, and stomach and is therefore related to the pancreas and thoracic duct. **Bones:** The breast bone, the ribs that are nearest to the stomach. **Muscles:** Intercostals (those between the ribs) and diaphragm (those used in breathing). **Arteries:** Diaphragmatic; those serving the stomach. **Veins:** Mammary, gastric, gastro-epiploric, diaphragmatic.

Health

The stomach being the principal source of affliction for this sign, it is essential that foods taken into it be pure, undefiled, or not inclined to cause fermentation. Foods should be well cooked, and stimulants avoided. Special care is required when the Moon is transiting through Cancer or Capricorn. Guard against colds or chills; avoid imagining diseases; avoid worrying about finances. Frequent changes of scenery are beneficial.

Desirable Characteristics

Patience, tenacity, conscientiousness, economy, domesticity, maternity, kindness, devotion, versatility, sociability, adaptability, sympathy, patriotism.

Undesirable Characteristics

Timorousness, variation, vanity, fancy, imagination, untruthfulness, changeability, sentimentality, touchiness, grasping, pride, disorderliness, resentment, indolence.

Associations

May, mother, holy water, Arthur.

Locations

Lakes, rivers, brooks, etc.; places where rushes or vegetables grow; homes, stalls, sheepfolds; taverns, public houses; wash houses, kitchens, water tanks; cellars, corner houses facing north.

Leo

Classifications

Fire triplicity, fixed quadrature. Hot, dry, masculine, positive. Long ascension, northern. Choleric, barren, bestial, commanding, fortunate, feral, broken, strong, bitter.

Planets

Ruler: The Sun. **Detriment:** The recalcitrant Uranus, who will bow to no king. **Exaltation:** Pluto. **Fall:** Neptune.

General Description

The Sun enters Leo on July 22. It is universally symbolized by a lion, whose nature it represents. It symbolizes the fervid heat of July and August when the Sun has attained its greatest power. It represents the type of electric, fiery mind whose expression is often destructive, whose energy is often rapacious, daring, kingly, and commanding, yet generous.

Symbols

Leo is represented by the ancients as the Nemean Lion, which leaped down from the skies and was killed by Hercules. Leo is the emblem of violence and fury in the hieroglyphic writings. In the ancient maps the lion is shown just above Hydra, the great dragon, with his claws about to rend the serpent.

Feasts and sacrifices formerly celebrated during the Sun's transit in Leo in honor of the Sun were termed *Leonitica,* while the priests who performed the rites were called *Leones.* Among the Persians these celebrations were called *Mithra.*

Biblical Correspondences

Archangel: Verchiel. **Angel:** Sharatiel. **Prophet:** Leo is said to correspond to the prophet Hosèa. **Apostle:** Peter. **Tribe of Israel:** Judah. Leo, the Lion, is one of the beasts of the cherubim. Jacob assigned this sign to the tribe of Judah, and the subsequent warlike and victorious energy of the tribe proved the allocation correct. Samson represents the Sun in Leo. Michael is the archangel of the Sun.

Stellar Symbols

Regulus is a mighty fixed star in the heart of the Lion (now about 29° Leo). Hydra forms the first decan. The second decan is Crater, "the cup." Corvus, "the raven," constitutes the third decan. The fixed star Algorab is in this constellation.

Anatomical Correspondences

Leo represents the heart, indicative of vital power, ardency, interchange, and generation, as well as the spinal marrow, nerves, and fiber. **Bones:** Dorsal vertebrae. **Muscles:** Those of the back and around the shoulder blades. **Arteries:** Aorta (coming out of the heart), anterior and posterior coronary. **Veins:** Coronaries.

Health

Physical disorders of Leo manifest in the various forms of heart disease, palpitation, fevers, spinal meningitis, heat exhaustion, sunstroke, pestilence, and inflammations.

As this is a vital and motive sign ruling the heart, temperate living is essential. Harmony, order and moderation in all things should be cultivated; excitement and haste curtailed. Heating and stimulating foods or beverages should be avoided, but nutritious, blood-building food is necessary.

Desirable Characteristics

Loyalty, outspokenness, ardor, kindness, tolerance, generosity, philanthropy, inspiration, magnetism, inspiration, hope, chivalry, industry, fearlessness, magnanimity, idealism, sincerity, hospitality, intuition, comprehension.

Undesirable Characteristics

Arrogance, dictatorial manner, overbearing, condescension, impetuousness, pomposity, dominance, sensitivity, promiscuity, gullibility, fussiness, striking, hotheadedness.

Associations

Adam, Abraham, David, Esau, Israel, Hercules, Judy, Osiris, Leonis, Richard the Lion-Hearted, Alphard, Lea or Lee. Its colors are orange, yellow, flaxen, and golden. Gold watches, rings, amber, gold coins.

Locations

High, round-topped hills, places inhabited by wild beasts, deserts, forests; hard, stony, gravelly ways or hills; castles, forts, theatres, playgrounds, dance halls; places for sports, gambling, speculation; formal social functions; fireplaces, ovens, solariums.

Virgo

Classifications

Earth triplicity, mutable or flexed quadrature. Cold, dry, feminine, negative. Long ascension, western. Melancholy, barren, nocturnal, scientific, human, maternal.

Planets

Ruler: Mercury. **Detriment:** Neptune. **Exaltation:** Mercury. **Fall:** Venus.

General Description

The Sun appears to transit Virgo between August 23 and September 22. Virgo is known to have a bearing on matters pertaining to sickness, hygiene, clothing, food, cereals, employees, servants, service, work, and domestic animals.

Symbols

In some ancient Zodiacs, this sign was symbolized as a virgin lying prostrate; in one hand she holds a "spica" and in the other a "branch" (often referred to as a bough, sprout, plant, root tree, stem, or rod).

Mercury, the ruler, is a messenger, Messiah, A-Rab, or wandering teacher.

Biblical Correspondences

Virgo, bearing the sheaf, was called "the house of corn" or Bethlehem and is sometimes related to Joseph. **Archangel:** Hamaliel. **Angel:** Shelathiel. **Disciple:** Andrew. **Tribe of Israel:** Nephtali.

Stellar Symbols

Virgo, the constellation, rises at midnight, December 25. In the first decan of Virgo is Coma; the second decan is Centaurus, "the despised" or "the pierced." The principal stars in it are Bungula and Agena. Bootes is the third decan of this constellation. Prominent fixed stars in the constellation and near the ecliptic are Caphir, "an atonement offering," and Spica, "seed."

Anatomical Correspondences

Virgo's domain is the bowels or abdomen. It is chiefly associated with the duodenum and peritoneum. **Muscles:** Rectal and abdominal. **Arteries:** Those serving the digestive system, particularly the intestines. **Veins:** The intestinal veins.

Health

Virgo indicates disorders pertaining to the bowel and abdominal functions, such as colic, cholera, peritonitis, constipation, malnutrition and afflictions of the intestinal regions. Virgo affects the nervous system considerably. Virgo people benefit by paying attention to diet, hygiene, sanitation, and mental poise. Hypochondria is characteristic of this sign, while absorption, assimilation, selection, and utilization are Virgo functions.

Diet is an important factor to Virgo people. Meals should be regular and food well masticated. Foods, especially cereals, that regulate the bowels properly should be chosen. It is said that a well-proportioned vegetarian diet is favorable. Strong drinks or condiments should be avoided.

Desirable Characteristics

Thoughtfulness, action, seriousness, conciseness, discretion, sensitivity, intuition, efficiency, caution, intelligence, perception, contemplation, domesticity, prudence, providence, industry, methodicalness, thrift.

Undesirable Characteristics

Calculation, mercenary, selfishness, anxiety, worry, irritability, apprehension, discontent, secretiveness, criticism, skepticism, cold, unresponsiveness, inconsistency, indecisive, quick temper, timidity, lack of self-confidence.

Associations

Astrea, Athene, Beth, Bess, Bula, Elizabeth, Celeste, Stella, Adorah, Virgin, Eve, Madonna, Paris, Notre Dame, Gene.

In mundane astrology, the sixth sign has special reference to public health, general conditions of working people, and of poultry and domestic animals. It also indicates matters relating to municipal or national service, army or navy, departments or labor, horticulture, agriculture, medicinal herbs, prophylactics, Red Cross, humane relief societies.

Locations

Gardens, cornfields, granaries, pantries, restaurants; places where fruit and vegetables are kept and where hay, wheat, barley, cheese, or butter are stored; places where books, papers, maps, charts, planes, or medicines are kept.

Libra

Classifications

Air triplicity, cardinal quadrature. Hot, moist, masculine, positive. Long ascension, equinoctial, western. Semifruitful, humane, scientific, sanguine.

Planets

Ruler: Venus. **Detriment:** Mars. **Exaltation:** Saturn. **Fall:** Sun.

General Description

The Sun appears to enter Libra September 23 and to transit this sign until October 22. Libra is a crossing place or meeting place of the ecliptic and equator, the autumnal equinox. The Sun passes over from north to south declination at the first point of Libra, and on that date the day and night are of equal length—they weigh evenly, are balanced.

Symbols

Libra is symbolized by the apparently commonplace scales, but the arms of that tilting beam reach out into eternities. The position of the attached bowls, which a feather's weight may change, indicates the destinies of ages, the fortunes of empires, the estates of immortality. The equipoise of the beam marks the adjustment of mighty feuds internal and external.

Biblical Correspondences

Archangel: Zuriel. **Angel:** Chedquiel. **Disciple:** Bartholomew. **Apostle:** Luke. **Tribe of Israel:** Asher.

Stellar Symbols

Two stars formerly in Libra: Zuben al Genubi, "insufficient price," and Zuben al Schemali, "the full price." Hydra, "the serpent," extends through the meridian of this sign also. On the south of this sign is the first decan, Crucis, or crux, meaning "cross"; on the north of Libra is the third decan, Corona Borealis, "the crown." Between these two and close to Libra is Lupus, "the wolf."

Anatomical Correspondences

Libra rules the lumbar region in general and the kidneys in particular. Its zone of influence includes the loins, ovaries, and the substance of the kidneys. Libra represents equipoise, distillation, sublimation, and filtration. **Bones:** Lumbar vertebrae, just below the ribs. **Muscles:** Those of the lower back and top of pelvic bone. **Arteries:** Those going to the kidneys and lower back. **Veins:** Those coming from the kidneys and lower back.

Health

Libra disturbances manifest through Bright's disease, nephritis, suppression of urine, neuralgia of kidneys, weak lower back, etc. Pains in the lower part of the back are symptoms that should be given attention. A well-balanced diet between acid and starchy foods is necessary. Plenty of fresh air, harmonious surroundings, and mild exercise are essential. Attention should be given to proper diet, especially concerning liquid foods, as the kidneys are the chief organs affected.

Desirable Characteristics

Thoughtfulness, impartiality, unprejudiced, conciliation, foresight, justice, grace, modesty, decorum, refinement, art, adaptability, persuasiveness, affection, peace, cheerfulness, sympathy, forgiveness, generosity, idealism, tact, balance.

Undesirable Characteristics

Indecision, uncertainty, extremism, recklessness, hesitance, susceptibility, impressionability, illusion, punctilious, pedantry, vanity, aloofness, shirking, carelessness, vacillation.

Associations

Justice, Justine, Zuben, Ruben, Corona, Sum, Luke, Harpocrates, Charles, beam, cross, scale weights, measures, pianos, tables, upholstered furniture.

It is said that Libra people usually make good buyers for large concerns, having good discrimination and intuition regarding what to buy that can be sold readily, especially in seasonable goods and quickly moving items such as novelties, fancy goods, perfumes, apparel, and jewels. They are also good as court attaches, bailiffs, clerks, and justices.

Locations

Places near windmills, straggling barns; where wood is cut or piled; sawpits; harbor for ships, where boats are made or launched; tops of mountains, mounds, or hills; trees; ground where hunting or hawking is practiced; golf links, sandy or gravelly places; tops of buildings with cupolas or domes; closets, guest chambers; tops of dressers, wardrobes, jewel cases.

Scorpio

Classifications

Water triplicity, fixed quadrature. Cold, feminine, negative. Long ascension, nocturnal, western. Fruitful, phlegmatic, reproductive, violent, mute.

Planets

Ruler: Mars was the traditional ruler of Scorpio, but when Pluto was discovered in 1930, it proved to have a great affinity for this sign. **Detriment:** Venus. **Exaltation:** In the ancient tables of dignities and debilities, Scorpio was left blank as to exaltation. No planet was exalted in Scorpio, but modern astrologers assign it as the exaltation of Uranus. **Fall:** The Moon.

General Description

The Sun appears to transit this sign yearly between October 23 and November 21.

Symbols

Scorpio is symbolized by a scorpion or sometimes by a snake or eagle. Scorpio in Arabic and Syriac is Al Akrab, meaning "wounding, conflict, war." In Coptic it is Isidis, "attack of the enemy." In the Hebrew Zodiac, Scorpio was ascribed to Dan. The banner of the tribe of Israel was originally a scorpion, but afterward was an eagle.

Biblical Correspondences

Archangel: Barkiel. **Angel:** Saitziel. **Disciples:** Judas Iscariot is the disciple indicated by Scorpio. Philip is also assigned here. **Tribe of Israel:** Dan. The cherubim had the head of a bull (Taurus), the head of a lion (Leo), and the head of an eagle (Scorpio), as well as a human head (Aquarius).

Stellar Symbols

In the three decans—the parts outside the Zodiac in the constellations that in older days corresponded with the longitude of the sign—we see pictured in the star map the serpent, Ophiuchus, and above, Hercules and the three-headed dog of hell, Cerberus. Beneath all these is the scorpion. The bright star in the Hercules constellation is Rasel Gethi, meaning "head of him who bruises."

Anatomical Correspondences

Scorpio is concerned with both the reproductive and destructive processes, procreation, and re-adaptation, exercising special influence over the generative organs. The parts of the body coming within its zone are the bladder, ureters, pelvis of the kidney, urethra, prostrate gland, groin, rectum, colon, nostrils, and sense of smell. Scorpio is responsible both for producing the subtle scents of sexual excitation and for picking them up. **Bones:** The pelvic and pubic bones. **Muscles:** Those governing the openings of the bladder, rectum, and urethra. **Arteries:** Those serving the pelvic region. **Veins:** Those serving the reproductive organs.

Health

Physical disorders manifest as rupture, fistulas, hemorrhoids, and afflictions associated with the generative organs, including injuries to the groin.

Desirable Characteristics

Energy, action, positiveness, fearlessness, tenacity, penetration, thoughtfulness, optimism, pleasantness, eloquence, devotion, patience, ambition.

Undesirable Characteristics

Severity, callousness, causticity, sarcasm, suspicion, destruction, vindictiveness, dogmatism, shrewdness, parsimoniousness, tyranny, passion.

Associations

Isidis, Frons, Antares, Shiloh, Lesuth, Judas.

Scorpio indicates success in positions requiring patience, perseverance, and concentration, and produces good surgeons, chemists, detectives, researchers, and in lines where courage, strength, and personal effort are necessary.

Locations

Low gardens, vineyards; muddy, sluggish streams; ill-smelling ponds, peat bogs, quagmires; slaughter-houses, meat markets, operating rooms; lavatories, sinks, drains, cesspools; places where junk or old iron is stored; garbage dumps, compost heaps; tanneries, incinerating plants, chemical laboratories, crematories.

Sagittarius

Classifications

Fire triplicity, mutable of flexed quadrature. Hot, dry, masculine, positive. Long ascension, southern. Choleric, dual-purposed, motive, bilious.

Planets

Ruler: Jupiter. **Detriment:** Mercury. **Exaltation:** The South Node of the Moon. **Fall:** The North Node of the Moon.

General Description

The Sun appears to transit this sign between November 22 and December 21, yearly.

Symbols

Sagittarius is pictured as half man, half horse, the man an archer with a bow and arrow: a Centaur or Centaurion. The symbol of Sagittarius is pictured by a sharp instrument like an arrow or spear; an armed horseman or warrior represents this fiery sign. The Greeks called him Chiron.

Biblical Correspondences

Archangel: Adnachiel. **Angel:** Samequiel. **Prophet:** Zephaniah. **Apostle:** James, son of Zebedee. **Tribe of Israel:** Benjamin.

Stellar Symbols

The first decan, or side piece, of the constellation of Sagittarius was Lyra, "the harp," the oldest of stringed musical instruments, the invention that the ancients ascribed to the gods. The harp connects the archer with superior joy, delight, gladness, and praiseworthy action, all typical of the characteristics of the advanced sons of Jove as we know them today. Vega, meaning "victory," the brightest star in the northern skies, was in Lyra.

The second decan of Sagittarius was Ara, called, by the Arabs, Al Mugamra, "the completing." In the third decan we see Draco, "the dragon." Its chief star, once the pole star (four to six thousand years ago) had several names as Al Waid, "who is to be destroyed," Thuban, "the subtile," and Al Dib, "the reptile."

Other stars in Draco are Etanin, "long serpent," Grumain, "the deceiver," El Athik, "the fraudful," El Asieh, "the humbled," and Gianser, "the punished enemy."

Anatomical Correspondences

Sagittarius rules the sacrum and the sciatic nerve that proceeds down from it, enervating the upper and back parts of the legs, the hips, and the thighs. Tradition gives it rulership over the liver, although Virgo and Cancer are probably more influential here. **Bones:** The sacrum and tibia. **Muscles:** Thigh muscles, buttocks. **Arteries:** Those serving the thighs and buttocks. **Veins:** Those serving the thighs and buttocks.

Health

Sagittarians are susceptible to felons, whitlow, abscesses, suppuration, and septic inflammations, as well as injuries through horses and falls. Being opposite to Gemini, the sign Sagittarius also is given to afflictions denoted by that sign, i.e., lung and nerve trouble. Disease may also manifest as enteric disorders, sciatica, rheumatism, gout, dislocations of the hip joint, feverish ailments, blood disorders, cuts and wounds, and volitional disturbances.

This sign has a tendency to over-activity; therefore moderation and deliberate action are essential when ailing. The great open spaces is their sphere; the outdoors, with sports, physical exercises, and hiking. Its herb is pimpernel.

Desirable Characteristics

Sincerity, honesty, frankness, justice, generosity, foresightedness, prophecy, perseverance, dependability, buoyancy, geniality, joviality, hope, logical, charitable.

Undesirable Characteristics

Boisterousness, overconfidence, rashness, changeability, bluntness, brusqueness, aggression, defiance, uncompromising, prodigality, independence, speculation, sportiveness.

Associations

Jove, Jehovah, Vega, Terebellum, St. George, Swift, horseman, victory, obelisk, Oedipus, Leviathan, Victor. Incense burners, harps, racehorses.

Locations

Highest places in the land, hills, ground that rises higher than the surrounding country; the topmost room in a house; places near fire or where it has been; stables for war horses or racers; also long, slim, pointed things such as arrows, spears, swords, etc.

Capricorn

Classifications

Earth triplicity, cardinal quadrature. Cold, dry, feminine, negative. Short ascension, solstitial, southern. Tropical, melancholy, quadrupetal, serving.

Planets

Ruler: Saturn. **Detriment:** The Moon. **Exaltation:** Mars. **Fall:** Jupiter.

General Description

The Sun apparently transits Capricorn between December 22 and January 19. From the astronomical standpoint, the Sun is seen to come yearly to the lower part of the great cross at the winter solstice in Capricorn, reaching its lowest point in southern declination (23° 27') called *the grave* on December 22, remaining in that degree for three days, after which on December 25 it ascends out of the grave like a new birth or a resurrection.

Symbols

Capricorn in modern astrology is symbolized by a goat, but in ancient uranographies it was portrayed as half goat, with the tail of a fish. In early religious history, the goat was a sacrificial animal. The Philistines connected Dagon, the half-fish god, with Capricornus. The Babylonians connected the half-fish god Oannes with Capricornus.

Biblical Correspondences

Archangel: Hanael. **Angel:** Saritiel. **Prophet:** Nathum. **Disciples:** Simon, Peter, and Thomas. **Tribe of Israel:** Zebulon. Capricorn is related to Nephtali, the son of Jacob.

Stellar Symbols

The first decan of Capricorn is Sagitta, a heavenly arrow speeding to its aim. The second decan shows Aquila, "the pierced and falling eagle." Its principal star is Al Tair, meaning "the wounded." The third decan to this sign is a beautiful cluster of stars named Delphinus or Dolphin, a vigorous fish springing upward.

Anatomical Correspondences

The two words "catabolism" and "metamorphosis" adequately describe decay, death, and rebirth, attributes of Capricorn, which also signifies contraction, limitation, dry epidermis, nucleolation, and induration. The joints come under Capricorn's influence, particularly those of the knee and the patella bone, as well as the bony structure or skeleton, as indicated by Saturn. **Muscles:** The muscles of the knee. **Nerves:** Those in the knees. **Arteries:** Those in the knees. **Veins:** Those running through the knees.

Health

As Capricorn governs the epidermis, morbid action registers in skin diseases such as eczema, impetigo, and pruritus; falls, bruises, and dislocations are indicated, as well as hysterics, rheumatism, and colds. Because of the tendency of this sign toward depression, melancholia, despondency, discontent, worry, and nervousness, special attention should be given to transcending these tendencies. Cheerful company and comfortable, congenial surroundings are helpful. Heating and stimulating foods are usually required as well as those that are laxative. A fair amount of physical exercise is beneficial. Its herb is dock.

Desirable Characteristics

Dignity, prudence, caution, reverence, practicality, thoughtfulness, particularity, diplomacy, profundity, positiveness, magnetism, ambition, organization, concentration, service.

Undesirable Characteristics

Nervousness, limitation, conceit, jealousy, selfishness, discontent, capriciousness, suspicion, authoritativeness, gloominess, depression, avarice, impatience.

Associations

Messiah, mediator, atoner, sexton, set, stone, priest, winters, Calvary, Golgotha, St. Peter, Simon Peter, church, Vatican, religion, cross, gates, groves, Janus, Naphtali (son of Jacob), Pan, Bacchus, Father Time, King Winter, Jack Frost, Dionysius, caper, Adolph.

Things ruled by Capricorn include ice chests; leather for harness, belts, shoes; logs, old trees; coffins, ashes, stones, tile, cement, lime brick; ice, snow, frost; brimstone, rock salt; goats; bones, skeletons, knees, horns; quince, hemlock.

Locations

Jails, cells, vaults, sepulchres, tombs, etc.; mangers, goat pens, corrals, etc.; thorny or barren ground; cellars, deep pits; frozen places, fallow ground, dungeons, convents, old churches, caves; thick, dark forests.

Aquarius

Classifications

Air triplicity, fixed quadrature. Moist, masculine, positive. Short ascension, southern. Sanguine, human, scientific, electric, serving, eloquent, intuitive.

Planets

Ruler: Uranus. **Detriment:** The Sun. **Exaltation:** Neptune. **Fall:** Pluto.

General Description

The Sun appears to transit through this sign between January 20 and February 18.

Symbols

Aquarius is symbolized by a man emptying a water pot. In some of the Zodiacs, he holds a rod, branch, or wand in one uplifted hand. In some of the older Zodiacs, Aquarius is pictured as a woman. Always associated with Aquarius is the urn, or the cupbearer. The Hebrew name for Aquarius was Delphi, or "water urn," signifying a pouring out or baptism, related to atonement. The waters poured by the heavenly man are the waters of life, the beneficence of fresh, sparkling water to parched humankind on earth.

Biblical Correspondence

This is one of the four fixed signs constituting the Cherubim mentioned in the scriptures (Taurus, Leo, Scorpio, and Aquarius). It is believed that it corresponds with Jacob's son Reuben. It is also associated with John the Baptist. **Archangel:** Cambiel. **Angel:** Tzakmlqiel. **Prophet:** Habukkuk. **Disciple:** Matthew. **Tribe of Israel:** Reuben.

Stellar Symbols

The first decan was the Southern Fish, Pisces Australis; the second decan, Pegasus, a great horse rushing forward with huge wings at his shoulders. The stars in the constellation are Markab, "the returning"; Scheat, "he who goeth and returneth"; Enif, "the branch"; Al Genib, "who carries"; Homan, "the waters"; Matar, "who causeth plenteous overflow." The third decan is that of a beautiful swan, which, though injured, circles and mounts the Milky Way; it lies in the midst of the great Galactic Stream of nebulous stars. The principal stars in it form a beautiful cross. Its brightest stars are Deneb, "the Lord Judge to come"; Azelfafage; Sadr, "who returns in a circle"; Adige, "flying swiftly"; and Arided, "he shall come down."

Anatomical Correspondences

Aquarius rules the coccyx at the base of the spine, the calves and ankles, and the cones and rods in the eye. **Bones:** Coccyx, lower leg bones, and shins. **Muscle:** Calf muscles, those in the ankles and shins. **Arteries:** Those in the lower leg. **Veins:** Those in the lower leg.

Health

Aquarius inclines to falls; sprained, broken, or swollen ankles; anemia; spasmodic and nervous diseases, blood poisoning, hay fever, heart weakness, and cramps.

As Aquarius has much to do with the water in the bloodstream, the blood should be kept in good condition and any sign of impurity suggests prompt remedial attention. Fresh air and good water, with plenty of vegetables and fruit, are necessary, as well as music and harmonious surroundings. Brain and blood-building foods are required, but stimulants and fat or greasy foods should be avoided. The eyes should be given proper care. Its herb is dragonwort.

Desirable Characteristics

Leadership, truthfulness, scientific, sincerity, earnestness, humane, cooperativeness, sociability, service, consideration, unbiased, patience, steadiness, invention, philosophy, intuitive, pleasant, progressive, cosmopolitan.

Undesirable Characteristics

Unnecessary radicalism, mental fanaticism, emphasizes ideas over feelings or irrational, subjective material, political extremism, derives enjoyment from shocking people, gullibility where social injustice is involved.

Associations

Cup, water pot, Delee, Ganymede, fountain, Pacha, chief, Cygnus, smoke, steam, rain, ferries, bridges, railways, roundhouses, cars, airplanes, gas, motors, telephones, radios, electricity, wool, hair.

Locations

Hilly and uneven places where rivulets run, near springs or conduits; vineyards; roofs of houses, eaves; highways, railroad crossings, stop signs; broadcasting stations, power lines, electric power houses, uranium mines, garages.

Pisces

Classifications

Water triplicity, mutable or flexed quadrature. Cold, moist, feminine, negative. Short ascension, eastern. Fruitful, lymphatic, serving, psychic, emotional, inspirational, bicorporal.

Planets

Ruler: Neptune. **Detriment:** Mercury. **Exaltation:** Venus, Neptune's octave. **Fall:** Mercury.

General Description

The Sun appears to transit Pisces between February 19 and March 20 annually.

Symbols

Pisces is pictured by two fishes, one headed toward the north and the other parallel with the path of the Sun. They are some distance apart, but bound together with the undulating band that falls upon the neck of Cetus the whale, and under the leg of the Lamb.

Biblical Correspondences

Archangel: Amnitziel. **Angel:** Barchiel. **Prophet:** Joel. **Disciple:** The younger James. **Tribe of Israel:** Simeon. Ephraini, the son of Israel is associated with Pisces.

Stellar Symbols

The first decan is the constellation named the Lizard. The second decan is the constellation Cepheus; the figure of the king stands in an attitude of power. In one hand he holds aloft a scepter. The star on his right shoulder is Al Deramin, "quickly returning"; in the girdle is Al Phirk, "the redeemer"; and in the left knee, the Shepherd. The north fish reaches right over into the third decan, Andromeda, a woman in chains that are broken.

Anatomical Correspondences

The feet and toes come under the domain of Pisces, particularly the soles. Also the lymphatic system, all the extremities in general (for instance, the fingers, the tips of the nose and ears), the duodenum, and the cecum. The Pisces/Virgo axis rules peristaltic action as well. **Bones:** Those in the feet and toes. **Muscles:** The muscles governing the movement of the feet and toes. **Arteries:** Those in the feet and the extremities. **Veins:** Those in the feet and the extremities.

Health

Physical disturbances manifest through deformities of the feet and toes, bunions, gout, discharges, edema, glandular softening, lung trouble, bowel troubles. Danger through contagious diseases and by the use of drugs.

As the recuperative power may be weak, attention to the rules of hygiene, diet, and sanitation is necessary. There may be a tendency to take too much liquid; stimulating beverages should be avoided. It is said that the dandelion is very beneficial because of its tonic effect.

Desirable Characteristics

Inspiration, idealism, concentration, hospitality, service, peace, refinement, purity, perception, psychometry, order, method.

Undesirable Characteristics

Negativism, diffidence, dreaminess, lethargy, carelessness, indolence, indecisiveness, easygoing, improvidence, apologetic, submissive, variation, self-depreciation, inferiority complex, timidity, sensitivity, self-pity, loyalty, criticism.

Associations

Nuno, Picot, Okda, holy water, fishnets, boats, aquariums, submarines, deep-sea divers.

Locations

Oceans, fishing places, fish ponds, canneries; grounds overflowed with water; damp, wet, boggy places; places formerly underwater; oil fields, oil tanks; spiritualistic churches, séances.

ASCENDANTS

The following delineations of the effect of Ascending Signs are for the signs alone without any planets in the First House. A planet in the First House will modify these testimonies. A fortunate planet will increase the good and diminish the adverse qualities; and vice versa if the planet is malefic.

The physical descriptions denoted by the Sign Ascending may be termed the ideal that may be expected from each sign. In actual practice, however, it will be observed that they frequently vary from the normal in some respects. The variations are mainly due to the effect of the sign in which the planet ruling the Ascending Sign is located; whether it is in one of similar or contrary nature; the nature of the planets strongly aspecting that significator, etc. Racial characteristics, hereditary peculiarities, early training, environment, occupational traits, and geographical influences all have some effect in molding the physiognomy.

The planet ruling the hour of birth also has a considerable effect on the physical and mental make-up of a native.

Aries Ascending

Personality

Those who are born at a time when the sign Aries is rising are at their best when they can guide, control, and govern themselves or others, as they have the ability to plan and map out the future and lay out modes of action. They are lovers of independence, fond of their own way and happy only in activity and command. The desire is to be at the head of things and leaders in thought and action. They are enterprising and ambitious, quite versatile and usually rather headstrong and impulsive; forceful and determined in effort and expressive in speech; intense when interested, vehement when excited. Somewhat inclined to be fiery or quick-tempered, ready to resent abuse or imposition, and also liable to go to extremes through indignation, they do not hold a grudge for any great length of time. They admire scientific thought and are quite philosophical; and do not become discouraged easily as they possess a sharp, penetrating willpower. They do best in vocations requiring quick action, decision, executive or mechanical ability, and responsibility. Motive temperament. The planetary significator is Mars.

Physical Appearance

Middle stature or rather above it, spare body, long face and neck, ruddy complexion, head broad at the temples and narrow at the chin, thin features, mark or scar on head or temples; bushy eyebrows, sharp sight, eyes gray to grayish brown; rough or wiry hair but sometimes fine in youth, varying in color from dark to sandy, sometimes going bald at the temples, sandy whiskers.

Mental Tendencies

Ambition, activity, energy, courage, enterprise, impulsiveness, ardor, combativeness, and ingenuity.

Taurus Ascending

Personality

A self-reliant, persistent nature capable of working hard and long in order to accomplish their purposes. Gentle while unprovoked, but "mad as a bull" when really angered, and when opposed are stubborn and unyielding. Usually quiet, dogmatic, and somewhat secretive or reserved concerning their affairs. They have a great deal of endurance, latent power, and energy; are practical and have organizing ability; usually sincere, reliable, and trustworthy. They are fond of pleasure and love beauty in nature, art, music, and literature; are influenced greatly by sympathy. Possessing a magnetic quality, they are able to benefit those who are irritable or nervous. They are careful, steady, and able to carry to completion the projects they undertake. They have the ability to earn money for others and are good at all executive work. Matters connected with the earth and its products succeed under their supervision; vital temperament. The planetary significator is Venus.

Physical Appearance

In stature short to middle height, inclined to plumpness and often stoop-shouldered; square face and square build of body; short, strong neck; full forehead, nose, lips, cheeks, and mouth; heavy jaw; dark eyes; hair wavy, dark, and sometimes curly; round and prominent eyes; hands plump, short, and broad.

Mental Tendencies

Persevering, constant, conservative, determined, obstinate, proud and ambitious of power, yet sociable, affectionate, and loving, but can also be very unreasonable, prejudiced, and stubborn as a bull. When angry will not stop at anything. Usually slow, but good, steady worker. The undeveloped types are sometimes very indolent and sensual.

Gemini Ascending

Personality

Ambitious, aspiring, curious. and given to inquiry, investigation, and experimenting; also apt, dexterous, active, and capable of engaging in two or more pursuits at the same time. The nature is sympathetic and sensitive, the mind is intuitive, perceptive, and imaginative, also quite idealistic and fond of all mental recreation. There is a liking for pleasure, adventure, science, and educational pursuits. At times restless, anxious, high-strung, and diffusive, mentally timid, indecisive, irritable, and excitable. Love change and diversity and must be constantly busy to be happy, because inactivity creates impatience. As a rule, Geminis are very clever as they are progressive, inventive, mechanical, ingenious, and possess inherent conversational and literary ability. They do best in occupations where there is variety of activity, and where the mind and hands can be engaged in several different things. The literary and educational world is their best outlet. Mental temperament. The planetary significator is Mercury.

Physical Appearance

Tall, slender, erect but lithe figure; quick, active walk; long arms and fingers; thin features, long face, nose, and chin; sanguine complexion; hazel or gray eyes; dark hair, usually brown.

Mental Tendencies

Quick to learn, fond of reading and writing, inquisitive, capable of acquiring a good education; dexterous, lively, ingenious, quick witted; inclination and admiration for music, drawing, painting, languages, dancing, travel, and invention. Sometimes shy or retiring, good disposition, humane. Nervous and restless.

Cancer Ascending

Personality

Changeable, sensitive, and retiring disposition with many changes and ups and downs of position and occupation. They have a fertile imagination, are somewhat sentimental, sympathetic, and talkative. Fond of home and family; have a tenacious memory, especially for family or historical events; industrious, frugal, economical, and anxious to acquire the goods of life. Fear of ridicule or criticism makes them discreet, diplomatic, and conventional. They appreciate approbation and are easily encouraged by kindness. The emotions are strong and they delight in beautiful scenery and in romantic or strange experiences and adventures. They have psychic and mediumistic faculty, are very conscientious, receptive to new ideas, and have the ability to adapt themselves to their environment. They are adapted to pursuits of a fluctuating nature, such as catering to public needs and desires. Vital temperament. The planetary significator is the Moon.

Physical Appearance

Not usually above average height, tendency to stoutness, sometimes an awkward or heavy gait; round face, full cheeks, tendency to double chin, short nose sometimes prominent at the tip; gray or light blue eyes, pale complexion, wide chest, hands and feet small; uses crablike positions and motions of the arms.

Mental Tendencies

Fond of novelty, change, and traveling, yet usually attached to relatives and home, inclined to public life. Desirous of possessions, cautious, prudent, careful with money yet often imposed upon; sympathetic and changeable. As a rule, some psychic or occult faculty manifests.

Leo Ascending

Personality

Good-natured, philosophical, generous, kindhearted, noble disposition. Leo natives are frank, free, outspoken, independent, impulsive, forceful, and demonstrative in manner. Their nature is electric and inspiring. They have great hope, faith, and fortitude; are energetic and lavish in the expenditure of energy and vitality when their sympathy or interest is aroused. In affection they are ardent, sincere, and passionate. They are philanthropic, charitable, loyal, aspiring, conscientious, adaptable, inventive and intuitive; are imperious and fond of power and command; usually popular and leaders in their social sphere. They are generally good-tempered, though high-strung and quick to anger, yet are very forgiving and do not hold a grudge for long; high ideals. They receive and grant favors readily and are usually fortunate in the long run. They succeed best where they have authority or hold some high or responsible position in managing or executive departments. Motive temperament. The significator is the Sun.

Physical Appearance

Broad shoulders, large bones and muscles, tall, upper part of body better formed than the lower; thin waist, prominent knees, upright carriage; hair soft and wavy, usually light in color with tendency to baldness; head full-sized and round, gray eyes, ruddy or florid complexion.

Mental Tendencies

Ambitious, generous, honorable, frank, warm-hearted, self-confident, fearless, impulsive, determined, persevering, and conscientious; fond of power and distinction; liking for art; cheerful, optimistic.

Virgo Ascending

Personality

Modest, conservative, thoughtful, contemplative, and industrious. Virgos have a desire for wealth but require extra effort to save money; are very active, not easily contented and learn readily and quickly;

have good endurance and do not show their age. Of a speculative turn and often give way to worry and over-anxiety; are sensitive to surroundings and to the conditions of others. They are quite discriminative and careful of details. Cautious regarding their own interests and will not neglect the interests of others, being diplomatic, tactful, and shrewd. They are prudent, economical, and practical, and usually act with forethought. The Virgo native should avoid drugs and animal foods as much as possible, and study hygiene in connection with diet to maintain health. Commercial and business affairs and matters connected with the earth and its products succeed under their careful supervision. Usually mental-motive temperament. The planetary significator is Mercury.

Physical Appearance
Average height or a little above, moderately plump, well formed; oval face, dark hair, eyes, and complexion; straight nose; active walk.

Mental Tendencies
Fond of learning, active mind, good mental abilities, critical, thoughtful, methodical, precise, ingenious; sometimes rather undecided, nervous, and lacking self-confidence.

Libra Ascending

Personality
Love justice, neatness, order, peace, and harmony and are usually very courteous, pleasant, and agreeable people; although quick to anger, are easily appeased. They are fond of beauty in all forms: in nature, art, music, literature, etc., and can enter with zest into refined and cultural pleasures and amusements and greatly enjoy the company and society of brave, happy, sunny, mirthful people. They are affectionate, sympathetic, kind, generous, and compassionate; idealistic, artistic, adaptable, constructive, intuitive, impressionable, and inspirational. They admire modesty and refinement; are ambitious but dislike unclean work and all discord. The best outlet for their talents is in the professions and they have ability for lines requiring good taste, an artistic touch, and a fine finish. Mental-vital temperament. The planetary significator is Venus.

Physical Appearance
Well-formed body, tall, slender in youth but tendency to stoutness in middle age. Hair smooth, brown to black; blue or brown eyes; Grecian nose; round or oval face with regular features; often have dimples; good-looking, youthful appearance; good complexion.

Mental Tendencies
Good mental abilities, keen sense of perception with foresight and good comparison; imaginative or artistic, good-natured, hopeful, cheerful, genial, humane, just, orderly; usually amorous, loving but

changeable, fond of society and amusements. Like to go places and do things, be in-style or up-to-date. Fond of fine clothes and jewelry.

Scorpio Ascending

Personality

Reserved, tenacious, determined, and secretive, somewhat inclined to be suspicious, skeptical, and stingingly sarcastic. They are quick-witted, quick in speech and action, alert, forceful, and positive. They are often blunt, brusque, and seemingly fond of contest; nevertheless they make staunch and splendid friends. They possess grit and enterprise that will enable them to reach high attainments. They accomplish their purposes by subtlety and strength of will, or by force if necessary. They have mechanical skill and much constructive (or destructive) ability.

They enjoy travel, are fond of investigating mysteries and things occult. Although appreciating luxury, can be very frugal and economical. They are natural detectives, sheriffs, bailiffs, chemists, surgeons, and contractors and gifted in accomplishing things requiring muscular skill or aggressive enterprise. Motive-vital temperament. The planetary significator is Pluto.

Physical Appearance

Average height or slightly below, tendency to stoutness or at least full form, often square type of face and build of body; thick, dark hair curly or wavy, sometimes crimpy or frizzy; prominent brows and perceptive faculties, aquiline or Mediterranean type of nose and profile, dusky complexion.

Mental Tendencies

Quick, keen, shrewd, critical, penetrating mind, and keen judgment. Strong will and determination; self-reliant, bold, fixed views. A subtle mind hard to influence, not easily imposed upon, willful, courageous, energetic, and active when interested but at other times indolent. Sarcastic or impulsive and very angry when provoked. Frequently interested in some form of occult or chemical research and fond of mystery. Some are very practical, matter-of-fact, executive, good businessmen, contractors, etc. They make good officers, naval men, workers with or dealers in liquids. Inclination to surgery or some practical scientific research or pursuit.

Sagittarius Ascending

Personality

Inclined to be jovial, bright, hopeful, generous, and charitable. Love liberty and freedom, are very independent, and will allow no one to order or drive them. Usually good-humored and honorable. In disposition, frank, fearless, impulsive, demonstrative, outspoken, nervously energetic, ambitious, sincere, and quick to arrive at conclusions. They are sympathetic and loving, possess good calculation and foresight, are intuitive and prophetic, and, although often appearing blunt or abrupt, they rarely miss the mark in their deductions. At times they are restless, over-anxious and high-strung. They respect religious customs, enjoy outdoor sports, are fond of animals, and interested in travel, law, medicine, and philosophy. In the professions or commercial world, Sagittarians are generally aggressive, progressive, and aspiring, quick to see and take advantage of opportunities and to consummate business arrangements. In speech they go straight to the point and aim directly at the mark. They like wholesale, big business and large financial undertakings. Motive-mental temperament. The planetary significator is Jupiter.

Physical Appearance

Tall, slender, well-made figure inclined to stoop; generally long or oval face, rounded forehead, expressive blue or hazel eyes, clear complexion, hair brown or chestnut inclining to baldness especially near the temples; tendency to stamp or scrape the feet.

Mental Tendencies

Generous, goodhearted, good-tempered, just, frank, free, cheerful, charitable, and friendly; active and enterprising; sympathetic, humane, and somewhat impulsive. Inclination for philosophy, law, medicine, or religion; fond of traveling, voyaging, and outdoor sports and exercises.

Capricorn Ascending

Personality

Serious, quiet, thoughtful, contemplative nature, possessing dignity and self-esteem enough to look after their interests well. They are cautious, prudent, economical, and practical and usually act only after due premeditation. They are ambitious and persevering and can work hard and long without becoming discouraged. Capable of much endeavor where opportunity is afforded, especially in business. They possess organizing ability. Determined and persistent, cautious and calculating, of profound thought and concentrative ability, they are able to plan and carry out schemes of considerable magnitude. They are not demonstrative in feeling and do not readily show their sympathy; they prefer ideas to words and acts to promises. They are industrious, self-reliant, and thrifty; respect religion, are given to investigation, interested in theology, and explore any chosen subject or science deeply. If Saturn, the significator, is much afflicted in the horoscope, they meet with many delays and disappointments and are inclined to give way too readily to adverse circumstances. They may be restricted by poor health. Otherwise they do well in matters connected with the earth and its products and with large corporations and public utility concerns. Motive or motive-mental temperament.

Physical Appearance

Stature average to short; generally defective walk and liability to rheumatism in the joints or marks and scars about the knees; sometimes thin and bony; prominent features usually long and thin; long or prominent nose, thin neck, long chin, hair dark or black, not overplentiful, thin beard; usually not very handsome.

Mental Tendencies

Self-willed, strong in purpose, ambitious, reserved, pensive, and secretive. In disposition quiet, cold, sometimes despondent, much mental ingenuity and fertility, changeable, capricious, conniving, and determined. A great desire for wealth, power, position, and a tendency to look out for themselves. Ability for managing and organizing. They succeed by perseverance and forceful, steady action, rather than by spasmodic effort.

Aquarius Ascending

Personality

Determined, quiet, patient, unobtrusive, and faithful nature as a rule. Aquarians are philosophical, very humanitarian, and usually refined; fond of art, music, scenery, and literature. In disposition reasonable, thoughtful, discriminative. Have a good memory, are clear reasoners and very capable of dealing with facts. Everything in the mental world appeals to them and they are sincere and practical, fond of honor and dignity, active in reforms, progressive in ideas, and possess a sympathetic, goodhearted, pleasant, generous nature. Have strong likes and dislikes, usually sociable and of large acquaintance; intuitive, fond of occult research; peculiar, radical, or eccentric in some ways. They succeed in pursuits where steady application of mind and concentration of thought are necessary or where sociability and friends are required. They have inventive genius and literary ability. Mental-motive temperament. Uranus is the planetary significator.

Physical Appearance

Medium stature, full or square build, strong, well-formed; tendency to stoutness in middle age; good, clear complexion, oval or long, fleshy face; hair varies from light to dark, flaxen, brown, etc.; usually good-looking, friendly countenance.

Mental Tendencies

Intelligent, good memory and reasoning faculty, very capable of dealing with facts; possess good concentration and appreciate knowledge. Kind, humane, self-controlled, constant, persevering, happy disposition; ingenious, inventive, sometimes incline to psychic or socialistic matters; love for humanizing influences, pursuits, and occupations; often become physicians; have many friends.

Pisces Ascending

Personality

Kind, loving, trustful, confiding, sympathetic nature. The disposition is courteous, affable, hospitable, and methodical. Pisces are idealistic, imaginative, impressionable, emotional, mediumistic, receptive, and quiet. Orderly in manner. Quick to observe deficiencies in others or lack of completeness in anything. They are usually lacking in confidence and self-esteem, are modest and timid, and hesitate about putting themselves forward. At times they are inclined to be over-anxious and become disheartened, indecisive, and lacking in life and energy. Capable of developing fine psychometric, telepathic, intuitive, and inspirational faculty. They love music, scenery, and animals. They usually succeed in occupations that require industry, discretion, and power to make the best of circumstances; also in any employment that brings some kind of change, or where attention to details and completeness is necessary. Vital temperament. The planetary significator is Neptune.

Physical Appearance

Middle to short stature with short limbs, inclining to corpulence especially in later years; full or fleshy face, pale complexion, tendency to double chin; full eyes, wide mouth, plentiful hair, dark brown to black, small hands and feet.

Mental Tendencies

Quick in understanding, inspirational, versatile, easygoing, good-natured, uncertain, changeable, psychically receptive, emotional, and fond of music; passionate, affectionate, charitable; sometimes reserved, secretive, or mysterious in their way of doing things.

MIDHEAVENS

The sign on the Midheaven in the birth chart indicates the ground upon which self-understanding can grow. The Midheaven (MC) is an indicator of our status in the world and how we see ourselves. To summarize in general terms, the fire signs at the MC indicate that self-awareness develops through intuitive means, supported by concrete interactions in the social, family, and work environments. Earth signs indicate a practical, conscious path to self-understanding, supported by subconscious intuition. Air-sign Midheavens learn about the self through logical intellectual processes, supported by clarity of judgment based on less conscious feelings, while water signs do just the opposite—make judgments based on feelings, supported by intellectual analysis. Each time a planet conjoins the MC or the MC conjoins a planet, energy is applied to the system to impel you to greater self-awareness.

Aries Midheaven

Mars reflects energy and action. Midheaven-Mars aspects, or Aries Midheaven, indicates ego-conscious action. The ability to decide what to do and the action itself are closely connected to the awareness of self. This connection between self and action leads to organizational ability, independence, and determination. It also indicates prudence, a quality not normally associated with Mars, because the individual is bringing self-awareness to his or her activities. The integration of ego-consciousness with action results, then, in more orderly activities and fewer missteps. That is the constructive side. A less constructive expression can result in careless action, due largely to the lack of cultivation of thinking processes.

Taurus Midheaven

The Taurus Midheaven, or Midheaven conjunct Venus, indicates the persistent pursuit of goals. This individual does not waver, but pushes ahead steadily. Thus outcomes are predictable, if sometimes slower that desired. Early in life the individual may not be aware of the tendency to be somewhat hard to please, as the desire to have one's comforts may not be fully conscious. Later in life, the understanding of this desire leads to very direct, forthright actions, based on clear understanding of one's personal needs and desires. The Taurus Midheaven indicates a general tolerance that is grounded in awareness of one's own limitations.

Gemini Midheaven

The Gemini Midheaven, or Midheaven conjunct Mercury, addresses self-knowledge through thought processes that are immediately available for self-examination. The Gemini Midheaven indicates that inner conflicts are resolved directly through self-awareness, or ego-consciousness—you are the catalyst for your own change. The individual may go years without being particularly conscious. However, when the difficult moments arrive, the individual is often able to generate swift, effective change, based on the capacity to look at the ego for what it is. These individuals cultivate the ability to think logically and clearly, and then apply this ability to understanding the philosophical side of life.

Cancer Midheaven

When the Midheaven is in Cancer, or when it is conjunct the Moon, there is a direct connection between ego-consciousness and the soul. The emphasis on inner spiritual meaning and values becomes a catalyst for self-understanding. Preconscious or unconscious motives are always close to the surface of conscious awareness involving soul, relationships, and changing objectives. Emotions stimulate events. Changes in work and relationships affect the deepest levels of being, and bring new understanding of social position home to one's awareness.

Leo Midheaven

In terms of consciousness, this position addresses the very goals of life. Individuals with the Midheaven in Leo, or with the Sun conjunct the Midheaven, are often more in touch with their own consciousness because what they are and self-awareness are focused in the same direction. There is a strong focus on advancement toward success. One knows oneself well enough to recognize direction or mission clearly, and then to go after the desired objective.

Virgo Midheaven

The Virgo Midheaven, or Mercury conjunct the Midheaven, indicates a personal drive for security. Career is very likely to involve a focus on money and material things, and the details of satisfying one's needs and desires. It seems obvious that self-awareness is essential to this task, as knowing oneself can make all the difference in the choices one makes. If the Virgo Midheaven resorts to bickering or petty criticism, then the lack of self-awareness is apparent to others, if not to the individual. A possible weakness is susceptibility to faulty logic when it comes dressed in elegant language. The strength is the capacity to take a critical look at what one is offered, and decide if it is really what you want.

Libra Midheaven

The Libra Midheaven, or Venus conjunct the Midheaven, expresses through art and harmony, involving either the physical world or interpersonal, social relations. The Taurus Midheaven indicates that women or the feminine principle are active in the person's life. This energy arises within the self and affects relationships with others. There is a steady development of self-awareness concerning the capacity to love, the nature of attachment to someone or something in the world, or the stage of falling in love with someone or something.

Scorpio Midheaven

The power of Pluto manifests directly in the Scorpio Midheaven as a force to shape one's individuality. Through sheer force of will, Pluto (and Scorpio) at the Midheaven pushes the individual to discover a mission in life and to fulfill it. No longer simply thoughts, the mission becomes a guiding force for transformation. As the ego-consciousness is focused on the life's mission, personal power is mobilized to attain success, to organize one's life, and to express personal authority. Any misuse or misdirection of personal power can lead to disaster. Power out of control is like a racecar without a conscious driver, dangerous in the extreme. Then the power of will inherent in the Scorpio Midheaven is best managed through self-awareness.

Sagittarius Midheaven

Jupiter indicates expansion, optimism, and religious or spiritual interests. The Sagittarius Midheaven, or conjunction of the Midheaven to Jupiter, emphasizes the nobler facets of human expression as a result of consciousness. The urge to expand is joined with self-awareness to produce direction and optimism. Frequently there is success throughout life because the higher, more comprehensive awareness of cosmic law is so closely linked to ego-consciousness. It is as though the two are one expression for the individual. The desire to accomplish something important can be a powerful motivation; it can also lead to a sense of self-importance, depending on other aspects of the Midheaven.

Capricorn Midheaven

The Capricorn Midheaven, or Saturn conjunct the Midheaven, relates the structure of things to the ego-consciousness and can lead to rigid ideas about the world. The Capricorn Midheaven is less about awareness of change and more about the limitations we find in the physical environment. There is a focus on the structure of one's own personality rather than on things outside the self. Because the individual does not develop a strong sense of the structure of social systems, there is a tendency to be self-critical, sometimes leading to an actual loss of ego-consciousness. Ego-consciousness is not placed within the framework of the world, and thus does not have solid ground on which to develop. The result is a difficulty in career and relationships that can only be overcome through steadfast adherence to one's goals. Once again, the need for sufficient practice in thinking is apparent; clear thought processes will negate the tendency toward depression and mental disorder.

Aquarius Midheaven

For the Aquarius Midheaven, or Uranus conjunct the Midheaven, rhythm, independence and even rebellion are keys to self-awareness. There is a state of being ready to take action, coupled with a strong intuitive sense of what direction to take with one's life. When the mind is well trained, the thinking process provides equilibrium in one's life, as the individual can foresee conditions and events clearly. When the mind is out of control, emotional imbalances result and chance runs one's life. The more out of balance the Midheaven seems, the more it indicates a lack of self-awareness. Attention to oneself is essential for the Aquarius Midheaven.

Pisces Midheaven

Uncertainty is the keyword for this Midheaven, or for Neptune conjunct the Midheaven. Ego-consciousness is frequently not available, or only after great effort. The individual with this combination must work hard to manifest the higher qualities of psychic awareness. The strength gained from the contemplative practice of meditation can compensate for dreaminess and aimlessness. As people move into the twenty-first century, they will find better ways to work with Pisces and Neptune energy, thereby relieving the depression and mental disturbance that occur with this Midheaven. Actually there is tremendous depth and strength available. The prerequisites are training of mental focus and grounded connection to the material world. Definition in the physical realm balances any lack of definition.

Ascendant and Midheaven

The relationship between the Ascendant and the Midheaven is significant in the development of the personality and self-awareness. The optimum angle between the two is 90 degrees. In this case the individual is balanced in his or her receptivity to the environment as well as assertiveness toward the environment.

When the angle between the Ascendant and Midheaven is greater than 90 degrees, the greater the angle, the more the individual tends to be responsive to the wishes and desires of others. The Midheaven inclines away from the Ascendant, and self-awareness inclines away from the personality and toward others.

The reverse is true for a smaller angle between the Ascendant and Midheaven; the Midheaven inclines toward the Ascendant, and self-awareness inclines toward the personality.

This key piece of information can be very helpful in understanding individual motivations and strategies. The same planetary configuration will work quite differently in different charts. Where the Midheaven is oriented to the Ascendant in a mode responsive to the environment, a pattern will reflect the absorption of information and feelings. Where the Midheaven inclines toward the Ascendant, the pattern will reflect a natural tendency to exert oneself in the world, according to the nature of the pattern.

THE PLANETS

It is interesting to note that in everyday affairs we unconsciously employ astrological terms, as all words are originally the attempt to communicate in definite terms human urges or reactions to planetary influences.

In this chapter Llewellyn George carefully listed a number of words chosen for their relation to the planets. Only the more commonly used words were allocated, therefore the list is by no means complete and is subject to amplification. The words are arranged in alphabetical order under three headings: Characteristics, Occupations, and Other.

The sagacious student will find among these keywords many that may be used effectively in horoscope delineations.

The Moon

People ruled by the Moon are usually sensitive, emotional, and domesticated, possessing a love for home and kindred. They usually pursue a career related to the family tree, are very patriotic, and have a good memory for events in history. They are interested in public conditions of some sort. They are very sympathetic and the women are easily led to tears. Having a fertile imagination and being also very conscientious, they meet with many ups and downs in life. They are quite receptive or mediumistic and frequently possess musical talent. They like water and natural beauty and should never live for long in a dry, barren place.

When undeveloped, that is, unenlightened, they may be either too easygoing and given to self-gratification and over-indulgence in eating, drinking, or pleasure, or are too changeable, negative, and uncertain.

In astrology we refer to the Moon as being cold, moist, feminine, fruitful, and convertible in character; that is, being fortunate or unfortunate according to its position and aspects in the horoscope.

It rules public or common commodities such as groceries, liquids, etc., that pertain to the domestic side of life. Monday is the day of the Moon; metal: silver.

The Moon exerts considerable influence over the general or ordinary and common affairs of daily life. It makes a complete transit of the Zodiac every 27 days, 7 hours, and 43 minutes. In other words, it makes one complete revolution through the horoscope of every individual in that length of time. As it passes through the various houses and forms the different aspects to the planets' places at birth, it produces conditions, events, feelings, and states of mind or health accordingly. As no two horoscopes are exactly alike, the Moon's monthly transit produces all manner of varying conditions.

Characteristics

Adaptable, agreeable

Beaming

Changeable

Domestic, dreamy

Emotional

Feminine, frivolous, fruitful

Generative

Inconsistent

Maternal, mobile, moist, moody

Nocturnal

Pale, passive, peaceful

Queer, quiet

Rambling, receptive, restless

Serene

Tender, timid

Vacillating, vulgar

Weak

Occupations

Baker

Caterer, cook

Fisherman

Gardener, grocer

Janitor

Laundry worker

Maritime worker, midwife, milk deliverer

Navigator, nurse

Obstetrician

Restaurant worker

Scrubber, security guard

Waiter, washer

Other

Baby, baptize, bathroom, boat, breasts

Cabbage, canal, cheese, china, conception, crescent, crying

Dock, duck

Eel, evening

Faint, family, fermentation, fish

Geese, glass, groceries

Harbor, hen, home, hotel

Infant

Juice

Kitchen

Lady, lake, lighthouse, liquid, luncheon

Mammal, melon, menses, milk, month, mother, mushroom

Night, nutrition

Omen, owl, oyster

Phantom, plastic, pond, the public

Queen

Rabbit, reflector, restaurant, river
Saloon, shellfish, silver, sleep, snail, stomach
Tides, turtle
Umbilical

Voyage
Wake, water, willow, womb, women
Youngster

Mercury

In astrology the influence of the planet Mercury is known to be variable, convertible, neutral, and dualistic. That is, it expresses a nature in accordance with the character of the planet that it aspects: benefic when with fortunate planets or when in favorable aspect, and malefic otherwise.

Mercury has a particular influence over the nervous system, bowels, hands, arms, shoulders, collarbone, tongue, sense of sight, perception, understanding, interpretation, and expression.

Persons who respond to Mercury as a ruling planet are active-minded, quick to discern, eager to acquire knowledge, fond of investigation, inquiry, research, and exploration, and are usually much given to reading. If Mercury is well placed in the horoscope at birth, they are fully capable of maintaining any position where adaptability, dexterity, perception, skill, quick wit, imagination, and good memory are required. They usually conduct their work in an orderly, methodical, systematic, and handy manner, being adept at simplifying arrangements.

When Mercury is ill placed at birth and afflicted, the native has the same inclinations as those just mentioned, but not the expert power of execution, and they carry out ideas rather than create them.

When Mercury is afflicted, it inclines to excessive nervous activity both of body and mind, and unless controlled by willpower, the tendency is to worry, haste and irritability, which inclines to mistakes, forgetfulness, and controversy.

The influence of the afflicted Mercury may be much improved by cultivating continuity, concentration, deliberation, and patience.

Among the ancients, Mercury was known as Thoth, Hermes, and the Messenger of the Gods. Its speed in orbit is approximately 95,000 miles per hour. It was usually portrayed as a youth, flying with wings at his heels, bearing a caduceus made of olive wood about which were twined two serpents, the rod being surmounted with a pair of wings.

This symbol represents well the essential qualities of the planet: duality, speed, and wisdom. It is noticed that Mercurial people have a youthful appearance.

Characteristics

Adroit, alert, analytical
Cheating, clever, critical, cunning
Debating, dexterous, diplomatic
Eloquent
Fanciful, forgetful

Glib
Handy
Imaginative, inconsistent, ingenious,
    intellectual
Juvenile
Literate

Meddling, mediating, memorizing, mental

Neurotic

Perceiving, persuasive, perverting, petty

Restless

Sensitive, shifting, shrewd, skillful, speedy, stammering, subtle

Talkative, thinking, trembling

Understanding

Variable, versatile

Witty

Youthful

Occupations

Accountant, advertiser, architect, astronomer

Bookkeeper

Child monitor, clerk

Distributor

Educator

Graphologist, grocer

Handyman

Interviewer, interpreter

Journalist

Lecturer, linguist

Mail carrier, merchant, messenger

Orator

Printer, publisher

Reporter

Secretary, storekeeper

Teacher, tennis player, translator, typist

Writer

Other

Account, acoustics, agreement, ant, arm, autograph

Bargain, book, bowels, brothers

Cereal, communication

Diary, diet, double

Education, errand, essay

Fingers, fox

Greyhound

Hare, herald, hound, hygiene

Illusions, imagination, imbecile, information, inquiry

Journal, journey, juggle

Kernel, kin

Language, lilac, literature

Mail, merchandise, mimicry, mischief, monkey

Neighbors, nerves, newspaper, number

Observation, opinion

Pair, paper, parrot, parsley, pen, perjury

Question

Record, relate, rumor

School, shoulders, sisters, squirrel

Telegram, theory, thermometer, thought, tongue, travel, twin

Wednesday, wheat, words

Youth

Venus

Venus is fruitful and productive, and is called a feminine planet as it governs the gentler and more refined attributes. Men and women ruled by this planet are noticeably kind or sociable.

When well aspected in a chart, Venus endows the native with a pleasant or handsome countenance, symmetrical form, and graceful manners. It inclines to harmony and, as it rules the sense of touch, favors art, music, and decoration. By their pleasing personality, the subjects of Venus are natural peacemakers; their refined natures soften the ruffled feelings of friends and convert anger to pleasure. As Venus is the promoter of pleasure, these people are splendid entertainers and excellent hosts.

When adversely aspected in the horoscope of birth, Venus bestows less beauty. The native is apt to cultivate the social and pleasure-giving tendencies to an extent that is detrimental to other interests, for when living too much on the personal plane, the real, or finer, attributes are submerged and the emotions dominate.

When afflicted, Venus produces unsatisfactory domestic conditions, anxiety in love, and difficulty with friends or through finances. It rules the skin, throat, veins, ovaries, and internal generative organs, and these are adversely affected by over-indulgence in amusements, eating, and drinking.

Venus aids the faculties of comparison and perception as related to order, form, size, weight, color, tune, and time. It also acts on conjugality, amorousness, friendship, mirthfulness, and agreeableness. On the days when Venus is well aspected by the Moon or other planets, the activities of those faculties are accentuated and manifest the best of the native's capabilities, according to the moral status or soul unfoldment, and they are conversely affected in the same manner when Venus is afflicted by transit or by directions in the progressed horoscope.

Venus is feminine in nature. It rules the sense of touch and has much to do with the disposition. It inclines to all that pertains to the higher attributes of the mind: music, singing, poetry, painting, drama, and all refined amusements and adornment. Venus is beneficial and fruitful and expresses through the character of an individual by generosity, good humor, and love. Colors are all the pastel shades and especially the clear blue of turquoise; some also give to Venus the clear red of crimson. Metal: copper.

Characteristics

Affectionate, amiable, amorous, artistic
Beautiful, benign
Calm, cheerful, clean, compassionate,
     courteous
Delicate, dissolute
Elegant, erotic
Feminine, flirting, frivolous, fruitful
Genteel, gentle, graceful
Immaculate, immodest, immoral, indolent,
     indulgent
Kind
Laughing, lazy, lenient, lewd, loving, luxurious
Mirthful, modest
Normal, nourishing
Peaceful, pleasing, plump, poetical
Queenly
Refined, rejoicing
Sensual, sociable, soothing, sympathetic
Tame, tender
Untidy
Warm
Yielding

Occupations

Artist
Beautician
Dancer, dramatist, dressmaker
Entertainer
Florist
Gardener
Haberdasher, hotel keeper, horticulturist
Jeweler
Milliner, musician
Opera singer
Tailor, theatre worker
Vocalist

Other

Adolescent, adultery, amusement, approval

Balm, bedroom, bridal

Calf, candy, caress, clothing, club, copper, courtship

Deer, dimple, dining, dolphin, dove, drama

Embellishment, emerald, engagement

Fair, Friday, furnishings

Garden, gem, gown

Honeymoon, hussy

Jewelry

Lady, leisure, loins, luxury

Marriage, maiden, matinee, myrtle

Neck, negligee, nosegay

Orchestra, ovaries

Party, partridge, peach, perfume, picnic, plum

Rose

Sapphire, sheik, society, sofa, song, swan

Thanks, throat, tint

Unify, upholstery

Vacation, vineyard, violet

Wardrobe, warm, wedding, wine

Yarrow

The Sun

The Sun apparently passes through all the signs of the Zodiac in one year, leaving one sign and entering the next on about the twenty-first day of each month. The Sun is always on the ecliptic and is therefore void of latitude. It rules the sign Leo and has but one sign for its home.

If not hampered by unfavorable aspects from other planets, and dignified by position in the horoscope, the Sun bestows a nature that is ambitious, proud (but seldom admitting it), magnanimous, frank, generous, humane, firm, and honorable. Leo natives aspire to positions of rulership and by their earnest nature inspire others with a respect for their abilities, so they usually attain positions of trust, responsibility, and honor where they are perfectly at home and capable of practical execution to a very satisfactory degree.

But when the Sun at birth is unfavorably aspected and otherwise undignified, the native is inclined to be too forceful, lordly, domineering, arrogant, and extravagant, inclining also to sickness of a feverish, inflammatory nature, eye afflictions and heart disorders, as well as losses of position, credit, or esteem due to impulsiveness.

All the adverse testimonies, particularly those owing their origins to the mind and physical condition, can be corrected and greatly improved by studying psychology and by taking a deep interest in advanced thought, subjects with a view to unfolding latent qualities, developing self-control, and harmonizing the environmental conditions. The early morning sunshine should be sought, and the heat of day avoided. When making a conscious effort along constructive lines, Leo people will find frequent exercise conducive to inspiration, vigor, and harmony. Many important events will occur on Sundays.

The Sun by nature is hot, dry, masculine, and life-giving. It has much to do with health and the vital principle. It has dominion over individual progress and social success. It rules positions of rank and title and high office generally. In the human anatomy it governs the sides, back, heart, and the right eye of the male and left eye of the female.

Characteristics

Absurd, ambitious, ardent, arrogant,
authoritarian
Boastful, bombastic, brilliant
Candid, charitable, commanding,
condescending
Dignified, disdainful, dry
Egotistical, energetic
Famous
Gaudy
Haughty, healing, honorable, hot
Illustrious, imperialistic, inflammatory,
influential
Kind
Loyal, luminous
Magnanimous, majestic
Omniscient, optimistic
Prominent, proud
Radiant
Scrupulous, stimulating, sumptuous
Vigorous, virile
Warm, wasteful
Zealous

Occupations

Actor
Biologist
Healing professions
Leader
Park attendant, playground director
Supervisor
Theatre worker

Other

Ablaze, alive, amber, animation
Ballroom, boss
Cardiac, central, circle, coliseum, conscience,
cooperation
Daylight, desert, dictator, diurnal
Elevate, exalt
Faith, flame, flaxen, fire, frankincense
Game, gift, glow, gold, grand, grant
Halo, health, heart, heat, helium, honor, hope
Joy, juniper
King, kingdom
Light, lion, living
Mansion, midday, marigold, monarch, myrrh
Noon, nucleus
Orange
Palace, peacock, president, prince
Quality, queen
Radiation, rank, recuperation, respect, rosemary,
ruler
Salamander, spirit, starfish, sunburn, Sunday,
sunstroke
Theatre, throne
Walnut

Mars

Mars is significant of energy, the form that energy assumes depending upon its position, aspects, and location in the horoscope. Manifests as hot, dry, and masculine and has much to do with the ambitions, desires, and animal nature.

People ruled by Mars are noticeably ambitious, positive, and fond of leadership. Being quite inventive and mechanical, they become good designers, builders, and managers and usually make their way to the front in whatever they undertake.

Being averse to the dictatorship of others and unhappy in subordinate positions, they usually find the best outlet for their special abilities when in business for themselves or in positions where they can direct the work of others.

On the undeveloped plane they are the cruel boss, the domineering husband or wife. But when intelligently enlightened and spiritually inclined, they are excellent healers and teachers and may be found at the foremost of movements for the advancement of public welfare.

Mars has a two-year cycle, and every fifteen years Mars reaches its smallest distance from the earth, i.e., about 36,000,000 miles, when it shines with a splendor like that of beautiful Venus.

Mars rules strength, force, and courage. Its manifestation is constructive or destructive, according to the nature of the aspect and what use an individual makes of the vibrations as compared to his or her desires, the nature or quality of effort, and the degree of his or her understanding.

Anatomically considered, Mars governs the external sex organs, muscular system, head, face, left ear, sense of taste, and the bladder, and these parts are the most readily affected with disease when the health has been abused or neglected. Mars predisposes one to injuries through accidents and hurts by cuts, scalds, surgery, firearms, etc., and to feverish or inflammatory complaints. Metals governed by Mars are iron and steel.

Characteristics

Abusive, aggressive, angry, antagonistic

Bellicose, boastful, bold, brave

Caustic, combative, compelling, courageous

Daring, defiant, destructive, disruptive, dreadful

Energetic, exciting

Feverish, fiery, forceful, furious

Headstrong, hostile

Impulsive, industrious, inflammable, invincible

Keen

Loud, lusty

Muscular

Obscene, obstinate, oppressive

Poignant, positive

Quarrelsome, quick

Reckless, resentful, resourceful, ribald, rough

Sensual, sharp, stimulating

Turbulent

Uncouth, urgent

Valiant, victorious

Willful

Occupations

Athlete

Barber, bootlegger, builder, butcher

Carpenter, construction worker

Dentist, designer

Engineer, executive

Firefighter, foundry worker

Garbage collector, guard, gunner

Jailer

Locksmith, lumberjack

Machinist, manager, mechanic

Police officer, prizefighter

Saw-filer, salesperson, steel worker, soldier, surgeon

Wrestler

Other

Accident, action, arena, armor, army

Battle, bile, bladder, burn

Cannon, cayenne, chimney, contagion, crime,
    crow
Danger, dart
Eagle
Fever, file, forge, friction
Gamecock, guns
Hardware, hawk, house
Iron, implement
Junk
Knife

Lamb
Measles, missile, motion, mustard
Nail, navy, needle
Onion, operation
Panther, puncture
Radish, ram, rape, rash, razor, red, regiment, rifle
Scar, scorpion, steel
Thistle, tiger, torture, Tuesday, turbine
Violence, vivisection
War, weapon, wolf

Jupiter

The typical Jupiter native is usually termed jovial, owing to the fact that Jupiter gives such characteristics as sociability, hope, benevolence, veneration, compassion, justice, honesty, and spirituality, and also well-developed faculties of proportion, calculation, and location. Jupiter people are usually quick to hit the mark, as their symbol is the Archer, and they love outdoor exercises; in fact, they require considerable such recreation in order to overcome uneasiness and develop poise.

In the business world they become interested in large, popular enterprises. Science and medicine, insurance, and commercial traveling often engage their attention; also affairs of philanthropic, charitable, religious, or benevolent import, as well as other matters in the professional world.

Jupiter is termed *the greater fortune,* and indeed, it seems well named, for, unless Jupiter is ill placed in the horoscope, it bestows luck and opportunity, based on the nature of the sign it occupies. Where Jupiter is placed by sign and house, the individual meets people who are fitted for positions of dignity, trust, or power in business and social circles. Having a logical, broad mind, considerable self-possession, self-confidence, and determination, they usually inspire confidence and attain responsible positions.

If Jupiter is not dignified or if adversely aspected in the horoscope, it causes restlessness and uncertainty, giving liability to losses through misjudgment, unfortunate speculation, investments, and trusts.

Jupiter in nature is said to be warm, moist, sanguine, temperate, social, expansive, masculine, and moderate. Has dominion over the blood, liver, veins, arteries, and thighs. Rules higher education and philosophic reasoning. If Jupiter is unafflicted in a person's birth chart, the native will be a good, sound, and correct reasoner, whereas if it is ill dignified or badly aspected, the native will often exhibit poor, uncertain, and unreliable judgment.

Characteristics

Abundant, affluent, ample, auspicious
Benevolent, big
Careless, charitable, comfortable, correct, costly
Dull

Erroneous, excessive, expansive, expensive,
    exorbitant, extravagant
Formal, flourishing
Gluttonous

Hazardous, honest, hospitable, huge, humorous

Illicit, immense, indulgent

Jovial, judicious, just

Lavish, lucrative

Magnificent

Noble

Peaceful, philanthropic, philosophical, professional

Rational, reckless, religious, respectable, rich

Sporting, successful

Tactful, temperate, thriftless, truthful

Unimpeachable

Valuable

Wholesome

Occupations

Academician, ambassador, appraiser, archer

Banker, barrister, broker

Cashier

Diplomat

Financier

Gambler, golfer

Hunter

Judge, jockey

Lawyer

Minister

Physician

Scholar

Other

Abscess, apoplexy, aristocrat

Bishop, blood, boil, bond

Ceremony, collegiate, customary

Default, development, disburse

Finances

Gambling, good will, growth

Hale, ham, heir, hips

Income, inherit, insurance, interest

Jubilee, judgment, jury

Knowledge

Legacy, legal, leisure, litigation, liver

Maximum, millionaire

Official, opportune, ordain

Precious, profit, prosperity

Quality, quantity

Racehorse, ransom, right, rubber

Shares, smell, success, supply, surplus, stocks

Tallow, thigh, thunder, Thursday, tin, tour, treasury, truth

Value, voyage

Wager, wart, wealth, whale, winnings

Saturn

The influence of Saturn is commonly called evil, and in this respect it is much maligned, as in reality there is no evil, since all things work together for good ultimately. Saturn acts as a deterrent and because it brings denial and necessity into some lives, it has been considered an oppressor, a Satan. "He that filleth with pride will suffer a fall," for Saturn will bring him to his knees, humble his nature, and by means of restrictions, limitations, and adversities, will cause the individual to ponder, study, and seek to find the source of woe, that in the future it may be overcome. Thus, while Saturn is a destroyer (of false ideals), it is also a redeemer in that it brings the mind to a state of introspection and stimulates effort toward perfection and victory.

People born with Saturn well placed and aspected in their horoscope have a serious and practical nature; they are wisely economical, prudent, conservative, executive, and profound, being good organizers and managers. Their special ability depends upon which planet most strongly and favorably aspects Saturn in the chart.

Saturn children are extremely sensitive, but they hide their feelings and emotions under a mask of reserve. If frequently censured, they withdraw from association and their progress and development are much delayed.

When adversely aspected in a chart, Saturn does indeed seem to produce a train of adversities, for delays, restrictions, disappointments, and sorrow are plentiful and usually these lead to misery, poverty, and ill health.

Saturn governs the knees, teeth, spleen, and bones, and these parts are most readily afflicted when any inharmony prevails. As its influence is cold and dry, heat and moisture are the antidotes. For the native of Saturn, critical and important years are those in which Saturn will transit in adverse aspect to his or her birth position; that is, between the years 14 to 15, 21 to 22, 29 to 30, 36 to 37, 44 to 45, 51 to 52, 59 to 60, etc. Avoid new undertakings during these periods, rest as much as possible, seek the society of cheerful people, and live in a light, airy, new place. Persistent metaphysical treatment, plus cheerful associates and environment, will do much to overcome the adverse effects of Saturn's influence.

Characteristics

Afraid, aged, apprehensive, ascetic, astringent, austere

Bitter

Calculating, callous, chronic, cold, conservative, contemplative

Deficient, depressed, doleful, dry

Earthly, economical

Faithful, firm, frigid

Glum, grasping, grievous

Haggard, harsh, heavy

Immovable, inscrutable, introspective

Jealous

Laborious

Malevolent, materialistic, methodical, miserly, morose

Needy, nonchalant

Obnoxious, old

Patient, poor, practical, prudent, punctual

Querulous, quiet

Realistic, retarded

Scrupulous, secretive, sober, sordid, sour, stiff, stoic, suspicious

Taciturn, tardy, tense, thin, tight, tired, tranquil

Vested

Weary

Occupations

Cement worker, coal miner

Fanner, framer

Hearse driver

Leather worker

Mason

Priest, prison worker

Refrigeration worker

Tanner, timekeeper

Undertaker

Other

Acoustic, adhesive, agriculture, ash, astringent, atrophy

Ballast, bankrupt, basic, bones, brick

Calendar, carbon, cave, clock, coal, continuity, crystallization

Debts, decay, delay, destroy, doom, drudge

Emaciation, embargo, envy, ephemeris

Failure, famine, fear, firm, foundation, frigid, funeral

Garter, gather, glue, goat, gravel

Harness, hate, heap, hearing, hearse, heavy

Ice, inert, inside

Jackass, join, junction

Keep, kill, knees, knot

Labor, lack, land, late, leather, lime, limitation

Matrix, mines, misfortune, monument, morgue, mortgage, mum

Necessity, no, nunnery

Paralysis, past, permanence, pottery, prison

Quarry, quit

Ranch, rheumatism, rocks, ruin

Sedative, sepulcher, skeleton, soot, space, spleen

Taint, tan, tar, task, teeth, terror, threadbare

Underneath, uphold, urn

Valley, vault, vow

Wall, wedge, woe

Yeoman, yesterday, yoke

Uranus

Those who are born during that period of the year ruled by Uranus, or who have Uranus strongly posited in their horoscope, are usually attracted to some form of occult research; in fact, they are reformers and pioneers in advanced lines of thought. Such people often appear odd, eccentric, or peculiar, and are said to be living ahead of their time. It attracts one to such subjects as astrology, phrenology, occultism, mesmerism, magnetic healing, telepathy, electricity, inventions, Freemasonry, etc; it predisposes to the antiquated, curious, new, odd, and everything out of the ordinary.

When Uranus is well aspected by other planets in the nativity, it endows the native with strong intuitive tendencies, giving also metaphysical and inventive ability. With keen foresight they can predict the outcome of business or the results of action quickly and with considerable accuracy in a manner not dependent upon the reasoning process, but by *knowing*. They have strong and constructive imagination and can see a way to improve upon almost everything. Their premonition and intuition guide them in the path of progress and freedom.

When Uranus is adversely aspected in the horoscope, it gives all the aforementioned intuitive activity and inventive genius, but it inclines to make one overly forceful, abrupt, brusque, erratic, willful, sarcastic, and easily offended. The native is liable to accidents through explosions, electricity, or vehicles of transportation. All the mental malformations can be improved and accidents avoided by those who firmly unite effort with aspiration. Great aid in this matter may be obtained by finding the dates on which Uranus is adversely aspected, and then taking care to maintain poise and self-control and to avoid risks with the things that Uranus rules.

The planet Uranus makes a complete transit of the zodiacal circle every 84 years. It requires about seven years for Uranus to pass through each sign.

The nature of Uranus is cold, dry, airy, positive, magnetic, strange, occult, and malefic. It inclines to acts without premeditation. It governs the faculties of curiosity, invention, and investigation, and all things of a curious or wonderful nature; modernistic art. It rules the ankles and the intuitive intellect. Its metals are platinum, aluminum, uranium, and radium. Uranus also has dominion over radioactive elements in general, and wireless communication.

Characteristics

Abnormal, abrupt, acute, adventurous,
     antiquarian, audacious
Bizarre, brusque
Clairvoyant, communistic, contrary,
     cooperative
Defiant, dire, disruptive, drastic
Electric, erratic, explosive
Fanatic
Garish, grotesque
Humanitarian
Illegitimate, incompatible, ingenious
Kinetic
Lawless, liberal
Magnetic, meddlesome, modern
Nonconformist
Original
Paradoxical, peculiar, premature
Quaint
Radical, raving, rejecting, roving
Spasmodic, spectacular
Telepathic, turbulent
Uncertain, unconventional
Vibrant
Whimsical

Occupations

Astrologer, auto mechanic
Broadcaster
Distributor, dynamiter
Electrician
Humanitarian
Inventor
Lineman
Metaphysician, motorman
Telegrapher, tractor driver
X-ray technician
Zookeeper

Other

Abortion, air, alarm, ankles, aura
Battery, bicycle, bomb, brotherhood
Colonize, commoner, crisis, cyclone
Detour, disaster, divorce
Earthquake, electronics, emancipation
Firecracker, flying, freedom, freelance
Garage, gases, generator
Hangup, hobo
Illegal
Kilowatt
Liberty, lightning
Magnetic, microscope, mutiny
Outlaw
Panic, pioneer, prodigy
Quest
Radioactive, revolt
Satire, separation, shock
Tantrums, telescope, tornado, trespass
Uranium
Vapor
Whim, whirlwind, wireless communication
Zealot, zigzag

Neptune

The influence of Neptune upon humankind is that of a mediumistic order, and those who are responsive to the vibrations of this mysterious planet are often subject to queer and indefinable feelings, sensations, and emotions.

At times it produces negative states in which the subject takes on the influence of surrounding conditions, either consciously or unconsciously, and acts or feels, for the time being, in harmony with the nature of persons contacted.

When this planet is well aspected in a horoscope, the native is endowed with aspiration and correct premonitions and is apparently often directed to do just the right thing, or to be in just the right place at opportune times.

Such people are frequently clairvoyant and have feelings about things that should be carefully analyzed. Neptune gives psychometric faculties that can be developed to so fine an order that its subjects can give truly interesting facts through the sense of touch and feeling, when handling an article for that purpose. They can also very correctly interpret dreams if they make a careful study of that subject. It usually bestows some artistic gift, which is susceptible to high development.

In fact, briefly stated, Neptune represents inspiration, psychometry, mediumship and inner feeling, as Venus, its octave, rules touch or outer feeling. It rules things or conditions of a mysterious, hidden nature, such as séances, "silence" meetings, or affairs of a secret order. Its influence is considered neutral, because the character of its expression is dependent upon the quality of the aspects made with other planets and its position in sign and house of the horoscope. It represents the feet in the human organism, but in its esoteric sense it governs the very base of understanding and knowledge of things as they are and not as they seem to be.

When Neptune is found adversely located and aspected in a chart, it leads to over-receptivity, inertness, and states overly negative and passive, states that result in various ills or defects of character, allowing weakness to temptations when strength and resistance are most needed. The emotions seem to predominate. If allowed to run to extremes, emotions produce unnatural appetites, changeability, uncertainty, indolence, vague imagination, intrigues, and confusion, bringing troubles through schemes, plots, deception, and secret enmities.

When well aspected, Neptune bestows some gift, but when afflicted it gives some weakness that should be discovered early in life and properly transmuted. With Neptune afflicted, the native, being quickly affected by the environment mentally and physically, should investigate the philosophy of all things mysterious before trying the phenomena.

The planet Neptune seems to be in a nebulous state and its influence appears to be more psychic than physical or material. It represents spirit, feeling, sensing, or inner perception. It governs the receptive faculties. Its nature is neutral and spiritual (not necessarily from a religious standpoint). It is not known to rule any metal, mineral, or other material substance, as do the other planets, but is related to gas, drugs, chemicals, and anesthetics. It is dualistic in character; on the one hand it may represent chaos, and on the other hand, fine spiritual insight. It has affinity for oil, liquids, beverages, tobacco, and the sea; impressionistic art.

Characteristics

Abstract, adaptable, assuming
Beguiling, bewildering
Cataleptic, counterfeit
Distraught, dreamy, doubtful
Elusive, emotional, exceptional, exotic
Fanciful, formidable
Gullible, glamorous
Hysterical
Idealistic, imaginative, indulgent
Limpid
Mediumistic , mysterious
Naive, nebulous, nude
Obscure
Poetical, psychic
Questionable
Receptive
Scheming, spiritual
Toxic, tranquil
Uncanny, undulating
Vacillating, vague, visionary
Weird, whimsical

Occupations

Alchemist
Bootlegger
Diver
Irrigation worker
Marine, medium
Oilfields worker
Poet, psychic
Seafarer, sorcerer, submariner
Yogi

Other

Alcohol, alibi, astral
Bath, beach, bribery, bogus
Camouflage, coma, communism, confusion,
   conspiracy
Defile, delusion, dike, dive, dope
Engulf, ether, evade
Fantasy, fiddle, film
Gasoline, gelatin, graft
Hallucination, harem, hydraulics, hypodermic
Incense, irrigate, intrigue
Kelp, kerosene
Liquid, lure
Moron, morphine
Narcotic, nautical, nymph
Obsession, ocean, oil, opiate
Poison, pool, pretense, prophecy
Quack
Rendezvous
Scandal, seclusion, seduce, seer, siren, swim
Tangle, tea, trance, tobacco
Utopia
Vapor
Wade, waves, wet
Yacht, yeast

Pluto

At the time of the writing of the original edition of the *A to Z* in 1910, Pluto had not yet been discovered. After its discovery in 1930, Llewellyn George made revisions in his text to accommodate this new planet, relying heavily upon classical mythology.

In mythology, Pluto was the god of the outer regions, the ruler of the dead. In no sense was he depicted as a tempter or seducer of humankind, like the devil of Christian theology. Pluto was certainly depicted as stern and pitiless, but he was only so in discharge of his duty as custodian of the dead.

Pluto is called masculine, stern, somewhat inscrutable, not itself malignant but dealing with high potencies; invoked by or responsive to music, especially jazz.

Pluto rules the underworld, the subconscious workings of the body, the fluxing influences, the contest between acid and alkali; the fusing actions; burning out of dross material; all those processes whose transmuting actions tend to regenerate the body; to sustain, repair, renew, or perpetuate it through the burning up and casting out of dead material—from death to life. It also rules the conscience, that inner prompter that helps us judge right from wrong, subconscious activities, the underworld, stern, incorruptible judges. Its keywords are regeneration, levitation, transformation, materialization, metamorphosis, and transfiguration.

The positive aspects to Pluto favor the discovery of error, detection of injustice. Revitalizing ideas and incidents that tend to promote health, preserve life, and encourage freer expression of the subconscious activities are probably due to Pluto's vibrations.

The adverse aspects to Pluto incline to inversion of its better qualities, low morality, lack of conscience, indecency, disrespect of law, and underworld proclivities.

Characteristics

Anonymous

Betraying

Callous, corrupt, covert

Defiant, degenerate, depraved, destroyer

Enigmatic

Fiendish, foul

Grave, guilty

Indifferent, insatiable, inscrutable, immoral, immortal

Lawless

Nefarious

Obscene, odious, outrageous

Passionate, putrid

Rotting

Sadistic, sardonic, severe, sexual, sinister, subnormal

Taciturn, terrible, terse

Unscrupulous, ungodly, unknown

Vindictive

Wasteful, wicked

Occupations

Gunner

Psychoanalyst

Other

Abyss, atlas, ambush, amnesia, atom bomb

Brimstone

Chasm, conscience, covert, crematory, criminal

Defiance, demon, dice

Erase, evolution

Felon, fumigate

Hag, holocaust, hoodlum

Kidnap

Loot, lust

Magic, marsh, menace, monster

Null

Pollute, purgatory

Racketeer, recuperation, regimentation, reproduction

Scavenger, sewer, siren, spoil, steel, swamp

Transformer

Underworld

Vampire, vanish, vermin, victim, virus

THE PLANETS IN THE SIGNS

The Moon

The Moon in Aries

Strong imagining faculty, positive, forceful, masterful, independent, self-reliant, courageous, and practical. Enthusiastic in whatever line is of interest at that time; changeable, restless, uneasy, and dislikes to be ordered about or held to any one line. Generally quick-tempered, inclined to be persistent, impulsive, and aggressive. Imbued with activity, energy, enterprise, originality, and inventive ability. Fond of traveling and of original and independent ventures. Will attempt to hew out a path of their own and apt to be at the head of some undertaking or in some way prominent in their sphere of influence. If afflicted, some danger of drowning and trouble through women, changes of occupation and position. Indicates aches or pains in the head.

The Moon in Taurus (Exaltation)

This bestows a courteous and affable disposition inclined to friendship, love, and marriage. Determined, and not to be thwarted in their aims. The nature is conservative and resists forced changes or outside influences. Hopeful, ambitious, and desirous of excelling. Goodhearted, sympathies easily aroused. Tends to the acquisition of friends, possessions, houses, and lands. Favors occupations connected with the earth and its products and all dealings in such things; success in chemistry or hygiene, in business and in places near the water; sometimes assistance in a financial or business way through the opposite sex. Intuitive and as a rule has good judgment.

The Moon in Gemini

This location of the Moon gives the subject an agreeable, warm-hearted, sympathetic, humane, progressive, and ingenious nature, with the capacity to be very reserved in some matters, such as personal or domestic matters, but fluent concerning local or national affairs. Strengthens and enlivens the intellect, inclines to literature, and gains pleasure from books or scientific pursuits. Gives an active body and a versatile, receptive mind, responsive to new ideas and capable of following artistic, literary, or professional occupations.

Dislikes quarreling and warfare. Subject to many changes and some journeys. Apt to be drawn into embarrassing or difficult positions through lack of caution, discretion, or prudence.

The Moon in Cancer (Home)

This indicates one whose desire is to work along lines of least resistance; friendly, sociable, and domestic in manner and usually much attached to his home; feeling and emotion are active and usually for good. Somewhat changeable, influenced greatly by the surroundings, and is sensitive to outside influences; in other words, this person senses conditions psychically (consciously or unconsciously).

The native is kind and agreeable to all, sympathetic and humane. Sometimes allows imposition without an act of resentment; sometimes is elected to posts of honor. Good, conscientious, sensitive, superior nature; hard struggles, great obstacles, voyages. Loves traveling, also home; attraction to the mother. It favors dealing with the public in liquids, chemistry, catering, shipping, and a residence near the water. Fond of the occult, antique and curious things, family history, and history in general, patriotism and cooking.

There is some ability for acting and expressing the thoughts or emotions of others, and usually for poetry or music. The Moon in this sign heightens sensitivity to all things of a feeling nature.

The Moon in Leo

This makes one ambitious, self-confident, self-reliant, loyal, honorable, generous in money matters, high-minded, magnanimous, candid, and warm-hearted; a persevering, lively, and penetrating mind; organizing ability; generally a leader among his associates; popular with the opposite sex; sincere love; fond of home and honor; particular in dress and very orderly in conduct. It favors intuition and genius and gives a freehearted nature with a love for pleasure, music, art, and sports.

This location of the Moon has a tendency to uplift the native, mentally and socially, and place him in positions of trust, respect, and responsibility or in control or management of enterprises.

The Moon in Virgo

Good mental ability, receptive mind, good memory and ability to learn easily; capable of following some intellectual pursuit. Fondness for science in general and things occult. Often has clairvoyant, psychometric, or intuitive faculty. The native is usually quiet, unostentatious, and unpretentious, though talented and quietly ambitious, preferring to earn his or her way through merit of mental ability; fertile imagination, fondness for change, travel, and investigation.

Although somewhat reserved, has many friends, especially of the opposite sex; usually has secret sorrows through marriage. Trouble with stomach and bowels until proper discretion is observed in diet.

There is likelihood of many short journeys and changes. This location favors a variety of occupations in literature or as teacher, secretary, bookkeeper, clerk, messenger, traveler, chemist, druggist, confectioner; sometimes success with the earth and its products, but more especially when the subject has an earthly sign rising at birth, or the planet ruling the Ascendant is in an earth sign.

This location of the Moon makes a good, trustworthy servant, and the native is usually fortunate through those who serve under him or her, unless a malefic is in the Sixth House.

The Moon in Libra

This location of the Moon, taken alone, favors or inclines to unions, partnerships, and general popularity. Fond of pleasure, society, amusements, and the company of young people. The native is affectionate, good-natured, agreeable, courteous, warm-hearted, affable, mirthful, inclined to love and marriage; kind in manner and makes friends easily. Liking for fine clothes, adornment, luxury, approbation and all refining and harmonious influences.

The life is considerably affected by other people, and the Libran usually prefers to work in association with another.

Appreciation for music, painting, scenery, and all the fine arts generally; considerable skill and ingenuity along these lines if Mercury is in good aspect.

The Moon in Scorpio (Fall)

Inclines to vigorous activity. The native has enterprise, will, determination, practical ability; is firm and self-confident enough to push forward and gain success in undertakings and take care of his or her own; somewhat abrupt and impulsive. It gives a fondness for pleasure, comfort, and desire to satisfy the tastes. The nature is energetic, forceful, independent, masterful, aggressive, courageous, and positive; will not tolerate imposition, nor be swerved from his or her purpose by opposition, yet will often sacrifice a great deal in return for kindness; sometimes quick-tempered. It inclines to interest in the occult or mysterious in nature, and, if there are any conforming aspects, will advocate and assist in carrying out revolutionary changes, employing sarcasm or satire.

Taken alone, this location signifies attachments or attractions and difficulties with the opposite sex and inharmony in the marriage state. Dangers through voyages. To women, it inclines to dangerous childbirth.

The Moon in Sagittarius

Shows the native to be generous, benevolent, humanitarian, charitable, kindhearted, sociable, good-humored, jovial, sometimes quickly angered but forgiving, of ready promise, hopeful, frank, and free; shows love of beauty, harmony, and sports.

Usually has a quick, restless, and unsettled manner, either in mind or body, and often both. Inclines to travel or change the place of residence frequently; active, never averse to physical exercise, a quick walker and worker; fond of children, pets, and sports; some inclination for the investigation of religion, philosophy, law, commerce, and foreign affairs generally. A natural teacher; very philosophical and often has something of the prophet in his or her nature, usually being correct in judgment regarding the outcome of movements or enterprises. Ingenious, talented, and has ability for science.

This location of the Moon tends to bring one out before the public in some manner, and the native may assist in carrying out great religious, educational, or political reforms. Benefits through women. It is somewhat significant of inheritance if Sagittarius occupies the cusp of the Eighth House.

The Moon in Capricorn (Detriment)

Tends to bring one before the public in some manner, but whether beneficially or otherwise depends upon the other indications in the chart.

If the Moon is well aspected at birth, especially by the Sun, may attract attention as a prominent and respectable person. If the environment has been good, it may manifest as rulership, generalship, and administrative ability.

If the mental rulers (the Sun, Moon, Mercury, and rulers of the Third and Ninth House cusps), are afflicted and the early training was neglected, it gives a vague, indeterminate mind, lack of creative energy although ambitious; misfortune through women and lax control of the appetites. Usually has enemies whether merited or not, and some drawback or difficulty attached to the occupation or reputation of the native. If the aspects in the chart are generally good, it indicates honors and prominence; the native has ability to interest others and inspire confidence; a good organizer and welfare worker.

This location is also indicative of care and caution in money matters. The nature is often too cold and calculating and at times disrespectful of the feelings of others.

The Moon in Aquarius

Active, intuitional, agreeable, friendly, and courteous disposition. The native is sociable and sympathetic in manner; broad, humane, independent, and somewhat unconventional. Gives liking for the strange and curious with an inclination for subjects that are unusual, original, or eccentric; inventive ability.

It tends to political, educational, and scientific work, interest in astrology, occult matters generally, secret societies, etc. It gives a good faculty for image-making; mental sensitivity; sorrow and changes occasioned by friends.

Troubles through women and liability to sorrow and wandering life, if badly aspected.

The Moon in Pisces

Kind, benevolent, quiet, retiring, sympathetic, fond of luxury, comfort, diversity, change, beauty, and harmony. Meets with many misfortunes and obstacles that tend to make the native feel irresolute, inert, downhearted, and easily discouraged at times. It gives a taste for reading and keen perception of romance, having a powerful and fruitful imagination. As a speaker, writer, or composer, the native is copious, fluent, earnest, and very correct in details.

Inconstancy is indicated in the love affairs; generally has a hard time saving money. If the Sun also is in a water sign or a water sign is ascending, the native is likely to grow corpulent.

With the Moon in this location, the native is often very receptive, mediumistic, or inspirational, and responsive to psychic conditions generally. Suffers both physically and mentally through adverse environment, uncongenial surroundings, and misunderstandings.

Mercury

Mercury in Aries

Impulsive and fiery, quick in thought and speech, good in repartee or argument and often contentious, antagonistic, and disputative; expressive, earnest, and demonstrative; apt to enlarge or exaggerate unconsciously, but is liberal, inventive, unique, interesting, and clever.

Fond of reading, writing, literature, and literary people. Inclined to enter quickly into projects and given to changes of opinion. The faults are want of mental continuity, lack of order and method, and general restlessness, although a friendly aspect from Saturn will largely correct these and give much more stability.

Mercury in Taurus

Pleasant and happy disposition, fond of the opposite sex, pleasure, recreation, music, art ,and intellectual or refined amusement. Very practical and determined mind, especially where mental development is concerned. Good reasoning and judgment, persevering and somewhat obstinate; however, discreet and diplomatic although of fixed opinions and strong likes and dislikes; desirous of acquiring money, possessions, and an established income.

Mercury in Gemini (Home)

Quick, ingenious, clever, inventive, and resourceful mind. Sympathetic, unbiased, very seldom prejudiced, usually good-humored and generous. Perceptive, observing, shrewd, and executive in detail; good orator, lawyer, or business person. Informed on topics of the day.

Fond of travel, change, novelty, speculation, reading, literature, science, and the acquisition of knowledge, especially of the occult.

Mercury in Cancer

Diplomatic, tactful, discreet, faithful, and good-natured. The intellect is clear and reasonable with retentive powers. Readily adapt themselves to surrounding conditions and capable of changing their opinions quickly; sociable disposition. Fond of pleasure, picnics, and family reunions.

Very impressionable and sensitive. Easily influenced by kindness and encouraged by approbation.

The mind is somewhat restless and requires an abundance of material for reflection. Usually spiritually inclined and interested in psychic investigation. Appreciation for the poetry of motion or of rhyme and music; liking for journeys by water and public entertainment. Gives the ability to mentally understand, verbalize, and communicate the personal emotions.

Mercury in Leo

Denotes an ambitious, confident, persistent, determined, lofty mind, fiery, quick-tempered. Kind-hearted and sympathetic; dignified and aspiring; intuitive intellect and high, noble ideals; will seldom stoop to low action. Positive mentality and governing, controlling, or organizing ability. Willpower of progressive and expansive development; concentration. Fond of children, pets, music, singing, drama, fine arts, sports, pleasures; tendency to self-indulgence. Danger through drugs, etc., which affect the heart action.

Mercury in Virgo (Home and exaltation)

Good intellect: comprehensive, cautious, prudent, discriminative, practical, versatile, inventive, intuitive, perceptive, and possesses ability for study and memorizing. Power of persuasion; a good scholar or linguist; fluency as a writer, well informed, capable in detail, sequence, and expression; innate love of mystery or of occult investigation.

Quiet or somewhat serious nature, but at times critical and skeptical; must see, know, and understand thoroughly before he or she will be convinced.

Taste for mathematics or literature; capable of undertakings that require ability, planning, and dexterity. Interest in hygiene, prophylactics, nursing, healing, or chemistry.

Mercury in Libra

A refined, good, and broad mind; quiet, just, tender, dispassionate disposition; fond of comparison, capable of judgment and reason. Taste for mental pursuits, often musical, splendid natural abilities, aptitude for delicate mathematical work or invention. Very favorable location for all intellectual development. Good for club, fraternal, or social welfare work.

Mercury in Scorpio

A bold and somewhat obstinate, sarcastic, forceful, positive, and reckless nature, but ingenious, keen, shrewd, and desirous of gaining knowledge and mental ability. Often has troublesome friends, relatives, and neighbors; fond of the opposite sex and partial to company and pleasure-seeking; many disappointments. Fond of occult and mystical subjects and the different "ologies" and "isms"; very careful of personal interests; somewhat critical, curious, suspicious, and distrustful. Mesmeric ability, suggestive mental healing qualities, mental resourcefulness, fertility, and practical utility.

Mercury in Sagittarius (Detriment)

The nature is ambitious, sincere, just, generous, very independent, and often rebellious, with some tendency toward rashness or impulse.

The mind becomes prophetic, wise, and philosophical, inclining to freedom of thought and speech. Very active mentally or physically, somewhat changeable but progressive. Appreciation for the beautiful in nature, fond of change and travel, also of home and family; likes authority, also likes sports and animals. Inclination toward mental development through philosophy, religion, science, law, or medicine.

Mercury in Capricorn

Acute, sharp, penetrating, tactful, curious, diplomatic, and critical. Somewhat suspicious, peevish, fickle, discontented, or restless. Careful, economical, and painstaking, especially toward perfecting the intellect. Constantly busy with something. Interest and ability for literature, science, chemistry, philosophy, and the occult. Influenced only through kindness. Serious, thoughtful, contemplative, and practical nature. Observant, discriminating; organizing ability. Many generals and military strategists have benefited from this placement of Mercury.

Mercury in Aquarius

The mind is refined, comprehensive, critical, original, penetrative, observing, and keen in judgment of human nature, possessing good reasoning and concentrative powers. Makes acquaintances readily.

Fondness for science generally, also the occult and metaphysical. Apt in study, mathematics, invention, business methods, political or lodge work.

Great readers, deep thinkers, sociable and kind; expounders of humanitarian principles. Delight in discussing ideas, original thought, and mental stimulation. Often seek the company of intellectual, unusual, or elderly persons.

Mercury in Pisces (Detriment and fall)

The intellect gains in knowledge not so much by deep and profound application to study as by intuitive perception. Possesses an understanding not acquired from books; knows things in a peculiar manner; rarely at a loss to explain any condition and are often called "walking encyclopedias."

The mind is imaginative, impressionable, and quickly adapted to the requirements of the moment; possesses great absorptive capacity and the power to memorize. Tends to psychic or mediumistic qualities, but attended with some danger or inconvenience through over-receptivity in nature. Fond of pleasure, recreation, and travel, especially on the water. Numerous abilities, often changes employment, good judge of human nature. Analytical, diplomatic, cautious, just, good-humored, versatile, ingenious, and dexterous. Interest in hygiene, prophylactics, nursing, healing, hospitals.

Venus

Venus in Aries (Detriment)

Fondness for travel, music, painting, sculpture, decorative art, singing, poetry, romance, theatres, entertainment, and all genteel muscular and mental recreation.

The nature is ardent, affectionate, demonstrative, generous in the bestowal of affection, fond of love and admiration, warm-hearted, passionate, and attracted to friends of the opposite sex.

This location of Venus inclines to popularity, many friends, and, if other testimonies in the chart warrant, an early or hasty marriage. However, there are usually many inharmonies in the marital relation. The disposition is charitable and the feeling and sympathies quickly respond to appeals for worthy assistance; free and generous in gifts and expenditures.

Venus in Taurus (Home)

This location of Venus endows the native with deep feelings and lasting emotions; an affectionate and faithful love nature. Precise, careful, and correct with regard to form and custom in connection with pleasure, sociability, and friendship. Fixed and stable in feelings, decided and tenacious in opinions. Fond of money for the pleasure and comfort it brings, and generous with it in that respect.

Venus in Taurus is generally favorable for money and possessions gained by the native's personal efforts in business or profession and by the occupations of Venus. If other testimonies in the chart permit, it assists to gain by legacy, partnership, or marriage. This location inclines to marriage, but it is sometimes delayed.

Venus in Gemini

The native may find pleasure and profit from travel and Mercurial pursuits. Money is gained from more than one source; several occupations. If Mercury is in good aspect, or the education complete, much can be accomplished through writings, speaking, music, art, and drama. This location of Venus tends to refine the feelings and intellect, giving clear ideas, intuition, originality, inventive ability, good humor, friendliness, sociability, and keen appreciation for all light, airy, mental recreations.

Dual love affairs, inconstancy or tendency to flirt, likelihood of several love affairs, one with a relative; many loving friends. Venus in Gemini inclines to marriage, and if other testimonies in the chart permit, more than one union.

If unafflicted, much good will between brethren, cousins, and neighbors. Spiritual tendencies of a progressive or mystical nature.

Venus in Cancer

This location gives a love of home, domestic attractions, strong affection for the mother. The nature is sympathetic, kindhearted, loving, receptive, imaginative, and quickly responsive to the emotions. Several love affairs, secret attractions, union with one of occult tendencies or with a considerable difference in age.

Venus in Cancer is not wholly fortunate for marriage, as it indicates obstacles, either on account of parents, money, or occupation; unforeseen difficulties. Friendships among inferiors and connection with some obscure, unpopular, or plebian occupation.

Ability in occult arts, psychic research, and in matters connected with the unseen world; love for mystical religion. Gain by matters associated with water, refreshments, and, if other indications in the chart show it, gain through houses, land, or parents. Mediumistic gifts.

Venus in Leo

The nature is sympathetic, charitable, kindhearted, free, and generous. Earnest, sincere, and ardent in affection. The native is attracted to the opposite sex, fond of social display, pleasure, friends, entertainment, and amusements of all sorts. There may be real talent for something signified by Venus: music, poetry, singing, acting, art, etc.

Gain through young people, superiors, those of good position and social standing. If other testimonies in the chart warrant, the native will gain by judicious investment, speculation, inheritance, and by occupations connected with pleasure.

Venus in Virgo (Fall)

Venus in Virgo has a tendency to endow the native with a quiet nature and a deep sympathy seldom expressed. Some delay and disappointment in love, secret or dual attachments, union with one of a different station, possibly an employee, invalid, or a doctor.

Money is gained through servants or subordinates or by the native himself occupying such positions; gain by matters connected with drugs, medicine, nursing, food, farming, gardening, and through vocations associated with the earthly elements. If other testimonies in the chart permit, gain by careful speculation, investment, and through the partner.

Venus in Libra (Home)

Contributes to kindness, sympathy, pure and refined affections, and a rich love nature. It conduces to marriage, friendships, sociability, popularity, a fruitful union, and talented offspring.

Venus in Libra gives a love for fine arts, music, poetry, singing, painting, drama, opera, and all refined, cultured amusements and social functions.

Preference for friends and associates among philosophical people and those of good social standing, also affection for cousins or relatives.

The native may earn money through the things signified by Venus, and, if other testimonies in the chart permit, will gain through marriage and partnership.

Venus in Scorpio (Detriment)

The native is free, generous, and even lavish in expenditures. Money may be earned through the watery elements, catering to the tastes or by matters connected with the dead and, if other testimonies in the chart warrant, gain by gifts, legacy, partnership, or marriage, but there will be some delay or trouble in connection with them.

This location of Venus increases the passions and emotions and gives a love of sensation, luxury, and pleasure; ardent in love, demonstrative in affection. It attracts to the opposite sex and brings trouble, disappointment, delay, or loss in courtship or marriage. Sorrow through disagreement or jealousy, attacks upon the honor, death of partner.

Trouble or failure in social affairs; friends with mystical or occult tendencies, also friendships with some of doubtful repute. If Venus is much afflicted, liable to death by poison or by suicide due to unhappy alliances.

Venus in Sagittarius

This location of Venus refines the nature, making the native lighthearted, impressionable, intuitive, imaginative, prophetic, generous, and of loyal intentions, fond of beauty, fine arts, traveling, voyaging, romance, animals, and all outdoor sports and amusements. It inclines to charity, benevolence, and justice; to religion of a mystical or spiritual nature; to respect for literary and intellectual work, philosophies, philanthropy, and all lines leading to harmony and involving the higher attributes of the mind.

Money may be gained from two sources and through things signified by the sign Sagittarius, also through horses, shipping, traveling, sports, etc., and if other testimonies in the chart agree, through speculation, investment, legacy, and partnership.

The love nature is susceptible and attracted to the opposite sex. This location inclines to more than one union and affection for a foreigner or one from a considerable distance. Gives many friends, some of good position and social standing. Friendship with partner's relatives, and friends among educators, scientists, ministers, and mariners.

Venus in Capricorn

This location tends to uplift the native and place him or her in positions of trust, responsibility, authority, and profit, giving the favor of employers, superiors, and elders.

It inclines to business, commerce, banking, investments, stocks, shares, and executive positions that bring contact with many, also to affairs connected with the earthly elements. It conduces to social and business popularity, and friends of high standing, with gain and advancement through them.

The love nature is ambitious, diplomatic, and careful of honor. Marriage is usually for convenience or for social purposes. There is disappointment in love, domestic unhappiness, coldness or indifference on the part of the partner. If other testimonies in the chart agree, marriage is delayed for reasons arising out of age, parents, money, or occupation. Either the native or the partner is likely to be older, more serious, calculating, wealthy, or of a different position in life, or hold a different and maybe an indifferent attitude.

If Venus is afflicted here, it gives liability to business treachery through associates; loss and trouble through alliances with inferiors or those of doubtful repute.

Venus in Aquarius

This location of Venus gives fondness for pleasure and social life. The native makes friends easily and readily forms acquaintances with strangers. Friends among inferiors and also with those of wealth and refinement.

The nature is intuitive, philosophical, generous, reserved in opinions, and sincere in convictions; liking and ability for fine arts and all cultured and intellectual pursuits. Fond of romance and pleasure, friends among the opposite sex, faithful and earnest in affection, secret alliances, remarkable or strange, sudden, and unexpected experiences or events in love, union with one of a Uranian nature; possibly marriage in middle life or later years, and to one of a different age.

Indicates gain financially through friends, societies, and public enterprises. If other testimonies in the chart agree, it signifies gain through partnership, association, companies, and firms, also through speculation, investment, and inheritance. Many hopes and wishes realized.

Venus in Pisces (Exaltation)

Venus in Pisces bestows a nature that is charitable, philanthropic, easily moved to sympathy, inclined to relieve suffering and to assist the weak or afflicted; interested in work connected with institutions. The native is compassionate, sensitive, psychic, mediumistic, emotional, idealistic, and inspirational.

Fond of all things beautiful: poetry, music, painting, and fine arts generally. Cheerful, genial, hospitable, fond of society and friendly intercourse; desirous of peace, ease, comfort, and luxury; at times indolent.

Money is gained through friends, charity, gifts, Venusian occupations, or through obscure, subordinate, or plebian pursuits. There is apt to be more than one marriage and the native may be careless or fickle in matters of affection. Attraction to an inferior; secret alliance. If Venus is much afflicted here, the native may have a hard time gaining money, or if he possesses it will lose heavily through fraud, deception, and unscrupulous methods and maybe by his own actions. Difficulty, detriment, and loss through intrigue; obstacles, delays, and trouble in marriage.

The Sun

Occasionally the Sun may enter the sign a day earlier or later than the dates quoted in this chapter. If a person is born on one of the dates given as the change from one sign to another, it becomes necessary to note carefully the Sun's place given in the birth-year ephemeris to determine whether or not it had changed signs at the time of birth. An ancient rule states that when a planet reaches the twenty-eighth degree, it begins to influence the next sign.

Aspects to the planetary ruler of the sign the Sun occupies at birth, whether by transit or by progression, are important factors in producing events and changing conditions.

The Sun in Aries: March 21–April 19 (Exaltation)

In Aries the Sun gives much mental energy and quick wit. Natives of this sign are natural leaders, more or less headstrong or impulsive, ambitious, full of enterprise and new ideas. They do not like to be under the direction of a master and are inclined to be fiery and quick-tempered, quick to resent abuse or imposition but forgiving and do not hold a grudge long. Their great love of freedom and justice, coupled with their enthusiasm and self-will, makes them liable to go to extremes through indignation, hasty speech, or lack of discretion. They possess penetrating willpower, and are persistent, determined, and not easily discouraged. Are philosophical by nature, admire scientific thought, and are at their best when at the head of things, such as director, instructor, superintendent, or manager.

Mars is the planetary ruler of the sign Aries.

The Sun in Taurus: April 20–May 20

In Taurus the Sun makes the native self-reliant, determined, persistent, stable, firm, careful, and cautious. Taureans fear pain. They seem patient and will wait a long time for their plans to mature; gentle when unprovoked, but furious when angered and then headstrong and unyielding; secretive and reserved with latent energy and mental power; practical and constructive. Lovers of nature, art, music, literature, and amusement. Are usually capable of becoming psychics, mediums, and healers. Make good public servants, officials, and splendid executive workers.

Venus is the planetary ruler of the sign Taurus.

The Sun in Gemini: May 21–June 20

In Gemini the Sun makes the native sympathetic, kindhearted, affectionate, fond of home and children, and easily influenced by kindness, at times to his or her detriment. Is sensitive, intuitive, and idealistic. Fond of science and as a rule studious and usually endowed with great imaginative ability. Possesses an active mind and can be relied upon to act quickly in an emergency. Is an experimenter and investigator, quick reasoner, generally a good writer; likes to be busy and can engage in two or more occupations at once, but must be allowed to work in his or her own way. Changeable, inquiring, doubtful nature, hard to understand, but versatile, alert, dexterous, and skillful. Is ambitious, aspiring, and loves change and diversity.

Mercury is the planetary ruler of the sign Gemini.

The Sun in Cancer: June 21–July 22

In Cancer the Sun gives a quiet, reserved, retiring, sensitive disposition, yet inclined to publicity. Versatile, changeable; with many ups and downs, changes of occupation and position but desires to stick to his or her own course. Possesses a fertile imagination and dramatic ability, loves nature, adventure, and strange experiences. Is mediumistic, receptive, and influenced greatly by surroundings. Industrious, prudent, frugal, and very conscientious. Has a retentive memory. Loves approbation, sympathy, and kindness; fears ridicule. Fruitful and reproductive.

The Moon is the planetary ruler of the sign Cancer.

The Sun in Leo: July 23–August 22 (Home)

In Leo the Sun gives an active mind, good nature, generosity, many friends. Is a natural leader, ambitious, independent, determined, persistent, industrious, honest, and very conscientious; philosophical, philanthropic. Quickly angered but quickly appeased. Has a sunny disposition, is frank, outspoken, candid, forceful, and greatly appreciates affection in which he or she is usually ardent and sincere. Magnetic, intuitive, and inventive; fond of children, sports, drama, honors, and high office.

The Sun is the planetary ruler of the sign Leo.

The Sun in Virgo: August 23–September 22

In Virgo the Sun makes the native modest, thoughtful, serious, contemplative, and industrious, with a desire to refine the mind and acquire knowledge. Learns quickly, is philosophical and a good reasoner, and usually has a good command of language. It gives good endurance, reserve force, quick recuperation, and as a rule Virgos do not show their age. Quick-tempered but not a fighter, as Virgo prefers arbitration. Loves order, beauty, art, and literature. Not easily discouraged or kept down, although somewhat given to worry. Is idealistic yet practical, frugal yet speculative, ingenious, careful, cautious, and usually endowed with good forethought. Very active and seldom contented for a long period of time. Desires wealth but not able, as a rule, to acquire wealth easily. Interested in hygiene, diet, and labor conditions.

Mercury is the planetary ruler of the sign Virgo.

The Sun in Libra: September 23–October 22 (Fall)

In Libra the Sun gives love of justice, peace, and harmony. The native is courteous, pleasant, agreeable, and, as a rule, even-tempered, affectionate, sympathetic, and sensitive to surroundings and conditions of friends. Is a natural peacemaker, just, kind, amiable, and generous. Modest, neat, particular; loves art, refined pleasures, and amusements; artistic and dislikes unclean work. Is intuitive and has objective foresight. Usually marries young and generally more than once.

Venus is the planetary ruler of the sign Libra.

The Sun in Scorpio: October 23–November 21

In Scorpio the Sun gives strong characteristics and shrewd, keen judgment. The Scorpio native is critical, suspicious, skeptical but enterprising, reserved, tenacious, determined, and secretive. Fond of luxuries but economical and calculating; restless, energetic, fond of travel, especially on water, and admires grandeur in nature. Attends to own affairs in business but in matters of duty may make trouble for others.

In speech plain, blunt, sarcastic, and forceful; in politics or law very aggressive. At best, original, scientific, sagacious, daring, and creative, capable of much success through bold enterprise. Fine engineers, contractors, surgeons, chemists, detectives, and sheriffs are born in this sign.

Pluto is the planetary ruler of the sign Scorpio.

The Sun in Sagittarius: November 22–December 21

In Sagittarius the Sun gives a jovial, bright, hopeful, generous, and charitable nature: self-reliant, active, enterprising, frank, outspoken, honest, ambitious, persevering, and not easily discouraged. Loves liberty, freedom, and outdoor sports; dislikes a master and will not be driven. Generally has a strong will and is sincere, honorable, earnest, aspiring, energetic, and what he or she says goes right to the mark. Shows reverence for philosophy and science, has good calculation and foresight, and is usually prophetic as to the outcome of movements or enterprises.

Jupiter is the planetary ruler of the sign Sagittarius.

The Sun in Capricorn: December 22–January 19

In Capricorn the Sun gives a quiet, thoughtful, serious nature, deep mind and good reasoning ability; generally practical, economical, and given to investigation. Capricorns act with dignity and self-esteem, are somewhat particular, ambitious, and persevering; never entirely discouraged although often disappointed; thorough and hard workers. Careful, cautious, frugal, and make the most of opportunities. Usually meet with some heavy obstacles in the path of desires and progress, yet by dint of persistent, patient, and concentrated effort, often butt their way through and triumph over circumstances.

Saturn is the planetary ruler of the sign Capricorn.

The Sun in Aquarius: January 20–February 18 (Detriment)

In Aquarius the Sun gives a quiet, patient, determined, unobtrusive, and faithful nature, as a rule. The Aquarian is refined, pleasant, friendly, generous, charitable, dignified, and humanitarian; fond of art, music, scenery, and literature; cautious, steady, intelligent, intuitive, discriminative, concentrative, studious, thoughtful, and philosophical. Good reasoner, practical as well as theoretical; strong likes and dislikes and often has very radical and advanced ideas; is cheerful, sincere, and honest, easily influenced by kindness, slow to anger but will not be driven; loves liberty and is fond of occult research.

Uranus is the planetary ruler of the sign Aquarius.

The Sun in Pisces: February 19–March 20

In Pisces the Sun generally gives a kind and loving nature, confiding, honest, amiable, sympathetic, and especially kind to defenseless animals and people in distress. There is sometimes a sense of blessedness, or of being protected by the forces of nature, which either the native or those around him or her sense. Neat, particular, and a lover of order and completeness; modest, often timid, and lacking self-confidence. As a rule, Pisceans are industrious, methodical, and logical in their processes; idealistic, imaginative, inspirational; often gifted with mediumistic faculty and usually fond of secret, occult, or psychic investigation. The Pisces is retiring and humble.

Neptune is the planetary ruler of the sign Pisces.

Mars

Mars in Aries (Home)

Gives force, positivity, self-assurance, combativeness, activity, industry, enterprise, originality, and mechanical ability. The native is enthusiastic, electric, and inspiring. Philosophic and idealistic in spirit. So frank and free that he or she usually meets with little success in concealing anything. Very independent and often acts hastily and forcefully on impulse.

Possesses a keen sense of enjoyment, a love for sport, pleasure, and adventure. Has a strong dislike for all bonds, limitations, and restrictions, preferring to be free to explore and pioneer into all new lines of thought and activity.

Self-interest is strong and the native will usually push his or her affairs forward with very little outside encouragement, sometimes without any and in the face of discouragement. Mars in Aries increases the vitality but makes the native subject to danger by fire, surgical operations, fevers, inflammatory and mental complaints, accidents, wounds, and scalds.

If Mars is afflicted, it gives a hasty temper and trouble through the head, face, and eyes. It usually gives a mark or scar of some kind on the head or face.

Mars in Taurus

Gives practical qualities, quiet ambition, quick wit and foresight, good executive power, ability to organize and direct: a good manager capable of carrying plans and ideas into practical materialization. Not usually deterred or thwarted by obstacles; works determinedly and persistently where self-interests are concerned, gaining the desired end through tact, diplomacy, and sheer strength of internal force or confidence. This location of Mars indicates good earning powers, free expenditures and pleasure, as well as gain through the occupation.

If Mars is unafflicted, the native usually handles much money and gains by legacy. But if Mars is afflicted, the native will be liable to loss of money, property, and slumps in finances. The temper, during the period of affliction, is hasty and violent, and the native is irritable, acquisitive. When angry he or she is "mad as a bull" and quite apt to act "bull-headed." This position of Mars also indicates powerful opponents and legal difficulties, loss of legacy, unfavorable unions, some scandal, and monetary difficulties.

In either case, this location inclines to marriage, but trouble through it and also through the opposite sex.

Mars in Gemini

Sharpens the insight and perception, giving an acute, keen, quick intellect; mentally combative and forceful, plain-spoken; desire for educational attainments; active and nimble.

If Mars is well aspected, the native can write or speak well and is fond of reading, lectures, travel, science, law, or chemistry. Possesses a mind that is mechanical, inventive, and ingenious. In manner is practical, apt, and quick to make deductions and to arrive at conclusions.

If Mars is afflicted, often disagreeable and forceful in speech, satirical, fault-finding, and critical. Trouble through neighbors, relatives, and inferiors, also through writings, letters, education, and travel; difficulty, estrangement, or separation from brothers or sisters. The mind is restless, indecisive, and lacking in concentration. Pains in the lungs and injuries to hands, arms, shoulders, and collarbones.

Mars in Gemini tends to more than one union, to two attachments at the same time, or affection for a relative.

Mars in Cancer (Fall)

Makes the native bold, fearless, ambitious, and industrious, with sudden outbursts of temper and irritable tendencies; when offended, likely to nurse ill-feeling for a considerable time; fond of luxury and somewhat sensuous.

The subject is original, independent, and rebels against authority. Gives fitness for medicine or surgery, gain through enterprising business journeys and voyages, public concerns, and through physical effort. Somewhat changeable and lacking in continuity. Possesses some domestic tastes and liking for occult, mystical, psychical, and metaphysical subjects.

If Mars is afflicted, it indicates early death of mother, separation from or disagreement with her; trouble in home life and a discontented marriage partner; many worries, annoyances, sorrows, and changes of residence. Trouble through lands, property, and inheritance; accidents to home, such as fire, storms, earthquakes, theft, etc.; danger through the watery elements; many difficulties at close of life unless poise and harmony have been developed. Indisposition through the stomach and some trouble concerning the sight.

Mars in Leo

The native is candid, free, fearless, independent, enterprising, honest, and very conscientious. He or she is active, industrious, and capable of rising to positions of responsibility, trust, authority, management, and control. During good "directions" to Mars, success and good fortune through public appointments, government affairs, gain by speculation, investment, keen judgment in stock-exchange matters, insurance, and industrial concerns and through those of high rank. Sociable, fond of company, friendship, and esteem; warm-hearted, ardent in affection, love, and pleasure; often hasty and impulsive in love and sometimes too unrestrained in the emotions and passions. At times very forceful, positive, militant, aggressive, or defiant in manner, strong in argument and likely to arouse opposition and open enmity; but very magnanimous, generous, philosophical, reasonable; enthusiastic, broad, liberal, possessing a keen sense of justice and a determined will, and does not hold a grudge for long. Fondness for strenuous sports, adventure, risky enterprises, hazardous occupations, and for occult phenomena.

If Mars is afflicted, it threatens disappointment and sorrow in love, death of a loved one, separation or some irregularity in the union, death of a child. Trouble through superiors and also through inferiors; loss through speculation. Peculiar ailments of an inflammatory or timorous character, difficulty through accidents and fires, and trouble with sides and back. A responsive nature, amorous, forceful, bold and contemptuous of danger, quick in anger, though idealistic and fond of hazardous or strenuous pursuits.

Mars in Virgo

Makes the native quite original and interested in bold and scientific enterprises in which he or she is usually successful, yet has many struggles of a peculiar nature. This location of Mars puts difficulties in the way of the ambitions and desires for power and fame, helping to bring reversal, downfall, obstacles, and continual annoyance or opposition.

It favors profit through trading in common things and foreign produce and general business enterprises. The native is a good worker in employ but usually follows his or her own will quietly, being mentally very active, quick-witted, shrewd, and somewhat acquisitive; tactful and discriminative; possesses reserve force and energy. Mars in Virgo adapts one for science and is somewhat related to medicine, surgery, chemistry, pharmacy, hygiene, healing, and food products. It gives power to resist disease by study of hygiene and care in diet, but the nervous system and bowels are likely to suffer from complaints brought on or aggravated by Mars. There are also apt to be numerous ties, unions with inferiors, death of friends and helpers, or parting from them through quarrels or misunderstandings.

If Mars is afflicted in the horoscope, it will, at times, make one quite irritable, hasty, proud, obstinate, reserved, secretive, and revengeful. Suffers from loss of friends, servants, subordinates, co-workers, and false associations. Liability to accidents and sickness from overwork and trouble through labor difficulties and strikes.

Mars in Libra (Detriment)

Promotes development of the faculties of perception and observation. Gives clear vision, refined tastes, idealistic temperament, and an intuitive mind of a speculative nature. The native is enterprising and often placed in a position where he or she rules others. Love of sciences in general and refined occupations, business or professional. This location of Mars is good for a lawyer or surgeon. It also indicates many friends among scientific, philosophic, religious, legal, or business people. In the business world the native meets with trouble through competitors but survives enemies. Trouble also comes through other people; he meets with rivalry, opposition, enmity, and criticism, both open and secret. Troubles and sadness concerning deaths and losses of those related to the family circle.

Mars in this location inclines to an ardent, rash, impulsive, or passionate love. The opposite sex usually is a great attraction and exercises much control over the native. He or she is apt to become detrimentally entangled through the affections, causing much suffering, grief, or trouble. Other testimonies concurring, it causes an early marriage and quarrels with the partner. Usually, however, a disappointment in love delays marriage.

The experiences gathered through business, marriage, etc., lead the native, in later years, to a still higher education and unfoldment that produces fine judgment. Mars in Libra is a testimony for offspring and they are usually endowed with superior intellect.

If Mars is afflicted, particularly by Uranus, there are many separations, broken ties, and difficulties between the native and his or her partner, friends, associates, and relatives.

Mars in Scorpio

This gives a practical nature with the capacity to work hard and accomplish much. There is good executive power, mechanical and inventive ability. In character the native is firm, positive, determined, and forceful, with a matter-of-fact manner and a seemingly cold or unconscious disregard for the feelings of others. Somewhat selfish, rash, revengeful, and passionate. The mind is acute, sharp, keen, and diplomatic; native is quick and capable in government office, in secret missions and work of a peculiar nature in connection with the regular employment or with confederates or associates. This location is favorable for a chemist, surgeon, or any other profession or occupation that involves the use of liquids and tools. The native usually enters into projects with intensity of purpose and action, his or her motto being "Produce results." Fondness for hazardous enterprises, liable to accidents and a sudden or violent end. Likes to investigate things mysterious and at some time likely to become engaged in psychical research. There is likelihood of gain by marriage; romantic courtship experiences; long journeys and voyages.

If Mars is much afflicted in Scorpio, it tends to express as unsociable, ungrateful, quarrelsome, revengeful, overbearing, and selfish, with scant regard for the rights of others. Trouble through employees, severe illness, accidents, and operations.

Mars in Sagittarius

Makes the native free, frank, generous, enthusiastic, ambitious, and at times impulsive in speech and action. The mind is active and although fond of argument, is usually good humored, original, and independent in thought, morally and mentally brave, daring and fearless of the opinions of others; firm, fixed, and positive in his or her ideas, and frequently at variance with accepted opinions. Fond of travel and adventure; favorable results from investigation of the occult, particularly where the inspirational, prophetic, and intuitional tendencies are concerned. This location gives good mechanical ability, foresight, and ingenuity; also good for lawyers and surgeons, evangelists and explorers. It gives a love of pleasure, especially strenuous sports and athletics carried on outdoors. Conduces to a liking for military tactics and, if the chance offers, will hold military and naval positions. If Mars is not afflicted, it signifies gain through marriage, associates, legacy, and social means; likelihood of more than one union and concern regarding health of others in the domestic circle.

If Mars is afflicted, it signifies danger through journeys and traveling, possible loss of legacy, and loss through legal decisions; unfavorable employment and some risk therein. Liable to trouble through too much risk, overestimation, miscalculation, or exaggeration. Not favorable for brothers, sisters, cousins, and neighbors; disagreement with them, or one or more will die. Difficulty with religious persons or through religious or skeptical and unorthodox ideas and beliefs. In the early part of life the native is likely to be indisposed, and at the close meets with dual experiences.

Mars in Capricorn (Exaltation)

Gives courage, self-reliance, and assurance, a nature that is brave, bold, and not at all averse to adventure and excitement; often is very heroic. Due to disregard of danger, may meet with accidents, especially to lower limbs. Is ambitious, enterprising, industrious, and acquisitive. Capable of much responsibility and endeavor; possesses good executive and organizing ability. Desire for public life and in lines allowing plenty of scope for action. Being energetic and willing to assume responsibility, attains positions of authority and prominence; friends among powerful people and occult students.

In acquiring education, the intellect is slow but is sure in the assimilation of knowledge. The mind is subtle and gains much by intuition. There is some speculative tendency or liking for risks and a desire to acquire wealth. The native becomes a lover of duty, has good business ability, gains through commerce and science, also through industrious employees, travel, foreign affairs, and products of the earth. Honor and fame in profession; a successful sales manager, general manager, agent, or real estate broker. Marriage produces an important change in life, greatly affects the close of life, and may bring gain socially. There is likely to be an early affair of the affections with an inferior or an elderly person.

If Mars is afflicted, it indicates difficulties through friends and acquaintances; conflict with people in authority, superiors, and those of high rank. The native at times is irritable, quick in temper and passion. He or she may arouse rivalry, opposition, and criticism and is likely to suffer in honor and credit. Even though Mars is exalted in Capricorn, there may be a disagreement or separation between the native and a parent, or between the parents themselves, or one of them may die prematurely.

Mars in Aquarius

Makes a good reasoner who usually takes some unique, original, and unlooked-for point from which to reason. As a speaker he or she is a ready debater, forcible and convincing; he or she sums up facts and arguments clearly and often arrives at conclusions quickly. The native is intellectual, prudent, quick-witted, and scientific. There is some impulsiveness in manner and speech and at times he or she is rash, headstrong, and abrupt. The native is humanitarian and interested in reforms for public good; fond of literature and philosophy, occult studies, and science generally. Mars in Aquarius makes one ambitious, enterprising, and independent. The opinions may be fixed and not readily changed by others; when he or she makes a change, it is usually a complete one and undergone quite suddenly or abruptly. The native is original and unique in many things, inventive and fond of machinery, electrical, and aerial matters. This is a good location of Mars for medicine or surgery, hospital, philanthropic, or welfare work. Makes a good director and responsible official in connection with public companies or in governmental, municipal, and fraternal office. Gains by the professions, and financial success comes through public work. He or she is sincere and has refined tastes; makes friends readily through merit and ability.

If Mars is afflicted, it indicates that at times the native is apt to be too independent, abrupt, and blunt in speech and manner; apt to act hastily without realizing the consequences. This is likely to result in separation from friends and associates and suffering through opposition and hostility. Trouble occurs in connection with firms, companies, associates, societies, and partners. It is thought also to indicate the death of a friend, estrangement from one, or suffering through a false friends, also the early death of a parent or separation from them. The native may be rough and ready, faithful in affections, and capable in an emergency.

Mars in Pisces

The native is generous and free with money, yet anxious to accumulate wealth; somewhat timid or cautious; if angered or aroused, becomes bold and audacious. In nature the person is sympathetic, receptive, affectionate, and sensitive to imposition. Sometimes the native is quiet and retiring, easily depressed and gloomy, somewhat prone to indolence, vacillation, irresolution, or indecision, and too open to the influence of others, while at other times he or she accomplishes much quietly. Is desirous of popularity although may not gain much of it; endeavors to avoid conflicts and tries valiantly to surmount difficulties and misfortunes. Apt in details and successful in ordinary occupations and with the middle class of people, also with pursuits in connection with public or private institutions. Mars in Pisces gives ability as a detective, inspector, jailer, warden, hospital worker, sailor, marine engineer, fisherman, hotel keeper, and in occupations requiring a uniform. Friends among powerful people; help and gain financially from friends.

There may be some tendency to dissipation or passion, or overstimulated emotions, and danger through water and liquids generally; from drowning, scalding, poisons, food in liquid form, also through gas, anesthetics, and opiates. This location of Mars also tends to disappointment in love, to two attachments, and delay in marriage. Accidents and trouble to the feet.

If Mars is afflicted, it shows that the native will meet with many heavy misfortunes and difficulties; will suffer from secret enmity in various forms, such as theft, scandal, slander, false accusations, etc., whether deserving it or not. When Mars in Pisces is poorly aspected, one may suffer through overindulgence in any consciousness-altering substance, especially through drugs or drink. There may be a violent tendency or memory lapses while under the influence. This placement gives the subconscious more expression. One may become involved in trouble through lack of candor, truthfulness, and honesty, and this may be due either directly or indirectly to one's own fault. This placement indicates many changes in plans, views, disposition, and occupation.

Jupiter

Jupiter in Aries

Usually signifies a progressive person, ambitious, aspiring, generous, candid, high-minded, ardent, philosophical, and reasonable. Success is largely due to personal merits and through domestic relationship, social standing, and influential friends. The native is capable of holding positions of responsibility, government offices, etc., and where he or she has authority over others; military honors. Usually changes his or her pursuit sometime in life and has two occupations. Strong liking for literature, science, study, philosophy, traveling, and all that appertains to cultivation of mind. Shipping, voyaging, horses, sports, and outdoor exercises attract the attention. Usually respected and generally fortunate; a pioneer, in a way, and ambitious of advancement. An advocate of new ideas for improvement, and whatever the religious views may be, is sincere, earnest, and progressive therein. This location tends to benefit and gain through intellectual friends and acquaintances, shipping, travel, law, religious associates, children, young people, foreign securities, speculation, and insurance.

Jupiter in Taurus

Jupiter in Taurus gives love of justice. The nature is affectionate and generous, peaceful, reserved, and firm. Has great love for home and not much given to change. Seldom travels except for definite purposes such as those that relate to health, business, or learning. A patron of philanthropic movements and philosophy; fixed in religion and views generally.

This location is favorable for benefit through the opposite sex, sociability, church, philosophy, and matters connected with the higher attributes of the mind. Also for the things signified by the sign Taurus and Ninth House affairs. If other testimonies in the chart permit, it tends to gain through gifts and legacies, investments, speculation, children, young people, marriage, and partnership. If Jupiter is afflicted, there will be losses through these things.

Jupiter in Gemini (Detriment)

Gives a nature that expresses sympathy, charity, benevolence, and humanitarian tendencies. The disposition is friendly, courteous, truthful, and trustworthy. Fond of novelty, traveling, and mental recreation. The tendency is to intellectual development. The mind is lofty and aspiring, and although at times there seems to be restlessness and feelings of uncertainty or changeability, there is good comparison or mathematical faculty; also an ability for literature, occult investigation, psychic unfoldment, and prophecy. It indicates the possibility of an attraction to a relative or someone closely associated and two marriages. There may be some difficulty in marriage through relatives, writings, or travel. It inclines to success in literature, benefits through inventions, with large corporations, mail-order business and publishing. If afflicted, sudden difficulties or opponents; unprofitable or unpopular professions; differences or separation from relatives; trouble through publishing or publications.

Jupiter in Cancer (Exaltation)

The native is ambitious, enterprising, good-humored, humane, charitable, benevolent, sympathetic, kind, and sociable; popular, with friends among inferiors and also among those of good position. It tends to an intellectual view of life, intuition, useful imagination, and fondness for all fine arts and cultured amusements; patriotic, interested in public welfare and investigation in the occult and psychic fields. It shows a fondness for home and mother, also for voyages and travels for pleasure, health, or learning. It inclines to gain in public work through mental ability and, if other testimonies in the chart agree, through investment, inheritance, property, or marriage. A peaceful, honorable end abroad or far from the place of birth.

Jupiter in Leo

Makes the native good-natured, noble, and lofty-minded, magnanimous, loyal, courteous, generous, compassionate, benevolent, and prudent. This location strengthens the constitution, increases the vitality, and favors the birth of children. The love nature is deep, sincere, and honest; the subject is endowed with wisdom, good judgment, and willpower, capable of holding positions of trust and responsibility. Enjoys prestige, honors, grandeur, and great undertakings. The mind is intuitive, diplomatic, and inclined to higher sciences, philosophy, fine arts, religion, and culture generally. Favors government employ and positions of prominence. Gain through judicious investment and speculations. Benefit through long journeys, especially in connection with sports, education, or diplomatic affairs.

Jupiter in Virgo

This increases the mental inclination in all directions toward an intellectual or even somewhat materialistic view of things. The nature is cautious, not easily imposed upon, discreet, prudent, and discriminative, and therefore the native has ability for practical scientific and philosophical investigation and study, the mind being analytical, critical, and matter-of-fact, possessed of wisdom, knowledge, honesty, and an ability for the study of natural laws. Careful in choice of acquaintances, friendships among occult students. Rises above his or her sphere in life, has foreign associations and travel due to business. Marriage is in some way peculiar and possibly to a social inferior. If well aspected or unafflicted, success in business or professional pursuits; gain by employees, literature, investment, commercial and speculative dealings. It tends to the occupations of Virgo and Sagittarius. If afflicted, loss and trouble through these things and disturbances of the blood, liver, bowels, and hips; lack of application, method, and concentration.

Jupiter in Libra

The disposition is mild and temperate, sincere, earnest, kind, sociable, and obliging. The native is conscientious, compassionate, imaginative, and perceptive; loves peace, justice, mercy, and harmony. Charitable, philanthropic, fond of travel, music, art, and all intellectual and cultured entertainment. Benefit from the opposite sex, powerful friends, and those who are scientific, philosophical, or spiritual. If well aspected or unafflicted, gain through commerce, employees, science, medicine, law, professional associations, public institutions, theatres, hospitals, asylums, etc.; a happy marriage, fruitful union and good children; honors and esteem. If afflicted, trouble through legal difficulties, open enmity, and opposition, and through treachery from women, friends, or associates.

Jupiter in Scorpio

This gives powerful will, deep emotions, ardor, enthusiasm, perseverance, ambition, and generosity. The mind is active, resolute, self-confident, fruitful, subtle, analytical, lofty, proud, aggressive, both constructive and destructive; fond of chemical and mechanical experiments or occult and psychical research and all things of a mysterious nature. Association with governmental officials or connection with the government; power among associates and societies; professional secrets and information affecting the honor of others; friendships of a peculiar nature or open to criticism; intrigues with superiors; long voyages and strange adventures abroad. If well aspected or unafflicted, gain through occupations of Scorpio, by litigation, arbitration, death of partner, legacy, and public investments. If afflicted, jealous and powerful enemies; loss through questionable or unsound speculation and securities, etc.; death of child, danger, misfortune and liability to death through water and voyages; danger through social or political connections; liability to suffer from hereditary diseases, blood poisoning, or heart disease. Liability to quarrels and litigation; difficulty with those engaged in law, science, religion, or medicine.

Jupiter in Sagittarius (Home)

The native is endowed with a courteous, affable, tolerant, humorous, kind, generous, sympathetic, loyal, and noble nature. The mind is broad, just, liberal, merciful, compassionate, humanitarian, sincere, prophetic, and philosophical. Jupiter in Sagittarius tends to good fortune and general success. The native is usually successful in his or her enterprises, often receives honors and is a leader among his or her associates. It is favorable for matters connected with sports, horses, shipping, literature, and learned, scientific, philosophic, or religious bodies. If other testimonies in the chart concur, it tends toward gain through speculation, marriage, legacy, and voyages. If afflicted, troublesome social affairs, difficulty through sports, and loss by speculation or gambling.

Jupiter in Capricorn (Fall)

A mind that is serious, deliberate, thoughtful, and ingenious. The nature is constructive, capable, and creative with organizing ability. Is ambitious and attains some degree of popularity, power, credit, and esteem. Tends to economy, frugality, and the acquirement of practical education, taking part in the advancement of scientific, philosophic, or spiritual knowledge, industrial or political economics. It inclines to general success in the occupation, especially where the native is in authority over others or engaged in some public or governmental career. The tendency is to gain through commercial or foreign affairs and if other testimonies in the chart concur, gain through money or legacy from father or superiors. It is said to indicate a long journey or voyage and that the marriage is affected by the parents; also that the native is concerned with the sorrows and misfortunes of friends. If afflicted, it manifests as parsimony or inactivity; an unorthodox nature; trouble, difficulty, and obstacles in occupation; some discredit.

Jupiter in Aquarius

Makes the native cheerful, good-humored, obliging, just, merciful, compassionate, sympathetic, philanthropic, and congenial, disliking discord and in harmony. The mind is prophetic, intuitive, genteel, refined, liberal, broad, philosophic, humanitarian, and given to the investigation of new thought, social, spiritualistic, and reform subjects. Inclines to fondness for and pursuit of the out-of-the-ordinary, occult, curious, and mystical studies. Jupiter in Aquarius gives original, independent, and progressive views; often indifferent to the ordinary affairs of life; favors development of the higher attributes of the mind through hygiene, philosophy, science, literature, music, classical and ancient arts. It gives pleasure and benefit through good and sincere friends who are gained by personal influence. Pleasure and interest in congressional activates, public institutions, and public work. Gain and benefit through profession and, if in good aspect to the ruler of the Eleventh House, gain in employment with societies and associations or the government. Psychic and occult experiences; peculiar conditions and experience brought about by associates and friends. Acquaintances among foreigners and political executives.

Jupiter in Pisces

Gives strong idealism, interest in all philanthropic affairs; increases the emotions and imagination generally, adding to the intuition, spiritual perception, and psychic impressions. The native receives benefit from perusal of investigation along the lines of occult and psychical research in general and will experience some remarkable phenomena and prophetic dreams or visions. The native is studious, hospitable, quiet, unassuming, sociable, kind, charitable, fond of animals, sympathetic, always ready to help the sick and unfortunate, and possessed of many good talents. It disposes somewhat to traveling, especially by water. It inclines to honors, gain, favors, and high occupations through associations, companies, friends, mining, and shipping affairs, and institutions such as hospitals, sanitariums, laboratories, etc. If afflicted, loss through speculation and deception. The native is liable to become at times too lazy, changeable, overly fond of ease and pleasure, indolent, inert, inactive, or restless, unsettled, undecided, and easily influenced.

Saturn

Saturn in Aries (Fall)

Resolute, determined, ambitious for success. Prosperity through industry and perseverance. Contemplative, good reasoning faculties, easily angered, not at all averse to argument, and contentious when opposed. At times reserved and acquisitive. Jealous partner and probability of difficulties through marriage. Obstacles and troubles in first half of life.

Saturn in Taurus

Thoughtful, kind, quiet, but sometimes quick-tempered, stubborn, resentful, and not easily appeased. Economical, prudent, diplomatic, and somewhat reserved over personal affairs, especially finances. Fondness for botany, horticulture, or stockbreeding. Sorrow and loss through relatives; unfortunate domestic experiences; gain through thrift, economy, and judicious investment.

Saturn in Gemini

An observant, ingenious nature. Ability for scientific occupation in connection with literature, mathematics, etc. Adaptable and resourceful. Trouble and sorrow through relatives. Unfortunate legal affairs. Liable to false accusations, restraint, or limitation through some of the kindred or neighbors. Interest in current and advanced thought, ability for profound intellectual attainments.

Saturn in Cancer (Detriment)

Dissatisfied feelings causing many changes of residence and pursuits. Changeable moods; somewhat fretful, discontented, or jealous. Domestic troubles; anxiety and sorrow through attachments, parents, home, and children. Affected psychically by adverse conditions surrounding others. Pleasure through occult investigation and psychic sources; interest in domestic economy and public welfare. An industrious partner. Difficulties toward the close of life unless the native endeavors to develop and apply his or her highest qualities.

Saturn in Leo

Generous but quick-tempered, cautious yet bold in spirit, determined, ambitious, and strong-willed. Spiritual tendencies. Troubles and secret enmity through inferiors. At times receptive to psychic conditions, consciously or unconsciously, which affect the health. Danger through accidents and overwork or overexertion. Sorrows through love affairs and children.

Saturn in Virgo

Reserved, discreet, cautious, prudent, frugal, serious, quiet, and intuitive. Somewhat worried, anxious, doubtful, or mistrustful. At times very gloomy, depressed, and easily discouraged. Inclination for investigation of the mysterious; fond of the occult and profound or scientific studies. Gain by careful investment. Troubles and misfortunes through marriage and partnerships; difficulties, struggles, obstacles, and sorrows in first half of life. Liability to mental disease, headaches, and bowel weakness. Troubles in employment and through servants.

Saturn in Libra (Exaltation)

Refined tastes, respect and fondness for science, intellectual tendencies; somewhat given to debate or controversy. Generally has open or female enmities, sorrow through loss of one of deep attachment; separations, broken contracts, and domestic difficulties; troubles and opposition in employment. Often Saturn raises one to high position only to drop the native into severe disgrace or misfortune later. As it tends toward the necessary mental qualities, this is a good location for lawyers, doctors, and scientists generally. In a female chart it often bestows great beauty of the brunette type. Tends to delay marriage and to produce coldness on the part of the partner. Sometimes the life is stimulated by an adversary or through a difficult partnership.

Saturn in Scorpio

Sudden resolutions, violent temper, passionate, self-willed, acquisitive, jealous, independent, resourceful, and cautious; shrewd mind rather than profoundly intellectual. Sorrow through love affairs, secret alliances, intrigues, or domestic difficulties. Psychic ability and fondness for occult investigations, chemistry, or geology. Success through persistence and cleverness after many difficulties, obstacles, and trials, especially if necessary attention is given to development along the higher lines.

Saturn in Sagittarius

Frank, fearless, philosophical, kind, and obliging; humanitarian views and ever ready to assist in the advancement and promotion of domestic conditions or political economy. Occult tendencies, intuitive understanding, prophetic insight with regard to future welfare or scientific development. Opposition, antagonism, or reproof and censure hurt deeply, and by resenting such, the native often prevents his or her own elevation or honors, or makes it difficult to attain desired position; otherwise, it gives the power to create his or her own dignity through merit of ability. Trouble through public affairs, honor, and reputation. Sagittarians often engage in more than one occupation; gain by careful and judicious investment. Danger of nervous breakdown at close of life unless effort is made to safeguard the health by building up the system.

Saturn in Capricorn (Home)

Makes the native melancholic, serious, apprehensive, cautious, suspicious, discontented, and acquisitive; deep thinker, good reasoner, and grave or reserved in demeanor. Ambitious, very anxious to rise in life, and through tact, diplomacy, or persistence, generally succeeds. Liable to inferior attachments, unreliable friendships, sorrow through marriage and domestic affairs; chronic ailments and possibility of some mental affliction through worry, dissatisfaction, restricted pleasure and recreation, or repression. Success followed by failures.

Saturn in Aquarius

A courteous, affable disposition; a thoughtful, well-disposed, humane, grave, reserved, serious nature. Penetrating intellect, good reasoner and deep thinker; deliberate in action and very impressive in speech when interested; sociable, friendly, and usually unresentful. Generally become quite profound in what they undertake in the arts and sciences, refining the mind through study, observation, and experience. As a rule, gain good financial prospects through employment or profession by practical application, quiet determination, and faithfulness. Form many acquaintances and some romantic or lasting tie. The latter years are usually more fortunate than the beginning of life.

Saturn in Pisces

If afflicted, the subject suffers loss, hindrance, delays, deception, slander, and discredit though friends and acquaintances. Meets with many sorrows and disappointments in life, most of which he or she bears secretly, and attempts to present the best side of things.

Circumstances often decide his or her mode of procedure and compel the native to cope with lines of action entirely unexpected and undesired. Often reaches positions of honor or dignity but has difficulty maintaining them.

Misfortune, hard luck, and disaster usually mark attachments, or unfavorable ties are formed that severely handicap, retard, or sadden the life. Sorrow, romance, and tragedy are elements that accompany the affectional experiences. The sympathetic and emotional nature is strong, and the native is often the cause of his or her own misfortune and difficulty; desire is prominent, but hope, firmness, and continuity need developing.

The native is ingenious and aspiring, but lacks sufficient application, opportunities, and favorable conditions. The health is often adversely affected by psychic conditions, colds, and troubles through the feet, consumptive tendencies, and lingering illnesses. Regards money only as a means of acquiring the necessities of life and often seeks relief, understanding, and success through an investigation of psychic and occult affairs, which usually causes retirement and seclusion, the enlightenment proving somewhat beneficial.

Good aspects to Saturn in Pisces tend to mitigate the severe testimonies and assist the native to improve through steady, persistent effort and by means of psychical and occult research or large institutions. It gives practical execution, deep intuition, perception, and some mediumistic qualities.

Uranus

Uranus in Aries

Note: Uranus was in Aries from approximately 1843–1850 and 1927–1935.

This location of Uranus gives a love of independence and freedom, positiveness, force, and impulse. It increases the mental vigor, producing activity, energy, resource, originative, and inventive ability. Fond of machinery, electrical devices, and possesses mechanical ingenuity. Likes travel and often changes the residence. At times is abrupt, brusque, blunt, or radical in manner, disregarding tact and self-control; often impulsive in speech without intending to be so. Disputes and estrangements are frequent. Interest in children from a mental or intellectual standpoint.

Uranus in Taurus (Fall)

Note: Uranus was in Taurus from about 1850–1859 and 1934–1942.

Makes the native determined and headstrong, but when confronted with obstacles can usually extricate himself with resource and ingenuity. The native is naturally intuitive and can become an adept in occultism. It is a slightly evil location for marriage, causing jealousy on the part of the partner.

It causes ups and downs in financial affairs and some sudden losses. If well aspected, it signifies gain through partnership, marriage, associations, inventions, and original enterprise.

Uranus in Gemini

Note: Uranus was in Gemini from about 1858–1866 and 1941–1949.

Endows the native with versatility, and indicates some eccentricity in friendship and in expression. It increases mental power through originality, intuition, and ingenuity. The native loves science and invention, and favors new ideas, reforms, and out-of-the-ordinary subjects.

It is a favorable location for the study of electricity, aerodynamics, astrology, metaphysics, mesmerism, etc. Liking for travel, and friends among literary and scientific people. Telepathic or clairvoyant faculty.

If Uranus is afflicted, liable to estrangement from brethren, cousins, neighbors, and some trouble in education, examinations, letters, and journeys; unfavorable criticism.

Uranus in Cancer

Note: Uranus was in Cancer from about 1865–1872 and 1948–1956.

Gives mediumistic ability, the feelings and emotions being sensitive and easily touched; at times this makes the native eccentric, cranky, restless, impatient, peculiar, or radical.

Some domestic troubles or estrangement, although the native loves home and children. Loss and difficulty through the dwelling, land, or property. Stomach troubles. The native is patriotic, loves traveling, and is original in ideas and in expression. Interest in municipal or legislative activities.

Uranus in Leo (Detriment)

Note: Uranus was in Leo from about 1871–1878 and 1955–1962.

A mentality that is extremely industrious in its aspirations, yet the native may be physically disposed to great moderation. It makes the person, at times, headstrong, fiery, forceful, and eccentric, displaying a disregard for conventionality, a somewhat rebellious disposition, and often incurs the disfavor of others. Cannot tolerate being ordered about or contradicted. Great love of freedom, independence, and of daring or exciting adventures; strange aversions and attractions. Odd experiences in connection with the affections and in love affairs, and some danger of sorrow or estrangement therein. Obstacles in the home life in youth, and loss or difficulty in some way through the father. Some hindrance and annoyance in social affairs and through children, and probably sudden loss of a child.

If Uranus is well aspected, it indicates occult ability, success with electricity, machinery and inventions, and is good for a public or professional career of a unique or distinctive nature.

Uranus in Virgo

Note: Uranus was in Virgo from about 1878–1885 and 1961–1969.

The mind is subtle, independent, and original. The native is quiet, eccentric, stubborn, fond of curiosities and science generally, especially the occult in which he or she meets with great success. It makes a good mechanic or teacher and gives success in employment of others, especially in connection with electricity, electronics, dietetics, chemistry, metaphysics, or science.

It increases the intellectual ability and the desire for healthful comforts, also to make the most of the productive capacity in manufacturing and other enterprises in which the native is likely to have interest.

If well aspected it denotes gain through public occupations associated with the government or municipality.

If afflicted, it indicates many difficulties, disappointed ambitions, trouble through employees or through employment, and restrictions connected with the occupation. Strange or sudden bodily afflictions.

Uranus in Libra

Note: Uranus was in Libra from about 1800–1807, 1884–1891, and 1968–1974.

Makes the native a good reasoner, fond of traveling, eccentric, ambitious, quick-tempered, restless, and the possessor of good imagination, taste, intuition, and aesthetic faculties. This location favors scientific, artistic, literary, or judicial professions, gives telepathic and inventive ability and much personal magnetism. Interest in aerial affairs.

Sometimes it leads to a hasty engagement or marriage, but brings danger of separation, estrangement, divorce, or death of the partner. Unless well aspected, it is not good here for partnership. If afflicted, it is likely through some peculiarity of manner, to produce lack of sympathy or affection, also to arouse enmity, rivalry, opposition, criticism. Indicates broken friendships and trouble through schemes, politics, and strange actions of the partner.

Uranus in Scorpio (Exaltation)

Note: Uranus was in Scorpio from about 1807–1813, 1890–1898, and 1974–1981.

Gives the native strength of mind, will, determination, persistence, power of concentration, and a spirit that cannot be broken by resistance.

At times the native is bold, stubborn, sharp-spoken, shrewd, acute, reserved, secretive, aggressive, forceful, and rebellious; frequently at variance with other people and with accepted opinions. Uranus in Scorpio intensifies the activity toward self-advancement and personal gain. It gives a love for things mechanical and an inventive nature. There is mesmeric power, ability for practical occultism, industrial chemistry, and drugless healing methods.

If Uranus is afflicted, there is danger of sudden accidents, falls, wounds by firearms, explosions, electrical devices, and trouble on water.

Uranus in Sagittarius

Note: Uranus was in Sagittarius from about 1813–1820, 1897–1904, and 1981–1988.

This location of Uranus increases the imagination and inventiveness; it favors dreams, visions, intuition, premonition, and traveling.

The native loves science in general and takes an interest in all passing events of a scientific nature, especially inventions connected with locomotion and all means of travel.

Uranus here assists other influences that may be present in the chart to develop the higher side of the mind in almost any line where wide cultivation and higher education or understanding give scope. The native is progressive, daring, adventuresome, generous, and extremely fond of liberty of action and speech; enthusiastic in beliefs and undertakings that are not always orthodox or altogether free from risk or danger.

If much afflicted, strange difficulties arise through these things, and possibly some trouble through the partner's relatives and through religious or scientific people; also through foreign affairs and journeys.

Uranus in Capricorn

Note: Uranus was in Capricorn from about 1821–1828, 1904–1912, and 1988–1995.

Gives good reasoning faculties and generally a profound, penetrating mind. It disturbs the seriousness, reserve, and conservatism of the sign Capricorn; assists in intensifying the ambition, perseverance, executive ability, and independence. It tends toward bold enterprise and radical departures from established systems or accustomed methods, initiating innovations of a progressive nature. Foresight, intuition, business hunches, and the faculty of prevision often help the native anticipate public trends, conditions, or needs. Unique or original undertakings, and progressive or equitable attitude toward patrons or employees. It is a good location for success in governmental or public occupations; or those connected with special lines like electricity, manufacturing, machinery, radio, and transportation; also municipal offices, positions of power, authority, or responsibility.

There are times, when Uranus is disturbed by transits and directions, that the native feels restless or uneasy and acts eccentric, radical, stubborn, or headstrong.

If Uranus is afflicted, it indicates some family discord or trouble in early life, loss of the father, separation or estrangement from him, opposition from those in authority, reversals or difficulty in occupation; incurs the disfavor of superiors and severe public criticism.

Uranus in Aquarius (Home)

Note: Uranus was in Aquarius from about 1828–1836, 1912–1920, and 1995–2003.

Uranus in Aquarius increases the mental ability, giving originality, ingenuity, resourcefulness, inventiveness, comprehensiveness, strong intuition, and imagination.

The native is peculiar and eccentric in beliefs, fond of novelty, science, and unusual pursuits, possessing a great love of freedom. The disposition is pleasant, humanitarian, sociable, obliging, and gains many friends, some of whom are very peculiar or engaged in extraordinary occupations. The native usually succeeds in anything of a scientific or mechanical nature; also in association with others and in public life, municipal offices, large companies, railroads, radio, airway concerns; fraternal societies and social movements.

Uranus in Pisces

Note: Uranus was in Pisces from about 1835–1844 and 1919–1928. It entered Pisces in 2003 and will be in this sign until about 2011.

Gives a peculiar nature, fond of all occult investigations, mysteries, and psychical research.

It usually endows the native with some occult faculty and expresses in dreams, visions, and strange experiences.

It gives far-seeing, but not always on the brightest side of things; friends among occultists and those connected with public and private institutions. May be capable of originating formulas for medication or commercial chemistry or inventing useful methods of treatment.

If afflicted, it brings trouble, difficulty, estrangement from friends and public, lack of sociability or sympathy; opposition, hostility, critical, and scandal coupled with unexpected misfortune and reversals.

Neptune

Neptune in Aries

Note: Neptune was in Aries from about 1861–1875.

If well aspected, the native will take leading parts in mystical or secret societies and push forward popularity of psychic research.

It intensifies the feelings, emotions, and senses, softening or elevating the disposition through sympathy, benevolence, spirit perception, or inner understanding.

It gives a love of traveling, also some mystical experiences and original ideas with regard to religious or spiritual matters and naturopathic methods. It confers vivid impulses toward the correction of human ills or conditions, the reform of existing institutions, and an incentive toward a national, political, or public career.

If afflicted, it gives peculiar feelings, aversions, premonitions, and usually inclines to some habit for the gratification of the senses, such as smoking or excessive use of stimulants.

Neptune in Taurus

Note: Neptune was in Taurus from about 1874–1889.

If well aspected, it assists other testimonies in the chart for financial gain, especially through speculation, business, and secret or private organizations.

It gives a love for occultism, the old, curious, and mystical; in fact, it increases the aesthetic taste and adds a spiritual touch to the nature.

It denotes enthusiasm in beliefs, a companionable disposition, usually patient and good-humored and, although rather quick in temper, softhearted. A favorable location for friendship and marriage. It contributes an active desire to disseminate scientific knowledge, simplifying it as far as possible and popularizing the truth. It gives an insight to natural and psychic phenomena and a desire to undo the doctrines of materialism. It bestows a nature that senses mental achievements, seeing human progress years in advance of the times.

In business or profession, it seeks to simplify methods for practical application. The native is likely to be seclusive and lack certainty or persistence in acquiring the common pleasures of life, and to disregard the conventional or business trend of the present.

If afflicted, it adds to the sensuality and increases the mental alertness and desire for stimulants. It tends to negative and psychical states and a decided inclination toward imagination, mysticism, and luxury.

Neptune in Gemini

Note: Neptune was in Gemini from about 1887–1902.

When well aspected, increases the mental sensitivity, giving imagination, impressions, musical taste, and prophetic and symbolic dreams. It gives great linguistic or conversational capacity and an interest in drama, poetry, philosophy, and occultism.

It tends to sympathy and geniality. Favorable for quick perception, science, mathematics, invention, or anything requiring mechanical ingenuity or fine handiwork.

If afflicted, it inclines to excessive geniality and romantic friendships, mental restlessness or diffusion, likelihood of complications or misunderstandings with brethen, cousins, or neighbors, and difficulty or anxiety through too great mental receptivity. Deception in promises or agreements; misunderstanding of reports or rumors.

Neptune in Cancer

Note: Neptune was in Cancer from about 1901–1916.

Well aspected, adds delicacy, refinement, and idealism to the spiritual faculties. Increases strength of imagination, adds power to the impressions, and intensifies the emotions. It conduces to love of nature and natural science, love of home and domestic comforts, although likely to bring some important changes in residence and some peculiar or mysterious experience or development therein. It gives sympathy (especially for the mother), inspiration, and psychic or mediumistic faculty. Fondness for traveling, especially by water.

If afflicted, gives a highly impressionable and sensitive nature; restlessness, discontent, and strong desire for change are prominent. Indisposition through stomach and by receptive, passive, or negative states and inner nervousness or anxiety. Some complications or peculiar conditions in connection with home or domestic affairs.

Neptune in Leo (Exaltation)

Note: Neptune was in Leo from about 1914–1929.

If well aspected, indicates an ambitious, quiet, dignified, benevolent, and warm-hearted disposition; much sympathy, charity, and generosity, coupled with intuitive foresight.

The higher emotions are intensified, giving keen and accurate interpretation of human feelings. It bestows a high quality to the faculties of mind as expressed in spirituality and conscientiousness.

Fond of refined sports, pleasure, society, and of the fine arts such as poetry, music, painting, the opera, and drama. Peculiar sensations or feelings; mysterious or unconventional conditions arise through matters of affection; likely to suffer severe heartache through disappointment relating to the affections.

If afflicted, likely to indicate too much love of pleasure and trouble of some kind through allowing the senses, feelings, and emotions to sway the reason; also difficulty through an overly lavish expenditure of energy, impulsive sympathy, and generosity

Neptune in Virgo (Detriment)

Note: Neptune was in Virgo from about 1928–1943.

If well aspected, gives an intellectual trend to the spiritual faculties; a rather reserved nature, capable in mathematics and profound in the investigation of psychical phenomena; mediumistic tendency.

It adds gentleness, constancy, and patience to the disposition. The native may be unusual in some way and entertain peculiar ideas with regard to medication, hygiene, diet, and labor conditions.

It inclines to gain through employment in clerical work, pharmacy, chemistry, nursing, etc. Love of flowers, herbs, shrubs, fish, and small animals.

If afflicted, it tends to selfishness and deceit and indicates danger through the use of drugs, medicine, beverages, and trouble with the bowels.

Neptune in Libra

Note: Neptune was in Libra from about 1942–1957.

If well aspected, adds tenderness and compassion to the nature, increasing the imagination and giving poetical, musical, and artistic appreciations. It tends to general popularity, love, friendship, and marriage. It gives a love of science, especially the occult, interest in magic and motion pictures, social and economic equity.

If afflicted, may indicate too much sympathetic emotion, easily moved to tears, too great an attraction toward the opposite sex. Mysterious conditions arise out of unions and associations with others.

Neptune in Scorpio

Note: Neptune was in Scorpio from about 1955–1970.

If well aspected, intensifies the feelings and emotions and gives greater scope to the inventive ability; adds a love for secret arts such as chemistry and also for the recondite sciences. To the nature it lends persistence, reserve, secrecy, and a quick temper. It also tends to practical mediumistic or occult experiences and assists any other testimonies in the chart for gain by legacy.

If afflicted, likely to lead to an excessive love for sensation, luxury, or beverages, and may often be given to slander or rebuke and loss of legacy through treachery.

Neptune in Sagittarius

Note: Neptune was in Sagittarius from about 1970–1984.

If well aspected, it adds reverence, reason, determination, and ambition to the nature. It gives a love for traveling and much of it. It denotes farsightedness, dreams, visions, inspiration, and mystical experiences. Prophetic insight with regard to business, art, science, religion, foreign affairs, literature, and psychic research.

If afflicted, likely to give too great a love for change and travel, and overly sensitive emotions; vague, indefinite feelings such as strange and annoying dreams or visions and psychical states; afflictions in foreign lands; trouble through religious or political sentiments.

Neptune in Capricorn

Note: Neptune was in Capricorn from about 1984–1998.

If well aspected, strong faith and good reasoning powers; peculiar or psychic business insight; careful and cautious, but fearless when convinced. Indicates seriousness or spells of depression and also trouble or sorrow in family affairs during youth, especially in connection with the father. It gives interest in psychical affairs and profit through art, music, large business enterprises, and public and private institutions.

If afflicted, it will tend to make the nature somewhat indefinite and secretive. May indicate peculiar family relations and cause complications or scandal in business.

Neptune in Aquarius (Fall)

Note: Neptune entered Aquarius in 1998. It was there previously from about 1834–1848.

If well aspected, increases the intuition and inner perception, gives a love of nature, friendship, popularity, and sociability. The native is independent and original in religious and scientific views. Interest in social welfare, clubs, and congressional activities. Expansive, progressive, sympathetic, and humane.

If afflicted, the native is likely to be too independent and eccentric. Apt to suffer from disappointment in love and scandal with regard to social and marital affairs. Involved in the difficulties of friends.

Neptune in Pisces (Home)

Note: Neptune was in Pisces from about 1847–1862.

If well aspected, it lends dignity to the nature and gives an ability for quiet, serious, profound thought and contemplation. It is good for the inspirational faculty and intensifies the mediumistic and psychical qualities, usually conferring some occult ability and fondness for the investigation of mysticism and the recondite sciences.

The native is usually broad-minded, sympathetic, domestic, and charitable. Benefits through help and charity both given and received. It gives a love of travel, especially by water, and gain through occupations connected with shipping, etc.

If afflicted, the native is likely to suffer in health from psychic conditions and meet with losses and ill luck through thwarted schemes.

Pluto

Because Pluto spends from twelve to thirty years in one sign, its effects are felt on the collective unconscious, which is noticeable in generations and civilizations rather than in individuals.

Pluto in Aries

Note: Pluto was in Aries from about 1822–1851.

Revolutionary ideas in political, social, scientific, and economic fields. Inventiveness and eccentric thought patterns. Pioneering geographically and socially.

Pluto in Taurus (Detriment)

Note: Pluto was in Taurus from about 1851–1882.

Financial applications of new discoveries. Improved standards of living including agrarian reform, colonial expansion, and commercial application of natural resources. Favors new inventions in building, industry, and finances.

Pluto in Gemini

Note: Pluto was in Gemini from about 1882–1914.

Inventions in the fields of communications, transportation, and electronics. Favors psychoanalytical investigations, abolition of censorship, and rapid development of dialects and colloquial patterns of speech.

Pluto in Cancer

Note: Pluto was in Cancer from about 1912–1939.

Disruption of homes and families; rise in dictatorships, chauvinism, nationalism, racism. Inventions of labor-saving devices, especially in homemaking fields and child care. Disruption of customs and traditions. Improved methods of family planning and new family roles.

Pluto in Leo

Note: Pluto was in Leo from about 1937–1958.

Increased leisure and emphasis on recreation, entertainment, and the growth of the electronics entertainment media industry. Inventions in governmental systems and increased centralization of administration and information.

Pluto in Virgo (Fall)

Note: Pluto was in Virgo from about 1956–1972.

Emphasis on the work-related fields of automation, computerization, and specialization. Movement toward free trade and unrestricted flow of goods and services. Inventions in the health sciences, public sanitation, preventive medicine, and pharmacy. Environmental, nutritional, and ecological concerns.

Pluto in Libra

Note: Pluto was in Libra from about 1971–1984.

Redefinition of marriage and sexual codes and customs; new sex roles. Sweeping legal decisions and revisions of legal codes. Original inventions in artistic media and new standards of beauty.

Pluto in Scorpio (Home)

Note: Pluto was in Scorpio from about 1983–1995.

Increased military conflicts coupled with armament inventions and possible biological warfare. Psychic research facilitates occult breakthrough and possible extraterrestrial communication. Improved methods of birth control and increased longevity.

Pluto in Sagittarius

Note: Pluto entered Sagittarius in 1995 and will be in this sign until about 2008.

Increased long-distance travel effects a global familiarity with diverse ethnic cultures and a diffusion of national and racial distinctions. Religious revival. Inventions in education and publishing fields.

Pluto in Capricorn

Note: Pluto was in Capricorn from about 1762–1777.

Rebellion against authority and disruption of political patterns. Improved methods of governmental administration and organization. Emphasis on work ethic and social position.

Pluto in Aquarius

Note: Pluto was in Aquarius from about 1777–1799.

Astronomical and electrical discoveries. Humanitarian reform and rise of abolition movement. Increased suffrage and concern for the common man. Advent of many social movements.

Pluto in Pisces (Exaltation)

Note: Pluto was in Pisces from about 1799–1822.

Emphasis on mystical phenomenon, hidden motives, and dream analysis. Romantic interest in fine arts, music, religion, and philosophy. Improved methods of dealing with mentally deranged or mentally challenged people. Inventions in nursing and care of homeless, aged, or diseased persons.

THE PLANETS IN THE HOUSES

These interpretations are for the planets by their positions in the houses only, unaspected, unless otherwise stated. If a planet is aspected, its delineation by house will be subject to a modification. Consequently, before taking the following interpretations literally, note the sign placement, the aspects to the planet, and any dignity or debility, and modify the reading accordingly.

The nature of conflicts that will be experienced in the area of life represented by the house can be determined by the planet tenanting the house, the rulership of the house, and aspects to the planet. The placement of an afflicting planet will indicate the area of life that is in conflict with the house in question. The nature of the planets and signs involved will give an idea of the psychological and physical energies involved, while the aspect will show the type of tension in the conflict.

When the planet in a house is well aspected, and the ruler of the house is not afflicted, the area of life represented by the house can be easily expressed. Positive aspects to the planet in question will show what other resources of the life are in harmony with the particular house involved. If the planet in the house is well aspected, but the ruler of the house is afflicted, the difficulty with the tension will more likely be between the native and the environment, rather than within oneself; and vice versa, if it is the other way around.

As you consider more and more factors, make sure to differentiate them, understand where they fit in, and then join them together into a succinct statement.

The First House

The Moon in the First House

Change in fortune, residence, occupation, and employment; sensitive, intuitive, and receptive mind; fruitful imagination and nature; ambition, activity, and an inclination for public life; refined, ingenious, observant, and considerate.

In a mutable or cardinal sign, it denotes flexibility, inconstancy, often timidity, and a great desire for change or roaming. In the fixed signs, the nature is firmer, less changeable, and more contented if employed in some ordinary or popular occupation connected with the general public.

The tendency in the First House is to elevate the native in life and bring benefits and advantages from the public through social life in which the domestic interests largely enter. Dream and astral experiences.

The Moon is an important influence in a woman's horoscope, as it rules the periodical functions and shows health or illness according to the aspects.

Afflicted in a watery sign, shows danger from water and liquids.

Mercury in the First House

Mercury is neutral, sexless and convertible, its nature being such that it absorbs much of the character of the planets with which it comes in contact or aspect; consequently, close attention must be paid to the sign it occupies, in addition to the aspect it receives. Thus, Mercury assisted by the Moon is good for commissions; by Venus, good for music, singing, art; in favorable connection with the Sun, good for business and responsible positions; in good aspect to Mars, mechanical and constructive ability; if Jupiter assists, a good theologian; Saturn, a good statistician; Uranus, an originator and inventor; Neptune, foresight, prophecy, power for psychometrizing, and clairaudience.

Mercury gives adaptability, fertility of resource, an inquiring mind always on the alert for new information, quick comprehension; fondness for literature, writing, or speaking, and for books, reading, and learning.

Perceptive, studious, logical, sharp, persuasive, and expressive; fertile imagination. Many changes, journeys, spells of restlessness and anxiety. Quick in speech, thought, and action.

Venus in the First House

Denotes an amiable, trustful, cheerful, sympathetic, and affectionate disposition, responsive to the love and emotional side of the nature. Fond of company, enjoyment, society, and likes to make others in the environment happy. It gives an appreciation for art and beauty and a fondness for pleasure, music, singing, drama, opera. It shows a refined, generous, just nature, one who is usually much admired by the opposite sex.

The nature is fruitful. The tendency of this position is toward good fortune. If in aspect to Mars, the native marries early. If in adverse aspect to Saturn, it delays marriage.

Bad aspects to Mars, Saturn, Uranus, or Neptune indicate much discord and trouble in married life; afflicting Jupiter, much generosity, free and careless with money, yet fortunate in getting it.

Note carefully the influence or nature of the sign Venus occupies: Taurus, Gemini, Libra, Aquarius, and Pisces are the best for this position. The nature of Venus is feminine, so look to its aspects and note the tendencies. Inspiration for art comes from Neptune, but it requires a good aspect of Venus to manifest it, as Venus governs touch. This planet rules the groins, kidneys, and ovaries; also the throat, chin, and cheeks.

The Sun in the First House

Frank, free, generous, outspoken; ambitious, proud, firm, and stable; humane; strong moral nature; quick perception and constructive faculty that bestows a certain appearance of dignity and strength that impresses others. It gives an independent, combative, and defensive ambition, coupled with hope, confidence, and a love of power and authority that results in the native rising above his or her sphere in life and into positions of trust, influence, and responsibility. It strengthens the constitution and adds to the vitality. Tends to honor and general success, advancement, and good will of superiors. Lofty motives.

If afflicted by Mars, Saturn, or Uranus, it indicates heavy, sharp attacks of sickness; i.e., fevers, inflammation, and eye afflictions; also losses and reversals through impulsiveness.

The Sun rules vitality and indicates the strength of the constitution.

When afflicted, especially by Saturn, the recuperative power is not good.

Mars in the First House (Natural House)

Ambitious, confident, enterprising, aspiring, skillful, and assertive. Usually create a great deal of their own fate by impulse and strong desire nature. Have good, practical, executive ability; love of liberty and independence; free, audacious, courageous, combative, and positive, scorning defeat and reckless of danger. Somewhat fiery, amorous, aggressive, and defensive; at times, rash, headstrong, forceful, and impatient.

A great deal depends upon the sign Mars occupies.

By nature, Mars is masculine; both constructive and destructive; usually causes a mark or scar about the head or face and one on that part of the body represented by the sign occupied.

Danger of cuts, burns, scalds, falls, bruises, and other accidents. Look to the aspects carefully. A good aspect to Saturn is very beneficial to Mars.

Mars rules the muscular system and urinogenital organs, feverish and inflammatory troubles.

Jupiter in the First House

Optimistic spirit; cheerful, hopeful, jovial disposition; generous, faithful, just, prudent, and noble nature; sincere, humane, courteous, and amiable; pleasant manners.

The influence of Jupiter is always more or less fortunate. It gives executive ability, power, and dignity, and fits the native for leading positions in social, educational, and business circles.

Its tendency is toward good reasoning, a logical, broad mind, self-possession, confidence, and determination.

If unafflicted, it indicates one of high standing, such as bankers, judges, doctors, lawyers, professors, theologians, and government officials. Business connected with shipping, long-distance transit, wholesale business, or commerce on a large scale. When afflicted, clerk, assistant, clothier, draper, cashier, etc. Note carefully the sign Jupiter occupies and the aspects for judging wealth, station, and ability.

Jupiter as related to the body brings on disease resulting from impure blood, plethora, gout, liver complaints, excessive stoutness, varicose veins, etc., according to the sign occupied; super-abundant action of parts when afflicted by Mars or the Sun, or defective action when afflicted by Saturn.

Saturn in the First House

When well placed by sign and aspect, it denotes thoughtfulness and consideration for the welfare of others; contemplation, discretion, prudence, system, diligence, economy, respect, and careful attention to affairs generally.

The disposition is calm, serious, grave. They desire is to attain prominence as the result of merit, and to that end they labor with method, industry, perseverance, and steadiness, rarely entering into any project that is not premeditated and planned. Progress and success may be slow, but are sure to bring good reputation, honor, and credit through persistence, practical ability, worldly wisdom, and continual effort.

When weak or afflicted, it indicates liability to colds and trouble to that part of the body ruled by the sign it is in. Bruises to the head. The nature is faithful, chaste, reserved; thoughtful, mistrustful, subtle, acquisitive, penetrative, and careful of personal affairs; secretive and given to periods of gloom and discontent.

Loss and misfortune through negligence, habits, lack of opportunity, or fateful events and delays.

It also indicates many sorrows and disappointments, sometimes poverty and an uphill road generally.

Saturn rules the bones, teeth, right ear, knees, and spleen. Gives liability to suffer from colds, chills, and poor circulation, also through constipation, rheumatism, stone, gravel, obstructed growth; usually they are deficient in phosphate or calcium.

Uranus in the First House

Uranus signifies originality of thought, independence of mind, inventive genius, intuition, intellectual and metaphysical ability. It inclines to the occult, the antiquated, curious, new, and the odd; in fact, to everything out of the ordinary.

It attracts toward such subjects as astrology, occultism, hypnotism, spiritualism, psychic research, drugless healing, telepathy, psychism, Freemasonry, inventions, electricity.

It makes one appear odd, peculiar, eccentric, and many years ahead of the time.

It is significant of many changes in residence and occupation and is usually not good here for marriage, bringing about peculiar, unfortunate conditions, difficulties, and separations.

It is Uranus manifesting that makes these natives independent and revolutionary, apt to change their mind and position radically and suddenly, forming their own opinions regardless of what others may think of them. Estrangement from parents and kindred.

Uranus stands for freedom, equality, and progress. Its natives can always see how conditions may be improved even when they are good enough in the opinion of others. They are nearly always on the opposite side to things that are popular, formal, or limited, preferring expansion and upheaval, and therefore take the side of the unpopular in public movements, studies, sciences, religion, etc. They are often called cranks, but invariably their cranky notions become accepted facts after a time. They are usually forceful, not particularly quarrelsome or antagonistic, but are vigorous in the cause of the oppressed. They are not at all opposed to discussion or debate and seldom become angry in it; detest limitations and cannot stand control or dictation.

Uranus rules the originating or creating faculties: phrenologically expressed, the faculties of comparison and causality, without which there can be no invention or science.

Although Uranus gives originality and individuality of thought, and these natives may be fairly running over with good ideas, unless Mercury assists, they cannot utter them satisfactorily. Mercury gives the ability to learn, understand, interpret, expound, and express. Enlightened Uranians give all the freedom possible to those around them, knowing that their liberty is increased correspondingly. However, just how fine these natives will manifest or interpret the ray from Uranus depends upon the quality of the *aspects* to it in the birth chart.

Uranus afflicted shows quickness of mind, mental impulsiveness, originality, independence, and self-will. Makes the native changeable, impulsive, abrupt, erratic, eccentric, willful, brusque, sarcastic, critical, and easily offended. Gives inventive genius. It gives the ability to develop thought-reading and transference, clairvoyance, crystal-gazing, etc.

Danger through lightning, electricity, and hurts by machinery, inventions, engines, explosives, and vehicles of travel. Gives an interest in all occult affairs; rules the aura and personal magnetism; strange happenings.

Neptune in the First House

The influence of this planet is always more or less mediumistic, and the native will either consciously or unconsciously take on the conditions of the surroundings and of those with whom he or she comes in contact. Being a neutral planet, it depends upon *aspects* for the manner in which it will manifest.

It represents inspiration, trance, dreams, weird feelings, thoughts, and experiences; romance and emotion; a visionary or idealistic state of mind.

When well aspected, it gives good inspiration and spirit perception. It denotes far-seeing, the ability to estimate quickly and accurately. It attracts one to peculiar people, psychic centers, and mysterious, strange places.

It gives the ability to cultivate psychometry, clairaudience, and mediumship.

It exalts the artistic tastes, giving a love for beauty in form, color, and sound. It is also related to matters connected with the sea, water, and liquids in general, also mediumship and spiritualism. When it is weak or afflicted, it seems to open an avenue of temptation that appeals to the sense-loving and emotional side of the nature, bringing uncertainty and confusion through instability, indolence, or lack of energy. Danger through plots, schemes, enmities, and deception.

Although it indicates inspiration, enthusiasm and perception, it denotes a receptivity to psychic conditions that might run to extremes, allowing the feelings to get the upper hand of the judgment. Tendency to excitability, changefulness, morbid imagination, strange or unnatural appetites, intrigues, acts of indiscretion, deception, presumption, love of luxury; wandering disposition, many journeys, changes, ups and downs. Being readily affected both mentally and physically by the psychic conditions of the environment, individuals with Neptune in this house should investigate the philosophy of all things mysterious, rather than the phenomena.

There are times when people who are strongly influenced by Neptune should have nothing to do whatever with any occult phenomena, seances, drugs, medicines, gases, etc.; on the other hand, there are days when they should strive to develop their occult faculties. These times are when other planets come into aspect with Neptune, particularly the Moon.

Pluto in the First House

This position can give a lack of self-confidence to the point of self-abuse and neglect of appearance if Pluto is in detriment, debility, or poorly aspected; or an unrealistically high opinion of the self and an overestimation of one's ability if Pluto is in good aspect or dignified.

Periods of identity crisis and self-doubt according to the transiting aspects. The native is governed by subconscious drives that he or she cannot control—whether for good or bad depends on the aspects and sign position of Pluto. The drive for personal power is strong and often manifests in devious or underhanded ways.

This position bestows an aura of mystery due to the secretiveness of the native. The native thinks himself utterly unique and is often a loner, exile, or iconoclast; he has a sense of exclusiveness and isolation.

The native is subject to bodily violence, often self-inflicted or unwittingly brought about by himself. He has a tendency to get involved over his head and forms associations with persons of a tough, mean, or low nature, to his own misfortune.

This native projects varying images of himself to different people because his personality is not stable and undergoes violent, drastic changes, according to the transiting aspects.

The Second House

The Moon in the Second House

Gain by employment through public affairs and occupations, by dealing with liquids, commodities, and the wants of the common people generally. Money obtained through females or the mother, or matters related to the domestic life. Good for things ruled by the Moon and the sign it occupies.

If well aspected, it is favorable for financial success, although somewhat variable, since the source of profit will usually be some fluctuating commodity, or the whim of the public or the mass mind.

Mercury in the Second House

Denotes gain by letters, writings, speaking, traveling, teaching, clerical occupations, commissions, and ordinary business and commercial affairs generally; also through study, advertising, distributing, stationery, books, etc. Gain through any occupation corresponding to the nature of the planet in closest good aspect.

Venus in the Second House (Natural House)

By fortuitous circumstances, good will, and favors from others, money usually comes readily. It may be gained through artistic pursuits, music pleasure, social affairs, friendships, societies, marriage, jewelry, millinery, hotels, confectionery, and wearing apparel. A good deal of money is spent on adornment, luxuries, pleasure, friends, and social interests; nevertheless, they acquire it.

The Sun in the Second House

Money obtained by industrious effort and through the father and superiors; gain by affairs of government or through holding official appointments or other responsible positions. Benefit through superiors and persons of rank. The nature of the occupations depends much upon what sign the Sun occupies. The native is inclined to generosity in money matters, social intercourse, pleasure, luxury, and sports.

Mars in the Second House

Good earning powers but usually extravagant, overgenerous, or careless regarding the accumulation of wealth, and money runs quickly through the fingers.

It denotes gain by the native's own energy, activity, skill, and strength; by stock farming, iron, steel, chemicals, timber, business enterprise as agent, salesman, or promoter.

When well aspected to the ruler of the Eighth House, it denotes money by legacy; to the ruler of the Seventh House, by marriage.

If Mars is afflicted, heavy losses, expenditures, or extravagance and trouble, strife, and contention over finances.

Jupiter in the Second House

Increases the chances for success, wealth, and general prosperity. It has to do with government and responsible business affairs and tends to gain through law, insurance, banking, religion, science, education, literature, and travel. Money acquired through things indicated by the house that Jupiter rules in the chart and by the sign it occupies.

Saturn in the Second House

Saturn, unless well aspected, tends to make an uphill struggle and much work for little gain. The person may see many opportunities, but is seldom in a position to take advantage of them.

At times things run along apparently well and smoothly and then take a turn and go persistently wrong or suffer delay; lack of money. With this position of Saturn, one should become thoroughly acquainted with the directions operating in the chart to avoid failures and to increase chances for success in land, property, produce, mines, storage, investments, coal, lead, building, labor, etc.

When well aspected or favorably located by sign, prudent financial ability, thrift, economy, and solid, conservative investments bring steady but slow returns. Gains by father or employer.

Uranus in the Second House

Many changes in fortune; financial affairs very uncertain; ups and downs. Uranus has an affinity for unique occupations, affairs, and employment of all kinds, especially those of a curious or mental character and that require great ingenuity.

Gain through inventions, mechanisms, railroads, electrical affairs, occultism, astrology, extraordinary composition and sometimes music, especially when well aspected with Venus. Money is gained through friends, associations, or the government.

Neptune in the Second House

Neptune gives liability of financial affairs becoming much involved and loss through fraud and schemes.

Neptune rules hospitals, asylums, institutions, secret service, the sea, and its various industries, navigation, baths, public establishments, spiritualism, mediumship, mystical and secret societies. If well aspected, the native will gain through these things; afflicted, will lose through them.

Pluto in the Second House

Changes in financial position affect the personality of the native and can cause emotional trauma. Much worry and anxiety over monetary affairs. Ability to change financial situation.

Possible gain or loss of money due to the death of a benefactor, an inheritance or legacy; look to the aspects, sign position, and planets in the Eighth House for further indications.

Fields for successful financial enterprises include any industry that recycles waste or converts non-useable items into useable ones; industry that affects chemical change on raw materials; fields involved in combating pollution; sanitation, hygiene, garbage collection; all occupations dealing with death—funeral director, mortician, casket salesman, undertaker, grave digger, hearse driver, etc.; occupations involved in manufacturing organic fertilizers and compost; all professions delving into psychological motives; detective work of all kinds, including medical research and geological exploration.

A poorly aspected Pluto indicates associations with gangsters and criminal activity due to greed and materialistic motives. Gambling and speculation can bring sudden wealth, but unexpected losses always follow. Overpossessive of physical possessions as well as relationships. Self-indulgence in physical pleasures can affect the health. Gross appetites.

The Third House

The Moon in the Third House

Many changes of pursuit and occupation; desire for publicity of some sort; curious, active, and inquisitive mind that is ever alert for new information, and generally possessing a fund of knowledge regarding public conditions and new material for thought and action.

Usually there is not sufficient continuity; unfinished education or accomplishments. An unfavorable position for peace of mind, if afflicted.

If well aspected, good for learning and mental attainments along popular lines. Short studies of domestic science or social welfare and short journeys prove beneficial.

Mercury in the Third House (Natural House)

Many short journeys, much activity and writing.

The mind inclines to investigate whatever tends to enlightenment: to increase the consciousness and broaden the understanding; fond of reading, study, speaking, teaching, lectures, literature, new thought, science, news.

The mentality is quick and perceptive and usually interested in or anxious regarding relatives and neighbors.

When Mercury is afflicted, the native is inclined to excessive worry or anxiety. It is said that the mind reacts on the bowels, and that is likely true enough, as Mercury represents both, ruling Gemini and Virgo. Trouble through letters, promises, agreements, or reports.

When well aspected, successful travels, mental development, accomplishments and gain through Third House affairs.

Venus in the Third House

The mental quality is good. Strong inclination and liking for fine arts, music, singing, opera, paintings, light literature, and all that tends to uplift or refine the mind and give pleasure. The mind is cheerful, fruitful, optimistic, bright, and desirous of peace. It denotes favorable relatives or neighbors and aid or gain through them.

It is a good position for pleasure trips or pleasure and gain through journeys and successful travels. In fact, it is good for all things ruled by the Third House. Pleasant correspondence, many social acquaintances.

The Sun in the Third House

It is good for all things ruled by this house. It tends to respect, good will, and benefit from relatives and neighbors; successful travels for business and pleasure.

The mind is resourceful, creative, magnanimous, and ambitious of success and honor through mental qualifications; the desire is to uplift, enlighten, benefit, and assist others mentally. When afflicted, trouble with some of the kindred or neighbors and through proud, haughty states of mind. Discredit through letters, promises, agreements, or false reports.

Mars in the Third House

Liability to danger and accidents by journeys, trouble through travel, relatives, neighbors, writings, and litigation. The mind is alert, energetic, keen, forceful, combative, and likely to get out of control easily. The native is quick and prompt in speech and possesses executive power in literary or educational directions. At some time may be troubled with brain fever or deliriousness, and if Mars is afflicted by Saturn, Uranus, or Neptune, shows thought of suicide or violent tendencies.

The best sign for Mars in this house is Capricorn and the best aspects are the good ones to Saturn or Mercury, although a good one to Uranus will give genius in some line and inventive ability.

Jupiter in the Third House

Gain in all things ruled by this house. The mind is optimistic, philosophical, refined, cheerful, and sympathetic. Kind, thoughtful, just, and considerate in all matters of correspondence, publication, or exchange of thought; sincere, earnest, courteous, sociable, and reasonable in speech and writing. Capable of adapting themselves to conventionalities of thought that are prevalent and popular. Benefits through education, literature, publishing, traveling, brethren, and neighbors.

Saturn in the Third House

Trouble, loss, disappointment, annoyance, hindrance, and delays in connection with education, writings, relatives, neighbors, traveling, and changes. Coldness between brethren or sorrow through their demise.

The tendency of the mind is toward gloom, caution, acquisitiveness, worry, restlessness, anxiety, and misgiving, especially in youth. The mental condition improves with age and is much better in later life, becoming more contemplative, thoughtful, and capable of concentration on serious or profound subjects.

If Saturn is ill aspected or afflicted by the Sun, Moon, or Mercury, the melancholy expression is liable to run into extremes, despondency, morbid tendencies, or mental afflictions.

When well aspected, it denotes responsibility, tact, diplomacy, thought power, steady thinking, concentration and mental control, orderly reasoning; philosophic mind with ability for profound studies or writings.

Uranus in the Third House

Denotes estrangements from kindred and neighbors and strange experiences through them; sudden and unexpected news, journeys, and changes, odd happenings, meetings, adventures, and occurrences through travels. The native is peculiar or eccentric in some things, but usually intellectual and possesses ability to develop clairvoyant, clairaudient, or telepathic faculty in addition to magnetic healing. The mind is curious, inventive, ingenious, unconventional, and fond of the occult, mystical, new, extraordinary, profound, ancient, or unpopular studies, social and mental reforms; intuitive perception and understanding with regard to things occult. If Uranus is afflicted by Saturn or Mars, it shows danger of accidents, wrecks, or explosions on journeys, through vehicles of travel or treachery on the part of relatives or neighbors.

Neptune in the Third House

Denotes psychological faculties, spiritual perception; fruitful, inventive mind, given to the investigation of spirit phenomena and matters pertaining to the occult or mysterious; inspirational ideas.

Produces weird feelings or experiences. Signifies journeys, peculiar difficulties with relatives, schemes, plots, deceit, etc. Changes in name: nickname, nom de plume, or alias.

If Neptune is weak or badly aspected, it disturbs the mind with hallucinations, morbid fancies, imbecility, weak intellect, or depraved tastes.

When well aspected, it gives artistic taste or appreciation of an exalted order through a peculiar blending of the feelings and intuition and ability to contact the artistic realm inspirationally; possibility of independent or automatic writings.

Pluto in the Third House

Denotes a tendency to morbid thoughts and dwelling on death, decay, and excrement. Preoccupied with the seamy, sinister, and sordid side of life.

Mind liable to moodiness and brooding if poorly aspected. Depressions and negative thinking. Many changes of mind and second thoughts about decisions.

When well aspected, inspiration from unlikely sources, finds beauty in the commonplace and can use normally neglected articles. Ideas about recycling and conversion of waste products. Insights on death and the meaning of life, and desire to uncover the secrets of the universe.

Very opinionated. Holds on to ideas despite contradictory evidence and pressure from others, yet has the ability to uncover hidden motives and evaluate situations and people accurately in-depth.

This position indicates the need to talk, write, or express artistically the native's emotional state, thus providing a therapeutic release.

The Fourth House

The Moon in the Fourth House (Natural House)

Well placed or aspected, it shows gain and benefit through the parents, home, and domestic life; favors from the opposite sex; some chance of inheritance. Publicity or popularity through the parents; many changes in residence and fluctuation in affairs toward the close of life. If well dignified here, it shows an ultimate rise to success and independence through possessions, property, lands, farms, or orchards.

If Saturn afflicts the Moon, much disappointment will be encountered in desired success; in fact, great difficulty to keep from poverty and sorrow due largely to family affairs. Afflictions by Mars, Sun, or Mercury denote loss by theft, fraud, or deception. Jupiter adverse: denotes lack of opportunities and limitations through environment. Uranus adverse: sudden changes; difficulties with home affairs; estrangements from or loss of parents, probably the mother; loss through unexpected reversals and changes. Neptune adverse: mystery or complications concerning home affairs and property.

Mercury in the Fourth House

Inconstancy in affairs generally; change of residence through matters connected with business. Often the subject has no fixed abode; many traveling men have this position.

Worry and anxiety regarding disturbances in home affairs.

Good position for proprietors of private schools or other stationary places where literary or clerical work is carried on, such as land, mine, and real estate agencies, registry offices, newspaper offices, libraries, publishers, etc., or for business carried on in the home.

In bad aspect to Uranus, unexpected difficulties and disturbances toward the close of life or a sudden end.

Saturn adverse: denotes loss through deception, fraud, and theft.

Mars adverse: loss through imposition, controversy, or fire.

Sun, Moon, or Jupiter adverse: lack of opportunity or limitations and numerous losses.

Uranus in good aspect: unexpected gain in possessions; occult investigation and enlightenment before the close of life.

Saturn or Jupiter in good aspect: steadier, more satisfied, and studious; inclines to success, opportunities, and inheritance.

Sun, Moon, or Venus in good aspect: activity, popularity, and success before the close of life.

Venus in the Fourth House

Indicative of favorable domestic affairs and happiness through the parents; love of home and country. Chance of gain by inheritance, parents, houses, or property and investment; peaceful, comfortable conditions at the close of life. Sun, Moon, or Jupiter in good aspect is exceedingly fortunate, bringing general affairs to a successful issue.

In good aspect to Uranus or Saturn, success in old age. Benefit by pension or legacy.

The adverse aspects of Sun, Moon, Mercury, or Jupiter are not particularly evil, but affect the finances through extravagance or misjudgment.

Mars adverse: difficulty through generosity, carelessness, or extravagance toward the close of life.

Saturn, Uranus, or Neptune adverse: sudden, peculiar losses, disappointments, and sorrows toward the end of life.

The Sun in the Fourth House

A chance of honor in declining years, successful ambitions, hopes, and wishes realized. Good for houses, land, property, and occupations connected with them. Gain or chance of inheritance by or through the parents; fortunate heredity.

In good aspect to Moon, Venus, Jupiter, Saturn, or Uranus: gain through property or inheritance, financial success. To Neptune, it inclines to secrecy or investigation of occult or spiritual affairs; some psychic experiences in the home.

If afflicted, obstacles, limitations, troubles, and sorrows through the parents and home life; liability to loss and difficulty by living beyond the means or through heavy obligations. Weakens the constitution at the close of life.

The native will be content at home and amid family, and may become the stability of same, or greatly respected in the home.

Mars in the Fourth House

Domestic unpleasantness and much misunderstanding, in harmony or quarrels in the home life, especially if Mercury afflicts. Losses by theft, fire, and accidents in the dwelling place; early death of parent. Many difficulties, disappointments, and obstacles. Physical indisposition caused by bad digestion and acid condition. Liability to trouble over property, loss through speculations in property, lands, and mines. If Neptune, Uranus, or Saturn afflict, mental distress, suicide, or liability to sudden end by accident; unfortunate in the place of birth. The good aspects give much energy, force, activity, and enterprise in the acquisition of possessions.

Jupiter in the Fourth House

Tends to satisfactory, comfortable, and peaceful domestic affairs; successful home life and family surroundings; gain and favor through parents; benefit through land and possessions; good position and success toward the close of life.

If unafflicted, a fortunate, easy life; success at the place of birth, successful termination to business enterprises and affairs generally.

Jupiter afflicted gives trouble through the parents or their affairs, and extravagance; hereditary limitations.

Sun or Moon adverse: liability to sudden heart trouble or apoplexy. Mars adverse: danger of loss by fire.

Mercury adverse: danger of lawsuits over property or inheritance, and if Mercury afflicts the ruler of the Fourth House, lawsuits with or through the parents.

Mars or Saturn in good aspect: a religious or satisfactory end. Uranus favorable: occult tendencies, long life. The luminaries favorable: overcomes many adverse testimonies in the chart and shows a rise in life to opulence and popularity.

Saturn in the Fourth House

Difficulties and trouble through property, inheritance, or mines. Sorrow through parents, probably separation from the father either physically or emotionally. Acquisitiveness. Unsatisfactory domestic or home life. Much work, heavy responsibilities, and great difficulty in achieving ambitions. Unfortunate in the place of birth. Seclusiveness at the close of life. If well aspected, acquisition of property; gain through produce or mining.

Uranus in the Fourth House

Unsettled residence; many changes; a checkered career. Unfortunate in place of birth. Estrangements from parents; domestic troubles and family affairs. Exceptional domestic experiences. Loss of inheritance, if one is expected. Many ups and downs and tastes of poverty through peculiar circumstances.

Mars or Saturn adverse: danger of violence; liability to accidents in the home. Neptune adverse: threatens loss through theft, fraud, and deception, by accident, flood, or action of the elements. Jupiter adverse: loss through impulsiveness or misjudgment, law, storms, or by lightning.

Neptune in the Fourth House

Changes of residence. Voyages. Peculiar domestic and family affairs, some secrets or mystery regarding the home life; schemes, fraud, and misunderstandings, which affect the parents in some way, affect the native. Much depends on the aspects. The luminaries in affliction denote weakened vitality and poor health. Mercury adverse: peculiar nervous disorders in later life. Abides in unusual or peculiar conditions. Neptune is neutral; consequently, good aspects would show benefits through property and parents, according to the nature of the aspects.

Pluto in the Fourth House

Unsettled conditions in the home; many changes of residence. Possible secret in native's background or heredity; hereditary or sex-linked disease likely.

The end of life will be difficult with a long, lingering illness or gradual decline. This can be demoralizing if Pluto is poorly aspected or debilitated, or can serve to prepare the native spiritually for death if Pluto is well aspected.

Death of the mother greatly affects the native's mental condition, perhaps even causing emotional problems or trauma. Incest, sexual attraction to a relative, or marriage to a family member possible. Intense feelings for family often kept secret.

Difficult childhood can cause psychological problems later in life. Home and childhood very important to the native. If adversely aspected, this position indicates selfishness and overprotectiveness.

The Fifth House

The Moon in the Fifth House

Public success in connection with places of amusement, playgrounds, bathing resorts, or with children and young people; fondness for pleasure and the society of children and the opposite sex. Strong tendencies toward speculation or games of chance. Much activity and change in all enterprise. Changeable affections (except in fixed signs), yet the heart may be given to one who least deserves it and thus the affection changes to aversion, coldness, or indifference.

It is indicative of a child who achieves fame and popularity, if well aspected; also that the native will in some manner be closely connected or drawn to a child or young person. Several offspring, if the Moon is in a fruitful sign. If Neptune is in good aspect, may adopt a child.

If the Moon is afflicted, it brings loss through speculations and danger or sorrow and trouble through love, children, and morals.

Mercury in the Fifth House

Refines the pleasures and makes them more mental than muscular, more of the mind than of the senses, and is good for occupations connected with entertainment, schools, or travel.

This position denotes worry, anxiety, and sorrow through objects of affection, children, and their affairs.

A good aspect of Saturn or Jupiter much improves the position and brings success and gain through these things and also through speculation or investment. Luminaries favorable: indicates success in connection with traveling for public amusement and with children. Mars, Uranus, or Neptune adverse: denotes troublesome love affairs, scandal, separations, divorce, lawsuits. Losses through speculation.

Venus in the Fifth House

A fruitful union and beautiful children who may be endowed with artistic or musical ability; happiness, comfort, and gain through offspring, which are usually or mostly girls.

This position denotes gain and success through love affairs, friendships, etc., the ability to entertain others and enjoy success through all manner of social intercourse, pleasure, and amusement.

It indicates gain through speculation, investment, and general enterprise, also through theaters, singing, music, painting, children, schools, playgrounds, parks, or summer resorts.

If Venus is much afflicted, it gives liability of injury to the health through over-indulgence in pleasurable gratification. Saturn adverse: sorrow and disappointment through love, speculation, children. Mars, Uranus, or Neptune adverse: trouble and danger through the opposite sex, and careless, rash, indiscriminate, or unconventional bestowal of affection.

The Sun in the Fifth House (Natural House)

Honorable and successful attachments. Gain through speculation, investment, enterprise, children, pleasure, and places of amusements. Small family. This position often denies children and inclines to difficult or dangerous childbirth. However, this depends on the nature of the sign on the Fifth House cusp, whether barren or not, etc. If the Sun is afflicted here, it causes loss through speculation, troubles and jealousy in courtship, and sorrow through love, pleasure, and pride; trouble with children.

Mars in the Fifth House

Pleasure through the strenuous sports, athletics, muscular exercise; impulsive, rash, and unfortunate attractions toward the opposite sex. Sensual emotions or over-ardent affections, and too much indulgence in pleasure and amusement results in physical, financial, and social loss; danger of accident to the first child. In a woman's horoscope, this position shows difficult and dangerous childbirth. Loss by speculation, gaming, extravagance, pleasure, and excess of feeling. Trouble with or through children.

Neptune, Uranus, Saturn, Jupiter, Sun, Moon, or Venus adverse: threatens danger of ruin or disgrace through the opposite sex; loss through risky speculation.

Well aspected: gain through occupations and enterprises connected with pleasure and investment corresponding to the nature of Mars.

Jupiter in the Fifth House

Good and dutiful children who will be a help and comfort to the native. Success, happiness, and gain through love affairs and the opposite sex. Pleasure, success, and gain in connection with places of amusement, theaters, social functions, schools. A good position for gain through speculation, investment, and financial enterprise, especially if Mars or Sun is in good aspect. For a female, it usually denotes attraction to professional men, wholesale merchants, or those in good financial or social position. Increases the number of children and is fortunate for them. If Jupiter is afflicted, the good influences are modified, giving the same desires but trouble, losses, and obstacles according to the nature of the afflicting planet and house occupied.

Saturn in the Fifth House

Denotes disappointments, delays, hindrance, and sorrow in connection with love affairs; attraction to those who are older or more serious in disposition. For a female, it usually denotes an attachment to an elderly gentleman or widower or to one of a religious nature. Loss of child, troubles and unhappiness through children.

Loss by speculation, investment, and games of chance.

Danger from animals while on pleasure trips. Danger of drowning if Saturn is in Scorpio, and of heart trouble if in Leo. If Saturn is well aspected by either the Sun or Moon and not otherwise afflicted, it is a good position for investment in lands, mines, and property, and such things that Saturn governs. If afflicted by the Sun, Moon, or Jupiter, take no speculative chances of any kind.

Uranus in the Fifth House

Unconventional ideas with regard to sex union; strange, romantic, inconstant, secret, or impulsive love affairs. Social vexation, scandal.

Loss of first child through some sudden or extraordinary manner, or separation, anxiety, and trouble through children; difficulty through childbirth. Difficulties in domestic life and love attachments. Loss through speculation, risks, chances. Liking for odd, new, daring pleasures or unusual places of amusement.

Neptune in the Fifth House

Strange and peculiar experiences in connection with the feelings, emotions, and affections; abnormal conditions relating to sex matters. Sensuous pleasures, seduction. If afflicted, it denotes trouble, faithlessness, or confusion and sorrow in love affairs and loss through lax control of the desires and appetites; losses in speculation through deceit or treachery. If well aspected, the native will be assisted in self-development by a fortunate association with one of the opposite sex; gain by investment in oil, shipping, and such things as Neptune rules.

Pluto in the Fifth House

Compulsive gambler, usually in secret. If well aspected, can mean sudden wealth through gambling. Likes unusual, esoteric amusements and entertainments. Likes unconventional or perverted sexual relations. Inclines to secret love affairs. Much emphasis placed on sex.

Disappointments from children; illegitimate children, or baby given up for adoption. Factors surrounding the birth of a child cause anxiety or emotional instability later in life. Children unusual in some way.

Emotions often kept secret; relationships with people for reasons other than those given. Gives parties and entertains for ulterior reasons. Social climber. Arrogant and self-centered.

Finds emotional release in physical exercise and sex.

The Sixth House

In this section, pertaining to the Sixth House, there is no intention to indicate medical remedies in an advisory capacity. Bodily indisposition, as well as mental disturbance, should be remedied as soon as possible. Health is important to efficiency and happiness and should not be neglected. Therefore, when indisposed, it is wise to seek the aid of those who are trained in the art of healing, and, by whatever method of treatment seems best, strive to reestablish physical and mental equilibrium.

The Moon in the Sixth House

Uncertain health, especially in a woman's horoscope; much sickness and danger in infancy. Desire to serve the public in some professional capacity. The subject has better ability and opportunity of getting good results from serving others than from others serving him. Many changes among servants or employees. Success in domestic service or in catering to public desire for necessities, food stuffs, drinks, etc.

Good aspects to the Moon help the health and indicate success with small animals, servants, and through some subordinate position connected with the occupations ruled by the sign the Moon occupies. Moon afflicted gives poor success with employees, treachery, and dishonesty among them; poor success with small animals, poultry, etc.; weakness in the part of the body ruled by the sign the Moon occupies.

Afflicted in a mutable sign: danger from lung trouble and chronic diseases. Fixed sign: bronchitis. Cardinal sign: nervous derangements and stomach trouble.

The Moon afflicted by Mercury: indigestion, aches in head and teeth, bowel troubles.

The Moon afflicted by Venus: functional or skin trouble.

The Moon afflicted by Mars: inflammatory complaints.

The Moon afflicted by Jupiter: liver and blood trouble.

The Moon afflicted by Saturn: chronic disease, poor circulation.

The Moon afflicted by the Sun, Uranus, or Neptune: weak vitality, indigestion, indisposition through psychic conditions.

Mercury in the Sixth House (Natural House)

Many small vexations through servants; journeys on account of health. Good position for the study of hygiene, medicine, or chemistry. Gain in subordinate positions, through writings, clerical work, and Mercurial affairs generally.

Active mentality, but liable to become overstrung or impaired through anxiety, worry, or overwork, causing dyspepsia or a tendency to become easily affected by the surrounding conditions.

Any afflictions to Mercury here are unfavorable to the health through the mentality and nervous system.

Afflicted by Uranus: liable to abnormal mental states; suicidal tendencies due to illness.

Afflicted by Saturn: danger of serious illness through despondency or worry.

Afflicted by Mars: mental derangement or excitability; surgical operations.

Afflicted by the Sun, Moon, or Neptune: fevers, stomach trouble; indisposition through psychic conditions.

Venus in the Sixth House

Favorable to health, but common sense and discretion should be exercised to keep from excesses of all kinds, especially with regard to eating and drinking. Gain in the employ of others. It is favorable for success and benefits through servants, hygiene, medicine, nursing, and by clothing, small animals, poultry, etc. People with Venus here often take up work for the pleasure it gives them and the interest it creates. Love for pets, fine clothes, and adornments. If afflicted, it shows trouble to the health through indulgences, and to that part of the body ruled by the sign Venus is in or by the afflicting planet; skin diseases, kidney or ovarian trouble. Health usually improves after marriage.

The Sun in the Sixth House

This is a cadent house; therefore the Sun, the ruler of vitality, placed here is not a very good position for health, as it may slightly weaken the constitution. If afflicted by Neptune, Uranus, or Saturn, the recuperative power is not good, and it indicates a great deal of indisposition, liability to contagious diseases, and danger from epidemics.

When the Sun is well aspected, the native seems to understand intuitively how to safeguard the health and in that way avoids illness.

Any aspect of Mars strengthens the constitution. A good aspect of Mars, Jupiter, or Venus would show success and gain through servants and service rendered; success, promotion, and fortunate conditions in employments that benefit others, such as healing, chemistry, hospital work, etc. In fact, the Sun well dignified or aspected here indicates that the native can do great work in relieving the sufferings of humanity.

The Sun afflicted in a fixed sign: tonsillitis, bronchitis, asthma, diphtheria, heart trouble, weak back and sides, and nervous disorders; organic troubles. Afflicted in a mutable sign: chronic diseases; troubles with respiratory organs, liver complaints. Afflicted in a cardinal sign: nervousness, weak chest and stomach, rheumatism. Also liable to some permanent injury; functional derangements.

Mars in the Sixth House

Disputes, quarrels, losses, and theft through servants or employees and much difficulty and annoyance by their taking liberties and advantage of the native. The native is usually an active, energetic, and enthusiastic worker and liable to overdo himself, especially in other people's employ.

Mars rules the tastes, and this position of Mars tends to impair or injure the health and cause suffering through excesses, acts of indiscretion, carelessness, extravagance, and by accident.

Its position here is usually significant of incision with steel to that part of the body ruled by the sign it is in; surgical operations.

Mars afflicted: inflammation or accidents to that part of the body ruled by the sign occupied; difficulty in employ; danger, loss, and trouble through employees, animals, poultry, pets.

Mars gives a tendency to inflammatory complaints in the bowels and troubles in that part of the body represented by the sign occupied in about the same manner as does the Sun when in the Sixth House and in a like sign (see *Sun in the Sixth House*).

Saturn adverse: danger of death due to operations and injuries by animals.

Uranus adverse: danger of fatal accident or suicide.

Neptune adverse: danger of foul play, accidental poisoning, etc.

Jupiter in the Sixth House

Gives health, but if indisposed the subject receives kind treatment, good attention, and many comforts; in fact, is likely to gain through sickness. The native's care and presence would be beneficial and healing to others in distress.

If the person should become a physician, likely to be successful financially and with patients.

Gain and profit through employment, especially in high circles; also through servants and inferiors, and through religious, philanthropic, and social tendencies. Success with domestic animals, poultry, etc. If afflicted, the health will suffer from over-indulgence or intemperance in diet; difficulty with the chest, bowels, liver, blood, and digestive organs.

Saturn in the Sixth House

Denotes much sickness through exposure and circumstances over which the subject has little control: neglect, privation, sorrow, disappointment. Many lost opportunities through the state of health. Troubles according to the nature of the sign Saturn occupies; somewhat similar to Mars in the Sixth House.

Not a good position for employment or success with servants or inferiors, denoting loss and trouble through them. Ill success and loss with small animals, etc.

Afflicted by Uranus: incurable diseases.

Afflicted by Mars: dangerous illness, accidents, and operations.

Afflicted by the Sun, Moon, or Neptune: chronic ill health, poor circulation and recuperation, colds, rheumatism, psychic and heavy ills. Note the part of the body represented by the sign on the Sixth House cusp.

Saturn denotes poor digestion, constipation, obstruction, poor circulation, debility. When ill, seek the services of a doctor and accept the benefit of such aid by whatever method best suits the case: medicinal, surgical, mechanical, dietary, color, light, etc.

If Saturn is dignified or well aspected, it denotes benefit through laborious or sedentary occupations; mining, masonry, sculpture, cement work, plastering, plowing, excavating, etc.

Uranus in the Sixth House

Trouble through peculiar nervous disorders; neurosis. Sickness that is puzzling or not well understood. If much afflicted, the sicknesses are strange or incurable; liability to mental derangement; danger of illness through the employment and sudden events. Not a good placement for success, harmony, and happiness in employment, service, or with servants, employees, poultry, and similar lines.

Treatment by electricity, radium, hypnotism, etc., is apt to prove detrimental if Uranus is afflicted, but beneficial if well aspected, and a careful study of the diet and environment should be made.

Uranus rules the aura and sometimes the native is very sensitive to environmental conditions and should refrain from eating when tired, nervous, excited, or angry.

If Uranus is well aspected here, it may bring some unexpected or unique opportunity to perform exceptional service and obtain good results. Uranus well placed may give success as a metaphysician, mesmerist, or electrician; and through occult, electric, or drugless treatments.

Neptune in the Sixth House

Threatens some chronic, incurable disease, atrophy, inertia, wasting sickness, some inherited or psychopathic tendencies. Danger of some deformity through illness. If much afflicted, it shows severe sickness and trouble from gratifying the tastes or desires, especially if afflicted by Mars. Should carefully avoid narcotics and opiates, and if any medicine is taken, use only the simplest kind. Neptune rules the mediumistic faculty and this house rules clothing, food, etc.; consequently, the native should not take food into the stomach received from a sick person or one of undesirable habits, nor should any apparel be worn once used by another. Use only the freshest and purest food obtainable and little or no animal matter.

Generally no success with poultry and other things ruled by this house. Theft, schemes, plots, deceit, or loss and difficulty through employees.

This position of Neptune may keep the native in seclusion, retirement, or servitude. If well aspected, the native has the ability to develop fine psychometrizing powers, especially for sensing surrounding conditions. He should always pay attention to his own intuition in regard to food, clothing, environment. Neptune people need to exercise great care regarding the physical condition and habits of their associates or of those whom they engage to treat them. Being very receptive, they absorb what others are throwing off and often this proves detrimental rather than beneficial, although the intentions may be good. People who indulge in tobacco, liquors, or who engage in vivisection or cruelty in any form, should not be allowed to treat the body of an indisposed Neptune person. Kindly suggestions, verbal and mental, and natural methods seem best for them.

Pluto in the Sixth House

Interest in the welfare of servants, pets, all people and animals dependent upon the native. Often unusual ideas and practices in employment and high turnover of employees or jobs. Problems at work cause physical upset.

Health very dependent on the emotional state. Tendency to blood disorders. Health variable and nature of illness often difficult to diagnose and treat. Prone to unusual, rare diseases, and susceptible to esoteric treatments. Sensitive to faith healing and psychic healing. Health also dependent on healthy sex life.

If well aspected, this is a powerful position for a healer. The native has the intuitional ability to diagnose and cure the true cause of other people's illnesses.

If poorly aspected, overly critical, picky, fussy, difficult to please; sometimes obsessed with these characteristics.

The Seventh House

The Moon in the Seventh House

In a female chart, it indicates a union with one whose affections are variable, fond of change and travel, of an unsettled nature, and engaged in public work. If well aspected, it favors an early marriage, partnership, public favor, popularity and social success, also money or property by marriage. Unless the Moon is well aspected and located, this is not a favorable position as it indicates the death of a partner, public opposition, unpopularity, female enmity, trouble and loss through litigation; changeful relations with the opposite sex and with partner and associates.

If the Moon is well aspected to the ruler of the First House, it helps offset the adverse testimonies and magnify the good ones. In bad aspect to Mars: discord, discontent, hasty speech, and action; enmities, assaults.

Saturn adverse: disappointment, loss, and sorrows through unions. Uranus adverse: separation, estrangement, peculiar experience in connection with the unions; unexpected enmities or attacks.

Mercury adverse: matrimonial and business worries.

If the Moon is applying to any aspect of Uranus, the native is likely to marry suddenly and meet another to whom affection is given afterward. Taken alone: inclines to journeys and removals (especially when in a cardinal sign) in the interests of business for others.

Mercury in Seventh House

The native usually carries on Mercurial pursuits in partnership or association with others and is fortunate or otherwise thereby, according to the aspects.

Unsettled married life; many inharmonies; the partner is quick in thought and action. If Mercury is afflicted, sarcastic, untruthful, and hasty-tempered; if well aspected, shrewd, active, clever, and progressive. The partner is usually younger and oftentimes is an employee or is related in some way. Marriage is generally the result of writings or traveling and is more of the mind than of the senses or emotions. If Mercury is much afflicted, many small strifes, worries, vexations through writings, speech, contracts, traveling, legal affairs, and business dealings with others.

Venus in the Seventh House (Natural House)

With marriage come social and financial pleasures. The native usually marries early and enjoys much happiness; love of offspring; successful partnerships; peaceful termination to strifes and success in public relations.

If badly aspected, it shows delay and sorrow in marriage; probably a dissipated partner; loss through litigation and partnerships.

The Sun in the Seventh House

If well aspected, success and rise in life after or through marriage; a proud but magnanimous, warm-hearted partner, firm and lasting attachment, happiness. Good for partnership and general popularity, especially with business people and superiors.

Difficulties averted by arbitration or mutual consent; gain through business, contracts, and associations.

If afflicted, delays, opposition, disappointment, loss, etc., according to the nature of the aspecting planet.

Mars in the Seventh House

If afflicted, impetuous in love, an early or rash love affair or union, possible separation through excessive demonstration of affections and combative or forceful nature of partner. Death of partner; troublesome opponents.

In a female chart, danger of sudden death of husband or severe accident to him. If Mars is in Cancer or Pisces, he is apt to be worthless through dissipating habits.

In a male chart, the partner is industrious but assertive, positive, or masculine.

Loss through litigation or partnership; business enemies; much strife, sometimes resulting in violence; criticism and opposition are frequently met. When Mars is well aspected or located by sign, much of the above is modified; the native may marry a Mars person and benefit thereby.

Jupiter in the Seventh House

If well aspected, success, gain, and happiness through marriage, the partner being faithful and good.

The partner is usually of good social and financial standing; usually older, more patient, profound, or religious than the native. Success in partnership and in dealing cooperatively with others; friends and popularity with and through business people; gain through litigation or legal affairs. Jupiter is weak in Virgo and Capricorn.

If afflicted by Uranus or Mars, loss through litigation.

Saturn or luminaries adverse: marriage is delayed or indicates marriage to an unfortunate person, or to a widow or widower.

Saturn in the Seventh House

If well aspected or in Libra, gives a sincere, prudent, faithful, and well-disposed partner, or union with one older and more serious than the native, not demonstrative or emotional, but stable in affections, possessing property or children.

If afflicted, grief, sorrow, death, or enduring coldness on the part of the partner, who may be of Saturn disposition and habit, according to the sign and aspects.

Ruin by contracts and partnerships, persistent opponents, litigation, business enmities, and treachery. Marriage at about the age of twenty-eight or after; incompatibility with the marriage partner.

Uranus in the Seventh House

When well aspected, union with one of genius, intuition, ability, or an unusual character.

A romantic, sudden, impulsive, secret, or irregular union with likelihood of inharmonious results.

If afflicted, a hasty or impulsive union or attachment followed by unhappy results; misunderstanding, separation, estrangement, scandal, or death of partner.

Loss through strangers, partnerships, law, contracts, opponents, willfulness, opposition, open enemies, and public contests. Unexpected opposition. Conflict with municipal or federal authorities.

Neptune in the Seventh House

Threatens domestic troubles, jealousy, scandal, death of partner, or marriage to a deformed or deceptive person; much sickness; peculiar affairs. Not a good position for partnerships and public dealings unless well aspected.

When afflicted, some mystery, confusion, and deceit in connection with unions. Two engagements or marriages.

Pluto in the Seventh House

Pluto in this house indicates difficulty with relationships. The native intellectually understands and desires a close relationship but, because of circumstances or through the wrong choice of partners, is unable to consummate an intimate, fulfilling relationship. If poorly aspected, the native is bound to a relationship that is meaningless, but freedom is denied. If well aspected, the native's partnership is dissolved, and he learns a valuable lesson that can be applied to the next relationship. This position generally indicates a series of partnerships.

This is a good position for working with the law and the legal system, and with the public, particularly indirectly as through the courts. Energy is used in dealing with others as a group, such as a corporation or other collective bargaining unit. This work may sublimate unhappy personal relationships.

The Eighth House

The Moon in the Eighth House

When well aspected, gain in the public affairs and finance through the business or marriage partner and the mother; gain by inheritance or goods of the dead, probably through the mother's connections; natural death.

Taken alone: ability to develop latent occult tendencies for practical results; astral-plane experiences.

In a female chart, it tends to increase the number of children, but signifies the death of some, especially if afflicted.

The native's mother is likely to die early; in a male chart, also the wife.

If afflicted, unsettled fortunes after marriage; death of a public nature, accident, drowning, etc.

Neptune adverse: death by treachery, drugs, or water, or by obscure or infectious complaint.

Uranus adverse: extraordinary, peculiar, sudden, or accidental death.

Saturn adverse: demise through slow or chronic disorder.

Mars adverse: violent or sudden demise.

Sun adverse: weak vitality and serious sickness, but death usually in the presence of others.

Venus adverse: urinary troubles.

Mercury adverse: stomach, bowel, or lung trouble.

Mercury in the Eighth House

In a female chart, trouble, quarrels, dissension, and difficulties with the partner regarding money; worry in connection with the financial affairs of partners and others.

The native inquires into occult subjects, literature, lectures, and meetings regarding the continuity of life. The mind is conscious and active at the time of death.

Death of a brother, sister, cousin, employee, or neighbor causes much grief and mental anguish. A journey on account of death.

If afflicted, indicates liability to brain or nervous disorders that in some way are related to death.

Venus in the Eighth House

Gain in financial affairs through marriage or partnership. Gain by legacy or through goods and affairs concerning the dead. Denotes a natural, peaceful, or easy demise.

If afflicted, death may be caused by the pursuit of pleasure; kidney, bladder, or functional derangement; death of marriage partner, loss, grief, and disappointment in love.

The Sun in the Eighth House

Steady fortunes after marriage; gain by marriage, partnership, or inheritance. Fame often comes at death that should have come before, or the end may be due to self-sacrifice or heroic deed. The Sun in this position tends to increase vitality and prolong life.

The foregoing is to be considered when the Sun is well aspected.

Taken alone: about the forty-fifth year may be a critical period. Death may be due to heart affliction or constitutional weakness, due to some honorable activity; or there are honors connected with passing. The tendency is to gain through death and through the partner, who is apt to be overly generous and extravagant.

If afflicted, the likelihood of a premature, sudden, or violent end; the father may expire before the native; in a woman's chart, the husband may die first; vice versa, in a male's chart. Sharp attacks of sickness during transits and directions afflicting the Sun bring danger of death.

Mars in the Eighth House

Trouble regarding financial affairs after marriage; the partner is usually extravagant and spends the money of the native if allowed to do so. Difficulties concerning legacies or property of deceased persons. Death usually comes quickly as the result of short sickness, shock, or accident.

If afflicted, liability to violent or sudden death, loss, or legacy, financial loss through partner. If Mars is in a water sign, danger of death by drowning; if in an air sign, mental afflictions or aerial accidents; in a fire sign, by fire, accident, or violence; in an earth sign, heavy sickness, inflammatory complaints; if Mars is the ruler of the Fourth House or afflicts Jupiter, danger of loss by fire and theft.

Jupiter in the Eighth House

If unafflicted, marriage brings prosperity; the partner is or will be well-off financially. Gain by legacy, affairs of the dead, and through occupations denoted by this house and sign; also through the handling of other people's money.

Success in the investigation of the occult, happy dreams, natural and peaceful death.

If afflicted, denotes heart trouble and danger of blood poisoning, foul growths, or consumption.

Saturn in the Eighth House

The marriage partner is apt to be poor, financial difficulties after marriage, no gain through business partnership, or legacy, delay, and disappointments with regard to goods of the dead. Restrictions due to a lack of capital.

If well aspected, moderates all the above and denotes a long life; death from natural causes.

If afflicted or weak, lingering or slow death resulting from some chronic ailment; distressing dreams although not always remembered; death of the father.

If Saturn is in a water sign, danger of drowning. When afflicting Mars, Uranus, or Neptune, danger of fatal accidents.

Uranus in the Eighth House

When well aspected, sudden and unexpected benefits and gains through the marriage or business partner and inventions.

Taken alone: difficulties in financial affairs after marriage, sudden losses through partner and through the financial losses of others, trouble through legacy; sudden, unexpected, or peculiar death; interest in occult affairs and subjects dealing with the continuity of life; peculiar psychic, dream, and astral experiences.

If afflicted, worry and annoyance regarding legacies or goods of the dead; unexpected conditions arising in connection with deaths and through financial affairs.

Liability of death through some extraordinary or sudden event; violence, heart disease, epilepsy, paralysis, or some uncommon nervous disorder; by electrical devices, explosion, or vehicles.

Neptune in the Eighth House

When well aspected, the ability to enter upon spirit planes and gain knowledge through the experience; gains in peculiar manner through others and possibly through the partner.

Strange psychical and dream experiences; desire to investigate spiritualism and other mystical subjects; peculiar death. Danger of death on water. Danger through poisons, opiates, and anesthetics.

If afflicted, trouble in money matters after marriage, loss through complicated money affairs of others; fraud and deceit regarding legacy; partner is usually careless in money matters. Nightmares, strange dreams, weird feelings, trance conditions, astral experiences. Peculiar death.

Pluto in the Eighth House (Natural House)

Pluto in this house indicates an interest in or preoccupation with death and all aspects of the passage from this world into the next. It usually indicates a strong life force; but if afflicted, this force is dissipated through degeneracy and base sensuality. If well aspected, this force is directed to the higher planes of spirituality.

This position is favorable for extrasensory and higher consciousness experiences. The native has psychic abilities that may manifest on many levels: astral projection, dreams, mediumship, healing abilities, etc. Clairvoyance likely.

The native is apt to be financially independent, because of a legacy, inheritance, or lucky streak. If poorly aspected, he uses others for his own gain. If well aspected, he receives unexpected and unasked for bequests.

The Ninth House

The Moon in the Ninth House

When well aspected, an ingenious mind; inventive, progressive, penetrative, reflective, fond of investigation; gives a love for traveling and indicates benefit or improvement through change. Keen imagination and high ideals. Interested in inventions of a public nature, especially modes and means of travel and learning. Benefits through relatives by marriage.

Taken alone: signifies voyages, life in foreign lands; legal or clerical inclinations; keen, romantic, fanciful, and idealistic mind.

Remarkable dream or psychic experiences. Fond of change, diversity, and novelty. Publicity of some sort regarding science, religion, philosophy, traveling, or mysticism.

Sun adverse: overly enthusiastic in religion or unorthodox, probably both, at some time. Saturn adverse: sorrow and difficulty through religion, travel, publications, and partner's relatives. Uranus adverse: romantic, eccentric, fond of adventure; liberal religion.

Mercury in the Ninth House

When well aspected, a keen, clever, ingenious, studious mind; literary ability, taste for art, science, and all higher educational or enlightening subjects; love of knowledge. Success in journeys, clerical or legal affairs, and publishing.

Taken alone: a busy, active mind; danger of legal worries; taste for reading, science, literary pursuits, and every form of knowledge. Desire for life in foreign countries or travels to and knowledge of distant places. Mercury in a cardinal sign is a sure indication of travels. In an air sign, interest in aerial affairs.

If afflicted, tendency to worry and scatter the forces by engaging in numerous activities instead of concentrating on one thing until completed; too much doubt, not enough decision; difficulties with clerical or legal affairs; fruitless and troublesome journeys.

Venus in the Ninth House

Kind, sympathetic, helpful, gentle disposition and cultured intellect; philosophical, optimistic; appreciation for every form of mental improvement. Fond of fine arts, music, operas, high-class literature, lectures, social intercourse, and literary persons. Favorable for social and domestic welfare interests.

Benefits from relatives by marriage, pleasant journeys, success abroad. Venus here will modify many adverse testimonies regarding mental qualities and helps the native avoid trouble.

Indicates marriage abroad, or to a foreigner, or to one of a spiritual, scientific, literary, or artistic disposition.

If Venus is the highest planet in the map, it is a splendid position, denoting honors, success, good marriage and good fortune generally. If Venus is afflicted, it gives longing, high ideals, and desires that are hard to materialize and disappointments through their unattainment.

The Sun in the Ninth House

Success or honors in connection with church, universities, or law, also through travel and social intercourse; desire to investigate science and philosophy to find truths worthy of giving out to benefit others. Dignity or success abroad, or residence in foreign countries; faithful, earnest, sincere, consistent, and constant in religious beliefs, whether orthodox or liberal.

Ambitious, firm, self-reliant, and confident. Taste for fine arts, music, science, literature, and intellectual development.

Mars or Uranus afflicting: extreme, enthusiastic, or peculiar in religious beliefs; trouble in foreign countries, also with legal affairs and partner's relatives; accidents in travel.

Jupiter adverse: unsuccessful in legal or clerical affairs. Trouble in foreign lands and through educational affairs or publishing.

Saturn adverse: hindrance through perversity, pride, etc.; unsuccessful in clerical or legal affairs. Losses in foreign lands.

Jupiter favorable; success and honors through popular reasoning, in science, religion, literature, or philosophy; a good counselor; favor of partner's relatives; international recognition or honors.

Saturn favorable: love of justice, ability for profound or responsible undertakings; philosophical.

Mars favorable: patriotic, courageous, and vigorous in defense of justice.

Mars in the Ninth House

Much strife, generally through legal or religious matters; danger of violence in foreign places; trouble through journeys and spouse's relatives; distressful dreams or fancies.

Enthusiasm or impulse in religion or philosophy; liberality and freedom of thought; forceful in beliefs.

If afflicted, forceful, fanatical, irregular, or skeptical ideas regarding religious matters; preconceived or early religious teachings are overthrown; many troubles, litigation, disputes; danger while traveling, disagreement with some of the relatives, changes in religion or indifference.

If well aspected, active in defense of his rights; successful in law; enterprising in self-development.

Jupiter in the Ninth House (Natural House)

When well aspected, good intuition, clear foresight; success and honors in religious, collegiate, legal, philosophic, or philanthropic affairs; favorable for travel and success abroad; prophetic faculty and prophetic dreams; peaceful, logical, and optimistic disposition; international interests.

Mars adverse: danger of shipwreck, fire, or accident on journeys; liable to go to extremes in religious matters or trouble through them.

Uranus adverse: unexpected loss, difficulties, and experiences through journeys, religion, law, philosophy, relatives.

Mars or Uranus favorable: inclination toward occult philosophy, higher science, originality of thought, invention, and means of travel.

Saturn in the Ninth House

When well aspected, the mental attitude is scientific and philosophical; the nature is studious and meditative, given to the investigation of law, geology, mineralogy, metaphysics, psychic and occult subjects generally.

Sun in good aspect: denotes a very faithful, devotional, or religious spirit. Interest in geology, archeology, or political economy.

Taken alone or afflicted: trouble in foreign lands, dangerous voyages (especially if in a water sign); loss through legal affairs, troubles through relatives by marriage; self-deception, lack of comprehension of the profound or higher sciences or philosophies, likelihood of religious bigotry and mental afflictions.

Mars adverse: perverse mind, danger of mental derangement, or accidents in travel. Narrow religious ideas may be the cause of friction and conflict.

Uranus in the Ninth House

Trouble in foreign lands or through relatives by marriage; peculiar, unexpected, adventurous, dangerous voyages; taste for philosophy, occult, metaphysical, or unusual knowledge.

Original, inventive, peculiar, eccentric, or reformative and progressive ideas. Desirous of traveling and investigating. Prophetic intuitive faculty and sometimes engaged in antiquarian, Uranian, or aerial research.

Neptune in the Ninth House

Clairvoyant or other psychic faculties; a highly inspirational nature; strange dreams, feelings, and experiences. Astral experiences.

Psychic studies or investigation of spiritualism, psychic phenomena, and philosophy. Voyages if in a cardinal or water sign.

If afflicted, distressful dreams; ominous forebodings; trouble through travels; legal involvements; complicated affairs with wife's relatives. Adverse psychical experiences; impressionable and simulative nature.

Pluto in the Ninth House

Pluto here indicates that the native's religious and philosophical ideas will undergo drastic change during his life. A complete religious conversion is likely and he may repudiate his former beliefs, often violently. The native is drawn to emotional and sensual religious rites, and undergoes the ecstasy of religious inspiration, visions, or communion with otherworldly beings.

When well aspected, the native is eloquent and persuasive in defending his beliefs; when poorly aspected, he is violent and quarrelsome; a fanatic. In either case, the native believes that his religion is the only true one, and thinks that everyone should convert to his beliefs.

Contacts with foreign cultures and ideas confuse and disturb the native and cause an unsought-after questioning of his basic beliefs.

The religious ideas may embrace occultism and sex magic, and may either deteriorate into obsession and perversion, or may become purified of emotional content and reborn. The native may even be psychically preyed upon by living or disincarnate personalities who claim spiritual powers or knowledge.

The Tenth House

The Moon in the Tenth House

Inclines to public life, changes in business, occupation, and employment, instability of position and popularity, rise in life followed by reversal or downfall. Voyages in connection with business, if in a cardinal sign. Women influence the position in some way according to the aspects; strong attraction to mother. If well aspected by the Sun, Venus, or Jupiter, favors success, popularity, and prosperity. Indicates carefulness in money matters and usually gain in property and possessions. Public business; catering to the masses.

Mars adverse: public scandal, notoriety, or discredit, obstacles in business. Taken alone, it gives the ability and tendencies to employment of a changing nature, such as shipping, voyaging, traveling, dealing in public commodities, novelties, etc.; affairs connected with common people generally, also with things ruled by the sign occupied.

Mercury in the Tenth House

The honors and success in business or occupation depend upon the sign and aspects, Mercury being neutral.

Good position for public service or for holding responsible positions under superiors.

The vocational tendencies and abilities may be seen by delineating the planet in most powerful aspect to Mercury, as though the planet in question were actually in the Tenth House, thus:

Uranus most strongly aspecting: novelists, reporters, lecturers, teachers, travelers, electricians, railroad employees, occult professions generally, psychologists, dealers in occult literature, antiquities, inventions.

Taken alone, it gives a taste for literature; several professions, occupations, or undertakings; mercantile work, commissions, agencies. If in an air sign, retentive memory and fluent speech, used effectively in business activities. If much afflicted by Mars or Saturn, a restless nature, subtle and deceptive; impulsive speech or untruthfulness; trouble in business or failure.

Signifies an active, able, penetrating, adaptable mind used resourcefully in business.

Venus in the Tenth House

This position favors honors, popularity, and friendships; the native has merit and ability, possesses an agreeable and pleasant manner; usually marries above the station in life and enjoys success in dealings with women.

Generally well disposed and of good moral stamina, dislikes quarreling or trouble of any sort and delights in all that is social, pleasant, and harmonious. It favors gain through the parents (probably the mother), general prosperity, and artistic or musical pursuits. This position is fortunate for parents and home life or for the occupations of Venus and those designated by the sign it occupies. Preference for business that is beautifying, harmonizing, comforting, or entertaining.

If well aspected by the Sun, Jupiter, or the Moon, the subject meets with social distinction, honors, and financial success, and the favor, good will, and support of those in good position, government officers, superiors, and responsible persons, especially along social or entertainment lines. When afflicted, it indicates limitations, and the native suffers a lack of opportunities to manifest his abilities or may occupy a lowly position in high-class undertakings. The occupations of Venus are those that deal with artistic, refined, and entertainment matters; all business directly connected with females; adornment, jewelry, finery, luxury, beauty, amusement.

If in good aspect with Mercury, it makes fine musicians, artists, painters, speakers, writers, librarians, speculators, actors, singers, stage directors, band or choir masters, bailiffs and other political officers, secretaries, printers, decorators, housekeepers, carpenters, druggists, confectioners, dyers, and good character readers; public work in professions that require considerable traveling or that bring one into contact with many people; influential posts; positions or trust and refinement.

The nature of the profession depends largely upon the nature of the sign in which Venus is located.

The Sun in the Tenth House

When well aspected, honor and success, distinction, authority, independence, prosperity, high patronage, and favor of those in power and good position. This position usually indicates a good birth and favorable parental influences. The native's success is generally steady in whatever business, profession, or occupation he adopts; positions of trust, responsibility, honor, or governmental office; good vitality; high moral standards; favorable environment.

If afflicted, love of power; dignity, pride, opposition, reversals. Although the Sun in the Tenth House is always beneficial in some respect, great difficulties will be met according to the nature of the affliction.

Mars in the Tenth House

Unless Mars is in the sign Capricorn, impulse and feeling are likely to predominate, reason and intellectuality often being overridden by the passionate or forceful side of the nature.

The native meets with much turmoil and strife through excessive ambition, independence, domination, or force and aggressiveness.

A spirit of freedom and desire for conquest spur the subject on, at times to his detriment. It is significant of extravagance or extremes in some form. Scandal, discredit, and disrepute, whether deserved or not. Death of parents or disagreement with them.

The native has plenty of courage, energy, enterprise, and force, and is consequently capable of being in business for himself, but will succeed best in the occupations corresponding to the nature of Mars and the planet that best aspects Mars.

When well aspected, gain and promotion through business acumen, salesmanship, bravery, and industrial pursuits; benefit through the father and also by legacy.

Mercury in good aspect indicates the engineer, carver, sculptor, designer, athlete, mechanic, soldier, sailor, officer, dentist, surgeon, surgical instrument maker, hardware dealer, and all lines where courage or daring is necessary, or where skill is combined with muscular energy and the use of tools, such as iron or steel instruments and machinery.

If Mercury afflicts, mason, laborer, iron worker, tanner, cattle man, butcher; bath, lavatory, or laundry attendant; worker in metal and where there is an element of risk and danger. Saturn adverse: laborious employments and likelihood of failure in business.

Jupiter in the Tenth House

Usually indicates a good birth; help from relatives or those in high position. The native has good moral standards and will occupy secure influential or important positions at some period.

Gain through the occupation, marriage, sports, and public or political office. This is a good position for rise in life, honors, favor of superiors, public appointments, dignities, esteem, good will, social, political, and financial success.

Uranus adverse: reversals of fortune, difficulties.

Saturn adverse: downfalls, obstacles, losses. Luminaries adverse: difficulty in social life and through changes and travel; unfavorable publicity.

Mercury favorable: good judge, minister, ambassador, philosopher, banker, merchant, government official, stock broker, trustee, etc., and is good for positions of distinction, honor, responsibility, trust, and social welfare.

If Mercury afflicts, minor or laborious government offices, bank clerk, clothier, upholsterer, draper, provision dealer, or catering to the public; liability to loss or discredit through dishonesty.

Saturn in the Tenth House (Natural House)

A great deal depends upon the sign and aspects. When well aspected, ambition for power and advancement; the native rises above his sphere in life by steady, persevering industry.

When afflicted by aspect or weak by sign, rise and success are followed by downfall or adversity. The native is usually persistent and has ability, but lacks opportunities and meets with obstacles, delay, dull periods, and disappointment. In business, financial ruin is threatened; in professional life, dishonor and failures, whether deserved or not; in political matters, defeat. Public affairs fail and bring loss and discredit. These take place during adverse transits and directions. If the native has a good situation, he had best keep it and not branch out into new undertakings that entail heavy liabilities or great responsibility.

Mercury in good aspect helps improve the conditions and denotes government officials, land surveyors and dealers, managers, organizers, solicitors, stationers, binders, lawyers, scientists, geologists, architects, contractors, builders, mining engineers, coal dealers, and other employments where care and skill, patience, or organized and concentrated efforts are required; diplomatic occupations. If Mercury afflicts, miner, printer, bookbinder, bricklayer, coal handler, grocer, gardener; general and practical work connected with the earth and its products; country preacher, notary public, night watchman, etc.

Uranus in the Tenth House

A strange and eventful career; many important changes of position and credit.

Originality is a marked feature. The native is unique in that he originates new lines of activity for himself, follows uncommon lines of thought and employment and establishes customs and codes of his own, apart and opposite to the conventional.

All effort is made for freedom and to undo and overthrow all bonds of limitation. Very independent, erratic, eccentric, and unconventional. Difficulties with employers; opposition from public functionaries or governmental bodies. Threatens discredit and reverses; extraordinary experiences in public or business career.

In a mutable sign, two simultaneous occupations are indicated. Estrangement from parents and kindred, unless good planets occupy the Fourth House, not necessarily through trouble unless parental ruler afflicts.

In good aspect to Mercury, it fits the native to reconstruct the old, undertake new and improved methods, create new professions and new plans of work, and follow uncommon pursuits; investigator, explorer, reformer, teacher, inventor, flier, metaphysician, electrician, astrologer, psychologist.

If Mercury afflicts, novelist, reporter, hypnotist, occult student, antiquarian, dealer in curiosities and antiquities, lineman, engineer, employee having to do with transit and mechanism, people of peculiar genius, and extraordinary or hazardous employment.

Neptune in the Tenth House

A highly inspirational nature, capable of attaining honor or position through some unique achievement. Professional people become municipal officers of sanitary, hygiene, health, or hospital boards. A chance of honor in some artistic or scientific field. The subject becomes interested in the mysterious nature and seeks to arrange deductions for practical application. This position endangers the life of one of the parents while the native is yet young, but if well aspected may bring inheritance from a parent or gain through some pursuit connected with psychism, liquids, health springs, hospitals, or sanitariums. Taken alone, it signifies all occupations where mystery, secrecy, inspiration, a nom de plume, or a title are employed; the sea and the various industries connected with it; secret service; inspirational writing; singer, actor, musician, artist, medium, psychic, diver, fisherman.

Being a neutral planet, the occupation indicated depends on the planet in closest or strongest aspect. Neptune here in the sign Taurus, trine to Mercury, gives an active desire and ability to simplify science, to popularize it as far as possible and present it in the most reasonable and practical manner. Also to investigate and carry on occult, philosophical, and spiritual philosophies of life. Useful inspirational ideas; unique distinction.

If unfavorably aspected, it indicates a strange and peculiar career, some disgrace or scandal, whether deserved or not; peculiar circumstances, separation from the parents, unfortunate business or professional complications.

If Neptune is well aspected, it reverses the unfavorable indications and the native gains through mediumistic or spiritual friends.

Pluto in the Tenth House

Strong drive for power and public recognition. If poorly aspected, this drive is fed by greed, ruthlessness, and utter selfishness. If well aspected, the native desires power in order to help others, or to fulfill some obligation. In either case, there is a tendency to believe the ends justify the means and to use other people for his own gain.

The Eleventh House

The Moon in the Eleventh House

Large circle of acquaintances, unreliable friends, few lasting attachments, unless in a fixed sign and well aspected; success in dealing with children and young people. When well aspected, gain through acquaintances and hopes realized; good for social life and popularity; friends among celebrities.

If afflicted, especially by Mars or Uranus, troubles, sorrows, and losses through friends, disappointing friendships; sudden changes among friends and separation from them. Saturn adverse: sorrow, loss, delay or limitations occasioned by friends or through legislative enactments.

Mercury in the Eleventh House

Many acquaintances but few lasting friends; some association with literary or scientific people and with those who are younger. When well aspected, inspiration, mental development, and gain through friends. If afflicted, unreliable and troublesome acquaintances. If Uranus, Saturn, or Jupiter is in adverse aspect, the native should in no way rely or depend upon friends for assistance or provide security or bonds for them, as they will cause worry, anxiety, trouble, and loss through wrong advice and carelessness in handling facts or the truth, or their circumstances will so change that their promises cannot be kept.

Venus in the Eleventh House

Gain and happiness through friends who desire to forward the interests of the native; social success and popularity.

Favors from women, socially inclined; friends are usually of an artistic nature; fruitful marriage.

Saturn adverse: unfortunate friends whose advice, if followed, leads to trouble, loss, and scandal; disappointments and delays in hopes and wishes. Mars adverse: possibility of trouble through excessive pleasure with friends. Uranus or Neptune adverse: unreliable, eccentric, or seductive means.

The Sun in the Eleventh House

Definite and lofty ambitions and desires; respect for dignitaries or superiors and those of loyal mind, honesty of purpose, self-respect, dignity, worth. Association with those of power and good position; gain in reputation, honors, and esteem through friendships; successful, ambitious, well-regulated hopes; firm, honorable, and constant friends; social success.

Mars in the Eleventh House

Disagreement with acquaintances, some social unpopularity, contention, alienation, and deaths among friends and troubles with others in social life; few real friends; friendships are likely to lead the subject into trouble through impulse or some form of extravagance.

Saturn or Mercury in affliction: violation of friendship or treachery among friends.

Jupiter or Sun adverse: difficulty through wrong advice, law troubles, financial losses, rash men, etc.

Venus or Moon adverse: over-indulgence with friends.

Uranus adverse: disaster, extraordinary events and attachments; trouble with legislators.

Neptune adverse: losses and unfortunate complications through unreliable friends.

Jupiter in the Eleventh House

True and fortunate friends; associations with prominent persons, legislators, senators, judges, bankers, doctors, professors; gain through acquaintances of good position; social success, popularity, and credit. Ambitions are often attained and hopes brought to a successful issue due to the instrumentality of powerful or influential friends. In a cardinal sign: executive ability, progress. In a fixed sign: jealousy or pride among friends. In a mutable sign: scientific or religious friends.

Saturn in the Eleventh House

If Saturn is exalted or well aspected, few friends; gain through acquaintances who are older, profound, scientific, or serious.

Taken alone or afflicted: false and deceitful friends, or unfortunate acquaintances by whom the subject is liable to sorrow, loss, and ruin, especially if in a cardinal sign. Friends among the lowly, ill, or unfortunate.

In a fixed sign: delay and hindrance through friends.

In a mutable sign: hopes are likely to be unachieved and ambitions often frustrated; sorrow through friends.

Uranus in the Eleventh House (Natural House)

This is the natural house of Uranus, but whether its presence therein will benefit the native or not depends upon the aspects. When well aspected, friends among occult or peculiar people, unusual or extraordinary acquaintances, geniuses, inventors, writers, government executives, etc. Unexpected benefits from friends; progressive hopes and wishes. Taken alone or afflicted: peculiar or remarkable friendship, eccentric or unreliable acquaintances; sudden, unexpected estrangements, impulsive attachments often ending in coldness; peculiar hopes and wishes, strange and romantic attachments. Radicalism and humanitarianism are not uncommon. The native has strong ideals.

Neptune in the Eleventh House

If adversely aspected, unfavorable attachments, unsatisfactory friendships, strange and unaccountable attractions and associates, seductive friends and alliances, treachery among supposed friends, unreliable advisors and losses and troubles thereby; complications among friends.

If Neptune is well aspected, it reverses these indications, and gives friends among mystics, psychics, poets, musicians, swimmers, yachtsmen, nightclub workers. Gain through mediumistic or spiritual friends.

Pluto in the Eleventh House

With Pluto in this position, great care must be taken in the choice of friends, as the native is easily led and influenced by others. He is a natural leader, but the people he leads seem to be an accidental combination. If well aspected, he uses his magnetic personality to lead others in a social welfare, humanitarian, or charitable cause. If poorly aspected, he becomes an underworld gang leader, a criminal egging others to do his dirty work for him. There are likely to be sudden breaks with friends and associates, and people enter and leave the native's life unexpectedly. He is apt, at the height of his power, to abandon his goals and set out in an entirely different direction.

The native is fiercely loyal to the cause and people of the moment, and demands the same sacrificing loyalty from his acquaintances. He is ruthless in pursuing his goals, and his expectations are often unrealistically high. Demanding a lot from himself and others, he inspires either great admiration or intense hatred from those around him.

The Twelfth House

The Moon in the Twelfth House

Love of mystery, occultism, secret arts, or romance. Liability of the senses dominating the reason, causing indiscreet love affairs, sorrow, and loss thereby.

Hindrance and limitations are prominent, but benefit is indicated in out-of-sight work, in occupations that require seclusion rather than publicity, in hospitals, institutions, or in isolated positions, in remote, quiet, obscure places. Voyages. Mystery.

If the Moon is well aspected and not in Scorpio or Capricorn, it shows development and progress, particularly through the occult.

When well aspected, success with large animals; ability for occult arts.

If afflicted, lacks firmness and stability and is led into acts of indiscretion, resulting in worry, trouble, secrets, and female enmity. Liability to restraint, enforced retirement, or sickness in a hospital; fanciful fears.

Mercury in the Twelfth House

Fond of investigating occultism, chemistry, medicine, or secret arts, and of risks and adventures of a secret or dangerous nature; of unusual lines of thought generally. Love of mystery; petty worries and annoyances; many small enmities, frequently caused by writings or scandalous reports. The subject possesses ability but lacks power or opportunities to manifest. When well aspected, tends to success ultimately. Benefit through rest, quietude, and seclusion.

Venus in the Twelfth House

Inclines to romance and adventure; love of the mysterious in nature, and for investigating the secret arts, medicine, chemistry; pleasure and success with horses and other animals.

Gain by an obscure or plebeian occupation, also benefit through charitable or public institutions; enjoys peaceful or voluntary seclusion.

Secret love affairs or intrigues leading to enmity of women; an early union (especially if Mars is in aspect), affection for another after marriage, and if Saturn afflicts, separation or divorce and sorrow or disappointment through the opposite sex.

Scorpio, Capricorn, or Cancer are the worst signs for Venus here, giving too great a love for physical and emotional pleasures; detrimental to the native because of excess.

The Sun in the Twelfth House

Occult and psychic tendencies, uncommon tastes and inclinations. Success over enemies and success in medicine, chemistry, occult affairs; in some quiet, secure, obscure, or unpopular occupation; or in connection with hospitals, prisons, or other institutions; seclusion. Life in places far from birth. Help and charity received when needed.

If in a water sign: strong mediumistic faculty.

When well aspected, self-sacrificing, enduring, and rises out of seclusion, obscurity, or difficulties by his own efforts after the first third of life has passed.

If afflicted, sorrow and misfortune through things indicated by the sign occupied; inflammatory conditions.

Mars in the Twelfth House

Danger of injury, slander, scandal, loss of reputation, or treachery from enemies or misplaced affection; grave trouble through impulse, lack of frankness, or candor; liability to imprisonment.

Unfortunate adventures, secret enemies, danger of injury through large animals and burglars; death in seclusion or restraint. The partner is subject to feverish complaints.

If Mars is in Libra or Pisces, it denotes poverty or limitations and privation.

Saturn adverse: injuries or imprisonment, illness requiring hospital service; labor troubles.

Jupiter adverse: financial and social ruin.

Luminaries adverse: distressful circumstances.

The good aspects of the Sun and Venus or the sign Capricorn here improve this position of Mars.

Jupiter in the Twelfth House

Success in medicine, chemistry, or occult studies; respect for ancient wisdom and teachings; success through asylums, hospitals, or public institutions, through benevolence and philanthropy, in places remote from birth, in quiet places and with animals; charity given or received; the native readily helps others.

The subject prevails over enemies. They become friends and he eventually gains through them; reversals followed by success.

Peculiar experience in connection with the affections, religious, collegiate, political, or foreign affairs, which, however, may result in ultimate benefit.

Aid from friends and others quietly or secretly; success about the middle part of life.

Saturn in the Twelfth House

When well aspected, success in seclusion or in quiet or laborious occupations.

If unaspected, secret enemies who work for the native's downfall; losses and bruises through animals. The nature is acquisitive, reserved, and inclined to solitude; desires to work secretly, unobserved, and live peacefully or alone. Secret sorrows, fear, and disappointment; liability to false accusations and even imprisonment or confinement.

Uranus adverse: unexpected or strange enmities, disgrace, loss of credit and honor; labor troubles.

Mars adverse: danger of violence, robbers, or suicide.

Mercury adverse: mental disorders, hallucinations, severe sickness; loss by theft.

Luminaries adverse: tendency to despondency, melancholia; sorrow through death of loved ones.

Uranus in the Twelfth House

Estrangement from one's native state or kindred; difficulties with animals; secret, romantic, mysterious affairs and attractions; occult investigations; psychic and mystical experiences.

If afflicted, eccentric, peculiar, violent tendencies; threatens disgrace and troubles from psychic and occult sources; mysterious and unexpected misfortunes; restraint in public institutions; strange and unexpected enmities; eccentric people perplex and annoy by underhanded actions. Sudden illness.

When well aspected, success through occult affairs, institutions, and extraordinary, secret, or out-of-sign avocations.

Neptune in the Twelfth House (Natural House)

When well aspected, success in mediumship, psychical research and occult investigations; through secret, secluded, and quiet methods, detective work or laboratory research; benefit though large institutions.

If afflicted, danger from psychic sources and through deception, schemes, fraud, secret enemies, scandal, disgrace, and secret sorrows. Vague or weird apprehensions. Sickness necessitating hospitalization.

Pluto in the Twelfth House

The native is a private person, close and secretive about his true feelings. His natural desires are to help others and to give himself utterly to service to humankind. However, if Pluto is poorly aspected, all efforts to this end are thwarted, and the native ends up requiring more help than giving it. If well aspected, the service can have a therapeutic role in aiding the native find himself while working for others.

There is a tendency to let others take advantage of his sympathies and the native suffers when not able to have enough time to himself. This can lead to self-pity and depression. The native must combat blaming himself for the problems of others, and to avoid involving himself in problems that do not affect him.

INTERPRETING THE ASPECTS

Not everyone with a preponderance of good aspects is successful in life; some may be too easily satisfied or contented. Nor does everyone with a preponderance of inharmonious aspects achieve success through stimulating effort; they may be too easily irritated and develop obstacles in their path through enmities, injuries, etc.

So it will be seen that aspects are the modifying influence in a horoscope. Unless aspects are properly computed, the necessary modifications cannot be read and the delineations not properly made. The influence of a planet in a house is qualified by the aspects it beholds.

Much of the skill and art in reading horoscopes depends upon the correct recording of aspects and knowledge of their influence. The first requisite is the ability to calculate and collect the facts about aspects. Although this text gives the influence of each planetary aspect, the saying of Ptolemy should be observed: *Judgment must be regulated by thyself, as well as by the science.*

Consider the different applications of the same aspect in several cases, as a person in the penitentiary, or lying ill in a hospital; a youth off on his or her vacation; a person in charge of a flourishing business; a person chiefly concerned with his or her family of children.

A physician does not diagnose until he is familiar with the history of the case; likewise an astrologer should not render judgment until he is familiar with his client's station in life, his condition, and his activities, in order that he may properly anticipate the nature of the person's response to the vibratory action of an aspect. To do this correctly, he must have made no mistake about the aspect.

In fact, the aspect must first be diagnosed along these lines:

1. Quality of aspect, good or adverse.
2. Platic (wide orb) or partile (exact aspect).

3. Forming or separating.

4. Is the aspecting planet sinister or dexter? How many degrees away from the aspected planet is the one that is doing the aspecting? How many degrees plus or minus the exact aspect?

5. Is the aspecting planet angular, succedent, or cadent?

6. Is the aspecting planet in a cardinal, fixed, or mutable sign?

7. Is the aspecting planet in a fruitful or barren sign?

8. Is the aspecting planet a so-called benefic or malefic?

9. What house of the horoscope does the aspecting planet occupy?

10. Does the aspecting planet have any other aspect at the same time? If so, compare them and decide whether one accentuates or modifies the other.

11. What is the nature of the aspected planet, malefic or benefic?

12. What house does the aspected planet occupy? Is it elevated above the aspecting planet, or below it in the chart?

13. Is either of these planets in its sign of dignity or debility?

14. Is either of them retrograde?

The most important of these questions are (1) What is the nature of the aspect? and (2) Is it applying or separating?

Combined Influences of Houses, Aspects, and Planets

The influence and effect of planets in a horoscope depend largely upon their aspects, and an aspect, favorable or unfavorable, to any planet will alter its indications in the chart as judged without an aspect. The reading given for a planet in a house must be modifed or arranged to coincide with the aspects to the planet in order to delineate a horoscope correctly.

For example, Mercury in the Third House unaspected gives mental perception, mental activity; learns much by observation; ability in matters of speaking, writings, or commissions.

Mercury in the Third House well aspected, for instance by Jupiter, gives a jovial mind with very good judgment. Ability for collegiate studies, inclination to medicine, law, or philosophy. Success in writings, travel, and professional matters. Gain through brethren and neighbors.

Mercury in the Third House afflicted, for instance by Mars, gives a clever, sharp, shrewd, active mind. Quick-tempered, sarcastic, resentful, impatient, impulsive, and forceful in speech. Difficulty through writings and trouble with brethren and neighbors. Careless with facts and hasty in drawing conclusions.

Thus it is essential not only to render judgment on a planet in a house according to the quality of its aspect, but also by nature of the planet with which it is aspected.

As a planet often has more than one aspect, it is sometimes necessary to make a combination judgment, especially where one aspect is good and the other adverse. Saturn in the Second House in good aspect to Jupiter and in evil aspect to Venus would show success where property, land, and investment were concerned, but loss through women or excess of pleasure.

The Planetary Aspects of the Moon

The Moon in Favorable Aspect to Mercury

Indicates that the native is quick in wit, perceptive, ingenious, comprehensive, reasonable; has splendid mental abilities, keen and penetrating, productive, versatile, expressive, fluent, and copious in speech or writing. If any of the air signs ascend, it gives admirable elocution and the ability to acquire languages with ease.

The mind responds readily to new ideas and is fond of change and variety; optimism, imagination, and intuition are increased, also mental sympathy, receptivity, and adaptability. Fond of art, music, pleasure, literature, and journeys.

The Moon in Unfavorable Aspect to Mercury

Anxiety, worry, quick, sharp, turbulent, and sarcastic states of mind. Impressionable, mutable, imaginative, indecisive, speculative, and overly sensitive. Tendency to change, not enough continuity, fixity, firmness, and stability of mental attitudes. Poor memory for dates and facts in history. Nevertheless, dexterous, ingenious, or clever, and possesses many good qualities.

Temporary derangements of the health through the nervous system, stomach, or bowels. Unsuccessful or unpopular writing; public criticism. Business losses, litigation.

The Moon in Favorable Aspect to Venus

Good-natured, kind, and cheerful; neat and tasteful in dress and pleasing in manners; fondness for the beautiful in nature, music, and all things artistic; taste for pleasure, light literature, drama, and public functions; fruitful nature, good intellect.

Gentle, refined, agreeable, affectionate, and attractive; sociable, maternal, and sympathetic.

Endowed with respect and company of the opposite sex; enjoys sociability, friends, and general popularity. General public or business success through engaging personality and cheerfulness.

Profitable employment in connection with the common classes. Assistance or approval of parents.

This aspect is favorable for money and possessions, for Second, Fourth, and Seventh House affairs, and for the things ruled by the house that Venus occupies. It tends to success and frugality.

Gain through catering to public tastes and necessities in confectioneries, bakeries, restaurants, hotels, boarding houses, etc.; also through dealing in houses, lands, and the fruits of the earth.

The Moon in Unfavorable Aspect to Venus

It indicates over-indulgence in pleasures, a tendency to carelessness in habits and manners; changeful affections, usually amorous; losses and difficulty in connection with money, property, and possessions, or in business pursuits.

Trouble in partnerships, love, or marriage; disapproval of parents or may suffer unpopularity, slander, and scandal, whether deserved or not.

To a female, it threatens ill health periodically.

The Moon in Favorable Aspect to the Sun

Sincerity, energy, will, loyalty, ambition, and adaptability. Strengthens the constitution of both male and female natives; indicates success in life, rapid promotion, prosperity, and assistance from influential persons; seldom has difficulty in obtaining employment and usually receives a good salary. Gain through speculation, investment, enterprise, and responsibility. With a good aspect of Jupiter also, it indicates the accumulation of great wealth and fortunate, congenial marriage.

The exact conjunction of the Sun and Moon is often adverse, especially when at the same time in ill aspect to the malefics, the nature of which will signify the difficulty; but of itself the conjunction is apt to make the native mutable, inert, indifferent, lethargic, sensitive, volatile, irresolute, self-centered, but harmless, and may experience a lowering of vitality every month when the conjunction occurs.

The Moon in Unfavorable Aspect to the Sun

Ambitious, venturesome, egotistical, irresolute, sensitive, compelling, and immoderate.

Difficulty in financial affairs, accumulating money, or in obtaining and keeping employment; loss by speculation, ill health, inferiors, disappointment, and overconfidence; misfortune or poor success with those of high position; weak constitution, and if Saturn be in affliction, long and serious sickness; difficulty through women.

The Moon in Favorable Aspect to Mars

The subject is ambitious, energetic, firm, brave, ardent, and resolute.

This aspect in the chart tends to offset many testimonies regarding sickness or weakness. It gives strength to the whole system, muscular and circulatory; increases the activity, force, and vitality. It is a good aspect for those whose work requires strength for occupations carried on outdoors.

Success and promotion through resourcefulness and enterprise in business, personal affairs, or employments of responsibility and publicity. Results are largely accomplished through quick action, energetic, commonsense methods and hard work that inspire confidence and trust from others.

If any testimony of legacy is shown, this aspect strengthens it and brings benefit, possibly through the mother's connections.

It is good for things ruled by the house the Moon occupies, also for Fourth House affairs, property, timber, commodities, etc.

The Moon in Unfavorable Aspect to Mars

Brave but headstrong; inclined to acts and words that are indiscreet or rash, causing regret, humiliation, and sorrow.

The temper is quick, resulting in disputes, strife, and difficulties. Self-confident, egotistical, domineering, daring, and venturesome. The desire is for freedom and liberty of expression; obstacles and opposition or lack of opportunities cause fits of passion. Apt to suffer from disregard of regulations, carelessness of consequences; through appetites, sex impulse; and through scandal, criticism, and enmity.

An unfortunate aspect for domestic happiness; indicates loss of legacy, sorrow through the mother, difficulty over property and in dwelling place, loss through partnership and theft. Not favorable for health, showing liability of trouble to the sex organs, head, eyes, breast, and stomach, sometimes causing indigestion and nervousness. Danger through excitement, fevers, operations, accidents, ruptured blood vessels, fire, and water. The native should avoid low, swampy, or stagnant districts and beware of danger on water. In a female's horoscope, it threatens ill health, annoying periods and many difficulties.

The Moon in Favorable Aspect to Jupiter

Increases the imagination, intuition, and appreciation for beauty; indicates clear, sound, and usually correct judgment and reasoning. Strengthens the vitality, fertility, and resourcefulness. Inclines to honesty, justice, benevolence, compassion, sympathy, friendliness, and sociability. Jovial, generous, humane, hopeful, and popular.

Success in literature and general affairs, especially those things ruled by the houses these planets occupy, and also the Fourth and Ninth Houses, if they are unafflicted. This is one of the good aspects that assist in the acquisition of possessions, happiness in marriage, and good health. Gain and development through the occult, spiritual and educational affairs, and publishing; also through the mother and family, especially if the Tenth and Fourth Houses are unafflicted.

The Moon in Unfavorable Aspect to Jupiter

Unfortunate for speculations, games of chance, and risky ventures. Loss through misplaced confidence, loans, deception, dishonesty, excess, lack of candor, concealment of motives, irresolution, wrong judgment, either of self or by others.

Trouble through changes and voyages; likelihood of slander and false accusations. Severe illness, misunderstanding or separation from the mother. Rather an adverse aspect for health generally, giving liability to derangement of the stomach and liver, blood disorders, and tumorous growths. An unfortunate aspect for health in a woman's chart.

The Moon in Favorable Aspect to Saturn

Denotes a thoughtful, conservative, prudent, sober, and contemplative mind; not much given to gaiety, but provident, careful, and attentive to business and affairs generally.

Popularity, credit, respect, esteem; diplomatic, self-reliant; systematizing, organizing, and constructive ability; accomplishes most by subtlety, tact, and method rather than by force.

Favorable aspect for occupation, public advancement and attainment to positions of trust and responsibility through persistent effort; approval or benefit through parents, friends, elders, and employers.

Gain in business and by such things as Saturn rules: mines, lands, and produce. If Jupiter is also in favorable aspect, it leads to the acquisition of great wealth. If the Sun is in good aspect, it denotes a rise in life to a very prominent and distinguished position through perseverance.

The Moon in Unfavorable Aspect to Saturn

Indicates that the person is poor, or loses his money and becomes so, and has a hard struggle to make both ends meet.

He is earnest and ambitious, but his plans do not materialize as expected; a hard worker but generally receives little gain; usually fails in business though careful and persevering; unlooked-for obstacles, delays, disappointments, rebuffs, and reversals constantly arise, coupled with a lack of opportunities and unfavorable circumstances at the critical or needed times.

It is an unfortunate aspect for marriage, yet if the planets are in mutable signs, usually marries more than once.

A bad aspect for speculation and such things as Saturn rules by nature, also by the sign and house it occupies in the chart.

The native meets with persecution, slander, or scandal; disapproval of seniors, parents, or employers; difficulties and sorrows through parents, property, and possessions. Sorrow through death of young people and mother.

Temporary derangements of the health, colds, falls, and accidents. The native should employ healthful exercises.

This aspect affects the disposition, causing the subject to become somewhat selfish, subtle, careful of his own interests, given to periods of worry, anxiety, doubt, mistrust in self, gloom, and despondency. A good aspect of the Sun, Jupiter, Mars, or Venus will help offset the severity of the above.

The Moon in Favorable Aspect to Uranus

The native is active, firm, enterprising, and scientific. Fond of friendship and the opposite sex.

Success and gain through the occult, and through original, inventive, and progressive people.

The aspect tends to awaken the imaging faculties, quickens the thoughts and intuition, leads the mind into original lines, and gives interest in new methods, inventions, curiosities, etc., giving mesmeric and psychic faculty; good for healing and telepathy. Benefit through business and novelties. A good aspect for an electric expert or worker.

Inclination for and benefit through astrology.

Advantageous changes and removals. Favors traveling, and if either planet is in the Third or Ninth House, many journeys. If in the Fourth House, many changes of residence.

The Moon in Unfavorable Aspect to Uranus

Unfortunate changes, journeys, and removals.

Impulsive, sarcastic, abrupt, peculiar, electric, and independent; danger on or near the water; trouble through the opposite sex, difficulties, annoyance, and possibly separations; troubles through occult affairs and unreliable friends.

Not good for health, tending to upset the stomach and digestion, causing mental disturbance of different kinds, sudden or peculiar changes in feelings, emotions, likes and dislikes.

Restless, active mind, ever desirous of new scenes, new working material and surroundings; cannot stand limitations. It usually produces extremes and reversals.

The Moon in Favorable Aspect to Neptune

Inclines to success in things ruled by Neptune and as indicated by the sign and house it occupies; good for boating, swimming, shipping, dealing in liquids, choice foodstuffs, canned goods, delicacies, and things calculated to please the tastes of the public.

Strong inspirational and imaging faculty; mediumistic qualities; fond of investigating spiritualism, psychism, and the mysterious in nature, or some form of the occult. Would make a good psychometrist, having active emotions and impressionability. If Venus or Mercury is also in good aspect, it shows inspiration for art, music, singing, writing, speaking, or acting.

The Moon in Unfavorable Aspect to Neptune

Threatens fraud, deception, or slander; difficulties through things ruled by the house Neptune occupies; misfortune through the opposite sex, delays or obstacles in regard to marriage in a male chart; desire to gratify the tastes, which leads to injury of the health, especially if either is in a water sign.

Strong inspirational, psychic, emotional, and imaging faculty; subtle feelings, quick impressions, and eccentric, undefined, or unexplainable acts. It attracts to peculiar people, exquisite tastes, luxuries, odd colors, odors, and bohemianism or unconventionality.

Impulse is liable to predominate over reason, or through over-enthusiasm the feelings may get the upper hand of judgment, leading to acts of indiscretion. Quick response to environmental influences. It affects the nervous or mental health through bodily disorder (note the signs they occupy).

In mutable signs, it affects the brain and nervous system; in fixed signs, the glandular and secretory processes; in the cardinal signs, the circulatory and absorptive systems.

The Moon in Favorable Aspect to Pluto

The native is resilient to change, able always to make the best of circumstances. He is emotionally sensitive, and able to influence others subtly.

The conjunction cannot be considered a favorable aspect in this case, since the Moon is in its fall in Scorpio. Moodiness and depression may appear, due to vulnerability to strong emotional drives. The individual will be psychologically keyed into powerful interpersonal emotional interactions at an unconscious level.

The Moon in Unfavorable Aspect to Pluto

The native is subject to severe emotional trauma, but internalizes this, so that intense feelings may erupt violently from time to time. Lack of self-control or self-discipline. Overly sensitive and lacks emotional discrimination. The native is usually prejudiced, because the rational facility is weakened.

The Planetary Aspects of Mercury

Mercury can never be more than 28° away from the Sun in either dexter or sinister position. Therefore, Mercury can only form the following aspects to the Sun: conjunction, parallel, and within 2° of a semisextile.

Venus can never be more than 48° away from the Sun in either dexter or sinister position. Therefore, if Mercury were 28° away from the Sun on one side, and Venus 48° away on the other, the extent of their possible distance is 76°. Mercury can only form the following aspects to Venus: conjunction, parallel, semisextile, semisquare, sextile, and quintile, all of which are considered good, except the semisquare.

Mercury in Favorable Aspect to Venus

The mind is intuitive, cheerful, merry, witty, mirthful, good-tempered, and hopeful. This aspect gives a sociable, friendly nature, amiability, and general popularity, especially with the opposite sex. Fondness for pleasure, refined entertainment and recreation, also for all the fine arts and sciences or anything requiring finish, touch, daintiness, color, and culture. It tends to mental pleasures, harmony, and mirth.

It favors gain in money, property, and possessions.

Indicates marriage, friendships, and associations.

Oftentimes it indicates that the native has two attachments, marriages, or partnerships, or marriage to someone of kin.

It is good for employment and money earned by the wits, speaking, writing, art, manual dexterity, entertainment. Neat, artistic touch.

If Mercury is more prominent than Venus, Third and Sixth House (Mercurial) affairs are favored; i.e., gain through mental accomplishments, writing, speaking, designing, short journeys; clerking, advertising, publishing, science, commercial affairs, commissions, kindred, neighbors, business, literary and professional people.

When Venus is more prominent, it favors pleasure and profit through talents, accomplishments, refinement, and good taste; all things luxurious, pleasurable, and beautiful; music, singing, poetry, painting, art, theaters; dealing with women and children, doctors, nursing; also in confectionery, stationery, jewelry, fancy work, millinery, dressmaking. Fortunate for things ruled by the house Venus occupies.

Mercury in Unfavorable Aspect to Venus

The only adverse aspect they can form is the semisquare. This aspect is not very malignant or important. It gives fondness or desire for all the aforementioned, but not so much ability for their execution, and some minor obstacles and hindrance in Venus and Mercury affairs.

Mercury and the Sun

Mercury never moves more than 28° away from the Sun and is best when more than 8° in advance of that luminary. Under the latter influence, the native will be ambitious, aspiring, quick-witted, intuitive, thoughtful, intelligent, ingenious, adaptable, studious, observant, and capable. Good business ability; learns with facility and ease.

If Mercury is in Pisces, the mind should receive careful but gentle training. In Scorpio, it tends to make fine physicians or surgeons. Mercury in exact conjunction with the Sun is not considered favorable for the best reasoning and business judgment, unless located in a favorable or scientific sign, or in good aspect to other planets.

Mercury in Favorable Aspect to Mars

Makes the native quick, lively, bright, alert, witty, humorous, satirical, constructive, ingenious, practical, skillful, dexterous, and businesslike.

Enthusiastic, fluent, animated, and magnetic when interested. It shows a great deal of energy, activity, force, and enterprise; splendid mental abilities.

Inclination or ability for drawing, music, carving, designing, chemistry, medicine, engineering, surveying, and science; inclines toward investigation and application of new practical methods in commerce and industry, mechanics, literature, or business.

It favors association with or development through literary, educational, or professional people and those connected with the practical sciences.

Mercury in Unfavorable Aspect to Mars

Good intellectual powers; the mind is acute, shrewd, clever, and sharp. The disposition is impulsive, forceful, quick-tempered, sarcastic, argumentative, resentful, and impatient; the mind is fired with desires, but doesn't have enough continuity, the aspect being separative rather than unifying.

The subject possesses great mental activity and is therefore liable to brain troubles through overwork, excitement, or lack of suitable opportunity for expression of his particular ability, which results in irritability and periods of weariness or exhaustion, and disorganization of the stomach and digestive organs.

Apt to create enmity, opposition, and disagreements through sharp, critical statements or impulsive actions. Likely to meet with difficulty through relatives, superiors, servants, and neighbors. Losses through theft, risky enterprises, correspondence, contracts, litigation, carelessness with facts, hasty conclusions, and criticism.

Danger through traveling, tools, machinery, instruments, and electrical contrivances; also drugs, operations, wounds from insects, reptiles, and small animals.

This aspect indicates difficulties, obstacles, and disorganization through things ruled by the signs and houses occupied by Mars especially. Trouble through neuralgia, headaches, accidents. The aspect is worse from water signs, usually showing the tendency to drink and other ruinous habits.

Mercury in Favorable Aspect to Jupiter

Inclines to general success in life through the houses they occupy, especially if unafflicted. Denotes a broad, philosophical mind with the ability to think clearly, deeply, and seriously, and to develop good judgment through comparison and learning; capability for collegiate studies.

The mind is versatile, vigorous, and creative, combining conscientiousness with hope, good cheer, good nature, contentment, and joviality.

The disposition is generous, kind, candid, humane, honest, sincere, liberal, and fruitful. Indicates beneficial changes, journeys; inspirational ideas, thoughts, and conclusions.

Success with literature, accomplishments, science, and in professional lines. Good aspect for mail order, governmental, law, or church affairs. To occult students, it is good for visions, psychic and inspirational experiences, independent and automatic writing.

With Mercury in an air sign, it gives discrimination, discernment, understanding, knowledge, appreciation, perception, compassion, sympathy, and forbearance.

Mercury in Unfavorable Aspect to Jupiter

Obstacles and difficulties arise regarding matters ruled by the houses they occupy, Mercury more particularly, through unfinished education or accomplishments.

It shows liability to deceit or poor judgment leading to changes, journeys; unreliable ideas, wily thoughts, dissension, disagreements, and sometimes legal troubles. Misfortune and difficulty through investments, speculation, contracts, agreements (especially verbal), writings, church affiliations, social affairs, foreign and financial matters.

Liable to suffer from scandal, slander, or false reports, and accidents in travel.

The mind is active, keen, alert, and impressionable, but not sufficiently steady or confident. Unfavorable changes, travels, and letters. It tends to weakness in the parts of the body ruled by the signs occupied by Mercury and Jupiter.

Mercury in Favorable Aspect to Saturn

Good intellectual abilities: memory, order, method, reasoning, and judgment. The mind is contemplative, substantial, practical, studious, and fond of science generally.

Success with teaching hygiene, or as a physician, mental healer, or in any capacity with large corporations, especially railroads, mining, produce, and commission concerns.

Gain through tact, diplomacy, caution, and perseverance.

The aspect inclines to the study of geology or mineralogy. It favors travel in connection with business; some association or business with the father or brethren, probably both; may gain some prominence through societies, church, or established concerns, as agent, secretary, representative.

If Mercury is in the First, Third, or Ninth House, it is very good for scientific or intellectual pursuits, writings, publishing, lecturing, traveling.

Denotes strength of will, steady persistence, and determination; good memory, strong, sensible, practical, and sound judgment. The native has ability for politics, public appointments, official positions of all kinds, large public undertakings, brokerage, speculative, commercial, or financial affairs, and business where much prudence, caution, and sobriety of judgment are required. Mercury in conjunction with Saturn (if not otherwise afflicted) gives a very comprehensive and profound mind, capable of achieving much in whatever direction it is turned.

Mercury in Unfavorable Aspect to Saturn

The subject has great ambitions and desires for activity, success, and mastery in lines coming under the Third, Sixth, and Tenth House affairs, but his efforts are attended with delay, disappointments, obstacles, and limitations, and in some cases he meets with criticism and opposition, open or secret, and his efforts are frequently thwarted and hindered or his plans overthrown.

Encounters difficulty in acquiring an education and in all matters pertaining to books and studies.

The retentive or memorizing faculty needs developing even though memory of events is strong.

This aspect signifies great sorrow through the death of brethren or the father, probably both, or their ill health, separation, or estrangement from them, although not necessarily through quarrels, but more as the result of circumstances.

Trouble is occasioned through slander, false reports, forged letters or documents, unfriendly writings, delayed and misunderstood letters, and the subject may himself cause difficulty through these things. The effect on the nature is to make one sarcastic, bitter, impulsive, and somewhat dissembling with periods of gloom, pessimism, or exasperation, grave anxiety, worry, constant disturbance of the mind, errors of judgment caused by fear, circumstances, lack of initiative, procrastination, and continuous restriction of actions. This leads the mind to meditate and endeavor to discover the reason for these undesirable manifestations, and from this attitude one may be prone to seek recourse in the study of occult subjects and spiritual philosophy, and thus improve his responses to the aspect.

If either planet is in or rules the Third or Ninth House, it gives an inclination for science and occult learning, which considerably improves the reactions to this aspect, but still there is liability to loss through failures, theft, fraud, and deception; difficulty or loss in employment or through lack of employment, poor health often interfering; troubles through neighbors, servants, societies, associations, messengers, travelers, and by things ruled by the sign and house occupied. This is a bad aspect for the teeth, causing decay; also causes slow or poor circulation or digestion, bowel afflictions, weakness, obstructions, and constipation. People with this aspect and annoyed with these latter troubles should avoid strong drinks or highly seasoned food.

Mercury in Favorable Aspect to Uranus

Intuitive perception, inventive ability, original and eccentric nature. Fond of old and curious things, occult science, astrology, and advanced thought generally.

Gain through invention, originality, speculation, and unique enterprises. If either is in the First, Third, or Ninth House, or is the ruler thereof, it promotes success in literature and the ability to become a great scholar, excelling in the arts and sciences; fine comprehension.

Good character reader; successful in connection with electrical affairs as salesman, telegrapher, bookkeeper, stock manager, etc., for electrical, aerial, or transportation companies. Much ingenuity and unique enterprise.

Successful advertiser, publisher, writer, inventor, researcher, or explorer.

Mercury in Unfavorable Aspect to Uranus

Active mentality; impulsive, irregular, and sarcastic turns of mind; very observant, ingenious, and critical; unsuccessful in literary pursuits; public criticism probably through the press; difficulty through societies, friends, and kindred. Skeptical and peculiar; a reformer's spirit and extreme or radical ideas; constant desire for new fields or modes of action; sudden and unexpected adverse changes and removals. Restless, dissatisfied, discontented, daring, audacious, defiant, adventurous. Subject to accidents, especially in travel.

Mercury in Favorable Aspect to Neptune

Fertile imagination; practical, quick, sensitive, and resourceful mind; versatility of genius; receptivity to new ideas and methods. Gives ability to develop mediumistic and psychic qualities, clairvoyance, psychometry, crystal gazing, automatic writing, trance, and inspirational speaking.

The native is attracted to psychic centers and people, spiritual investigations, unconventional healing, and hygienic methods or hydrotherapy, and success with same. It gives visions or prophetic dreams.

The Third and Ninth Houses are the best for the above.

Improves mental receptivity, psychic understanding, and adaptability. Occult experiences.

It favors matters relating to liquids, chemicals, oils, drugs, bever ages, canned goods, fish, the sea, hospitals, and private institutions.

If Venus also is in good aspect, the subject will have remarkable faculty for music, poetry, art, literature; inspiration.

Mercury in Unfavorable Aspect to Neptune

Conducive to an interest in all of the above, but attended with unreliability, obstacles, and misfortune.

The memory is apt to be poor, the mind vacillating and somewhat unpractical, affected by spells or periods of mental aberration, abstraction, lack of concentration, absentmindedness, dreaminess, or irresolution. It tends to nervousness, sensitivity, restlessness, changes, and liability to trouble through slander, deception, imitation, fraud, intrigue, bribery. Danger through drugs and poisons.

Difficulties through changefulness, unexplainable psychic conditions, lack of cautious self-control, and the liability to be led by the impulses, sensations, appetites, emotions, sympathy, and by the ideas, thoughts, and advice of others, resulting in nervous, restless excitability, which exhausts the vital processes. The native should benefit through the study of dietetics.

Mercury in Favorable Aspect to Pluto

Mental flexibility; the lack of fixed ideas allows the native to easily size up a new situation and change his tactics to meet the changing reality. Strong suggestive personality, able to persuade and even dominate others mentally. Analytical mind penetrates through the obvious, searching for the causes of things. Sees connections between externally unrelated objects, ideas, and feelings.

In the conjunction, there is a possibility of self-centeredness, and using the power to subtly control others for his own benefit.

Mercury in Unfavorable Aspect to Pluto

Snap judgments made; ideas are grasped quickly, but the native shows impatience with others who do not think in the same manner. Skepticism and cynicism may turn into fanaticism and obsession. Mental turmoil causes physical disorders. An inner restlessness may drive the native to an obsessive search for new knowledge and occult information. Preoccupation with death.

The Planetary Aspects of Venus

As Venus is never more than 48° away from the Sun, only these aspects can be formed: conjunction, parallel, semisextile, and semisquare.

Venus in Good Aspect to the Sun

Fondness for company and hospitality, delighting in sociability, pleasure, ease, luxury, comfort, and places of entertainment.

The nature is generous, warm-hearted, sympathetic, courteous, amiable, kind, affectionate, impressionable, and cheerful.

This aspect is fruitful and creative, good for gaining money through business, profession, speculation, or public occupation; it shows popularity and promotion in employment, and preferment in social affairs. Liking for music, opera, the fine arts generally, and some ability along these lines.

The conjunction leads to warm attractions, love affairs, and marriage, even when there are adverse testimonies denying union.

Venus in Unfavorable Aspect to the Sun

As Venus is never more than 48° from the Sun, the "combust" and semisquare are the only adverse aspects Venus can form to Sol.

Neither is a very important aspect in itself, but at times may make the native extravagant, overly fond of pleasure and luxury, amorous, and mutable in the affections.

Some delay or misfortune in love affairs and in dealing with the opposite sex. Loss through speculation and extravagance, or carelessness.

Venus in Favorable Aspect to Mars

Fond of pleasure, adventure, and the opposite sex; aspiring, ambitious, confident, amorous, affectionate, and demonstrative.

Gain through enterprise, pleasure, sport, practical artistic ability, music, and matters requiring artistic and mechanical skill.

It is a good aspect for money; not for saving it (that requires a good aspect to Saturn, acquisitiveness), but for getting it, earning it through energy, activity, ingenuity, responsibility, and business instinct, and through things ruled by the house Venus occupies and rules. The native is free and generous in money matters, a cheerful spender; in business, for advertisement, show, and display; in social life, for pleasure, adornment, music, and entertainment.

If the chart shows any indications for inheritance, this aspect strengthens it. The aspect also shows social popularity and indicates marriage either early or suddenly.

Venus in Unfavorable Aspect to Mars

Very fond of pleasure; impulsive and amorous; difficulty through excesses and the opposite sex.

Loss through overly liberal tendencies or carelessness and extravagance; also through fires, partnerships, and too freely entering into business or speculative enterprises.

At times the social popularity or standing will be adversely affected; danger through dishonesty or loss; opposition through friends or jealousy, separation, and enmity. Trouble through marriage and partnerships.

If Venus or Mars is in a water sign, the tendency is to gratify the tastes and pleasurable emotions in dissipating habits.

Venus in Favorable Aspect to Jupiter

Strengthens the imagination and the idealistic and poetical side of the nature, giving a keen appreciation for beauty in form, color, sound, and touch. High motives, ambitions, and aspirations.

It gives social and general popularity, preferment, esteem, and respect.

Inclines to acts of charity and sympathy. The nature becomes generous, kind, thoughtful, amiable, loving, sociable, hospitable, philanthropic, liberal, talented, good-humored, and optimistic; fond of pleasure and elegant, dainty, and costly surroundings.

Gain through refinement, accomplishments, social intercourse, traveling, foreign affairs, influential persons, companies, associations, and corporations. A good indication of fortunate events, love and marriage; favors success, gain, and general good fortune. Generally is associated with wealth and culture, and handles considerable money or other valuable assets.

Fortunate for things governed by the houses they occupy and also those houses that they rule in the nativity.

Venus in Unfavorable Aspect to Jupiter

Strong desire for grace, refinement, talent, beauty, and luxury, but forced to be content with these to an ordinary or limited extent and satisfied with the best show or substitute possible.

Unless other testimonies offset this, it is not a good aspect for the accumulation of money, as a great deal is spent for appearances in dress, ornaments, luxury; inclines to an easy good nature and fondness for pleasure, producing a lack of accurate business instinct, resulting in loss through carelessness, fraud, deception, desertion, separation, prosecution, speculation, and unsound investments or securities. Difficulty in love and marriage through faithlessness or misrepresentation. Liable to overdo in the gratification of desires for pleasure and amusements; apt to be overly liberal, extravagant, and amorous. Blood or skin disorders; loss through floods.

Venus in Favorable Aspect to Saturn

Sympathetic, modest, prudent, chaste, frugal, and sincere. It favors success in courtship and marriage and steady attachment to the partner and family. Faithfulness in love and friendship.

The tendency is toward thrift, economy, and accumulation of money. It endows the native with the capacity for business, tact, method, and system, and the ability to make the most of opportunities. Much good luck, good will, and many presents.

Gain through elders, superiors in position and by investments, associations, banking, lands, and solid, secure methods.

Venus in Unfavorable Aspect to Saturn

Disappointment and trouble in courtship and marriage or partnership; censure, unpopularity, disapproval, interference, reversals, or misfortunes through elders, parents, or relatives. Danger through deception, avariciousness, sensuality, jealousy, and theft.

Sorrows and difficulties through the opposite sex; marriage probably delayed until the twenty-eighth year or after; trouble through difference in age, social, or pecuniary affairs or illness.

Diplomatic nature; liability to business losses; also through speculations, investments, lands, mines, companies, banks, drought, depressions, or epidemics; loss of accounts or salary.

Venus in Favorable Aspect to Uranus

Fondness, desire, and ability for the fine arts, leaning toward new or extraordinary conceptions, radical and progressive departures from the usual interpretation of art.

Attractive, magnetic personality that gains many friends and acquaintances and good fortune or success through them. A fortunate business aspect.

Bright, quick, intuitive, inspirational mentality.

Benefit and gain through fraternal, social, and progressive societies.

Success through such things as Venus and Uranus rule; gain by peculiar or unexpected circumstances and through strangers; favorite with the opposite sex. Friends among artists, inventors, congressmen, and extraordinary persons.

Venus in Unfavorable Aspect to Uranus

Trouble and jealousy through courtship and marriage; difficulty through the opposite sex. Unconventional; liable to hasty, impulsive marriage leading to divorce.

The mind is imaginative, curious, alert, and hastily influenced by unrestrained feelings, which make the native liable to be led astray; troubles by broken promises and scandal; separations, estrangements, and difficulty with friends. Losses through sudden and unexpected circumstances. An unfortunate aspect for matters connected with the opposite sex. Loss through unreliable friends, associates, or partners, and through risky ventures.

Venus in Favorable Aspect to Neptune

Inclines to fondness for art, music, singing, drama, and beauty in all forms. This aspect has a tendency toward benefit and pleasure through friends, associations, and acquaintances.

The feelings quickly respond to kindness, sympathy, love, and appreciation. Inspirational, ardent, and attracted to the opposite sex. Good aspect for benefit through mystical interests and success in speculation or as an actor if either is in the Fifth House, especially in connection with the cinema.

It is a fortunate aspect for making money out of large combines, trusts, or institutions; also for matters related to shipping, liquids, and amusement resorts, especially at places by water.

Venus in Unfavorable Aspect to Neptune

Disappointments, complications, deceit, and danger of scandal in love or marriage; instability and liability of fraud and deception on the part of the partner, especially if either planet is in the Fifth, Seventh, or Twelfth House.

Strong desires, with probability of injury and danger through catering to the gratification of the tastes, or through lack of proper emotional expression.

Caution should be observed with diet and beverages. There may be danger from ptomaine poisoning through wrong food combinations or impure substances.

Guard against loss and theft, misplaced confidence, and secret organizations and affairs. Beware of financial loss through schemes, trusts, cliques, or rackets.

Venus in Favorable Aspect to Pluto

A loving personality, always able to see the best in people. Strong emotional attachment for the underdog; empathy for other people's problems. Understanding nature. A strong and loyal friend, though the relationship may change many times.

In the conjunction, the sexual element is more emphasized. Intense love or lust, and strong procreative drive.

Venus in Unfavorable Aspect to Pluto

Jealousy and possessiveness enter relationships, ultimately causing loneliness in the native. A strong sex drive can lead to uncontrolled lust and immoderate behavior. Relationships are full of conflict. The native often loses friends without understanding the reason why. The native feels emotionally insecure and fears the inability to love or be loved.

The Planetary Aspects of the Sun

The Sun in Favorable Aspect to Mars

Tends to strengthen the constitution and give energy, vitality, determination, enterprise, vigor, animation, confidence, and courage.

The nature is frank, outspoken, assertive, aggressive, ambitious, venturesome, progressive, and generous.

The native has the ability to command and control; gives power of leadership through intensity of purpose, enthusiasm, activity, faith, and strength of will.

Capacity for games and sports where strength and muscular exertion are depended upon. If Mars or the Sun is in an air sign, powerful intellect and much will force. If either planet is angular, it denotes great executive power and leadership.

The native has quick perception and possesses practical, constructive, and engineering ability; meets with favor, promotion, and cooperation.

The Sun in Unfavorable Aspect to Mars

Many ups and downs and obstacles in the path of the desires. Impulse, pride, and anger cause many difficulties; deaths, separations, litigation, and enmities; hasty, fiery temper, though not lasting; ambition, love of enterprise, but not enough continuity of application, confidence, faith, and patience.

Outspoken, assertive, aggressive, combative, defensive, impulsive, forceful, overbearing, destructive, self-willed, headstrong, audacious, and sensual. Loses the esteem of superiors and those in high position.

Danger through impulsive action, assaults, quarrels, accidents, fires, fevers, inflammatory complaints, surgical operations; short, sudden, sharp attacks of sickness; cuts, burns, scalds.

If Mars is in Capricorn or the Sun dignified, it lessens the tendency to rashness, etc.

The Sun in Favorable Aspect to Jupiter

This increases the chances for success and rise in life; even with bad aspects from other planets, it still indicates some good fortune, because it tends toward a far-seeing, broad outlook and sound judgment.

The native is honorable, humane, benevolent, sympathetic, kind, philanthropic, charitable, generous, sincere, frank, candid, hopeful, social, genial, popular, executive, reliable, honest, and fond of sports.

Indicates influential friends and assistance or benefit through them. Inclines somewhat to religion or spiritual investigation. Appreciation of social life and its functions with a desire for the good opinion and favor of those in good position. The subject is usually "correct" with regard to fashion and customs and careful not to overstep the limits of good form.

Inclines to good health and abundant vitality. With a female, this aspect assists to a successful love or marriage.

Fortunate for those things ruled by the houses these planets occupy, especially Jupiter. If Uranus also is in good aspect, it signifies gain and the acquisition of wealth through railroads, inventions, governmental office, speculation, investment, banks, large theatrical enterprises, sports, transportation, publishing, and things electrical and political.

If Saturn assists, gain through investment and solid financial deals, government affairs, inheritance, or gold mines.

Mars also in good aspect: although not detrimental to the acquisition of wealth, it is not good for the saving of it on account of generosity and lavishness. It favors industrial success. Venus in good aspect: gain through refinement, pleasure, music, entertainment, and general good luck. Mercury in good aspect: gain through science, art, traveling, writings, and publishing. Moon in good aspect: gain through dealing with the public and possibly through shipping and public utility concerns.

The Sun in Unfavorable Aspect to Jupiter

Threatens business and financial loss through investments, speculations, loans, errors, miscalculations, etc.

Danger of difficulty through wrong advice, extravagance, legal or social affairs. A good aspect of the Moon will help modify these financial testimonies, but, in any event, it shows ill luck, probably through misjudgment, false "securities," pride, lack of careful reasoning or forethought.

The tendency at times is to be bombastic, irritable, haughty, egotistical, mistrustful, fond of display, pleasure, and comfort.

In a woman's horoscope, it indicates a good but somewhat unlucky husband.

There is tendency toward Sun and Jupiter diseases during the latter part of life and weakened vitality.

The Sun in Favorable Aspect to Saturn

This aspect is such that it aids general success and rise in life through the native's own efforts and meritorious qualities, and the ability to concentrate, appraise, organize, and coordinate the efforts toward a definite objective.

Makes the native sincere, considerate, conservative, methodical, responsible, discreet, discriminative, serious, confident, and capable of sustained effort.

The personality is strong and not easily affected by the opinions or protests of others; the mentality is contemplative and practical, authoritative, and capable of organization. If assisted by any other good aspect, it tends to gain and success through lands, mines, investments, and industrial enterprises.

If the Moon is in good aspect, the native gains municipal or other political honors and appointments.

The Sun in Unfavorable Aspect to Saturn

Indicates derangements of the health; the nature of the illness threatened can be seen by the signs that the Sun and Saturn occupy. It is bad for business affairs, especially of the kind signified by the two planets.

Obstacles, limitations, hindrance, and delays cause disappointments, sorrows, and losses. The ambitions are thwarted. Sometimes the native seems to be getting along splendidly, and success seems close and sure, but suddenly inevitable conditions and reverses arise, resulting in downfall and loss. The native incurs opposition, enmity, jealousy, and public disfavor.

All of these things indicate a tendency to become unsympathetic, careless of the feelings of others, selfish, pessimistic, skeptical, or disinterested in social and economic welfare.

It indicates the death of the father, disagreement or separation from him; enmity or disfavor of superiors, employers, or those of high position; unfortunate marital affairs.

In a woman's horoscope, this aspect signifies a denial of marriage or delay. Also indicates the death of the husband, or marriage to a widower. These marriages are seldom happy ones, the husband usually being domineering, exacting, selfish, or inclined to illness and misfortune.

If Saturn is in a water sign, the partner is liable to be given to drink or other dissolute habits.

The Sun in Favorable Aspect to Uranus

Denotes talent, perception, intuition, independence, originality, and enterprise. It indicates success through invention, public or governmental employ. Also a good aspect for connection with societies, associations, or brotherhoods; research, exploration, adventure, transportation, aerial and electrical matters.

Tends to preserve the health in old age and lengthens life. Friends among government executives and extraordinary persons.

Benefit through the occult; from metaphysical, electric, or magnetic healing; by strangers, elderly people, or occultists. (Many successful public astrologers have this aspect.)

It excites to strong attachments and generally to an early union. Interest in fraternities, reforms, and progressive movements.

The Sun in Unfavorable Aspect to Uranus

Unfortunate for marriage, causing disharmony, separation, broken vows and ties generally. Tends to make one impulsive, rash, spasmodic, erratic, radical, and unconventional; inclined to leap before looking; precipitate, fond of risky ventures, enterprises, and romance. It is worse in a woman's horoscope, indicating danger of scandal, disgrace, and unlucky unions.

Denotes a quick, intuitive, perceptive, and original mind, always alert for change, liberty, freedom, novelty, and new opportunities.

It gives interest in occult affairs, but denotes liability to losses and danger through unreliable friends, disasters, calamities, enmity, opposition, love affairs, partnerships, strangers, societies, intrigue, estrangement, independence, and impulsiveness. It tends to upset the health and indicates accidents, possibly through engines, inventions, vehicles, airplanes, explosions, storms, and things electrical. A good aspect from other planets helps modify these extreme indications.

The Sun in Favorable Aspect to Neptune

Gives an inspirational nature and an inclination for philosophy, religion, science, psychic research, photography, and motion pictures. Interest in modern sanitation, hygiene, naturopathy, sunbathing, swimming, yachting, motorboat racing, etc. If Mercury is near the Ascendant, angular, or in good aspect to these planets, the native is usually inspirational in speaking or writing and can develop considerable musical skill, especially in connection with stringed instruments.

The tendency of the aspect is to refine the feelings and emotions, giving a keen appreciation for the beauties of nature and art or music in its highest forms; love of refined pleasures, concerts, yachting, sojourning at the beach, traveling, and all fine luxury or elegance. The native is sympathetic, kind, and generous and usually benefits through mystical and spiritual subjects.

The Sun in Unfavorable Aspect to Neptune

Signifies that the person is liable to be the victim of fraud and also scandal, whether deserved or not; unstable or involved affairs generally; unfortunate for the things signified by the house that Neptune occupies.

Creates the desire for mysticism, romance, gratification of abnormal tastes, and inclines in some way to lax morality and seductive alliances.

The native is usually mediumistic and subject to weird dreams, feelings, and desires. It usually indicates peculiar or irregular love affairs, some difficulty with or through children, and loss through speculation, gaming, or deception concerning securities and investments.

Inclined to suffer from illnesses that require hospitalization and that are difficult to diagnose; from psychic conditions, fraud, enmity, and conspiracy. It is wise in such cases to study the philosophy of all things mysterious or occult rather than the phenomena.

The Sun in Favorable Aspect to Pluto

This native has a very strong personality and a marked influence over others. He is able to easily discard old habits, ideas, and possessions that hinder him in attaining his goals. These he usually attains, on strength of will if nothing else. The native fights for what he believes or wants, and welcomes new conflicts.

In the conjunction, the power drive may be overwhelming and there is a tendency to use this power selfishly.

The Sun in Unfavorable Aspect to Pluto

The native is egotistical, domineering, possessive, and above all ruthless. He will do anything to achieve his goals, and has complete disregard for his fellow man. The native lacks an ethical system, and can be bought for a price, though usually he is the one who does the buying.

The Planetary Aspects of Mars

Mars in Favorable Aspect to Jupiter

Frank, free, generous, straightforward, just, active, ambitious, enterprising, self-reliant, original, and constructive. Any course of action decided on is entered into with enthusiasm, confidence, determination, and practical execution. A good manager or leader; capable of creating enthusiasm and action in others. Liberal concepts, broad views, capable of large and responsible undertakings, especially in wholesale, industrial, and commercial affairs. Always ready to help those who are willing to help themselves. If the chart shows indications of legacy, this aspect tends to strengthen it.

Fond of all legitimate sport, travel, exploration, mechanical, professional, and industrial activities. Gain by personal industry, enterprise, and the exercise of good judgment.

Fortunate for those things ruled by the house that Jupiter occupies.

Mars in Unfavorable Aspect to Jupiter

Indicates excessive or impulsive generosity; careless regarding the accumulation of money and apt to suffer from the dishonesty of others.

Difficulty through and with religion, religious or political people. Loss through speculation and games of chance.

Suffers from indiscretion, dishonesty, deceit, treachery, broken contracts, desertion, misrepresentation, and quarrels.

Often the native is directly or indirectly the cause of misfortune through hasty judgment, impulsive action, extravagance, dissipation, or through carelessness, overconfidence, miscalculation, anger.

Dangerous or difficult journeys, trouble in foreign places and through legal affairs.

Feverish complaints, blood and liver disorders; danger and loss through fires and accidents, and if Uranus is adverse, through lightning, electricity, floods, or explosions.

Mars in Favorable Aspect to Saturn

Confident, ambitious, determined, energetic, desirous of leading and ruling, a pioneering nature. Courageous, self-reliant, daring, somewhat overbearing and forceful, reckless of danger or defeat, capable of obtaining marked results through concentrated or sustained action. Reserve force, muscular endurance, strong bones; active mentality, capability, vigilance, skill in execution. Rises to prominence or power but usually attended by danger of some kind; would make a good military, state, or city official; also practical lawyer, civil and mining engineer, surveyor, construction contractor, manufacturer, farmer, etc. Favorable aspect for legacy from the father.

Mars in Unfavorable Aspect to Saturn

The mind and senses are in conflict, causing discord, selfishness, quick temper, violence; rash, hasty, impulsive acts; deception, resentment, cruel, hard or revengeful feelings when opposed.

Trouble with parts of the body denoted by the signs occupied by the afflicted planets. Feverish complaints, wounds, falls. and accidents; danger of violence through enemies, reptiles, animals, riots, strikes, uprisings, revolutions, accident, war, or state. Notoriety, reversals, criticism, opposition, enmity, scandal, discredit; obstacles and difficulty in occupation, danger of loss and failure in business.

An unfortunate aspect for parents, denoting death, separation, or disputes; bad for legacies; difficulties with companies, partnerships, or in marriage. Liable to imprisonment.

If either planet is well aspected and well located by sign, much of the above is mitigated, but notice the houses that they occupy, as they indicate trouble for the things ruled thereby.

Mars in Favorable Aspect to Uranus

The subject comes before the public in some capacity through the talents. The mind is very alert, quick to act, and inventive; the nature is positive, self-confident, enterprising, original, expressive, energetic, impulsive, ambitious, resourceful, and practical; possesses practical business intuition, talent, and intellectuality. Once a course of action has been decided upon, it is followed with a good deal of originality or independence and determination, which is difficult to thwart or turn aside, for the subject generally gets his own way; he is usually generous and has occult sympathies.

Gain through invention, electrical engineering, construction, transportation, or industrial research, unique achievements, municipal employ, government positions, progressive professional pursuits, psychology, psychoanalysis, suggestive therapeutics, metaphysics, astrology. Also through travel, exploration, investigation, the antique and curious generally.

Mars in Unfavorable Aspect to Uranus

The subject has most of the aforementioned traits and qualities, but is somewhat over-forceful, restless, and unsettled; hasty and erroneous in judgment, quick in opposition, resentful, irritable, erratic, radical, imprudent, defiant, odd, eccentric, ungovernable, rebellious, fanciful, excitable, enigmatical.

Sometimes violent or revolutionary, seeking to throw off all bonds of limitation, restraint, custom, and conventionality.

An unfortunate aspect for affairs ruled by the signs and houses occupied. Danger of imprisonment and liability to violence, accidents, wounds, and trouble through firearms, explosions, lightning, fire, wrecks, machinery, vehicles of transportation, and electrical devices.

It denotes sudden and unfortunate events that upset prearranged affairs, reversals of plans, and changes in objectives.

Mars in Favorable Aspect to Neptune

Gives a fondness for curiosities and travel, for occult and metaphysical subjects. Favors marine activities and aquatic sports.

Increases the generosity, emotions, and enthusiasm, and the liking for mysticism, romance, adventure.

A good aspect for those connected with the water or with liquids, beverages, oils, drugs, chemicals, anesthetics, hospitals, sanitariums, or the sea, and with the occult in a practical way.

Mars in Unfavorable Aspect to Neptune

Gives a fondness for curiosities and travel; inclines to self-indulgence and feelings of self-sufficiency.

Liable to trouble arising from relations with the opposite sex, also through scandal. Somewhat vague, indefinite, or mysterious, obscure, and secretive. Danger of loss and accident on or by water or liquids; through poisons, drugs, or habits; also through thieves and acts of nature. Trouble through duplicity, deception, fraud, imitation, racketeering, bribery, false accusation, arrest. To psychic persons, it gives liability to distraction or obsession (possession) and produces derangements, hallucinations, and strange ideas. If Mars or Neptune is well aspected or otherwise dignified, these testimonies are considerably modified.

Mars in Favorable Aspect to Pluto

The native has a forceful personality; he shows great ambition, the capacity for hard work, is self-confident and courageous. He is able to achieve his aims through energetic and unpredicted attack. Enjoys competition.

In the conjunction, the animal self is strong and ruthlessness can be a problem. Impulsive.

Mars in Unfavorable Aspect to Pluto

The capacity for violence lies just beneath the surface and often overwhelms the native. Lack of purpose causes inner turbulence and restlessness, which may lead to irrational acts. The native has trouble controlling his impulses, and has difficulty living in a structured society. Sadistic tendencies. The native should learn to *carefully* analyze his reasons for taking actions of any sort.

The Planetary Aspects of Jupiter

The aspects between the slower-moving planets will be within orb for a long time, and so have less individual influence. The conjunction and opposition between Jupiter and Saturn recur every 21 years; between Jupiter and Uranus every 14 years; between Jupiter and Neptune about every 30 years; and between Jupiter and Pluto about every 12 years.

Jupiter in Favorable Aspect to Saturn

A fortunate aspect for those affairs, occupations, and pursuits ruled by these planets and for things ruled by the houses and signs that they occupy, especially Jupiter.

Good mental ability, capacity for deep or collegiate learnings, strength of character and power to overcome obstacles; serious, profound, philosophical, or scientific; succeeds in favor of elders and those of good position generally. Power of review, appraisal, comparison, concentration, synthesis, and arbitration. This aspect strengthens the credit and reputation; gives justice, contemplation, meditation, and practical benevolence; indicates sincerity, honor, esteem, honesty, thrift, and general prosperity.

Practical financial and executive ability; good judgment. Gain through father, friends, long journeys, investment, religion, science, publications, societies, companies, associations, and political offices; also through religious, medical, or scientific institutions. If the planets are in angles or cardinal signs, he acquits himself worthily wherever located and his work is of a beneficent and public nature.

Favorable for money and possessions, gain through the father and by legacy if the Fourth and Eighth Houses are unafflicted. If in fixed signs, they endow power for conducting affairs of great weight and importance.

The trine and sextile are better than the conjunction.

Jupiter in Unfavorable Aspect to Saturn

Losses through litigation, trustees, banks, etc. An unfortunate aspect for financial success in business or occupation; threatens trouble, pecuniary or otherwise, through the father, neighbors, companies; downfall or setback by loss of money, property, and credit; through miscalculation, poor judgment, or speculations; trouble in connection with education and travel. Impressionable, indecisive, and mistrustful; insufficient hope, confidence, and self-will; inclined to give in to circumstances and environments too readily; possibly through ill health. Danger of opposition, limitations, enmity, and treachery; subject to charity, or imprisonment. Difficulty through or on account of dishonesty and misrepresentation; danger through floods, earthquakes, epidemics.

Jupiter in Favorable Aspect to Uranus

A fortunate aspect for the things indicated by the two planets and especially in connection with the sign and house occupied by Jupiter.

It denotes a broad scope of mind and originality of thought, with interesting, surprising, or unique logic and manner of reasoning. It is an indication of benefit through legacy and general success; gain through Uranus occupations or studies, fraternal societies, foreign travel, means of communication, transportation, and learning, law, higher science, philosophy, publishing, religious or educational movements, research, exploration, invention, speculation, political office, or government.

The nature is just, refined, sociable, humanitarian, and progressive; intuitive, prophetic, and usually correct in foresight.

Jupiter in Unfavorable Aspect to Uranus

The tendencies are the same as the above, but attended by unexpected difficulties, obstacles, and limitations.

Loss through impulse, unwise judgment, and imprudent action, risky ventures, unpremeditated acts.

Through unfortunate decisions, changes, and events, the subject is hindered and delayed, or denied the achievement of his highest ambitions.

Troubles and losses by litigation; annoyance and difficulty over inheritance or property.

It threatens sudden, unexpected, and heavy losses by acts of nature, through friends, governmental or legal decrees, misinformation, wrong advice, misjudgment.

Jupiter in Favorable Aspect to Neptune

Improves the artistic and poetic qualities; refines the imagination and strengthens the social, philanthropic, and emotional side of the nature. Denotes honor, benevolence, courtesy, candor, and sympathy. Favors traveling, psychic experiences, remarkable dreams and visions. The subject is inspirational and given to the investigation of psychism from a religious or scientific standpoint. Becomes popular and successful in secret or mystical societies. Beneficial for matters relating to the sea, hospitals, sanitariums, clubs, or pleasure resorts.

Jupiter in Unfavorable Aspect to Neptune

Difficulties and troubles through the aforementioned affairs and things indicated by the house occupied by Neptune.

Losses through speculation, fraud, and treachery; secret sorrows. Peculiar religious benefits, emotional disturbances, uncertain health, danger from deceit and dishonesty, trouble through water, liquids, drugs, oils, chemicals, or beverages. Danger at sea or pleasure resorts.

Jupiter in Favorable Aspect to Pluto

The person is optimistic, always able to see the positive side of things. This makes him a natural leader who is generous, cheerful, and caring. He can subtly influence others for their own good, and has the ability to see beyond the superficial and get to the core of things. His wit is light and subtle, and he is always able to make a funny joke to lighten an otherwise tense situation. The native may be spiritually oriented.

In the conjunction, the leadership aspect is heightened and the native often achieves fame and recognition.

Jupiter in Unfavorable Aspect to Pluto

The individual has unrealistic expectations and dissipates a lot of energy on unobtainable or inappropriate goals. His self-opinion fluctuates from overconfidence to inadequacy. Inferiority feelings may be compensated by an overbearing attitude and the tendency to try to force others to conform to his will. He has the power to lead, but without the charm and popularity of the favorable aspects. Dogmatic, destructive.

There will be difficulty or inability to conjoin spiritual insight and training with emotional drives and ambitions. The emotional needs will be expressed contrary to confidence in spiritual realities, while the latter will not be available to assist in difficulties arising from the former.

The Planetary Aspects of Saturn

These aspects are long-lasting and infrequently occurring. The conjunction and opposition between Saturn and Uranus are exact every 43 to 47 years; between Saturn and Neptune about every 35 to 37 years. The aspects between Saturn and Pluto vary according to Pluto's eccentric orbit, and are between 31 and 38 years apart.

Saturn in Favorable Aspect to Uranus

Increases the strength of mind, giving thoughtfulness, seriousness, the ability to plan, control, systematize, and organize, and adds concentration, intuition, perception, penetration. Tends to success in undertakings due to resourcefulness, practical foresight, fixity of purpose, and determination. Inclines to interest in occult affairs and some occult faculty, such as telepathy or mental healing, and success through them. If the aspected planets are well placed, it favors success in investment with or through large enterprises connected with the railroads, steam or electric, or in dealing with aluminum, platinum, lead, coal, and inventions; also through large, solid public institutions. If one or both of the luminaries are in good aspect also, it tends to conserve the vitality and prolong life.

Saturn in Unfavorable Aspect to Uranus

The tendencies and desires are the same as before mentioned, but the subject doesn't have the capacity and ability to direct the forces to the same successful results and meets with general misfortune through things mentioned and indicated by the houses these planets occupy.

This aspect has an injurious effect on the health at some time, weakening the parts of the body denoted by the signs occupied, especially by Saturn, producing a heavy, complicated, and serious sickness, either long-drawn-out or else incurable. Liability to accidents by falls, falling objects, collisions, acts of nature, riots, or uprisings, and disregard for the rights or feelings of others.

Mentally it gives singular, imaginative, eccentric, and peculiar attitudes, sudden temper, impulsive, aggressive acts. Radical or destructive tendencies.

In a very weak or adverse chart, may invert the abilities and become thoroughly bad, treacherous, violent, or the aspect may manifest indolence, idleness, with an improvident nature, satisfied only in catering to the tastes and emotions. Disrespect for laws.

Saturn in Favorable Aspect to Neptune

Gives inspirational ideas, intuition, concentration, clairaudience, depth, and clearness of thought, and favorably affects those feelings that tend toward the mystical, weird, and psychic. Interest in industrial chemistry, oil, refining, mineral waters, refrigeration, preserving, or fishing.

Goodhearted; deep sympathies. Success and benefit through the occult, advanced studies, investigation, and self development; also through serious and elderly people, unusual occupations connected with liquids, oils, or the sea. When well placed, it favors success and benefit through property, investments, shares, stocks, and legacies.

Saturn in Unfavorable Aspect to Neptune

Loss and difficulty through plots, treachery, and failures, improperly timed activities, insufficient action, misinformation, misunderstanding, confusion, or lack of coordination. Distressful psychic conditions. Complicated financial affairs; loss through speculation and difficulty through things indicated by the houses these planets occupy. Weird feelings. Liable to scandal, discredit, disrepute, criticism. Doubtful tastes, improper diet, inadequate health measures and accidents are apt to require hospitalization.

Saturn in Favorable Aspect to Pluto

Serious, hard-working, reliable natives with a capacity for great self-denial and self-discipline. Frugal, moderate, patient.

The conjunction produces a native who is more serious and austere. Periods of despondency.

Saturn in Unfavorable Aspect to Pluto

As with other negative Pluto aspects, indicates jealousy, lust, dominance. The native strives for personal power and may withdraw himself from normal human contacts in order to achieve this aim. Destructive tendencies. Frustrated drives. Dishonesty regarding emotional interactions. Miscalculations of desire.

The Planetary Aspects of Uranus

The aspects between Uranus, Neptune, and Pluto affect a whole generation and are only personally relevant to the native when one of the planets is dignified due to house or sign position, rulership, or by aspects. The conjunction and opposition between Uranus and Neptune occur about every 171 years.

Uranus was conjunct Pluto in Virgo in 1965 to 1966. The previous conjunctions occurred in 1850 to 1851.

Uranus in Favorable Aspect to Neptune

Gives intuitive understanding, unaccountable attractions and aversions, peculiar attraction to psychic centers, curious feelings, impressions, and inspirations.

Liking for journeys, curiosities, exploration, experiments, investigation, secret missions, and adventure.

Interest in occult affairs and mystical or secret societies, metaphysics, mental healing, transcendentalism, and new thought. This aspect indicates interest in unusual subjects, occupations, and experiences. The native will have success in the development of any occult faculty he may possess and will also benefit through these things and through occult people. Inspirational ideas will present themselves and also some marvelous psychic experiences. Favorable for matters relating to the sea, large institutions, and federal affairs.

Uranus in Unfavorable Aspect to Neptune

This is not a very serious affliction; it gives the same quick, keen intuition and faculty for the curious, with attraction for and desire to investigate the mysterious and things occult, but indicates obstacles, difficulties, and danger in following extremes in the foregoing. The person is subject to psychic conditions, consciously or unconsciously, and therefore may be influenced by surroundings and environment to his detriment. Many inexpressible moods and emotions will be felt, such as from trance, ecstasy, and bliss to vague, semihysterical states. Subtle attractions and revulsions. Should exercise great discrimination in choice of friend, confidante, or confrere.

Uranus in Favorable Aspect to Pluto

The native possesses great originality, intuition, and understanding. It favors scientific and metaphysical studies.

The conjunction gives a more rebellious native.

Uranus in Unfavorable Aspect to Pluto

An intellectual approach to the mysterious aspects of life. Original and inventive.

The Planetary Aspects of Neptune

During the twentieth century, Neptune and Pluto have only made one major aspect: the sextile, and this aspect continues well into the twenty-first century. This gives a high spiritual consciousness and sense of justice.

PLANETARY HOUSE RULERS

The planet ruling the sign on a house cusp moderates the expression of that sign according to its placement and aspects. The house placement of the planet, delineated below, gives the environment that the planet expresses itself through. Thus, the house the planet rules will be the avenue of expression for the activities of the house the planet is in.

In former times, delineations such as these were used principally for horary astrology, but if understood and used correctly they may bring to light many points in the birth horoscope that might otherwise remain unnoticed. What follows are suggestions only as to the possible effect of the natural house rulers posited in other houses, regardless of aspects. The influence of aspects to each house ruler should be considered as a qualifying factor.

A planet is considered in a house as soon as it approaches within 8 degrees of the cusp. This is true of all the houses except the Ascendant. When a planet has arrived within 12 degrees of the ascending degree, it is read as though in the First House, more especially if it is in the same sign.

The Ruler of the First House

When Posited in the First House

Bestows power to create conditions and own dignity; power over enemies. Well aspected: a long fortunate life, good health, harmony, triumph over difficulties. Just the contrary if afflicted or combust.

When Posited in the Second House

Much work and time given to the effort to obtain money. Benefit through industrious activity. If weak or afflicted: losses and wants.

When Posited in the Third House

Mental development, voluntary short journeys; association and affairs with brethren or kindred; opportunities delayed. Afflicted: restrictions on education; troublesome relatives, journeys, and writings.

When Posited in the Fourth House

Gain through lands, mines, inheritance, and possessions; home connections and affairs with the father. Success late in life; occult investigations. Afflicted: difficulties through the above and demise in home land.

When Posited in the Fifth House

Delight in pleasure, amusements, sports, speculation, and children, with tendency to success through these. Afflicted: losses through the above, few children and difficulty through them.

When Posited in the Sixth House

A good healer; gain through humanitarianism, food, clothing, employees, and small animals. Afflicted by the luminaries: much sickness and a short life. If afflicted by Mars: a surgical operation on the part of the body ruled by the sign on the cusp. Fondness for pets, small animals, and work.

When Posited in the Seventh House

Partnerships and close association with others; fondness for the opposite sex. Afflicted: tendency to act in opposition to own best interests; loss and trouble with the law, unions, and open enemies. Marital unhappiness.

When Posited in the Eighth House

Concern over affairs of the dead and with money of the partner and the finances of others. Death through irregularity; occult experiences; mediumistic. Afflicted: disappointment over a legacy, trouble in financial matters. The luminaries adverse: tends to shorten the life.

When Posited in the Ninth House

Long journeys, religious or psychic experiences; liking for science, invention, law, philosophy, and all matters connected with the higher mind; prophetic dreams or visions; gain through the partner's relatives. Afflicted: trouble with foreigners and religious, legal, or educational affairs; fruitless and dangerous voyages. Experiences in foreign lands.

When Posited in the Tenth House

Merit, honor, preferment, and success; rises to high social and professional position. Afflicted: incites to displeasure of superiors or those in power; suffers indignities, limitations, and because of rights withheld; liable to slander and dishonor; loss of parents or trouble by them.

When Posited in the Eleventh House

Large circle of friends, assistance to and from them; much pleasure in life; hopes and wishes often attained; gain by success of employer. Afflicted: friends are a detriment; hopes often defeated.

When Posited in the Twelfth House

Fear of imprisonment; secret unhappiness; enmities; native is often the cause of his own undoing; gain and benefit through understanding of the occult. Afflicted: imprisonment or restraint unless in its own sign; secret sorrows, suffering, and misfortune. Well aspected: gain through occult affairs and secret missions. Success in middle life.

The Ruler of the Second House

When Posited in the First House

Money comes readily. Afflicted: obstacles and difficulties through money, which may be hard to accumulate.

When Posited in the Second House

Money through personal ingenuity and industry. Naturally interested in financial affairs. Afflicted: much work for little gain; heavy losses.

When Posited in the Third House

Gain through education, writing, brethren, neighbors, and short journeys. Afflicted: losses through these things.

When Posited in the Fourth House

Estate or benefit through parents; gain through household goods, lands, or mines. Afflicted: loss by investment in property or mines.

When Posited in the Fifth House

Gain by speculation, investment, pleasure, entertainment, young people, and children. Afflicted: loss and trouble by such.

When Posited in the Sixth House

Gain through inferiors, small animals, poultry, etc., or by humanitarianism, hygiene, and services rendered. Fondness for pets and animals. Afflicted: losses through sickness.

When Posited in the Seventh House

Gain by marriage, contracts, business, and dealing with others, especially the opposite sex. Afflicted: trouble in unions and through open enemies, competition, and theft.

When Posited in the Eighth House

Gain by legacy and goods of the dead or through money of the partner. Afflicted: loss of legacy, loss of money through the financial losses of others such as bank failures, etc.

When Posited in the Ninth House

Gain by books, trading at sea, long journeys, philosophy, religion, science, and the partner's kindred. Afflicted: loss through these.

When Posited in the Tenth House

Gain by occupation, profession, merchandising, government, the partner's parents. Afflicted: financial loss through the mother or employer.

When Posited in the Eleventh House

Gain or loss by friends and accidental fortune.

When Posited in the Twelfth House

Gain by affairs of a secret nature, through hospitals, sanitariums, occult investigations, and by large animals.

The Ruler of the Third House

When Posited in the First House

Journeys and removals; concern with affairs of brethren and neighbors, writings, learning, and accomplishments.

When Posited in the Second House

Money through educational affairs, short journeys, writings, music, etc. Afflicted: trouble with kindred over money matters.

When Posited in the Third House

Benefits through learning, accomplishments, writings, short journeys, and brethren.

When Posited in the Fourth House

Traveling and writing in connection with home affairs and property. Afflicted: trouble with brethren over same.

When Posited in the Fifth House

Pleasure journeys; mental pleasures through children, brethren, reading, study, accomplishments, and travel to pleasure resorts.

When Posited in the Sixth House

Sickness or injury through journeys; difficulty through brethren; interest in study and methods of healing or social economy.

When Posited in the Seventh House

Marriage as a result of journeys or writing, or marriage to one's kin. Afflicted: the union will be unfortunate. Danger of robbery while traveling.

When Posited in the Eighth House

Sickness and death of siblings; journeys on account of trouble or false accusations, or trouble on account of death or bequests.

When Posited in the Ninth House

Long journeys; gain through philosophy, publishing, and science; siblings are likely to journey to foreign parts and marry.

When Posited in the Tenth House

Professional or honorable journeys and gain through them; honors or renown through writings or other accomplishments. Journeys with the mother. Afflicted: the native's siblings cause mental anguish.

When Posited in the Eleventh House

Friends through journeys, or vice versa; fortunate conditions through siblings. Correspondence with friends. Hopes and wishes accomplished through progressive studies.

When Posited in the Twelfth House

Great sorrow through siblings; secret suffering; occult learning; seclusion or estrangement from brethren or kindred and difficulty through some of them. Danger of enmities and imprisonment while traveling.

The Ruler of the Fourth House

When Posited in the First House

Fortunate inheritance; gain through land, property, or parentage. Interest in domestic science.

When Posited in the Second House

Gains by deals in land and property and by the estate or condition of the parents.

When Posited in the Third House

Gain through siblings; if afflicted, the father is put to sorrow or difficulty by one of them. May reside and travel with relatives.

When Posited in the Fourth House

Gain in property and through old people or antiquities; assistance of the father. Benefit and profit in the place of birth. Loss through storms, floods.

When Posited in the Fifth House

Gain and pleasure by the father's good fortune; possessions descend to children. May reside near a school, public park, playground, or theatre.

When Posited in the Sixth House

Loss of possessions through sickness, servants, or small animals. Well aspected: gain through sickness, service, etc. May build his own house, etc.

When Posited in the Seventh House

Property by marriage; gain by land and the opposite sex generally. Afflicted: loss of property through marriage or partnerships.

When Posited in the Eighth House

Gain by legacy or estate. Afflicted: death of the father, danger to the mother during pregnancy; loss of property inheritance.

When Posited in the Ninth House

Gain in possessions through science, religion, long journeys, and wife's relatives. Afflicted: loss of foreign property.

When Posited in the Tenth House

Gain in possessions by trade, profession, public, or government work, or by the wise use of the resources of the earth and manipulation of natural resources.

When Posited in the Eleventh House

Hopes come to good conclusions; gain through friends. Many hopes and wishes attained in old age.

When Posited in the Twelfth House

The native's health is considerably affected by the parents taking a long journey; he suffers sorrow through one of them; loss of possessions through treachery. End of life in seclusion or devoted to the study of occult subjects.

The Ruler of the Fifth House

When Posited in the First House

A propensity to pleasure through gaming and children. Many love affairs.

When Posited in the Second House

Gain through investment, pleasure, and children. The native's children gain in possessions that he enjoys. Afflicted: his possessions are diminished by speculation, pleasure, or young people.

When Posited in the Third House

Journeys with or through children or young people. Pleasure through some of the kindred. Liking for travel, sports, drama, and adventure.

When Posited in the Fourth House

Estate or possessions through discovery, gaming, or parents in latter part of life. Well aspected: the native's children profit through gifts from their grandfather. Love of home.

When Posited in the Fifth House

Much pleasure; love affairs and adventures; speculations or investments; prosperous children and pleasure through them.

When Posited in the Sixth House

Sickness among children. Money through careful speculation or by children's earnings. Pleasure in hygienic methods, through pets and hobbies.

When Posited in the Seventh House

Pleasure, close association, or understanding with the partner, but discord with children. Loss by theft. Afflicted: trouble and loss through love affairs.

When Posited in the Eighth House

Suffers through children who may die before the native. Loss through speculations or gaming.

When Posited in the Ninth House

Dutiful children who travel and give pleasure and learning to the native. Offspring become preachers, scientists, or explorers. Pleasure in foreign lands.

When Posited in the Tenth House

Honorable children; renown in speculation, business enterprise, or in the theatrical world. Well aspected: pleasure or honor through wife's father or through own mother.

When Posited in the Eleventh House

Great attachment between the native and his children; friends through them; happy conclusions to hopes and wishes; friends through speculation or pleasure and among legislators, ambassadors, and sportsmen.

When Posited in the Twelfth House

Children cause secret sorrow; speculations cause ruin; pleasure through investigation of things of a mysterious nature. Afflicted: danger of imprisonment through gaining.

The Ruler of the Sixth House

When Posited in the First House

Sickness through irregularity or lax attention to laws of hygiene. Fondness for pets. Afflicted: servants and small animals prove troublesome or unprofitable.

When Posited in the Second House

Losses and limitations financially through sickness, servants, animals. Well aspected: money through service, employees, healing, and small animals.

When Posited in the Third House

Sickness of some of the brethren or kindred; journeys on account of sickness, and vice versa. Interest in studies and methods of healing and industrial economy. Likelihood of mental disturbance when sick.

When Posited in the Fourth House

Sickness of the father through changes and worry; sickness of the native through anxiety and troublesome home or domestic affairs. Trouble through servants in the home.

When Posited in the Fifth House

Enjoyment of health-promoting ideas or activities. Afflicted: illness by overindulgence in pleasure or sports. Concern for children's health.

When Posited in the Sixth House

Some severe illness. Well aspected: usually has good health; success in service and with employees, poultry, medicine, healing, or social service.

When Posited in the Seventh House

Quarrels with servants, employees, or physicians who insinuate themselves into inappropriate relationships to the native. Overly concerned with the health or activities of the partner.

When Posited in the Eighth House

Dangerous illness; death of servants, animals, poultry, etc. Financial rewards for faithful service.

When Posited in the Ninth House

Sickness abroad, at sea, or while traveling; illness of partner's relatives; danger through overstudy. Work in connection with foreign affairs or universities.

When Posited in the Tenth House

Sickness through dishonor; sorrow or affliction on account of the mother or wife's father. Well aspected: honors through service and healing or through municipal or national activities.

When Posited in the Eleventh House

Sickness among friends and family. Hopes depend too much upon acquaintances. Interest in legislative activities, political and social welfare.

When Posited in the Twelfth House

Imprisonment or private enemies through servants, animals, or methods of healing. Sickness or work in some large institution. Work of a secret or mysterious nature. Interest in archaeology or submarine life.

The Ruler of the Seventh House

When Posited in the First House

Public enemies, unions, partnerships, love of opposite sex and benefit through them. Connection with processes of the law.

When Posited in the Second House

Gain by marriage. Afflicted: loss of money through unions; partnerships, contracts, lawsuits, public enemies. Loss through opposite sex; death of partner and public enemies.

When Posited in the Third House

Enmities with some of the brethren or neighbors; marriage with someone of kin or to a neighbor; difficulty through writings or contracts. Legal or religious disputes, trouble on short journeys.

When Posited in the Fourth House

Marriage into a well-established family, possibly with land or accumulated family interests. A happy married life unless afflicted, in which case, a stultifying marriage that limits the expression of the native. When afflicted, litigation over property, or robbery of household goods is also possible.

When Posited in the Fifth House

The native marries one younger than himself and enjoys much pleasure thereby, but has troubles and enmities with children. Loss by speculation or gaming.

When Posited in the Sixth House

The native marries below his station mentally or socially, has a sickly partner and evilly disposed employees. Trouble over small animals.

When Posited in the Seventh House

Success in lawsuits, marriage in good family; a prepossessing partner, but likely one who grows cold or proves untrue or hostile.

When Posited in the Eighth House

Money or property by marriage; death of partner; some inheritance but difficulty over it. Afflicted: loss of money through marriage and partnerships.

When Posited in the Ninth House

Marriage to a foreigner; gain by partner's relatives. Partner journeys to foreign lands. Afflicted: contentions with religious people.

When Posited in the Tenth House

An honorable partner who is beneficial to the professional career. Afflicted: trouble by rivals through some office, honor, or employment. Public disgrace or scandal through a union or enemy.

When Posited in the Eleventh House

Friends become public opponents or enemies. Marriage to a widow or widower with children, but liable to trouble through them.

When Posited in the Twelfth House

Unhappy marriage, secret sorrows, jealousy, vexation, sickness. Partner or opponents cause imprisonment or fear it. Danger of death at the hands of enemies if the ruler of the Eighth House afflicts.

The Ruler of the Eighth House

When Posited in the First House

Legacies and money through affairs and matters connected with the deceased; assists in the accumulation of money and business of others. Afflicted: trouble through the above and through the losses of others.

When Posited in the Second House

Gain in finances by the money of the partner and the money of others. Fortunate in collecting debts. Gain through the deceased. Afflicted: loss and trouble through all such matters.

When Posited in the Third House

Danger of death on short journeys. Unfortunate brethren and death of same. Investigation regarding death and the continuity of life. Psychic and mysterious experiences.

When Posited in the Fourth House

Gain in property through the deceased, probably by the death of parents. The native dies at home unless this planet is in conjunction with the ruler of the Ninth House, then abroad. Afflicted: death of parents, danger through falls and falling buildings, floods, and storms. Trouble over inheritance, land, and property.

When Posited in the Fifth House

Unfortunate children or death of some. Danger through excessive pleasures, speculation, children, and their affairs.

When Posited in the Sixth House

Dangerous sickness. Death of pets, small animals, or servants. Loss of money earned by employment and through those in whose keeping it may be.

When Posited in the Seventh House

A rich partner or one to whom money comes unexpectedly. Affliction: death of partner and public enemies. Danger of death by violence, suicide, accident, or war.

When Posited in the Eighth House

Gain by the dead; a natural death; a comfortably fixed partner. Interest in matters relating to future life. Spiritualistic experiences.

When Posited in the Ninth House

The partner has trouble with relatives over money matters. Death in a distant land. Danger of death by drowning or while on voyages. Well aspected: the native has a positive philosophy toward death, seeing it as an adventure.

When Posited in the Tenth House

Death of the mother and employers. Danger of violent death probably through discharge of government order or through war. Business through matters connected with the dead. Well aspected: rise to high position through an inheritance. Other persons will gain or lose money by him, according to the planet's aspects.

When Posited in the Eleventh House

Death among friends. Well aspected: gain and legacies through friends.

When Posited in the Twelfth House

Difficulty over inheritance. Death of secret or private enemies. Great sorrow, fear, or anxiety concerning death or imprisonment. Death while in an institution. If afflicted by the ruler of the Seventh House, death or imprisonment through enemies.

The Ruler of the Ninth House

When Posited in the First House

Long journeys, learning, wisdom, prudence; fortunate with strangers, foreigners, partner's relatives, and voyages. Interest in science, invention, law, philosophy, or political economy.

When Posited in the Second House

Money gained by foreign merchants or the sea, science, learning, publications, travel, invention, or banking.

When Posited in the Third House

Journeys on account of beliefs and convictions. Learning, accomplishments, and progress through research, travel, investigations, explorations, travel, or writings.

When Posited in the Fourth House

Ecclesiastical or scientific inheritance. Possessions through partner's relatives. Travel on account of family affairs or partner's mother. Journeys home to die.

When Posited in the Fifth House

Liberal or unconventional ideas in regard to union. Free living. Child by strange consort, journey on account of children. Pleasure journeys. Takes pleasure in science, philosophy, voyages, air flights, sports, foreign investments, or speculation.

When Posited in the Sixth House

Sickness through traveling, or vice versa. Study of hygiene, medicine, healing, etc. Difficulty through work in foreign lands or in connection with exporting.

When Posited in the Seventh House

Public enemies through religious, scientific, or seafaring people. Marriage to a stranger of education or refinement whose relatives may be opposed to the native.

When Posited in the Eighth House

Persecution regarding religious, scientific, or educational convictions, also through publications. Gain by long journeys concerning legacies or goods of deceased persons. Death of partner's kindred. Psychic experiences.

When Posited in the Ninth House

Traveling for education, scientific, or religious purposes. Prophetic dreams. Many fine qualities. Splendid possibilities through culture and development.

When Posited in the Tenth House

If a benefic: honor, credit, and esteem through science, literature, or travel. Success in foreign affairs. The reverse if a malefic, unless well aspected.

When Posited in the Eleventh House

Suffering on account of religious or other convictions. Fortunate for making friends on voyages and friends among foreigners and in foreign countries. The native will have acquaintances among travelers, scientists, and legislators. Spiritual benefit will come from friends and organizations.

When Posited in the Twelfth House

Difficulty and sorrow through religion, science, journeys. If a writer or inventor, has a hard time completing his work and getting it to the public. In middle or latter part of life, seeks seclusion for development, occult learning, etc., and takes long journeys for same.

The Ruler of the Tenth House

When Posited in the First House

Preferment and dignities, honors through merit, success through industrious effort, high ambitions, gain through the mother and governmental office.

When Posited in the Second House

Gain in money by industrious work through trade, profession, or government office.

When Posited in the Third House

Respect among kindred and neighbors. Gain in honors and advancement through the partner's relatives. Honors through short journeys, writing, and accomplishments; business trips, governmental commissions.

When Posited in the Fourth House

Gain and honors through parentage, lands, and property, success at close of life. Interest in reclamations, colonization, cooperative movements, horticulture, mining, architecture, or archaeology.

When Posited in the Fifth House

The native's children suffer from sickness, but rise to honors. Gain and honors through speculation, pleasures, young people, sports, or the stage.

When Posited in the Sixth House

Modest worldly position, gain and honors through service, employment, the practice of healing, or army and navy affairs. Good relationship with employees or those in one's care.

When Posited in the Seventh House

Gain through lawsuits and dealing with the public generally. Honors and reputation assisted by honorable marriage and partnerships in responsible concerns.

When Posited in the Eighth House

Gain and honors in handling the estate and money of others, also through lawsuits, legacies, inheritance, insurance, etc., of deceased persons.

When Posited in the Ninth House

Honorable voyages, professional journeys; honors through learning, writing, publishing, research, or philosophy. A religious or intellectual mother with many fine qualities.

When Posited in the Tenth House

Gain and honors through profession, honorary office, or government employ. Success aided by the mother's care, training, and efforts.

When Posited in the Eleventh House

Eminent friends among legislators and those in high governmental or professional positions; an honorable fortune. The native is helpful to his associates and others. Ambitious ideals.

When Posited in the Twelfth House

Loss of office or honor, dignity, etc., through business associates who become secret enemies. Unfortunate environments and conditions. Professional secrets. Difficulty in employment. Limitations relieved by the study of recondite sciences or metaphysics.

The Ruler of the Eleventh House

When Posited in the First House

The native meets with real friends and supporters; can overcome enemies and obstacles through the support of acquaintances. Many hopes are attained; fortunate actions. Afflicted: makes an irritable friend.

When Posited in the Second House

Business and money by means of friends and acquaintances, through legislative interests, or through development of his own creations.

When Posited in the Third House

Friendship among kindred and neighbors; friends through writings and journeys.

When Posited in the Fourth House

Inheritance through friends; fortunate in property. Love for the father. Friends reside in the home.

When Posited in the Fifth House

Much happiness and pleasure in life through children, friends, and beneficial circumstances.

When Posited in the Sixth House

Friends among working people and those in army, navy, or air service; concerned with sickness among friends; faithful servants. Interest in social welfare.

When Posited in the Seventh House

A loving partner with desirable friendships and social connections. Success in lawsuits.

When Posited in the Eighth House

Death of friends; gifts or legacies from friends. An easy demise.

When Posited in the Ninth House

Gain and success through long journeys. Friendships through travel and learning. Friends among educators, ministers, writers, explorers, inventors.

When Posited in the Tenth House

Friendship among those of good position. Gain and honors through those of high standing in social, business, or governmental circles.

When Posited in the Eleventh House

Many friends and beneficial acquaintances; well-defined hopes and wishes; friends among unique, ingenious, original, or radical people.

When Posited in the Twelfth House

Deceitful friends who may cause much suffering. Sorrowful friends. Good friendships among occult people. Pleasure in peaceful, quiet, harmonious, or secluded places.

The Ruler of the Twelfth House

When Posited in the First House

Animosities difficult to overcome; heavy troubles; secret sorrows; limitations; all are lightened, however, by occult studies. Danger of imprisonment or disablement requiring hospitalization.

When Posited in the Second House

Gain through secrecy and the occult, also through large animals, if well aspected. Afflicted: loss of money through enemies and generally unfortunate conditions.

When Posited in the Third House

Disappointment, sorrow, and trouble through friends or neighbors. Troublesome short journeys and writings; occult learning.

When Posited in the Fourth House

Loss or great difficulty through involved property. Trouble through the father or wife's mother. Secret suffering, restrictions, or limitations at the end of life.

When Posited in the Fifth House

Secret sorrows and difficulty through love, speculation, children, or gaming.

When Posited in the Sixth House

Difficulty, trouble, and loss through small animals; trouble through employees. Limitations on account of sickness.

When Posited in the Seventh House

Trouble through deceit and treachery concerning unions, partnerships, contracts, and lawsuits. Sickness, discord, and opposition of partner; trouble through women generally.

When Posited in the Eighth House

An unsatisfactory end, many misfortunes; secret enemies die; troubles over inheritance.

When Posited in the Ninth House

Well aspected: love of seclusion for the purpose of study; monastic life. Great interest in spiritual and occult matters. Afflicted: loss through travel, lonely studies, feeling of separation because of religious ideas, or persecution.

When Posited in the Tenth House

Liability to disgrace, discredit, and persecution from superiors, government, or those in office above the native that is likely to result in a long journey or retirement and seclusion. Governmental employ in the interest of large institutions. Sorrow through the mother or trouble with the partner's parents.

When Posited in the Eleventh House

Unfortunate undertakings; peculiar hopes; great disappointments and obstacles; deceitful friends and losses through advice of acquaintances.

When Posited in the Twelfth House

Occult abilities, powerless enemies, secret investigations, fondness for animals. Limitations, afflictions, and adversities prove to be blessings in disguise by developing inner growth and understanding.

THE PART OF FORTUNE
AND THE MOON'S NODES

The Part of Fortune

The Part of Fortune (⊗) represents worldly success as indicated by the house and sign it occupies in the nativity. It has been said that it is influenced only by conjunctions and its house position, but Llewellyn George observed a number of cases where directional aspects both good and adverse to the Part of Fortune directly affected matters ruled by the house it occupied.

When Posited in the First House

Portends gain and happiness by the native's own industry, especially if Jupiter or Venus are favorably aspected. Saturn or Mars unfavorable to it lessen its benign significance.

When Posited in the Second House

Happiness and gain through property, and profit by employment and business. Protection and promotion through business friendships.

When Posited in the Third House

Profitable journeys; gain through intellectual affairs; also by means of amiable and honest kindred.

When Posited in the Fourth House

Gain through property, treasure, or other hidden things and products of the earth, minerals, metals, etc. Aids any other testimony for gain by inheritance; stable patrimony.

When Posited in the Fifth House

If afflicted, shows much loss and damage to the native through pleasure and speculation; losses in his estate by means of children. If well aspected, gain through fortunate investments and children, young people, and ambassadors. A goodly portion of pleasure in life and prosperity for the offspring.

When Posited in the Sixth House

It denotes happy and prosperous uncles and aunts who may benefit the native. It gives gain in employ and by means of those whom the native may hire, also profit by small animals, and other things ruled by this house.

When Posited in the Seventh House

Inclines to success in dealings with others and in marriage or partnerships: gain through bargains, contracts, and dealings with others; victory over enemies and gain in conquest. Afflicted: produces the contrary.

When Posited in the Eighth House

If unafflicted, signifies gain by inheritance; gain by means of those deceased, also through the use of other people's money. Interest in psychology.

When Posited in the Ninth House

Inclines to long journeys; success pertaining to churches or educational properties and by means of foreigners, invention, or books.

When Posited in the Tenth House

Favorable circumstances and lucky events assist the native to rise to honor in his sphere, also by means of business assets.

When Posited in the Eleventh House

Pleasure and gain through friends in good position, realization of hopes and wishes.

When Posited in the Twelfth House

Afflicted: property losses through the wiles of secret enemies. Unafflicted: gains from unexpected sources. Well aspected: gain from quiet and secret sources; accumulation of possessions develops with age.

The Moon's Nodes

Some writers believe that the Moon's Nodes (☊ = North Node, ☋ = South Node) have no influence in astrology and need not be used. But Llewellyn George observed many cases where the influence of the Nodes was marked. It requires nineteen years, according to its motion of approximately three minutes per day, for the Moon's Node to complete the circle of the twelve signs. It is very interesting to observe the effects of the Node's influence in nativities as they transit to a conjunction with the various planets in the chart. This frequently corresponds with important conditions and circumstances that cannot be accounted for in any other way.

When Posited in the First House

North Node: Inclines to honors, wealth, and favors through religious, educational, or scientific affairs. It adds power to the personality and gives opportunity for self-expression.

South Node: Inclines to tribulations, loss, and scandals; endangers the face and eyes and is one testimony of a short life.

When Posited in the Second House

North Node: Removes want and bestows affluence; fortunate heredity or gain by legacy and gifts; gain by science and learning; increases the possessions.

South Node: Inclines to misfortune in finances, indebtedness, loss and damage to estate; sorrow, fears, and worry concerning money matters.

When Posited in the Third House

North Node: Adds quality to the mentality and is conducive to interest in spiritual or educational matters and gives preferment in such; gains through brethren, neighbors, and journeys, writing or publishing.

South Node: Mental anxiety, trouble with brethren and neighbors; unprofitable journeys.

When Posited in the Fourth House

North Node: Augurs gain by means of property and in somewhat unexpected manners; fortunate in discovery or in findings. Ancestry noble, long-lived, and trustworthy.

South Node: Loss or confusion with land and buildings; waste of patrimony; jeopardizes the esteem and credit; turmoil in the lives of ancestors; family discord.

When Posited in the Fifth House

North Node: Frees the native from many troubles, calamities, and dangers. It is favorable for children who live long and are fortunate. The native gains some public employment or office and is fond of civil recreation, pleasure, and sports.

South Node: Denies children or else portends their destruction suddenly or violently; inclines them to adversity while they live, and makes them cross or disobedient to the native. Excessive or irregular pleasures produce much harm.

When Posited in the Sixth House

North Node: Favors the health and strengthens the body. Faithful and honest employees; gain through service; fortunate by means of the father's kindred and by small animals.

South Node: The native suffers because of various physical afflictions. Is crossed and deceived by servants and suffers loss through small animals. Danger of illness through bites by insects, reptiles, or animals.

When Posited in the Seventh House

North Node: Lessens the number of enemies, increases profit through dealings with others, and portends delight and gain through others whose influence may benefit the native. It is a testimony for a wise and wealthy partner.

South Node: Many oppressors, calumnies raised by enemies or competitors, contention and difficulty with the partner, but it also portends the death or destruction of enemies.

When Posited in the Eighth House

North Node: Promotes health and is conducive to longevity; testimony for gifts and legacies and gain by those deceased.

South Node: Loss of goods through deception; sudden or violent death.

When Posited in the Ninth House

North Node: Improves the mental qualities and gives success in educational, legal, or religious studies; favorable for voyages and foreign affairs; true dreams and prophetic intuition.

South Node: Afflicts the faculty of faith and portends miserable or unfortunate voyages; curious dreams, unreliable premonitions; trouble and danger of imprisonment in foreign lands.

When Posited in the Tenth House

North Node: Native achieves honors, credit, and high position by merit of industry and ability.

South Node: Loss of position through deception, treachery, and adverse public conditions such as sudden depressions, changes, or failures.

When Posited in the Eleventh House

North Node: Meritorious friendships, acquaintances assist in the realization of hopes and wishes.

South Node: Undesirable associations, loss of opportunities and frustration of hopes; wrong advice and false friends.

When Posited in the Twelfth House

North Node: Gain by secret methods or in seclusion; success in occultism.

South Node: Frequently harassed by the machinations of secret enemies; liability to imprisonment or restraint and restrictions unfavorable to health; inclines to self-undoing.

Part Three

ADVANCED TECHNIQUES

THE PROGRESSED CHART

From the location in the Zodiac, the aspects and the positions in the horoscope held by the planets at birth, an influence is exerted throughout the whole life. This fact can easily be discerned by watching the transit of a planet over the place held by one of the planets in the nativity (or over the cusp of a house in a natal chart), although the planet itself has moved away from the original place in the natal chart.

While the birth map may be regarded as permanent because it represents the structure and composition of the body (the physical vehicle and individuality), so may a system of progression be considered valid because it represents the changes taking place in the living being within the limits imposed at birth.

The twelve zodiacal signs rise and set in the twenty-four hours of a day. The planets continually traveling through the Zodiac change their relations to one another and also to the places they held at birth. For instance, if the Sun was posited in 1° of a sign at birth and Jupiter was in 20° of the same sign, the Sun would arrive at that degree held by Jupiter nineteen days after birth.

Note: With regard to the conjunction just used as an example: Jupiter being a benefic and the conjunction a good aspect, the effects would be very favorable. However, if Jupiter had been heavily afflicted at birth, good results would not occur.

The changes among the signs and planets after birth are classed under two heads.

First: The rotation of the earth on its axis apparently causes the signs to move at a rate of approximately 1° every four minutes; so in the course of twenty-four hours, the whole Zodiac of 360° has apparently crossed over the horizon of every point on the earth. In that twenty-four hours, the earth has also moved forward in its orbit 1°. Therefore the sidereal day and standard day are slightly different. Reference to the Sidereal Time column in an ephemeris shows that it advances about four minutes per day in accordance with the earth's daily orbital progress of 1°. This motion causes the Midheaven for any given standard time to move forward 1° per day. Therefore, as in astrological calculations one day equals one year, it is likewise called "one degree (on the Midheaven) per year." The natal chart therefore progresses at the rate of a day for a year and the Midheaven progresses 1° per year.

The Midheaven progresses uniformly at the rate of 1° per day, but this is not true of the other house cusps, due mainly to the inclination of the earth's axis, except at the equator. Therefore, each day counted forward to represent one year of life changes the Midheaven 1° each day. The other cusps change at different rates, as indicated by the Table of Houses.

The original places of the planets in the natal chart are changed by this sign motion, but not their longitudinal places. For instance, if a planet was in conjunction with the cusp of the First House at birth, every four minutes (every year) it would be carried up 1° into the Twelfth House and its distance from the horizon and meridian would change—the planet just mentioned would be exerting a Twelfth House influence and would sooner or later form aspects of sextile, semisquare, semisextile, conjunction, etc., with the degree constituting the Midheaven, or the cusp of the Tenth House, at birth.

Second: The second change that takes place is caused by the actual movement of the planets in the Zodiac. In this way a planet may move away from the location in the Zodiac held at birth and form new aspects to other planets and also aspects to its own original place.

The measure of time for the progressed chart is *one day for each year of life*, i.e., the aspects formed during the first day indicate the events of the first year of life; the second day the second year of life, and so on. The elements taken into account by *direction* are the places of the Sun, the Moon, planets, and house cusps. The Ascendant and Midheaven are of more importance than the other cusps. Any of these points may progress to an aspect with any other or progress to an aspect with its own place in the birth chart.

We use the word "position" for place in the chart and the word "location" for place in the Zodiac.

The word "natal" is used to designate planets or cusps in the birth chart and the term "progressed" for places and conditions in the progressed chart. After the birth, the signs and planets all move away from the places occupied in the birth chart. Because they all move at different rates of speed, they form new aspects at different times, not only to the various places in the birth chart, but also among themselves as they advance. A distinction must therefore be made between any planet or cusp as it exists in the map for birth and the same one as it is placed after having moved away from the place of birth.

Such a directional aspect as the one previously mentioned (☉♂♃) would be registered in this way: progressed Sun conjunct natal Jupiter (p☉♂n♃), meaning that the Sun by its progressed motion had come to a conjunction with the place held by Jupiter in the birth chart.

Progressed Jupiter would also have moved away from its natal place. As the Sun moves faster than Jupiter, it would in a few days (years) catch up to Jupiter and form another conjunction. This second conjunction, due to the progressed motion of both planets, is termed a *progressed mutual aspect* and would be written thus: progressed Sun conjunct progressed Jupiter (p☉♂p♃).

When tabulating aspects in charts, note that the progressed aspects are divided into two general classes:

First, *directions from progressed planets or cusps to natal planets or cusps (progressed aspects to natal).*

Second, *directions from progressed planets or cusps to progressed planets or cusps (progressed mutual aspects).*

Effects of Change of Residence on the Progressed Horoscope

Now and then a student inquires whether it is proper to make the progressed chart from Tables of Houses for the native's present place of abode instead of for the place of birth.

It is not practical to substitute house cusps of the present abode for those of the place of birth, because the further away the native has moved, the larger the number of degrees difference it would make on the house cusps. Making the chart for the longitude of the present residence may change the aspects to house cusps by several months.

Using the natal latitude (that of the birth place) even when the native has moved a significant distance in longitude makes a difference of only a few minutes in the house cusps. Regarding the difference in time between the place of birth and the present residence, the time would be earlier or later according to whether the native had moved east or west of the birth place. This difference of a few hours is of slight importance when one considers that it is a very difficult matter to set a particular day for the operation of a progressed aspect, especially those whose influence lasts a month or more. Aspects such as the progressed Moon conjunct the natal Ascendant (p☽♂nAsc) or the progressed Sun sextile the natal Midheaven (p☉⚹nMc) begin to exert an effect from four to eight weeks prior to the actual completion of the aspect by the Moon or many months by the Sun.

The progressed chart requires the natural progression of the house cusps, just as it does the planets. At the moment of birth, the planets have house positions according to the latitude of the birth place. At the first independent, in-drawn breath of a baby, the prevailing vibrations cast or set the tendencies of the body according to those house positions, as well as by the aspects and the signs occupied by the planets. Those particular house positions of the planets at that time are time markers of when certain conditions will appear in the life of that individual.

Thus, if Saturn is 3° below the ascending degree, its position in relation to the Ascendant denotes that when the Ascendant has advanced 3°, it will be in conjunction with the place of Saturn (pAsc♂n♄). Due to the planetary rays affecting that particular latitude at that birth time, certain forces were timed for manifestation and those times can only be correctly calculated by the use of the original longitude and latitude from which the native received his or her original cast.

Although it is not practical to substitute house cusps of the present abode for those of the place of birth, it may be well to use the cusps made for the present residence as a supplement for investigation, to see whether or not in such a chart the indications to cusps in any way coincide or conflict with the testimonies indicated by house cusps of the original progressed chart latitude (see *The Locality Chart* in part 4). In other words, moving from the original birth place does not change or negate the indications as timed or measured from birth, but a change of residence may create other conditions that tend to accentuate or modify those that are denoted by the original birth place.

TRANSITS

The transit of a planet is its passage by ephemeral motion in any year as shown by the ephemeris. Thus a transiting planet may pass over an important place in either the natal or progressed chart, or form aspects to those points.

Transits are particularly important in two ways:

First: When a transiting planet forms an aspect of a similar nature with a planet it aspected at birth. For instance, if Jupiter were sextile Saturn at birth, the transit of Jupiter to any good aspects with Saturn would be very beneficial, while the effect of an adverse aspect of transiting Jupiter would be almost nil.

Second: When a transiting planet comes into aspect with progressed planets that are forming an aspect, it will set off (precipitate) their influences before the date on which they would act of themselves. In cases where the progressed aspected planets are separating from an aspect, a transiting planet coming into aspect with them may prolong or revive the influence. Such transits afford the means of predicting events very precisely, sometimes to the very day, by noting the date when the transit aspect is exact.

Orb of Influence

Note: Transiting aspects must be forming. The orb of a transiting planet is 8°, except the Sun, whose orb is 12°. Most astrologers use much narrower orbs: 1° to 2° for progressions and transits.

Current year means the year in life that the progressed chart represents. In the example chart for September 11, 2001, the progressed chart was desired for the progressed year 2012–2013. The progressed chart was made for September 22, 2001, representing the year September 11, 2012 to September 11, 2013.

Transits of planets as shown in an ephemeris for 2012–2013 are those that would be considered in their relation to planets in the natal and progressed charts.

For instance, suppose that the Moon by its progressed motion is close to forming a conjunction with Pluto in the birth chart, and that Mars by transit during the coming year would square Pluto's natal and progressed place. It would then excite into action the natal opposition between Saturn and Pluto, whereas without such excitement the Pluto opposition to Saturn by progression would not occur until the year 2079. Note that transiting Pluto formed the exact opposition to Saturn in November of 2001, and because Saturn was retrograde, it formed the exact opposition to natal Pluto during the same month.

Therefore, if you find a direction aspect forming, look carefully through the current year ephemeris and see when the Sun or any of the planets (the major planets, especially) will cross over the critical points (or form aspects thereto), and thus learn the date when the effects will be felt.

The Sun, Moon, Mars, Jupiter, Saturn, Uranus, and Pluto, in particular, passing in aspect by direction or transit to the places of the planets at birth, or passing their own natal places, or passing the progressed places of the planets, are very important and bring about events, especially if the planets were in an aspect of similar quality at birth. Mercury, Venus, and Neptune are also important, but to a lesser extent.

Transits over natal planets or forming aspects with them are very effective, and likewise so in the progressed chart.

A directional aspect does not manifest continually throughout the year. Its influence may be accelerated or diminished according to the transits. This action of transits (exciting the progressed aspects) provides material for very interesting study. The student will soon learn that transits are a valuable feature connected with the progressed horoscope indications. The examination of transits should never be neglected. It is not a difficult matter to understand, and the student is urged to study this matter carefully because of its importance.

Lunar Transits

The Moon completes a transit through the circle of twelve signs in one month. In the course of its transit, the Moon forms every possible aspect to all planets and cusps in the natal and progressed charts. It is interesting and valuable to note its place in the current ephemeris each day, and from its given place to see what aspects it forms for that day in the natal and progressed charts. It is sometimes amazing to see how events, conditions, or moods correspond to the aspects formed. Take note of the house in the chart occupied by the transiting Moon from day to day, as the house positions largely determine what things will be affected by the aspects.

Effects of Transits

There is little difference between the effect of a transit and the same aspect by direction, the difference being rather in the time of duration than difference in influence. Because aspects by direction last longer than those by transit, the latter may seem different.

For example, Saturn conjunct the cusp of the Sixth House *by direction* might last for over a year. During this time, unless offset by other testimonies, the aspect would likely produce physical disability, obstructions, limitations, and restricted action, which might result in serious illness. In contrast, the *transit* of Saturn over the cusp of the Sixth House or over a planet in the Sixth House might cause a severe cold or an attack of the flu, but comparatively speaking, its effects would soon pass. If the nativity indicated much ill health, the native would likely suffer frequent spells of indisposition during the whole period of Saturn's passage through the Sixth House, which is the house of sickness, and the person would feel especially indisposed on the days when the Moon (as shown in the current ephemeris) passed through this house and over Saturn therein.

In a *progressed chart,* the effect of a transit over the degree of the Midheaven or Ascendant, or conjunct any planet, is more effective than an aspect thereto.

In a *natal chart,* transits by either conjunction or aspect are noticeable, the major aspects more particularly than the minor aspects.

To study the effect of transits, learn the effect of aspects by direction, but modify the delineations because of the shorter duration, and never predict something from a transit that is not promised by some configuration at birth. If a person has a good horoscope for health, finance, or marriage, there is no use predicting trouble because of a malefic transiting the First, Second, or Seventh House, because nothing more than slight annoyances are likely to occur.

Declinations

When looking up transits, the declinations of the transitor should not be overlooked, for when it compares with the declination of any planet or cusp in the horoscope, it constitutes a parallel and has an effect like a conjunction.

Duration of Influence

The duration of the effects of transits depends upon two things:

First: Note which planet is doing the transiting, for each planet moves through the Zodiac at its own rate of motion, the Moon being the swiftest and Pluto the slowest (see the table that follows).

Second: Does the transitor turn retrograde before it gets out of orb of aspect with the transited? Frequently a transiting planet reaches a certain point, and then turns retrograde and crosses over that point again; then it turns direct in motion and crosses that point for the third time, thus affecting that place or planet much longer than usual. Look in the current ephemeris and count how many days it requires the transitor in question to traverse 8° preceding the exact aspect. After the aspect is complete, the effect quickly diminishes, unless the transitor becomes retrograde and goes back over the aspect.

The Moon transits the twelve signs in 27 days, 7 hours, 43 minutes.

The Sun transits the twelve signs in approximately 1 year.

Mercury transits the twelve signs in approximately 1 year.

Venus transits the twelve signs in approximately 1 year.

Mars transits the twelve signs in approximately 22 months.

Jupiter transits the twelve signs in approximately 12 years.

Saturn transits the twelve signs in approximately 29½ years.

Uranus transits the twelve signs in approximately 84 years.

Neptune transits the twelve signs in approximately 165 years.

Pluto transits the twelve signs in approximately 248 years.

Table 7: Geocentric Period of Planetary Transits

It takes Neptune several years to form and complete an aspect, while Venus or Mercury would cover the same amount of longitude in a few days. During a period of good direction, the potency of good transits is enhanced and the adverse transits are diminished in influence.

Tabulating Aspects

Look in a current ephemeris and take note of the various planetary positions, then compare their ephemeral places with natal planets to see if any aspects are formed. Note the date in the ephemeris when the transiting planet begins the aspect (allowing an orb of 8° applying, 12° for the Sun) and the date when the aspect is complete (exact). This will show the length of the period of influence.

In every month, the transits of *Neptune, Uranus, Saturn, Jupiter,* and *Mars* should be noted to see if any of them cross over the planets in the natal chart, or form major aspects to some planets in the progressed chart that are themselves in aspect. In that case, the transit sets the progressed aspect into activity during the period of the transit. But generally speaking, the transits through the natal chart are the most important.

The transit of the *Sun* through the natal chart is important. The good and adverse aspects that it forms to natal planets indicate the favorable and unfavorable solar periods in each year. The Sun moves forward about 1 degree each day, hence, it is twelve days applying to an aspect. Do not seriously consider the minor aspects.

The transits of *Mercury* and *Venus* are not very important unless they are ruling planets. They concern the minor details of life, when considered as transits, yet in the lives of people who are concerned mostly with ordinary matters, these two planets are quite important. In the lives of those who are concerned with larger things, business and public affairs, the larger planets are more important.

The transits of the native's *ruling planets* (one ruling the birth month and the one that rules the ascending sign at birth) are very important. The aspects formed by rulers in transit that coincide with aspects they held at birth are very powerful compared with other aspects they may form. For instance, if Mars is a ruling planet and was in opposition to Jupiter at birth, then the adverse transits of Mars to natal Jupiter would be very strong, while its good aspects to Jupiter would bring little benefit.

Transits to the *Part of Fortune* and the *Moon's Nodes* should also be observed, especially the conjunction.

An Easy Way to Find Transits: From the birth chart, make a table for permanent use, showing for each planet the degree of the Zodiac that is in exact opposition, conjunction, sextile, square, and trine. Then look in a current ephemeris and note when any planet will pass through the degrees you have recorded. In that way you will know the dates on which your natal chart will be affected by transiting planets and will thus be enabled to prepare yourself, according to whether the aspect formed is good or adverse.

Those who wish to be very exact can amplify their table, or aspect reference sheet, by also finding the points of minor aspects. It is then useful to watch how aspects from planets in the progressed chart affect the points of aspect in the natal chart. Once the table is made, it is good for all time.

Transits in Relation to the Natal Chart

The influence of transits should be judged according to their natal indications; i.e., if a planet is in adverse aspect to another at birth, its adverse aspects to that planet by transit are of more significance than its good aspects. In other words, its adverse aspects being in accord with the original indication would stir up corresponding conditions. Its good aspects, being contrary to the original indications, would not have the power to produce any particular or noticeable advantages.

Aspects by transit that coincide with the original indication will act directly upon the native and in his affairs. Aspects that do not coincide will act indirectly, not upon the native and his own affairs, but more upon other people whom he is contacting during such transits. All aspects operate in some manner, but whether directly on the native or on others around him depends upon the original indications between the two planets in question.

If the planets are in adverse aspect at birth, a good aspect by transit is not likely to bring the native any particular benefit, but he will see others benefiting in a manner coinciding with the nature of this aspect as related to its transiting house and sign.

Example: If the aspecting planet is transiting the Seventh House in the sign of Scorpio, forming a *good* aspect to the natal Moon with which it was in *adverse* aspect at birth, it might benefit his partner or his wife. If he happened to be engaged in a lawsuit at that time, it would benefit the opponent. If the Moon at birth ruled the Third House and was posited in the Eleventh House, then that good transit would also benefit his brothers, sisters, neighbors, and friends.

On the other hand, if that good transit concerned planets that had been in *good* aspect at birth, then the native would benefit directly through the matters and people just mentioned and he might also be in a position to help them.

Lunations

The New Moon (lunation) is commonly used in mundane astrology to determine the trend of world or large-scale events. It has been found that the positions and aspects of the planets at this time indicate general trends on a global level.

Does the monthly New Moon affect individuals?

Some New Moons (lunations) are very important, depending upon whether or not the luminaries at their conjunction form any important aspects to planets in the individual's natal chart. When the lunation occurs in a favorable place in the horoscope and in good aspect to some of the natal planets, it betokens that the month, summed up in a general way, will be fortunate. This is especially true if no strongly malignant aspects testify otherwise, but even then such a lunation will tend to mitigate the evil. The contrary is to be judged when the lunation occurs in adverse aspect to planets in the natal chart, the evil being magnified should the lunation be an eclipse. The New Moon may be applied to the progressed horoscope in like manner.

The results of a lunation (good or adverse) are determined by the combined influences of the house in which it occurs, the houses occupied by planets aspected by the lunation, and the houses these planets rule.

As the lunation, or New Moon, is also a transit, the sign and degree of its occurrence each month in the Zodiac should be correlated to both the natal and progressed charts.

Favorable Days

Favorable and unfavorable days are indicated by the dates when the Moon (as shown by its place in the current ephemeris) crosses over or aspects important places in the natal chart. This is the main technique used in Sun sign astrology.

The Moon's aspects are the most important factor of all in determining the daily events in one's life. Observant students will soon learn how to apply these to their own horoscope, as the lunar transits are all of monthly occurrence.

Look in the ephemeris at the Moon's longitude on the first and second day of the month. Find that place in your own natal chart, and then note what aspects it will form to your natal planets during the day, considering the distance it moves during the day. The Moon's position may be listed in the ephemeris for both its midnight and noon positions. On average, the Moon moves about 1 degree every two hours. Keep in mind that the ephemeris time is Greenwich time, and make the necessary correction for your location. For example, if the Moon in the ephemeris is at 24♊36 at midnight, and you are in Chicago, then the Moon's ephemeris position for the Moon is actually 6:00 P.M. of the previous day, and that is the time from which to calculate aspects.

Aspects Formed by the Moon's Transit

The good transits of the Moon will be more powerful in the months when there is a favorable transit of some other planet operating at the same time or during a period of a favorable lunation.

The Moon's favorable transit will be much weaker in the months when the Moon is adversely aspected by its progressed position. The Moon's good monthly transit aspect to a planet will avail little if in the same month the progressed Moon is adversely afflicting that particular planet, and especially so if the previous lunation occurred unfavorably in the horoscope.

The Moon's Transit Through the Houses

The advantage of knowing the Moon's place and aspects as connected with your natal chart, lies in the fact that it has much dominion over general daily affairs. Its influence is important because it goes entirely around your chart each month, through each house, and forms every aspect to all the planets. Look in the current ephemeris and note its place, then find that place in your chart. When you see the Moon forming an aspect, judge its effect, and decide in advance what course of action is in keeping with the indications.

The house through which the Moon is transiting in the natal chart is important, as it helps color the aspect with the nature of things ruled by that house. See *The Transiting Moon Through the Houses* in part 3.

It is presumed that you are thoroughly familiar with the characteristics of the zodiacal signs and the influences of the planets, as well as the things signified by the houses. This knowledge should enable you to interpret correctly the influence of the aspects formed by the daily transits of the Moon in your natal chart. In this matter, it should be remembered that you are to use the current ephemeris and not the birth or progressed year ephemeris.

If you will make it a point to note the Moon's daily positions and aspects in your natal chart day by day, regularly for a few months, you will soon learn what to expect of each aspect as it occurs. This will be found of inestimable value in helping to determine the best course of action, especially on days when important business matters should be transacted.

Solar Periods

As the Sun in its apparent daily motion transits through the Zodiac, it moves away from the place it held on your birthday, passing through one sign each month and at the end of a year returning to the place of your birthday.

In the sixth months from your birthday, the Sun comes into opposition of your zodiacal sign of birth and its own place in your natal chart, and tends to produce a trying time generally. This is not a good time to make any important moves or ask for favors. In the third and ninth months, it forms a square to your sign, which is also an unfavorable period.

Your Adverse Solar Periods Each Year

From 78 to 95 days after your birthday.

From 168 to 185 days after your birthday.

From 258 to 275 days after your birthday.

Your Good Solar Periods Each Year

From 48 to 65 days after your birthday.

From 108 to 125 days after your birthday.

From 228 to 245 days after your birthday.

From 288 to 305 days after your birthday.

Table 8: Good and Adverse Solar Periods

During the four good periods, aim to extend your interests and advance your business. Your good days in these good periods are apt to be more favorable than at other times, while your adverse days are usually less severe. Likewise, your adverse days during your adverse solar periods are apt to be more so than usual, while the good days are less favorable.

Eclipses

Are eclipses effective only in natal charts, or do they also affect the progressed chart? Eclipses affect most the chart in which they form the strongest aspects. Generally speaking, the natal chart is more responsive to New Moons, eclipses, and transits than the progressed horoscope. For instance, if an eclipse occurred in such a sign and degree that it formed no aspects in either the natal or progressed chart, its influence would be felt through its house position in the natal chart more than by its house position in the progressed horoscope.

A New Moon, eclipse, or transit may cause an aspect forming in the progressed chart to be set off prematurely if they come into a like aspect with that formed by the planets. However, there is really nothing premature in nature. If the eclipse, New Moon, or transiting planet should form an aspect contrary to a progressed aspect in the process of forming, it would tend to retard the latter or modify its influence during the time the transit, New Moon, or eclipse would be effectively in operation.

Retrograde Planets

The term *retrograde* is somewhat misleading as no planet is actually retrograde. It is an appearance due mainly to the position of the planet in orbit and its relation to the earth. It might be briefly defined as follows:

Retrograde: A backward motion that the planets appear to have due to the relation of the planets to the earth in their various positions in the Zodiac.

Influence of retrogradation: The planet's influence does not change when retrograde, but the individual's response to the particular influence of that planet is different; the channel for expression of its special qualities or characteristics is not quite as good when retrograde as when direct in motion.

In the ephemeris, where the planets' positions are recorded daily by zodiacal sign and degree, when a planet appears to begin to move backward in the order of the signs, it is usually denoted by the symbol ℞. When it apparently turns direct in motion, it is usually indicated by "D." A planet is said to be stationary when appearing to be neither moving direct nor retrograde. While the longitude is increasing between one day and the next, you may know such a planet is direct in motion. When the longitude decreases between one day and the next, the planet is retrograde.

- Saturn is retrograde for 140 days and is stationary for approximately five days before and after retrogradation.
- Jupiter is retrograde for 120 days and is stationary for approximately five days before and after.
- Mars is retrograde for 80 days and is stationary for two or three days before and after.
- Venus is retrograde for 42 days and is stationary for approximately two days before and after.
- Mercury is retrograde for 24 days and is stationary for approximately one day before and after.
- The Sun and Moon are never retrograde or stationary.

We believe that the influence of benefic planets is weakened when they are retrograde. The condition of retrogradation is contrary or inharmonious to the regular direction of actual movement in the Zodiac; hence, when malefic planets are retrograde, their malefic is increased. Aspects to a retrograde planet fall short of their promise, and should both planets be retrograde, the things indicated by the aspect would be deficient or disappointing, hence retrogradation is considered a debility.

The Difference Between Retrograde and Direct Motion

In astronomical circles, much has been said concerning the phenomenon known as the *red shift*. It is concerned with the effects of motion on light, specifically the shift toward red found in the spectrums of light originating from bodies moving away from our vantage point at incredible speeds. The consistency of the phenomenon provides a method for measuring those speeds. It is reasonable, therefore, to assume that the same natural laws apply to planets as well as stars.

When Venus is receding from the earth, lines are displaced toward the red end of the spectrum. When Venus is moving toward earth, lines are toward the violet end of the spectrum. This fact clearly shows that there is a difference in the direction of the vibrations from planets that retrograde and from those that are direct.

This discovery in astronomy has been known for ages in astrology, which has always taught that there is a difference in the influence of a planet, determined by whether it is direct or retrograde in motion.

Note that lines in a spectrum are displaced toward the red end (Mars) of the spectrum when Venus is receding, which corresponds to a weakening of its beneficent powers when retrograde, as Mars is the antithesis of Venus. When Venus is direct, we note that lines are displaced toward the violet end of the spectrum. Violet is a color that harmonizes with the nature of Venus. When a planet is direct, the power of its own inherent nature is normal; when retrograde, the influence is subnormal among the benefics and abnormal among the malefics.

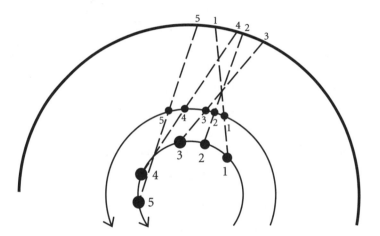

Figure 4: Retrograde Motion

Of course, the planets are never actually retrograde or stationary. Such apparent positions are phenomena caused by the relative positions of the earth and the planets.

EXAMPLE OF THE PROGRESSED HOROSCOPE

The progressed horoscope is a chart made for any year after birth, in which one may see what conditions are to affect the native during those twelve months according to the aspects that will come into operation.

Each day after the birthday is equal to one year. In the ephemeris, begin with the day after the birthday and count forward as many days (equal to the same number of years) to the year desired for the progressed horoscope. Having arrived at the desired date, make a chart as though you were born on this day, using the same birth time and birth place.

When the planets are properly inserted in the chart, you are ready to figure the aspects between the planets, but remember that in a progressed horoscope we consider only the aspects that are applying or forming and allow an orb of only 2°. This is because planets in their motion by direction require a year or more to move 1°, according to their rate of motion, with the exception of the Moon, which moves forward about 1° per month.

The influences in a progressed chart are discerned principally from aspects. If the aspects are all good, the native will have a very successful year, and vice versa. A planet crossing over the cusp of a house portends conditions according to the nature of the planet and the things ruled by the house.

The Moon, on account of its swifter motion, requires more consideration than the other planets. During a progressed year, it will move forward 12° to 15° and is therefore likely to form several aspects.

After noting the degrees through which the Moon will travel by progression during each month, refer to the natal chart to see if the progressing Moon will form any aspects to birth planets during the twelve-month period. When an aspect is formed, mark it beside the month and day in which it falls due, as before noted. The Moon by its direction or progressed motion produces effects whenever it comes to aspects of planets in either the natal or progressed chart. As this is true of all the planets by progression, we must look from each one in the progressed to each one in the progressed and note any aspects that may be formed between them, as well as the aspects they may form to natal planets. Remember to record only those aspects that are forming within 2°.

The effect of an aspect is the same whether it is formed in the natal chart or in the progressed chart. The nature of the influence is determined by the nature of the aspect—whether good or adverse. The conditions and events produced are indicated by the houses and signs occupied by the aspecting planets as well as by the houses they rule.

The declinations of planets in the progressed chart should be compared with the declinations of planets in the natal chart. When two planets have the same degree of declination, they are parallel, the effect of a parallel being the same as the effect of a conjunction. Parallels sometimes have an effect for more than a year and often tend to modify or accentuate the influence of other aspects, especially of the progressed Moon. For a detailed discussion, see *Parallels of Declination* in the aspects chapter in part 1.

After all the aspects have been calculated as directed, it is helpful to summarize their effects briefly, especially those of the Moon, from month to month, being careful to modify or accentuate its influence according to the presence or absence of parallels or aspects between the major planets, among which those of the Sun are most important. Be very careful not to predict anything that is not promised by some testimony in the natal chart. For instance, if the progressed Moon is coming to a conjunction with natal Venus, do not predict marriage if the natal chart denies marriage.

When the progressed chart has been erected, look in an ephemeris for the calendar year that the progressed chart represents and, tracing the movement (transit) of the major planets month by month, make note if they come into conjunction with any of the progressed chart planets. Tabulate the date when any conjunctions occur and look up the meaning in your textbook. Also note if any transiting planet forms a major aspect to any of the progressed chart planets, and tabulate the date when such an aspect occurs.

All the applications of transiting planets (in the current year ephemeris just mentioned) should also be made to the natal chart. When making these tabulations, record them in two lists headed *Transits to the Natal Chart* and *Transits to the Progressed Chart.*

As the effects of transiting planets are important, although they are not in operation as long as progressed directional aspects, it would be worthwhile to trace and record systematically the transits of the major planets, the Sun, Mars, Jupiter, Saturn, Uranus, Neptune, and Pluto.

Example Chart

On the next few pages is an example of the delineation of a progressed chart for John Lennon. This example is for February 15, 1964, when the Beatles appeared on the *Ed Sullivan Show* in Miami, Florida.

The aspects for this illustration are progressed aspects just before and just after the date of the performance.

You will note that two of the aspects are out of order in terms of the dates. This is because progressed Mercury and Midheaven move more slowly than the progressed Moon. Remember that progressions represent the movement of the planets, allowing one day's transits to represent one year in the life. Progressed Mercury is the slowest-moving planet being considered. Mercury turned retrograde a little over one year before the date under consideration, and was moving very slowly. Progressed Mercury first connected with the natal Moon in May of 1962 when it (Mercury) was direct in motion. It retrograded back to the Moon in September of 1964. Because Mercury moves so slowly when it changes direction, Lennon's progressed Mercury would not have gone forward to sextile the Moon again until August 14, 2000. Interestingly, the John Lennon Museum, a major monument to his memory in Saitama, Japan, opened on his birth date in the year 2000.

September 1, 1964—Progressed Mercury Sextile Natal Moon

When a progressed planet aspects a planet and then retrogrades to make the same aspect again, some central focus in the life is repeated or reemphasized. Because the Moon in this birth chart is the planet associated closely with the Cancer Midheaven, and the Moon is directly opposite the Midheaven, the Mercury sextile brought a career opportunity in May of 1962. The Beatles first single was released within weeks of this date.

Progressed Mercury turned retrograde and came back to sextile Lennon's Moon exactly on September 1, 1964. Keep in mind that Mercury was moving very slowly. It was within 1 degree of the sextile for about six years. During this period, the Beatles experienced incredible worldwide success. Their careers (Moon) were all about getting a message (Mercury) out to the world about peace.

February 27, 1964—Progressed Midheaven Sextile Natal Ascendant

The Midheaven and Ascendant are not planets. They are highly sensitive points in the birth chart, and as they move forward, they aspect one another several times during the life. The sextile represented an opportunity for John Lennon to gain greater understanding of himself. He was able to look at his own ego and its place within his personality. He perceived that his higher self was an integral part of his life and his career. He was able to direct his personality favorably at this time.

Because the Midheaven and Ascendant are not planets, they tend to take on the tone of planetary aspects. Now we turn to the aspects of the progressed Moon around the time the Beatles first came to the United States.

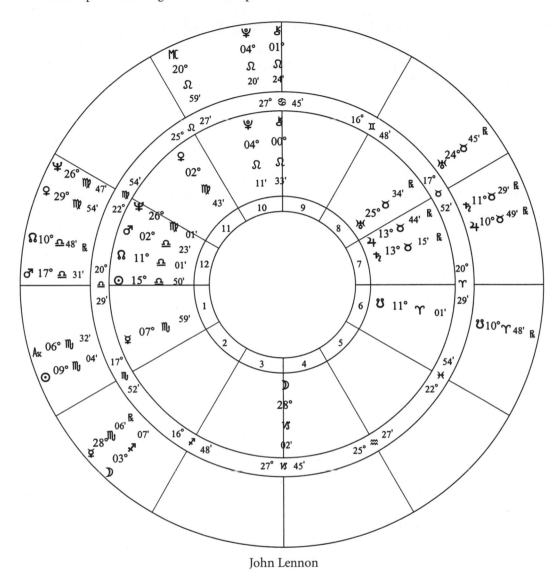

John Lennon

Inner Wheel: Natal Chart
October 9, 1940 / Liverpool, England / 7:00 A.M. Standard Time
Koch Houses

Outer Wheel: Progressed Chart for February 15, 1964
at 12:00 A.M. GMT
Koch Housess

Figure 5: The Progressed Chart

October 5, 1963—Progressed Moon Trine Natal Midheaven

Conditions were right for Lennon's inner beliefs to become part of his expression in his career. His inner experience came through in his music. He was developing an appreciation of his spiritual values, and they became an increasingly important part of his music.

October 12, 1963—Progressed Moon Sextile Natal Moon

When a planet progresses to an aspect of its own birthplace, the tendency is to excite or set into motion its indications in the birth chart, according to the nature of the aspect, whether good or adverse. The sextile brings many opportunities to fulfill the birth promise of the planet involved. In his birth chart, Lennon has the Moon in the Fourth House, making the following aspects:

- *Moon Opposite the Midheaven*   Awareness of the significance of one's soul; changing objectives in life, or becoming aware of significant objectives.
- *Moon Opposite Pluto*—Strongly emotional life with extremes of feeling, expressed in the direction of career because Pluto is in the Tenth House of the birth chart.
- *Moon Trine Mars*—Excitable and impulsive, with an intense expression of emotions. Potential for quarrels or intolerance.
- *Moon Trine Uranus*—Strong emotional tension and subconscious undercurrents. Potential attainment of sudden success. May experience large changes in personal circumstances.
- *Moon Trine Neptune*—Deeply sensitive to one's inner vision, and also to the emotions of others. Loves solitude.
- *Moon Biquintile Venus*—Inner creative potential that depends on the capacity to see into the self and then express one's feelings. Harmonious love relationships. Skill in understanding the true value of things.

Just this list of the Moon's aspects in the birth chart portrays the immense potential for career success that John Lennon experienced. All this potential is activated by the progressed Moon sextile birth Moon.

January 27, 1964—Progressed Moon Sextile Mars

Opportunities surrounded John Lennon at this time. He could grasp them impulsively (Mars), and tremendous emotion was a component of his daily life (Moon). It is as if he married into the Beatles group, for better or worse. There could have been significant disagreements expressed openly and sincerely.

February 4, 1964—Progressed Moon Square Venus

There was a strong desire to express feelings of love around this time. Artistic efforts made for harmonious connections, although there may have been some moodiness. Artistic talent was growing. There was feminine energy around him as well. The social processes were in full motion.

March 15, 1964—Progressed Venus Enters Libra

Venus had been in Virgo, indicating attention to practical considerations over those of the heart. There had been a strong focus on moral sensitivities. As Venus entered Libra, the focus shifted to a cheerful, obliging manner that attracted people to him. There is a primary focus on the artistic side. There was potential to be spread too thin between career and romantic relationships.

March 12, 1964—Progressed Moon Trine Pluto

Intense emotions pervaded Lennon's life at this time. The power was channeled in specific directions, and life may have become rather one-sided. Career goals were pursued (and achieved) without much concern for others. This period undoubtedly strained his marriage because of the intensity of desire to succeed. There was the potential to become self-absorbed. He was probably torn between his emotional sentiments and his career drive.

Transits

Once you have examined the birth chart and the progressed aspects in force during a period of time, you will want to turn your attention to the transits, as they often indicate the precise timing of events. On February 15, 1964, John Lennon had aspects from every transiting planet to his birth and progressed planets! Most notably, Pluto formed a quincunx to his Jupiter-Saturn conjunction, indicating a profound adjustment in his partnerships and in business matters. Transiting Uranus formed a sextile to Mercury, indicating again the opportunity to make something happen for himself and the group. Jupiter opposed his progressed Mars, indicating potential awareness (opposition) of the expansive (Jupiter) possibilities for action (Mars).

Summary

The majority of progressed aspects during this period were sextiles, with one square and two trines. Both sextiles and trines require some personal effort to manifest their highest potential. John Lennon and the group must have been working very hard at this time to perfect their sound and their image. Without this intense effort, they would have been good, but might never have achieved greatness.

The interpretations given here indicate that success does not come without its sacrifices. To pursue success, Lennon had to strain his personal relationships and his emotional balance, yet he had immense success and achieved worldwide popularity. The level of success is a measure of the way he was able to grasp the conditions and opportunities presented to him and the Beatles during 1963 and 1964.

INTERPRETING THE
PROGRESSED ASPECTS

The following delineations refer to all progressed aspects, whether formed to planets in the natal chart, in the progressed chart, or between one planet in the natal chart and the other in the progressed chart. The interpretations are general indications only and subject to modification and change according to the strength of the aspect (whether major or minor), the position of the aspected planets in the chart (whether angular, succedent, or cadent), and the strength by dignity or weakness by debility according to the signs occupied.

In reading these aspects, keep this fact constantly in mind that by direction a planet can only bring to bear the influence it indicated in the natal chart, whether good or otherwise, and in proportion to its power by house, sign, aspect, etc., in the natal chart.

Lunar Progressed Aspects

The Moon in Good Aspect to Mercury

Makes the mind active, studious, and creative. Inclines to success in journeys, writings, publishing, law, advertising, or business, and general prosperity; changes and activity with the inclination to read and study.

The Moon Adverse to Mercury

Tends to anxiety, restlessness, nervous disorders, and slander. An adverse period for lawsuits, publishing, letter writing, signing of contracts, journeys, and general business affairs. Friction with kindred or neighbors.

The Moon in Good Aspect to Venus

A happy, peaceful, healthful, prosperous, and fortunate period. The native inclines to the pleasures of Venus, and it is strong testimony for courtship and marriage, especially the parallel or conjunction. It indicates social and domestic pleasures, and the probable birth of a child, if such is indicated in the natal chart.

The Moon Adverse to Venus

Losses, disappointment, bereavement among friends, and sorrow in love and domestic affairs; extravagance, illicit relations, scandal, or quarrels with the opposite sex, excesses according to the sign Venus is in; often indicates the loss of a child. To females, ill health and disappointments in all Venus affairs.

The Moon in Conjunction or Parallel with the Sun

Not good for health, especially in a woman's horoscope, producing an inert, lethargic, indifferent condition, resulting in feverish complaints and ailments similar to an adverse aspect to Mars, a planet that the Sun closely resembles in aspects. Otherwise the mind is free, generous, and open. It brings changes, honor, gain in business, marriage, and public favor for both males and females.

The Moon Trine or in Other Good Aspect to the Sun

Good for both sexes. Produces honors, popularity, promotion, influential friendships, gain through superiors and parents; good health; the mind is dignified, lofty, ambitious; good for speculation, marriage, fame, and business. Success generally, especially in dealings with women and common people, as well as with those in high office.

The Moon Adverse to the Sun

Unfortunate for all affairs of life. Denotes ill health, bereavement, loss of honor, fame, office, business, friends, support of superiors or parents, and a very trying time generally. From water signs, the native may take to drinking, and is inclined to company beneath his own station; from the Twelfth House, danger of imprisonment. With a female, it affects the health particularly.

The Moon in Good Aspect to Mars

Good for business, health, journeys, new enterprises, and success generally. Shows gain through activity in Martian affairs; courage, generosity, a desire for active sports and exercise. Gain by military men, doctors, surgeons, etc., as denoted by Mars. Not so good with females, inclining to the society of the opposite sex; amorous and impulsive courtship and marriage, although good otherwise for activity and new projects.

The Moon Adverse to Mars

Inclines the native to rashness, quarrels, extravagance, recklessness, disputes, and litigation. He suffers discredit, slander, and dishonor. Danger of fevers, smallpox, and other Martian inflammatory disorders.

Liable to wounds, bites, kicks, broken bones, and accidents when traveling. If Mars is strong in the First, Second, or Seventh House, he may lose by theft, fire, or robbery. In fire signs, danger of high fevers, accidents by firearms, hurts by human hands; in earth signs, falls, hurts from animals, bites, etc.; in water signs, scalds, danger of drowning, from drink, or excesses. This is a very critical period for women as it signifies ill health, slander, discredit, attacks, or trouble through moral indiscretions.

The Moon in Good Aspect to Jupiter

An especially good direction for wealth, health, and attachments. Conduces to gain, fame, honor, and success generally; inclines to marriage, social advancement, and voyages. Very good for health, for women. A good period in which to start a new business or make investments.

The Moon Adverse to Jupiter

Bad for business. Trouble through the law or the church. Losses in dealing with landlords, politicians, lawyers, magistrates, or in speculation, through poor judgment and miscalculation. The disposition is free, extravagant, and profligate; the associates impose upon the generosity of the native, causing him to make bad loans and squander his money. It disturbs the health by impurities of the blood, headaches, stomach and liver disorders.

The Moon in Good Aspect to Saturn

Success in business, especially through elderly persons and Saturn things, popularity, new friends. The mind is active, patient, contemplative, serious, dignified, and cares little for society but is attentive to business; deep and profound with good organizing ability. Good for matters relating to land, property, produce, mines. Also beneficial for things indicated by the house occupied by the Moon.

The Moon Adverse to Saturn

Loss of friends, business, money, and danger of failure or bankruptcy, especially if either is posited in or the ruler of the Second or Tenth House. Dishonor, losses, grief, disappointment, and bereavement; morbid, melancholy, anxious state of mind; the health suffers from cold, lingering disorders; aches and pains according to the sign Saturn occupies. Unfavorable for the commencement of anything new. Very bad period for buying, investing, or assuming heavy liabilities.

The Moon in Good Aspect to Uranus

Produces pleasant journeys, advantageous removals and changes that are beneficial though sudden and unexpected, and according to the house in which the Moon is posited. Especially good for the above from the First, Third, and Ninth Houses. It sharpens the mental faculties and makes the mind curious, fanciful, eccentric, inventive, and inclined to the investigation of the occult; to research, exploration, and travel. Brings new friends; correct intuition. The nature is romantic and fond of adventure. It inclines to society of the opposite sex.

The Moon Adverse to Uranus

Causes sudden, unexpected, disastrous changes, journeys, and removals. Brings trouble through women, loss of credit or position, danger of accidents, slander, and disgrace; worry, anxiety, and restlessness. The mind is sarcastic, bitter, obstinate, rebellious, hasty, or irrational, and the actions indiscreet. Happening in the Seventh House, discord in marriage; in the Fifth House, illicit attractions, danger of loss in speculation, sorrow through children.

The Moon in Good Aspect to Neptune

Gain through the mediumistic, inspirational, and artistic faculties; also through schemes, secret alliances, and secret orders. Rise through the influence of women. Enemies are subdued and existing evils brought to light that were designed to discredit the native. The mind is restless, emotional, and given to pleasure. Prophetic impressions and premonitions. Favors matters relating to liquids, chemicals, oils, anesthetics, beverages, and the sea.

The Moon Adverse to Neptune

Produces secret enmities or intrigues against the native. Deception, fraud, plots, and schemes that tend to bring him into disrepute. The mind is uneasy, worried, and burdened with fear or strange forebodings. Seductive friends or associates. Bad for health, causing a negative physical condition; danger of food poisoning and danger on water. Confusion, indiscretions, or complications.

The Moon in Good Aspect to Its Own Natal Place

Changes, journeys, gain by females, new friends, increase in business. Inclines to female society.

The Moon in Adverse Aspect to Its Own Natal Place

Loss, disappointment, unfavorable changes, bereavement, unpopularity. To women it brings ill health.

The Moon in Conjunction or Parallel with the Ascendant

Change of residence and travel by land or sea; social or business preferment if the Moon is fortunate by sign or aspects. Otherwise, adversity, Lunar disease, or accidents and danger by water. Increased interest in public and local affairs.

The Moon in Sextile or Trine with the Ascendant

Active employment, friendship of women in authority or in social position; popularity, favorable publicity, general prosperity, marriage or birth of a daughter, according to the circumstances surrounding the native. Desire for change and travel.

The Moon Adverse the Ascendant

Controversies, strife, or disputes with women; conjugal misery, divorce, discord, jealousy, unpopularity, ill health, intemperance, etc., according to the position of the Moon in the natal chart. An unfavorable period for traveling by land or sea.

The Moon in Conjunction or Parallel with the Midheaven

If the Moon is strong and fortunate at birth, honor, renown, advantageous changes, traveling, and popularity. Men usually marry under this influence. But if the Moon is weak and adversely configured in the natal chart, losses and unproductive journeys or voyages result, and the wife or mother suffers. Public disfavor.

The Moon in Sextile or Trine with the Midheaven

Increase of substance, popularity, honors, gifts, favors from women. Active business and traveling are indicated, if in cardinal signs. To men, it may mean marriage, or an increase in business, improvement of position.

The Moon Adverse the Midheaven

This bring unpopularity, scandals, quarrels with women, suffering wife or mother, public discredit, and family disputes, according to the position of the Moon, whether in the Seventh, First, or Fourth House.

The Progressed Aspects of Mercury

Mercury in Good Aspect to Venus

Not of great importance, but increases interest in literature, music, dress, and comforts. Pleasure in the fine arts, new friends, and female acquaintances. Tends to refined society; adds a charm to the personality.

Mercury Adverse to Venus

Reverse to the above listing.

Mercury in Good Aspect to the Sun

Excites the mind to great activity and gives an inclination for books, study, literature, writing, and sometimes journeys if either planet is in the Third or Ninth House. Honor and promotion through Mercurial affairs; increased business activity.

Mercury Adverse to the Sun

Brings losses and annoyance through writings, publishing, letters, agreements, and possibly journeys, if either planet is posited in the Third or Ninth House. Criticism; loss of position.

Mercury in Good Aspect to Mars

Increases the activity of both mind and body, thereby adding new stimulus to business and gain therein. Resourceful, industrious, mechanical, constructive, enterprising, confident, practical, executive, and expressive.

Mercury Adverse to Mars

Inclines to low company, loose morals. Acting upon the mind, it inclines to quarreling, thieving, forgery, scandal, etc.; a sarcastic, suspicious mental attitude; liable to engage in law and disputes and may commit violence on impulse. Worried, anxious states of mind, trouble in business or employment and with relatives.

Mercury in Good Aspect to Jupiter

Strengthens the mind and gives good business judgment and foresight. Denotes popularity, promotion, and success in things ruled by these planets according to their indications in the nativity; good for things ruled by the houses occupied. Also for literary efforts, new studies, publishing, advertising, and travel.

Mercury Adverse to Jupiter

An unsettled mental condition. Losses through poor judgment and writings. If Mercury is not strong, it inclines to trouble through forgery, libel, perjury, loans, misstatements, miscalculation, misplaced confidence, extravagance, excesses, legal violations, and journeys.

Mercury in Good Aspect to Saturn

Gives a patient, persevering, systematic, studious, grave, dignified, practical mind; conduces to gain through discreet and prudent management of business affairs. If Mercury is in the First, Third, or Ninth House, it gives success in intellectual pursuits, writing, publishing, traveling, lecturing, and teaching. Favors matters related to land, property, produce, mines, science, geology, etc.

Mercury Adverse to Saturn

Trouble through slander, forged letters or documents, and things ruled by Mercury. The mind is sarcastic, gloomy, bitter, and given to much worry. Not good for health as it tends to poor circulation, indigestion, constipation and obstruction, and generous nervous derangement. Usually indicates trouble with landlords, tenants, employees, parents, or other relatives. Loss by small animals, property, mines, or lack of employment and illness. Hindrance, delays, disappointment, and a trying time generally.

Mercury in Good Aspect to Uranus

If from the First, Third, or Ninth House, or either planet the ruler thereof, inclines the mind to study and travel and gain thereby. Under this direction, the mind is active, witty, and original; gain through invention, electrical, aerial, or transportation companies, publishing, advertising, writing, radio, electronics, research, exploration, risky ventures, and such things as are ruled by these planets.

Mercury Adverse to Uranus

Unsettled, sarcastic, impulsive, radical, rebellious, chaotic states of mind; difficulty with friends, kindred, civil service or municipal officers. Unsuccessful in literary pursuits; press criticism. Trouble through writings, either letters or documents. Great inclination to travel and sudden changes, or upheaval in plans and affairs. Danger on journeys and through electrical contrivances, autos, engines, airplanes, etc.

Mercury in Good Aspect to Neptune

If occurring in the Third or Ninth House, and the nativity so indicates, it strengthens the mental qualities and psychic nature, producing automatic writing, trance, and inspirational speaking. Useful mental impressions and premonitions. Favors matters relating to food, hygiene, liquids, oil, beverages, the sea, and educational or healing institutions.

Mercury Adverse to Neptune

Defective memory and tendency to mental confusion, nervousness, restlessness, oversensitivity, lack of self-control, and liability to be led into dissolute habits. Deception and loss in business affairs and through things ruled by these planets. Misunderstandings, misstatements, concealment of facts, lack of proper information, perjury, forgery, and anonymity are likely to lead to distress and trouble.

Mercury in Conjunction or Parallel with the Ascendant

Change of residence, a journey, active business; a propensity for study, invention, and writing, the results of which will be fortunate or unfortunate according to the indications of natal Mercury.

If Mercury is very much afflicted at birth, an accident or serious sickness is threatened; many worries and annoyances. Trouble with neighbors or relatives.

Mercury in Sextile or Trine with the Ascendant

Prosperity, active employment, traveling; gain by literary work, teaching, or by speculating, if Mercury is in the Fifth House and well placed in Gemini or Virgo. May indicate the birth of a child (nephew or niece), a change of residence, new acquaintances.

Mercury Adverse the Ascendant

This influence gives a disinclination for study, failure to pass examinations; mischief by writings, promises, or agreements, or through the press; overwork; disease of the nature of Mercury and the planets with which it may be configured; troubles with children and young persons, scandal, slander, or discredit. To children, this aspect often brings bronchitis and convulsions, attended with danger.

Mercury in Conjunction or Parallel with the Midheaven

If Mercury is strong, in Gemini or Virgo, or in a cardinal house, gain by literary pursuits, traveling, teaching, etc. If Mercury is afflicted in the progressed or natal chart, libel, legal difficulties, unfortunate trading, many business worries and annoyances.

Mercury in Sextile or Trine with the Midheaven

Preferment, honor, and increase of business, according to the strength and situation of Mercury in the natal chart. Children are often first sent to school and young people to college, or honorary degrees are granted under this influence. It usually produces a change of residence or travel in connection with business.

Mercury Adverse the Midheaven

Troubles and losses are indicated, also danger of lawsuits, unjust sentences, libels, and false accusations. Death of a child, cousin, or neighbor frequently happens under this influence. Trouble through writings, promises, or publishing.

The Progressed Aspects of Venus

Venus in Good Aspect to the Sun

Honor and preferment in a social way and much pleasure in refined amusements. Gain through business, profession, speculation, public occupation; it produces a generous, harmonious state of mind. Good for health; conducive to love affairs and marriage; indicates gifts, honors, and promotion; inclines to the purchase of jewels, adornment, objects of art, furniture.

Venus Adverse to the Sun

Causes extravagance or excess of pleasure; grief through the offspring; misfortune in love affairs and dealings with the opposite sex; an amorous nature and mutable in the affections. Loss through speculation. Social rebuffs; difficulty through matters related to beauty and adornment; lack of funds and ill health.

Venus in Good Aspect to Mars

Inclines to the society of the opposite sex and a general good time. Incites to love and marriage. The native is daring and free, and delights in and gains through Venus affairs. Good for acquiring money through things ruled by these planets. Not good for morals, as no aspect between Mars and Venus tends to strict morality.

Venus Adverse to Mars

Inclines to low company, loose morals, scandal, debauchery, loss through speculation and extravagance; trouble with partners or associates. Especially bad for women, and particularly so if Mars is in the Fifth, Seventh, or Tenth House at birth or in the progressed chart.

Venus in Good Aspect to Jupiter

Good for the things governed by the houses occupied in the progressed or natal chart and also the houses that they rule. Inclines to refined society and amusements and gain thereby; social activity, gain in business, finances, new adornments, furnishings; travel for pleasure, education, or business.

Venus Adverse to Jupiter

Losses through speculations and a tendency to extravagance through overdress, women, and social amusements. Luxurious tastes, excessive pleasures, expensive undertakings. Liability to loss of money through loans, legal decisions, or gaming.

Venus in Good Aspect to Saturn

A modest, chaste, frugal, sincere state of mind; favors steady attachments in love and friendship. Gain by elders, superiors, and solid business investment. Much good luck of a substantial quality. Favors matters of practical, artistic value, also land, property, mines.

Venus Adverse to Saturn

Lax morals, bereavements, death of offspring, business losses, trouble in courtship and marriage, not good for speculation, investments, lands, mines, leasing, companies, or banks. Tends to delay, disappointment, restriction, loss of business or employment, and ill health.

Venus in Good Aspect to Uranus

Gain in the things that are ruled by the planets in question. Inclines to the company of the opposite sex. Romance, new friends, increase in business, new facilities, improved methods, new and pleasant experiences.

Venus Adverse to Uranus

Unfortunate for matters concerning the opposite sex. Extremely unconventional and indiscreet, liability to scandal and discredit thereby. Sudden and unexpected losses and estrangement from friends. Not good for speculation or risky ventures.

Venus in Good Aspect to Neptune

Promotes success through speculation, shipping, liquids, oils, and the occult sciences; pleasure and benefit through friends, associations, and acquaintances. Gain through secret organizations, by quiet, secluded efforts and things of artistic, pleasurable, or comforting nature.

Venus Adverse to Neptune

Financial loss through schemes, plots, theft, and trouble through secret organizations, friends, and associations; scandal and misrepresentation. Misunderstandings in love affairs, or financial loss from confusion, impractical procedure, and vague, indefinite, or involved ventures. Betrayed, fooled, duped, tricked, or cheated.

Venus in Good Aspect to the Ascendant

This aspect brings pleasure, gain, new friends, courtship, marriage, birth of children; purchase of articles of luxury, furniture, clothing, ornaments, etc., according to circumstances. If Venus is afflicted (especially in a water sign), the conjunction may incline to dissipation or extravagance.

Venus Adverse the Ascendant

Is not important unless Venus is very much afflicted, and then it will manifest according to the nature of the afflicting planet. It usually produces excess of pleasure, eating, drinking, etc., and ill health, accordingly; also extravagance and useless expenditure. To women, it sometimes disturbs the generative system; to men, danger of venereal diseases.

Venus in Good Aspect to the Midheaven

This brings mirth, gaiety, pleasure-seeking, renewal of furniture, clothing, free expenditure, advancement in artistic pursuits, the birth of children, and general prosperity. Love affairs commence and marriage often takes place under this influence. Indicates social distinction, honors, and favorable publicity.

Venus Adverse the Midheaven

Indicates scandal or annoyance on the part of women; loss of credit or reputation, extravagance, and, in some cases, dissipation. The mother, wife, or sister suffers in health or other inconveniences; business and financial troubles.

The Progressed Aspects of the Sun

The Sun in Good Aspect to Mars

Denotes changes, activity, preferment, honor, health, and strength. The mind is alert, quick in anger but soon appeased. The nature is frank, free, generous, candid, ambitious, progressive, venturesome, confident, and aggressive. The native is inclined to active or strenuous sports; possesses constructive qualities and self-assurance; meets favor, promotion, and success in Martian affairs; increased business activity and responsibilities. With women, it conduces to marriage but usually of a somewhat discordant nature.

The Sun Adverse to Mars

Denotes sharp, acute attacks of sickness; accidents, cuts, burns, bites, and danger from all inflammatory diseases and illnesses, such as smallpox, fevers, cholera, fluxes, etc., according to the sign occupied by Mars. In a female horoscope, danger in childbirth. Under this direction, one is liable to suffer loss by fire if either planet is in a fiery sign; inclined to fighting, anger, quarrels; danger of violence and robbery. A water sign conduces to drunkenness and excesses, if the nativity shows such.

The Sun in Good Aspect to Jupiter

Exceedingly good for honor, wealth, health, fame, law, and general success in all lines. If the natal chart indicates it, the native may expect advancement, preferment, and honors through influential friends and gain according to the house in which Jupiter is posited. Very favorable for marriage, speculation, expansion, extension of interests, and general prosperity.

The Sun in Adverse Aspect to Jupiter

Very bad for money matters, law, speculation, and health. It denotes liability to apoplexy, pleurisy, bursting blood vessels, and general derangement of the system if the Sun is hyleg or Jupiter is the ruler of the Sixth House. Do not buy, loan, speculate, or invest during this aspect. Loss through misplaced confidence, miscalculation, or poor judgment.

The Sun in Good Aspect to Saturn

Denotes substantial gain, public approval, honor, success in mines, lands, and things of a Saturn nature; preferment and advancement through those in authority and also through the native's own efforts. The mind is dignified, lofty, and austere, favored with concentration, confidence, good calculation, estimation, and appraisal. The native is quiet, patient, and persevering. A good period in which to make long-time investments, for building and buying.

The Sun Adverse to Saturn

Very adverse for health, wealth, and social standing. The native suffers loss of business, or credit and bankruptcy if the afflictions occur from the Second or Eighth House; sickness from the Sixth or Twelfth House, and possibly death from the Eighth House. The native incurs opposition, enmity, and public disfavor. The mind may become unsympathetic, without regard for the feelings of others, selfish, calculating, and pessimistic. It threatens the demise of the husband in a female horoscope. A very inauspicious time for new business, risky ventures, expansion, buying, investing, changing position, or traveling.

The Sun in Good Aspect to Uranus

Gain through the talents, inventions, public employ, popularity, fraternal societies, and voyages. The mind is active and enterprising. Beneficial changes brought about suddenly and unexpectedly. Good for health and general welfare. Advancement in occult science. Journeys, if not in fixed signs. New interests, friends, undertakings, and business improvements.

The Sun Adverse to Uranus

Sudden and unexpected losses, calamities, accidents, enmities; loss of honor, public favor, friends, and patrons. Uranus is separative in nature and causes trouble from any house in which it is posited or that it rules. Bad health, causing a disturbed, nervous, excitable, radical, or rebellious state of mind; very unfavorable for marriage as it tends toward separation, estrangement, divorce, or incompatibility.

The Sun in Good Aspect to Neptune

The mind is sympathetic, kind, and generous. Gain through the occult and spiritual sciences; inclines to pleasure and benefit through the artistic faculties and traveling; by things of a hidden or secret nature and those of authority and government employ. Harmonious, constructive, or enlightening impressions. Favors matters related to liquids, chemicals, drugs, oil, anesthetics, beverages, the sea, and large institutions such as theatres, sanitariums, hospitals.

The Sun Adverse to Neptune

Loss through fraud, scandal, schemes, and intrigues. Loss of standing with those in authority. Disadvantageous changes and loss of occupation. Bad for health; annoying psychic conditions. Danger through drugs, narcotics, beverages, or the sea.

The Progressed Sun in Good Aspect to Its Own Natal Place

Honor, esteem, popularity, promotion, progress, success in business, general prosperity, improved health, and many pleasures.

The Progressed Sun in Adverse Aspect to Its Own Natal Place

Loss in matters mentioned above and a trying time generally.

The Sun in Conjunction or Parallel with the Ascendant

If the Sun is strong and fortunate, in Aries, Leo, or Sagittarius, and has no adverse aspects, gain by public favors from powerful people, advancement, employment, increase of reputation and credit; but at the same time, liable to ill health through inflammatory complaints. To military men, great preferment is indicated.

If the Sun is afflicted by the malefics, danger to the life is threatened and trouble through the head, eyes, and heart especially. If the Sun is in conjunction with Mars, danger by fire or firearms and accidents of a Martian nature.

The Sun in Sextile or Trine with the Ascendant

Health of body, peace of mind, favor from persons in authority, new friends, some elevation in rank, according to the native's social position. Women usually marry or have a son under this aspect, or receive social distinction.

The Sun Adverse to the Ascendant

Disease according to the position of the Sun. Envy and enmity of persons in power; loss of employment and credit; danger to the father and in some cases danger of imprisonment, if the Sun was heavily afflicted at birth. Traveling, changes, speculation, risky ventures, excitement, and over-exertion should be avoided during this aspect.

The Sun in Conjunction or Parallel with the Midheaven

Honors, advancement, and increase of substance. To unmarried women, it usually indicates marriage. But if the Sun is adversely configured with the malefics, or in conjunction with fixed stars of a violent nature, it will bring disputes and possibly misfortune of a public nature; danger to the mother. Otherwise it denotes distinction.

The Sun in Sextile or Trine with the Midheaven

This is an elevating influence, and if the nativity promises it, brings renown, great advancement, honors, popularity, credit. It also benefits the native's parents. Public offices are often gained under this influence. To women, it brings marriage or employment of a public nature, and social advancement.

The Sun Adverse the Midheaven

This often brings loss of office or employment, bad trading, disgrace, and sometimes bankruptcy and imprisonment. One of the parents suffers or may die.

The Progressed Aspects of Mars

Mars in Good Aspect to Jupiter

Good for things indicated, according to the position of Jupiter in the nativity and by the place of Jupiter in the progressed chart. Tends to activity, determination, and vim; gain through personal effort. Elevates the desires and aspirations, increases business interests; promotion, expansion, success through practical endeavor, good judgment, and active execution.

Mars Adverse to Jupiter

Indicates losses and trouble according to the nature of the two planets and their indications in the nativity according to the houses occupied; possibly through law, foreign travel, religion, or competition, misplaced confidence or dishonesty. The subject may himself cause his own misfortune through hasty, impulsive action or extravagance, carelessness, hasty judgment, miscalculation, or dissipation. Danger through fires if these planets are in fire signs. Subject to accidents, feverish complaints, or strain.

Mars in Good Aspect to Saturn

If one or both planets are prominent, denotes activity, steadfastness, and credit through courageous acts and well-regulated business activity of a practical, conservative nature. Good for building, repairing, improvements; constructive, mechanical, or industrial activity; manufacturing, engineering, excavating, mining.

Mars Adverse to Saturn

Especially unfavorable if from the First, Seventh, or Tenth House. Inclines to a quick, violent temper, which leads to quarreling, fighting, jealousy, and perhaps crime. Danger of accidents and broken bones; loss in business or occupation; thefts; nervous apprehension and irritability; liable to sudden, sharp, serious attacks of illness.

Mars in Good Aspect to Uranus

Quickens the mind and increases power; indicates gain through invention, engineering, construction, contracts, exploration, investigation, energetic activity, unique enterprise, and extension of activities.

Since both are malefics, they usually produce no appreciable good, except through new, active methods or plans and aggressive business enterprise, personal industry, and progressive business acumen.

Mars Adverse to Uranus

From the First House, increase of temper, jealousy. From the Seventh House, intensifies and causes trouble with partners; divorce or separation. From the Tenth House, unexpected and sudden calamities and disgrace. Municipal or political enmity.

Otherwise, trouble through rash, hasty, forceful, and erratic expressions, premature speech and action, sudden radical changes and accidents.

Mars in Good Aspect to Neptune

Creates activity and enthusiasm in the investigation of occult subjects and secret missions and gain through matters connected with liquids, drugs, oils, beverages, chemistry, the sea, or large institutions.

Mars Adverse to Neptune

Danger from psychic conditions and phenomena. Tends to trouble by fraud, deception, scandal, bribery, and mental disturbance; loss or accident on or by water, oils, liquids, poisons, drugs, thieves, and habits. Avoid damp, unhealthy, foul, or ill-smelling places where disease or noxious influences may lurk.

Mars in Conjunction, Parallel, Square, or Opposition with the Ascendant

Tends to over-optimism; rash, hot-headed, sarcastic, combative attitudes.

Accidents or disease, according to the position of Mars. If Mars is in a fire sign, acute fevers or accidents by fire; in earth signs, danger of suffocation, especially if in bad aspect to natal Saturn; in Taurus, smallpox or diphtheria; in air signs, danger of homicide, or of being killed in a quarrel or battle; in water signs, danger of a fall from a height, or acute fever. Women will be in danger through the opposite sex.

Of course, if Mars was well placed in the natal chart and had no bad aspects, very little of the foregoing would transpire.

Mars in Sextile or Trine with the Ascendant

This inclines the native to travel, sport, health exercises; to enter the army or navy, study medicine, surgery, or chemistry, or become an engineer, according to the natal chart. Women sometimes marry under this influence. Benefits the health, strengthens the constitution, increases the passions. The native assumes new responsibilities, enters into new projects. Very active.

Mars in Conjunction, Parallel, Square, or Opposition with the Midheaven

This is an adverse influence as it denotes quarrels, losses, fires, thefts, and fraud. To military men and surgeons, the conjunction brings advancement, but it is attended with some danger. The parents suffer in some respect.

Misfortunes are sure to result if changes and speculations are made while this Martian aspect is in operation.

Mars in Sextile or Trine with the Midheaven

This signifies an active and prosperous period, especially for Aries. Busy, industrious, constructive.

The Progressed Aspects of Jupiter

Jupiter in Good Aspect to Saturn

Good for legacy, gifts, or promotion. Honors through science or law, gain through lawsuits and all things ruled by the planets and the houses they occupy, especially Jupiter. Substantial increase in general affairs, land, property, possessions, business, credit.

Jupiter Adverse to Saturn

Loss through law, business, educational institutions, religious bodies, and all things ruled by these planets. Loss of honor and credit, bad for health, peace of mind, and business generally. Unfavorable for new or important undertakings or assumption of heavy liabilities.

Jupiter in Good Aspect to Uranus

Gain through legacy, law, gifts of money, Uranian occupations, foreign travel, higher science, publishing, and religious or educational movements. Favors inventions, research, exploration, new studies, business expansion; interest in government and public welfare.

Jupiter Adverse to Uranus

Tendency the same as the good aspect, but attended by unexpected losses, obstacles, and difficulties. Much annoyance and trouble over lawsuits, inheritance, and financial affairs. Unfavorable for new undertakings or risky ventures.

Jupiter in Good Aspect to Neptune

Favors traveling, dreams, visions, psychic conditions, and honor through the investigation of religion from a scientific or occult standpoint; popularity and success in secret societies and through achievements in scientific research, medicine, chemistry, publishing, or large institutions.

Jupiter Adverse to Neptune

Losses through speculation, fraud, cheating, treachery; discredit through religious matters, secret societies, or foreign affairs. This aspect tends to disturb the health, necessitating care in diet, caution in use of stimulants, beverages, etc.

Jupiter in Good Aspect to the Ascendant

Stimulates growth and increases size or weight of the body. This is fortunate for health and all affairs, prosperity, conviviality, new friends, advancement, favors, marriage, birth of children, inherited property, according to the condition of the natal chart. Gives interest in travel, foreign affairs, education, philosophy, and philanthropy.

Jupiter Adverse the Ascendant

An indifferent state of health, often due to plethora. If Jupiter is afflicted by Mars, danger of measles, scarlatina, smallpox, pleurisy, etc. A bad time to deal with lawyers, bankers, brokers, or speculators. Extravagant expenditures, carelessness, conviviality, misjudgment. Loss through loans, indebtedness, heavy liabilities, or excessive overhead.

If natal Jupiter was in conjunction with the Ascendant or afflicted, it may bring serious illness (but not necessarily *fatal),* arising from some disease of the lungs, liver, blood, or hips.

Jupiter in Good Aspect to the Midheaven

Preferment, honors, increase of wealth, benefits from persons in power, general happiness and prosperity. Social advancement, business expansion.

Single women usually marry under this aspect. To merchants, it brings increase of trade; to the clergy, preferment; to lawyers, advancement and high repute. A good time to begin new undertakings if no other testimonies conflict.

Jupiter Adverse the Midheaven

This chiefly brings heavy expenses and disputes with professional persons; nothing very adverse unless Jupiter is much afflicted in the natal chart, which gives a tendency to loss through banks, speculation, or risky enterprises. Not a good time to loan money or sign bail bonds.

The Progressed Aspects of Saturn

Saturn in Good Aspect to Uranus

Quickens the mind and tends to a thoughtful, profound, and penetrating attitude; success through determination and fixity of purpose in the investigation of the occult on a mental plane, such as telepathy, mental healing, suggestive therapeutics, etc.; also through inventions, vehicles of transportation, railroads, either electric or steam, and mining of lead, coal, platinum, and aluminum. A great inclination for knowledge of the secrets of nature.

The aspects of these planets are more potent when occurring from the First, Third, Ninth, or Tenth House.

Saturn Adverse to Uranus

Unfavorable generally; unexpected obstacles and disappointment. Accidents. This is one of those aspects that lasts over a long period of time and is felt when excited by transits of an adverse nature, and usually affects the health.

From the Tenth House, loss of business, ill fame, and disgrace.

Saturn in Good Aspect to Neptune

Gives deep, clear, concentrated, inspirational thought and practical benefits through the psychical nature and the occult sciences generally; also benefit through elderly people, secret service organizations, investments, property, legacies, and large institutions.

Saturn Adverse to Neptune

Loss through plots, treachery, failures, speculation, and difficulty over legacies, business, etc. May suffer from psychic conditions. Health may be disturbed by improper diet, beverages, insufficient exercise, or excessive nervousness, anxiety, fear, and discontent.

Saturn in Conjunction, Parallel, Square, or Opposition with the Ascendant

If Saturn is oriental (in the eastern half of the chart, between the cusp of the Tenth and Fourth Houses), a serious accident or a broken limb; if occidental (the western half of the chart, between the Midheaven and Nadir), danger of severe illness. In some cases this indicates a heavy cold with danger of fatal results; in others, melancholia and suicidal mania. Depression, restriction, delays, disappointment, and many annoyances.

To women, dangerous internal diseases, possibility of disappointment or disgrace in love or matrimony.

Saturn in Sextile or Trine with the Ascendant

Gain by elderly persons, legacies, mining, building, purchase or sale of lands, houses. Benefits the health, strengthens the constitution, and produces many satisfactory conditions. Inclines to peace of mind, rest, and feelings of security.

Saturn in Conjunction, Parallel, Square, or Opposition with the Midheaven

This indicates family troubles and losses or the death of a parent or employer, loss of reputation and credit, theft, fraud, and unpopularity; merchants and tradesmen lose heavily in speculative transactions and through general depression and limitations. May also indicate difficulties on the job or finding employment.

Saturn in Sextile or Trine with the Midheaven

This shows monetary gain by farming, mining, building, legacies, favor and friendship of old people. Business and domestic conditions become more secure and favorable.

The Progressed Aspects of Uranus

Uranus in Good Aspect to Neptune

Increases the intuition and psychic ability; inclines to journeys, explorations, investigations, interest and gain in occult affairs, secret societies, and progressive matters generally. Inspiration for writing, healing, or social welfare.

Uranus Adverse to Neptune

Gives intuition and the same interest in the occult and mysterious, but investigation of such matters is accompanied by obstacles and difficulties; tendency to nervousness or vague apprehension.

Uranus in Conjunction, Parallel, Square, or Opposition with the Ascendant

This shows sudden losses (probably by railroads, airplanes, large corporations, or inventions), disappointments, and if Uranus is afflicted, injuries; sudden journeys (if in a cardinal or mutable sign), and changes of occupation. Estrangement and domestic difficulties. Strange feelings, thoughts, and desires; rebellious, eccentric, radical, impulsive, spasmodic, and given to sudden resolutions or changes in plans.

Uranus in Sextile or Trine with the Ascendant

Gain of a totally unexpected nature; fortunate journeys, removals, active business, also a desire to study or investigate occult science. Increases the intuition and inventive faculty. Favors telepathy, clairvoyance, and also new friendships; changes, reforms, improvements, and new interests.

Uranus in Conjunction, Parallel, Square, or Opposition with the Midheaven

This is often attended by a sudden death in the family; monetary loss and troubles of a strange nature; disappointment in love and marriage; separation or estrangements. Peculiar mental condition and impulsiveness. Great desire for change, unexpected opposition, governmental interference, business changes, discredit.

Uranus in Sextile or Trine with the Midheaven

Sudden and unexpected gain; sudden changes or traveling of an advantageous nature; favor and friendship of Uranian persons. Promotion and business advancement. Benefit by municipal or progressive affairs.

The Progressed Aspects of Neptune

Neptune in Conjunction or Parallel with the Ascendant

If adversely configured in the natal chart, it inclines to produce indescribable feelings and emotions, queer likes, dislikes, attractions, and aversions. Interest in things of a mysterious or psychical nature. Desire to travel.

Neptune in Sextile or Trine with the Ascendant

Pleasant and peaceful conditions. Interest in art, music, drama, and psychical affairs. Correct premonitions, impressions, or dreams. Gain by means of travel or liquids, oil, drugs, the cinema, and things of a mysterious nature.

Neptune in Square or Opposition with the Ascendant

Affects the health adversely and produces negative, lethargic states. Danger through liquids, drugs, anesthetics, and psychical affairs. Liability to domestic complications, also to deception, misunderstanding, or fraud.

Neptune in Conjunction or Parallel with the Midheaven

If badly afflicted in the natal chart, it brings on peculiar difficulties, discredit, deception, and business complications. But if well aspected in the natal chart, it will operate much the same as the sextile or trine.

Neptune in Sextile or Trine with the Midheaven

Increase of trade, benefits through voyages, shipping, liquids, oils, drugs, or psychical affairs. Credit and esteem through progressive or peculiar achievement.

Neptune in Square or Opposition with the Midheaven

Danger of loss, discredit, business complications, scandal, misunderstanding, deception, fraud, and treachery, especially in connection with the things mentioned in the preceding paragraph.

The Progressed Aspects of Pluto

Pluto moves so slowly through the Zodiac that its progressed aspects will not be significantly different from its natal aspects.

The Progressed Aspects of the Part of Fortune

The position of the Part of Fortune in a progressed chart has no influence on the character or health, but is said to benefit any house in which it may be posited, by gain in things ruled by such house, subject to the quality of the aspects it receives.

Benefic planets by progressed motion or by transit passing over or favorably aspecting the natal Part of Fortune are a favorable influence.

Malefic planets in like manner passing over or adversely aspecting it foreshadow loss.

The Progressed Aspects of the Moon's Nodes

The Moon's North Node passing the place of, or forming a major aspect with, the natal place of Jupiter, Venus, the Sun, the Moon, or Mercury indicates benefits to the native. A square or opposition to the benefics portends evil according to the house occupied by it and the nature of the planet afflicted.

The Moon's North Node passing in sextile or trine to natal Neptune, Uranus, Saturn, and Mars is beneficial in nature. The square, opposition, or conjunction to the malefics portends evil according to the houses occupied by it and the nature of the planet afflicted.

The Moon's South Node crossing over any planet is evil for the things ruled by the house occupied and the planet thus afflicted.

INTERPRETING TRANSITS

The Transiting Moon Through the Houses

The following delineations are the combined influences of the Moon and the house it is transiting without consideration for any aspects that may be formed. An aspect would modify or accentuate the conditions as stated, according to whether it is favorable or adverse.

This section should be used as an example for deducing the influences. The same method or style should be employed when treating the house transit influence of the other planets, based on their delineations given in previous chapters. The influence of the planets by transit in houses is similar to the delineations given previously for the natal house positions.

The Moon in the Ascendant, or First House

Affects the personality and brings matters of self into consideration. It brings desire for a change and overcomes conservatism by inclining to sociability. Increases action of moisture in the head and face.

The Moon in the Second House

Matters of finance will attract attention, and it is a good time to plan methods, ways, and means of increasing or conducting monetary considerations, especially those matters that involve dealings with the public or with commodities of a changeable nature. Good for vocal exercise.

The Moon in the Third House

Inclines to short journeys, dealings with neighbors or kindred, and correspondence. If you make up your mind about something when the Moon is in the Third House, you are very apt to change it, especially if not in a fixed sign. Good for study of public affairs, matters of mental enlightenment, and breathing exercises, as it affects the lungs; favorable for practice requiring dexterity of the hands and fingers.

The Moon in the Fourth House

Arouses interest in the home, the place of abode, and family or domestic affairs; also matters connected with land or property. This location of the Moon conduces to thoughts of change, if only to changing things about the house. It affects the breast and stomach, and one should be careful in eating and drinking.

The Moon in the Fifth House

Gives a speculative tendency, an inclination to take changes, to favor romance, gaiety, and the society of younger people. It conduces to happiness, mirth, a sense of freedom, and increase of affections. Favorable for attending places of amusement.

The Moon in the Sixth House

Conduces to matters of employment, employees, labor, food, clothing, animals, or sickness. It inclines to physical indisposition so that care should be given to hygienic methods. Overwork or overindulgence in any way is likely to result in sickness affecting the stomach and bowels.

The Moon in the Seventh House

Awakens interest in matters connected with partners, associates, marriage, opponents, and dealing with others. Unions, partnerships, etc., undertaken when the Moon is in this house are subject to changes and therefore care should be taken not to bestow too much confidence in the steadfastness of others. A good time to read a new book.

The Moon in the Eighth House

For the majority of people, the transit of the Moon through their Eighth House is not very perceptible in effect, but it inclines to attending to the monetary affairs or financial conditions of others, or the money of a partner or associate, and causes the mind to revert to those who are deceased. But in others, their interest turns toward the occult or psychology. This is a good time to turn within for self-examination, or to watch one's actions for psychological and emotional intents. Thoughts of jealousy, vengeance, or hatred should be released.

The Moon in the Ninth House

Turns the attention to higher channels of thought, matters of education, spiritual or psychical unfoldment, and thoughts of journeys and reminiscence of distant scenes. Dreams, when the Moon is in this house, are usually prophetic.

The Moon in the Tenth House

Inclines to business activity in a professional way or with professional people. It conduces to change in business methods or pursuits and brings up matters connected with honor, credit, or advancement. Interest in the mother's welfare and also that of the government or responsibilities. Use this period to reassess your goals and ambitions and your position in society.

The Moon in the Eleventh House

Usually brings one into contact with others in a social way, creates feelings of sociability and interest in friends. It usually produces new hopes and wishes and revives old ones.

The Moon in the Twelfth House

Gives interest in occult affairs or matters of a secret or mysterious nature, and hospitals or other large institutions. It is apt to bring to the fore many restrictions or delays that annoy the native, but by withdrawing the mind from external things and silently communing with the inner self, while the Moon is here, it is likely to shed light into the deeper recesses of the mind so that the way may be seen to extricate one's self from difficulty and find release from bondage.

Aspects Formed by the Moon's Transit

The Moon in Trine or Sextile to the Natal Sun

Generally an indication of one of the best days in the month in a business way, provided at the same time the Moon does not form an adverse aspect with some other planet, particularly with malefic planets in the natal chart.

The Moon in Conjunction with the Natal Sun

Good also provided the Sun at birth was unafflicted. The conjunction is good for business, but not as good physically, as it sometimes tends to lower the vitality.

The Moon in Adverse Aspect to the Natal Sun

The day is adverse for new undertakings or for dealings with people of high position, and is especially adverse for asking for favors.

The Moon in Good Aspect to Natal Jupiter

Next in power to the Moon's good aspects with the natal Sun. Including the conjunction and parallel, the good aspects to Jupiter are considered among the best aspects that occur monthly. These aspects favor general business and social activity.

The Moon in Adverse Aspect to Natal Jupiter

Not considered very malign, yet they incline to misjudgment, excess, extremes, extravagance, or overestimation in business calculations or decisions.

The Moon in Good Aspect to Natal Venus

Next in power, these include the conjunction and parallel. On the days when one of these aspects occurs, it makes one feel happier, more optimistic, more sociable, and more inclined to entertainment than usual. Very good for visits and dealings with women.

The Moon in Adverse Aspect to Natal Venus

Not very important, but doesn't favors the things mentioned in the preceding. For a person with bad taste, this aspect can accentuate the problem to a noticeable degree.

The Moon in Adverse Aspect to Natal Neptune, Uranus, Saturn, or Mars

All unfavorable indications, the worst one being the aspect with Saturn. New business should not be undertaken when the Moon is in adverse aspect with the place of Saturn at birth, if it can be avoided, for its tendency is to bring disappointments, loss, hindrance, delays, vexations, and anxiety.

The Moon in Good Aspect to Natal Neptune, Uranus, Saturn, or Mars

Tend to benefit through the things they rule.

The Moon Aspecting Natal Mercury or Natal Moon

These are not very important; however, when aspecting Mercury, it inclines the mind to excessive mental activity, and perhaps causes the native to be given more to talking and reading than usual. The aspects to the Moon incline to change and to a desire to be on the move, especially if the Moon is in a cardinal sign (Gemini, Virgo, Sagittarius, Pisces).

The Moon Aspecting the Natal Ruling Planets

The most important aspects of the monthly transit of the Moon are shown when it aspects the planet ruling the birth month sign, the planet ruling the ascending sign, or any planet that is in the Ascendant at the time of birth. When the transiting Moon favorably aspects a ruling planet, it is a good time for matters or things indicated by that planet; on the other hand, it is unfavorable for those things when that same planet is afflicted by the Moon.

The Influence of Planetary Aspects by Transit

General Indications of the Good Aspects of Mercury

Correspond, look after accounts, write, study, attend to educational and literary matters, read, make speeches, and attend lectures. Deal with commission and business people, also messengers, distributors, advertisers, publishers, editors, reporters, printers, book and stationery concerns, bookkeepers, architects, teachers, students, notaries, lawyers, scientists, and young people.

When the planet is well aspected, it will be noticed that the mind is keen, alert, penetrating, ingenious, comprehensive, reasonable, and versatile. The good aspects increase the intuition, imagination, mental sympathy, receptivity, and adaptability. It stimulates the mental activity, gives ready response to new ideas, and gives clear perception, as it acts directly on the perceptive faculties. Makes one quick, active, and businesslike. Things of a minor commercial character are accomplished with dispatch. Thoughts come clearly, and speech or pen are fluent in expression. A good time to attend to educational matters, advertise, draw up contracts, and seek information. Good for all affairs requiring a quick mind, fluent speech, nimbleness and dexterity in execution. Good for making minor changes, short journeys, dealing with neighbors, kindred, and business people generally. The mind is turned into an optimistic channel and finds pleasure and recreation in conversation, music, art, literature, novelty, and change. Deal with books, manuscripts, lessons, etc.

Adverse Aspects of Mercury

Keep from petty worries and over-anxiety, take no notice of trifling annoyances. Set a guard on the speech, act with prudence, write no letters, sign no contracts or agreements, make no important journeys, changes, or removals. Take no medicine. Avoid friction with brethren, cousins, neighbors, or employees.

The adverse aspects to Mercury produce unfavorable conditions and tend to disturb the stomach, bowels, and nervous system generally. The mental activity is intensified and one is unconsciously tense, leading to worry, anxiety, and turbulent or sarcastic states of mind.

It creates uncertainty, indecision, and sensitivity. We are apt to indulge in controversy and criticism or to say and do things that we do not really mean. In turn, we are likely to hear unpleasant news and meet with conditions that tend to disturb the mental equilibrium. During this aspect, one had best not have anything to do with litigation or new business. Misunderstandings and annoyances are apt to appear. Special attention should be given to keeping in mental harmony and in a pleasant state of mind, for in that way much of the aspect is overcome; at least, that part of it that depends upon you for its manifestation.

General Indications of the Good Aspects of Venus

A good time for all refined entertainment, pleasure, and amusement, also for courtship, love, marriage, social and general prosperity and popularity. Buy and don new clothing (especially when the Moon is new). Cultivate new friendships with the opposite sex, seek the favor of ladies, visit friends, hold parties, etc. Deal with confectioners, hotelkeepers, housekeepers, restaurant managers, milliners, clothiers, artists, singers, actors, musicians, drapers, jewelers, decorators, florists, and nurses. Make collections.

When this planet is in good aspect, it will be noticed that the mind strikes a lighter vein than usual, the feelings and emotions are easily aroused, and the desire is to respond readily to affection with perfect sympathy. The aspect tends to elevate, improve, and refine the mind, making it clear, bright, hopeful, cheerful, peaceful, gentle, kind, and mirthful. The native is good-natured and genial and more than ever inclined to neatness in dress and good manners. Gives appreciation for the beautiful in nature, art, or drama, and inclines to general public or business success through agreeable, attractive, and engaging manners and sociability. Personal benefit and financial gain may be derived from dealing with things that please the public's taste for delicacies, amusement, or adornment, and through people connected with those things; also through matters associated with houses, lands, and fruits of the earth. One should strive to make the most of this planetary influence for improvements in all affairs in either business, social, or domestic life.

Adverse Aspects of Venus

Avoid the opposite sex. Be moderate and refrain from excesses of all kinds, but especially with regard to eating, drinking, and amusement. Not a good time to obtain favorable results in matters of affection or pleasure, or in fact any of the things mentioned in the foregoing paragraph.

To women, this aspect sometimes denotes physical indisposition. It tends to produce trouble through overindulgence or carelessness in habits and manners. It indicates a liability to disappointment or disagreement in matters of affection and the feelings or emotions generally. It is likely to upset and disarrange domestic conditions. Attachments and social affairs are apt to cause anxiety and also matters associated with the occupation, finances, property, possessions, or partnership. The native is liable to be sensitive and easily wounded. During this aspect, one had best not engage in social affairs or new undertakings (of the kind this planet rules as stated previously), nor is it wise to cultivate new attractions. Quietly attend to present duties and associate with old friends; shun speculation. In this way, very much of the adverse nature of the aspect may be mitigated.

General Indications of the Good Aspects of the Sun

Ask favors of those in good position and authority, also of those in government office. Seek employment; try for promotion; give presents; seek that which is lost; make public announcements and advance notices. A good aspect for spiritual unfoldment and for the society of sunny, optimistic, and prosperous people.

The good aspects of the Sun promote loyalty, sincerity, ambition, energy, willpower, and adaptability; strengthen the constitution of both male and female. They tend to success, advancement, prosperity, and assistance from powerful, influential, or superior persons; also to popularity, progress, honor, esteem, and friendship. Gain through enterprise and responsibility and through good-hearted, generous, and radiant manners.

Adverse Aspects of the Sun

Avoid persons of wealth, position, and authority; also those in government office. Do nothing of importance; do not disclose your intentions; keep your own counsel. Begin only those things that are to be kept secret, private, or obscure; avoid being overheated or becoming excited. The adverse aspects of the Sun tend to make one over-ambitious, venturesome, egotistical, irresolute, proud, haughty, yet sensitive, compelling, immoderate, overconfident, somewhat domineering, and quick to take offense. Likelihood of difficulty in financial affairs through business or employment. This aspect also conduces to loss by speculation or through ill health and inferiors. Disappointment, misfortune, or poor success with those of authority and high position.

General Indications of the Good Aspects of Mars

Study, investigate, or attend to business connected with chemistry, surgery, assaying, construction, and mechanical affairs generally. Deal with animals by training, buying, selling, or transportation. Conduct business matters associated with engineers, contractors, structural iron workers, sewer builders, scavengers, carpenters, lumbermen, machinists, smiths, barbers, hardware dealers, agents, police, soldiers, stock raisers, butchers, dentists, and surgeons. Practice muscular development. Solicit, canvas.

The good aspects of Mars tend to make the native more ambitious, energetic, firm, brave, ardent, and resolute. It gives "tone" or strength to the whole system, muscular and circulatory; it increases the activity, force, and vitality, and is a splendid aspect for work requiring great strength in occupations carried on outdoors. Its tendency is also toward success and promotion through resourcefulness and enterprise in business and personal affairs, or employments of responsibility that owe their existence mainly to push, pluck, and perseverance, and in which results are largely accomplished through quick, energetic, commonsense methods and hard work, which inspire confidence and trust from others.

Adverse Aspects of Mars

The adverse aspects of Mars are a troublesome influence, and unless great care is exercised, it is likely to lead to accidents and injuries on journeys and difficulties or obstacles and much hard work in connection with changes and removals. While the aspect is in operation, be temperate in affection and avoid excessive demonstrations; cultivate no new acquaintances and beware of contentions with friends; avoid all disputes and controversy. Utilize the mental and physical force equally, i.e., be careful not to overdo in muscular effort, conserve the energy, restrain the passions, avoid hasty, forceful actions and impulsive speech, beware of accidents, cuts, scalds, burns, and bruises, be careful of the diet. Do not buy clothing, have no dental or surgical work performed. An unfavorable aspect for affairs connected with iron, steel, hardware, machinery, or construction. Have no dealings with engineers, contractors, iron workers, surgeons, dentists, agents, police, etc., as mentioned in the foregoing.

The adverse aspects of Mars have a tendency to make one brave but headstrong, inclined to acts and words that are indiscreet or rash and likely to cause regret, humiliation, or trouble. The temper is apt to be quick and the speech hasty, causing strife, difficulty, or opposition from others. It tends to make one feel very self-confident, somewhat egotistic, domineering, daring, and venturesome, but easily annoyed and irritated and apt to suffer from disregard of regulations or carelessness of consequences and through the sex impulse or through scandal, criticism, or enmity. It is an ill aspect for domestic happiness, and it often produces trouble in the dwelling place and also with regard to property.

General Indications of the Good Aspects of Jupiter

The good aspects of Jupiter vibrate a fortunate or benefic influence. It is a good time to open shops or places of business, begin new undertakings, ask for favors, speculate, sell, providing that there is not, at the same time, a malefic counteracting influence such as an adverse aspect of Mars, Saturn, or Uranus. Take counsel or conduct matters associated with judges, lawyers, bankers, merchants, brokers, commercial men, and physicians. Attend to affairs connected with education, colleges of law, business, science, and medicine; also with matters related to philanthropic, charitable, religious, or benevolent organizations. Make efforts for health or learning, study philosophy or healing. Conduct or attend important and formal social functions.

A good aspect of Jupiter conduces to clear, sound, and usually correct judgment; inclines more than ever to honesty, truth, justice, benevolence, compassion, sympathy, friendliness, and sociability. It increases the vitality and adds fertility and resourcefulness to the mental processes. It tends to make one jovial, generous, humane, hopeful, and popular.

Adverse Aspects of Jupiter

Avoid the law or dealings with lawyers, judges, bankers, treasurers, cashiers, bondsmen, stock and sharesellers, speculators, brokers, and woolen merchants. Have no dealings with philanthropic, charitable, religious, or benevolent affairs. Shun speculation and investment. Sign no bonds, bails, guarantees, or securities.

This is an unfortunate aspect for risky ventures or games of chance of any kind, as it is apt to lead to loss through misplaced confidence, dishonesty, excess, and wrong judgment either in oneself or in others. The aspect tends to disturb the liver, and for women it is not good for the general health.

General Indications of the Good Aspects of Saturn

Deal with plumbers, shoemakers, harnessmakers, hide and leather dealers, miners, masons, potters, excavators, gardeners, florists, farmers, agriculturists, landlords, coal and land dealers. Build, repair, dig, and deal with land. Converse with and seek the favor of elderly people. Practice concentration, autosuggestion, and mental healing. Study organization and economics.

The good aspects to Saturn tend to produce a thoughtful, conservative, prudent, sober, contemplative, and diplomatic mind, and help make one provident, careful, and attentive to business affairs generally. Increase of credit, popularity, and esteem; gives self-reliance, systematizing and organizing ability, constructive execution; the aims of the native are advanced by subtlety, tact, and method rather than by force. The aspect favors occupation and attainment to positions of trust and responsibility; the progress may be slow, but started under this aspect it is more secure and lasting. The good aspects to Saturn are favorable for matters connected with property, leasing, beginning a building, and other long-time projects. It tends to good, discriminative, conservative judgment in buying generally.

Adverse Aspects of Saturn

The adverse aspect to Saturn is an unfortunate influence. Therefore make no changes, removals or journeys, start nothing new, ask no favors, and seek not to gain. Rest, avoid worry, do not let any discouragement or melancholy feelings gain possession, and guard the speech. Do nothing of importance; it will pay to wait. One's judgment is apt to be very poor or warped during this aspect. Deal carefully with elderly people; keep away from old buildings, dark cellars, and gloomy districts; beware of falls, safeguard the health, guard against taking cold; seek optimistic and cheerful people, places, and things. Eat lightly and get plenty of sleep. Do not invest, buy, or exchange; have no dealings with landlords, builders, buildings, lands, mines, coal, or lead.

This aspect interferes with good concentration and has an adverse bearing on the physical condition, so the native will do well to guard against exposure and also depression, doubt, fear, gloom, or dissatisfied feelings. It is an exceedingly unfortunate aspect under which to be married. Any new undertakings commenced during its activity usually live long enough to cause regret, and eventually create a great deal of impatience through delays, hindrance, limitations, reversals, lack of suitable opportunities, and a train of other unfavorable circumstances; in fact, the fates seem to disfavor anything important set into operation at this time and especially those things that require quick consummation for their success.

General Indications of the Good Aspects of Uranus

Other aspects permitting, this is a good influence for traveling in the interests of business or science, also good for making changes and removals. Keep the mind active, study new thought ideas, astrology and inventions, as the vibrations of Uranus have affinity with things of that character. Investigate all things new, odd, unique, original, curious, and mysterious; experiment; practice telepathy, suggestive healing, etc. Work for social reforms and humanitarian principles. Take electric and magnetic treatments. Deal with reformers, electricians, railroad people, chauffeurs, inventors, metaphysicians, and experimental scientists. Take interest in Masonic, occult, and new thought affairs.

The good aspects of Uranus tend to make one active, firm, independent, enterprising, and businesslike. This influence is conducive to fondness and friendship for the opposite sex, and also to gain through the occult and through advanced thought people. It tends to awaken the imaging faculties, quickens the thought and intuition, and leads the mind into new, original lines of interest and investigation. It adds to the mesmeric and metaphysical faculty in a manner beneficial for healing and telepathy.

Adverse Aspects of Uranus

This is not a good aspect in which to travel, change, or move. Exercise extra caution in connection with engines, cars, airplanes, electric conveyances, electricity, machinery, inventions, and explosives. Avoid the opposite sex, do not confide in strangers or in aged people, restrain impulse and hasty speech. Enter into no contracts or partnerships or associations; one is very likely to use strange, unusual, or unexpected judgment during this aspect, change their ideas suddenly from what they had originally intended and afterwards wish they had not. Avoid electric, X-ray, radium, or magnetic treatments under this aspect.

The adverse aspects of Uranus act as a separative or explosive quality and tend to the unexpected and to extremes. They often affect the health, interfering with the aura, the stomach, and the digestive action, causing mental disturbance of different kinds, sudden or peculiar changes in the feelings or emotions; oppositions, aversions, repulsions, and strange attractions. Unless restraint is practiced, the native will be impulsive, sarcastic, abrupt, peculiar, odd, eccentric, very independent, and subject to separation, estrangement, or misunderstanding. This aspect also operates to increase the activity of mind, making it restless, easily annoyed, romantic, venturesome, unconventional, daring, radical, rebellious of limitations, and desirous of new scenes, and surroundings, and change of work.

General Indications of the Good Aspects of Neptune

Attend to business affairs connected with shipping, chemicals, perfumes, brewing, deep-sea fish, oil, paints, mineral and charged waters, and liquids in general. Take journeys by water, take baths and oil rubs. Sit for psychic development, inspirational ideas, hold séances, visit psychics, practice psychometry. Attend secret orders.

The good aspects to Neptune incline to success and benefit through choice foodstuffs, canned goods, delicacies, and things calculated to please the tastes of the public. They render active any latent emotions for romance and mystery and conduce to the reception of useful impressions and pleasant psychic influences.

Adverse Aspects of Neptune

Guard against fraud and deception, beware of schemers, do not invest or buy. Observe well the psychic conditions and be careful regarding the cleanliness and purity of people and things you may contact, avoid hospitals, prisons, and slaughterhouses. Be cautious with gas, ether, anesthetics, fetid odors, and poisonous liquids; use extra caution with canned or bottled foods; keep away from the waters. Drink no oils, restrain the desires, shun psychic phenomena, hold no séances. Enter into no partnerships, associations, and don't cultivate any new or doubtful friendships.

The adverse aspects of Neptune tend to produce seductive influences and confusion; likely to intensify any psychic emotions, bring subtle feelings and indefinable sensations. It leads to a desire for luxuries and to gratify exquisite tastes. Attractions to peculiar or mysterious people, to changeable colors and strange odors, sounds, etc. It leads to impressionability and psychic perception, but not of a desirable or satisfactory nature.

General Indications of the Good Aspects of Pluto

Good aspects of Pluto make the native aware of subtle changes, psychic vibrations, and ways that people are influenced and manipulated. Pluto reacts mostly on a subconscious level, so its vibrations may not be apparent to those with unrefined senses. Good aspects also increase the sexual awareness.

Adverse Aspects of Pluto

Natives tend to be more violent, hostile, destructive, lustful, and greedy during the adverse aspects. The desire for power and domination is increased. Restlessness and despondency may provoke change for change's sake without purpose or reason.

Part Four

CONTEMPORARY DEVELOPMENTS IN ASTROLOGY

Many of the astrological techniques in this section are not new. What *is* new is the way they are done. With the advent of computer capability in the field of astrology, many techniques have become much faster and easier to accomplish, and for this reason astrologers are turning to them in greater numbers.

In this section we expand on traditional techniques used by the advanced and professional astrologer. The descriptions of these subjects are not meant to be complete discussions of the techniques. Rather they introduce a number of the directions astrologers take as they develop their science and art.

RECTIFICATION

What was once a tedious problem of casting and recasting of many charts to find the birth time has become much faster with computers. Still, the basic steps in the process of rectification remain the same. For cases where an approximate time is known, the procedure is simplified. One of the main factors in rectification is the progressed Moon. This powerful direction is involved in most, if not all, major life events, and thus is a reliable factor to use in rectification.

Rectification Outline

1. Identify Key Events in the Life

The first step is to identify events in the individual's life that may be used for rectification purposes. This will vary from person to person, but there are certain classes of events that work well:

- Accidents that involve broken bones or other major injuries
- Surgery of any kind
- Major illness, when onset is acute
- Birth of a child
- Change of residence
- Graduation from school or college
- Beginning a new job
- Marriage
- Divorce

- Death of a parent or other close family member
- Any other event that changes one's health, physical appearance, or status in life

What all these events share in common is the fact that they are related to the angles—the Ascendant, IC, MC, and Descendant. What we expect for each event is a progressed or major transiting aspect involving the associated angle. The Ascendant will be aspected in any major event involving the physical body. The Midheaven is involved in events concerning a change in status. The IC is involved when the home is affected, and the Descendant is involved when partnerships are affected by events.

Some events involve more than one angle. For example, the birth of a child affects the mother's physical body as well. It also represents a change in status for both the father and mother. Graduation from college involves both a change in status, and very likely a change in residence. Often students marry close to the time of graduation.

Naturally, not every progressed or transiting aspect to an angle brings a major event. However, nearly every major event can be closely tied to angular aspects. These may be progressed or transiting aspects to natal angles, or aspects from progressed angles to planets appropriate to the nature of the event being considered.

2. If an approximate birth time is known, cast a chart for the mid-range of the time span.

For example, if the birth occurred in the afternoon, use 3:00 P.M. as a starting point. Calculate the position of the progressed Moon for several of the most significant events—five events is often enough.

2a. If a birth time is not known, cast three charts for 6:00 a.m., noon, and 6:00 p.m.

One of these charts will be within a few hours of the actual birth time. Calculate the progressed Moon positions for each event for each of these charts.

3. List the aspects of the progressed Moon for each date.

Calculate the orb, carefully noting whether the aspect is applying (use a +) or separating (use a –). This tells whether the Moon would have to be in a higher degree to be exact, or in a lower degree. Consider very narrow orbs only—1 to 1½ degrees.

4. Assess the results, and select the time that appears to be the most significant.

5. Evaluate the pluses and minuses, and adjust the birth time accordingly.

For example, if the majority of variation is on the plus side, adjust the birth time to a later hour. Keep in mind that the Moon moves approximately 1 degree every two hours. Thus if the pluses average 1°15', the time will be about 2½ hours later.

6. Recalculate the birth chart for the later (or earlier) hour.

7. Recalculate the progressions for each date.

8. If the results bring the progressed Moon and other progressed planets into very close aspects to the Midheaven, Ascendant, and other angles, then calculate the transits for each date.

Examine the results. You will find many aspects that are exact (this is always true for major life events). The key aspects you are considering are aspects to the angles, as these indicate the changes that are felt on the most personal (physical or emotional) level. The interplanetary aspects indicate the nature of the event. These will be evident, even if you do not know the birth time.

9. Select another event you have not already considered.

Calculate the progressions and transits for that date. Evaluate the chart as a confirmation of the birth time you have selected.

Example Rectification

For a woman born April 11, 1892, between breakfast and lunch, in Highland Park, Wayne County, Michigan, find a rectified birth time.

If breakfast is normally between 7:00 and 8:00 A.M., and lunch is between noon and 1:00 P.M., select a birth time of 10:00 A.M. Calculate the chart and the progressed Moon (the computer will calculate all the progressions).

In the following list, note that the early dates show the Moon progressing through the signs of the zodiac in order. For the third and fourth dates, the progressed Moon has made a full circuit of the chart. The last date, being many years later, indicates a progressed Moon that has gone completely around the chart almost two full times.

Date	Progressed Moon	Event
July 1, 1913	2♌33	Trip to Europe after college graduation
March 13, 1918	29♍51	Marriage
February 14, 1919	10♎48	Birth of first child
July 18, 1920	27♎36	Birth of second child
June 1, 1924	13♐59	Move from Michigan to Colorado because of husband's ill health
December 5, 1970	6♍49	Death of first child

Table 9: Progressed Moon Positions for Proposed Rectified Birth Time

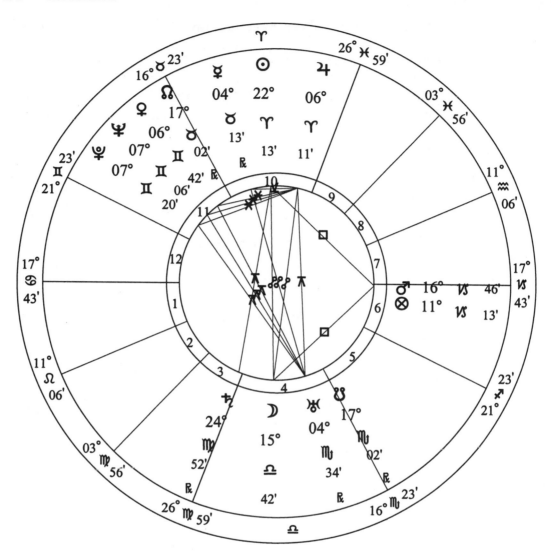

April 11, 1892 / Highland Park, MI (Wayne) / 10:00 A.M. Standard Time
Koch Houses

Figure 6: Tentative Birth Chart

In doing a rectification, you may have several lists of aspects for each event. The closer the birth time is known, the fewer lists you may need. The following is an example of such a list.

Date	Progressed Moon	Aspects
July 1, 1913	2♌33	None; p☽ in 1st House
March 13, 1918	29♍51	p☽☍Mc +2°51'
February 14, 1919	10♎53	p☽□⊗ +25'
July 18, 1920	27♎36	p☽⊼Mc +36'
June 1, 1924	13♐59	☽✳n☽ −1°43'
December 5, 1970	6♍49	p☽□♀ −7', □♆ +17', □♅ +31'

Table 10: List of Progressed Lunar Aspects for Proposed Rectified Birth Time

Most of the aspects have small plus denotations. This means that the proposed time is quite close. The marriage date marks a profound change of social status for this woman. To bring the progressed Moon into exact opposition to the Midheaven for the marriage date, the birth time needs to be later so that the Midheaven will be in a higher degree. A chart calculated for a birth time of 10:10:45 A.M. accomplishes this.

The date of death for the child has profound aspects from the progressed Moon to the planets Venus, ruler of the 4th House—the end of a matter; to Neptune, ruler of the 9th and 10th Houses; and to Pluto, ruler of the 5th House of children. The three natal planets are on the 11th House—ruling circumstances beyond the individual's control. A birth chart cast for the selected time, with secondary progressions and transits for the date of the child's death, reveals multiple aspects involving the angles:

p☽☍n3rd House cusp (The native lived a short distance from her child.)

p☽□n♀, □n♆, □n♅, ♐n☉, ✳p☉, ♐p♃ (All aspects from the progressed Moon are dependent on the birth time. These reflect the multiple levels of impact from the child's death.)

p☿☌nAsc (The news was delivered to the native at home, early in the morning.)

pMc⊼nAsc (past) (The native had been caring for the child, with the help of visiting nurses, for several months.)

t♇☍nMc (Pluto is usually present in charts indicating death. In this case, the death brought awareness of the finality of a long illness.)

t♂⊼nMc (This aspect is indicative of the profound adjustment this death caused. Mars is the ruler of the native's Sun sign, Aries, and the quincunx to the Midheaven indicates that the event caused the native to rethink her life and its purpose.)

Other Methods of Rectification
Several other methods have been used for rectification, with uneven results.

1. Planetary Hour Method—Use the planetary hour in which the individual requested the rectification as a potential Ascendant. When the planet rules two signs, careful consideration is necessary.

The problem with this method is that of knowing when the person first asks the question, and whether they have asked the question in their own mind before asking the astrologer.

2. The First Aspected Planet in the Partner's Chart—Consider the first aspect the Moon makes after birth in a man's chart, or the first aspect the Sun makes in a woman's chart. This planet very likely rules the rising sign in the partner's chart. The obvious problem with this method is that the Moon makes numerous aspects during each day, and the Sun may make more than one as well.

3. Arc of the Event—This method depends on first identifying the planet that is most closely associated with an event, and then determining at what hour that planet was placed so that it aspects the Midheaven or IC.

4. Prenatal Epoch—This method assumes a relationship between the Moon and the Ascendant at birth. It relies on a reasonably accurate given birth time. If the Moon is increasing in light on the birth date, then its degree and sign will be on the Ascendant in the prenatal epoch chart. If the Moon is decreasing in light, then it will be on the prenatal epoch Descendant. This method is quite complicated.

The advent of astrological computer programs makes these techniques less useful that the straightforward casting of charts. What used to take hours or days can now be reduced to minutes of computation time. Many programs have tools to assist in rectification as well, further lessening the time required.

Solar arc directions are very useful in rectification. They are often indicative of events in the physical world—the sort of events recommended for rectification purposes. They pinpoint the timing of events that occur at a specific time. Secondary progressions, partly due to the extended number of month or years that they are within an orb of 1 degree of exact, often indicate the emotional or psychological overtones of a period, and require transits to bring events to fruition. In the case of the example rectification chart, transiting Neptune was semisextile the solar arc Moon, and transiting Jupiter (often seen in charts where death occurs) was squaring solar arc Venus, Neptune, and Pluto.

Final Test of a Rectified Birth Time

Choosing an event not previously considered, erect a birth chart, along with progressions and/or solar arc directions and transits. Consider the following aspects:

- Progressed to natal
- Progressed to progressed
- Solar arc to natal (no need to do solar arc to solar arc, as they are identical to natal aspects)
- Transits to natal
- Transits to progressed and/or solar arcs
- Also consider the natal promise of the event in question—it must be in the chart

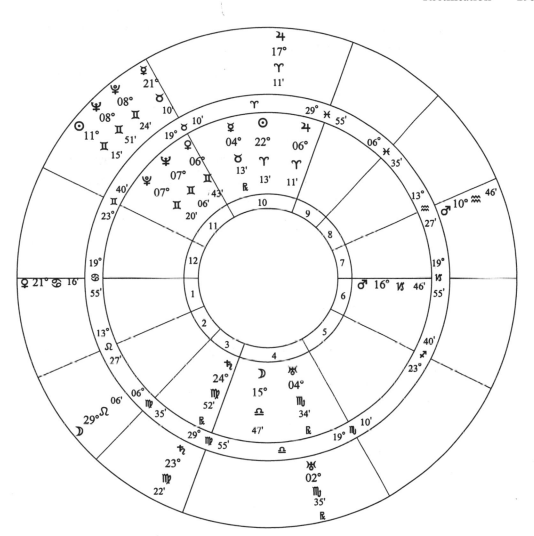

Inner Wheel: Rectified Birth Chart
April 11, 1892 / Highland Park, MI (Wayne) / 10:10:45 A.M. Standard Time
Koch Houses

Outer Wheel:
Progressed Chart for December 14, 1942, at 12:00 A.M. GMT
Koch Houses

Figure 7: Test Event for Rectified Birth Time

Solar arcs, secondary progressions, and transits all show strong indications of the birth of the grandchild. A sampling of the many aspects includes:

- Solar arc Moon sesquiquadrate Ascendant (Evidence of stress—the birth was six weeks early.)
- Solar arc Mars square Venus (The baby was a boy, and the native only had daughters. This boy was to later test her "grit.")
- Solar arc Uranus square natal Saturn (Premature delivery.)
- Solar arc North Node semisextile Neptune (Ruler of the 9th House of grandchildren.)
- Progressed Moon quincunx natal Midheaven (Another indication of the adjustment in status.)
- Progressed Jupiter semisextile North Node (An opportunity to form new associations, due to circumstances.)
- Transiting Saturn square solar arc Ascendant (Travel to see mother and child difficult because of winter conditions.)
- Transiting Mars trine natal Midheaven (Good news concerning the birth of her first grandchild to her first child.)

This partial list of aspects confirms the selected birth time. There are numerous aspects between planets, which would occur in any case. Those listed here focus on aspects that depend on an accurate birth time.

THE LOCALITY CHART

Moving from the original location of birth does not change or negate the indications shown in the natal, progressed, and transit charts, but a change of residence to another place may create other conditions that tend to accentuate or modify those that are denoted by the original birthplace. We cannot evade the duly timed operations of nature that were cast or timed at birth to manifest at certain periods of life, but moving to a more suitable environment may help improve our expression of the influence of aspects as they occur, so that one place may seem to be luckier or more fortunate than another.

Transits and Change of Residence

A student having moved from his birthplace on the Atlantic coast to his present residence on the Pacific coast, wanted to know whether it will have any effect on the aspects of the transiting planets.

Although Eastern time is three hours ahead of (later in the day than) Pacific time, that makes practically no difference in the effects of transits. While the change of residence alters the clock time in its relation to that of the birthplace, it does not noticeably alter anything concerning an aspect itself, except that it appears to begin and to manifest at an earlier hour. However, the time of the beginning of an aspect is an intangible matter, and even if known exactly would be of little importance because the inception of its influence is so subtle and gradual that some time must elapse before it produces any recognized or significant influence on either body or mind.

For instance, the Sun's apparent movement in the Zodiac is a transit of approximately 1 degree a day and it has an orb of influence of 12 degrees. Therefore, when approaching a planet in a nativity, the Sun begins the conjunction at some time on the twelfth day prior to its actual conjunction, regardless of where the native may then be residing. That beginning of the aspect is imperceptible, but day by day its influence grows in power and its expression becomes more noticeable until the day of its climax (partile), after which its influence rapidly diminishes.

When the Sun reaches the final degree constituting the conjunction, it transits through it during the whole day. In a nativity it would indeed be difficult to determine what time of that day the influence would be most strikingly manifest, although it would be but a simple problem in arithmetic to calculate the exact time of the conjunction, which of course would occur at a time that is three hours earlier on the Pacific coast than clocked in Eastern Standard Time.

As stated before, moving from one place to another does not alter the influence of a transit aspect, per se. There is a difference, but it is psychological rather than astrological. That difference is in the human response to the environment. In other words, a person's reaction to a planetary aspect when he is in Alaska will be quite different from his expression of the same aspect if he were residing in Florida, because environment determines much of the nature and quality of human activity. The channels for the manifestation of that aspect would be altered by the difference in climate, clothing, food, occupation, opportunities, personal contacts, mental attitudes, etc. Physicians often wisely suggest a change of climate to patients, but unless they understand astrology, they are not always able to suggest the place best suited to the purpose.

How to Find the Best Location

In the effort to choose a better location, several charts should be made, each for a locality the native has reason to believe would be advantageous with regard to climate, chances for successful employment, etc., and from them choose the locality indicated by the best chart.

The locality chart changes the natal chart house cusps and house positions of the planets, but does not change the planets' signs and degrees. This is true because the actual birth time does not change, only the birthplace. Moving to a new location provides a chart that shows the trend of changes to be experienced in the new place and the conditions to be met. Through the ability and characteristics with which the native was originally endowed, the natal planetary influences are expressed through different circumstances and environment.

For example, if Jupiter was originally in the Tenth House and moving took it into the Eleventh House, there would be a tendency to carry on the profession more through social endeavors. If Jupiter were carried into the Ninth House, the tendency would be to change the profession to embrace publishing, foreign affairs, law, science, or religion.

One of the rules to be observed is to avoid taking your ruling planet into the Twelfth or Sixth House; the former implies limitation; the latter, illness.

Choosing a New Location

Sometimes circumstances dictate where one will live. If one's parents move, there is very little choice. Members of the armed forces go where they are stationed. In such cases, examination of the relocated chart can be valuable in determining emotional, material, and other conditions in the new residence.

Often we have a great deal of choice about where to live. As adults, we can apply for jobs in distant cities; we can join the Peace Corps and choose the country where we will do our service. When we retire, we often choose to move back to the original birthplace, or to a warmer climate, or even to another country.

The charts on the following pages are for John Lennon in his birthplace (the basic birth chart that will always be the basis for any delineation) and in Miami, where the Beatles made their smashing debut in the American music market. Note that the planets have moved approximately two houses, or a bit more. This is correct, as Liverpool is about five hours east of Miami, and each house represents about two hours' time. As the time is earlier in Miami, the planets have moved counterclockwise from the Liverpool positions.

Lennon had the Moon exactly opposite the Midheaven in his birth chart. In moving to the Miami location, he now has Jupiter and Saturn close to the Midheaven.

On February 15, 1964, John and the Beatles performed live on the *Ed Sullivan Show* in Miami, to an audience of about 72,000 viewers. This was the beginning of their tremendous popularity in the United States—popularity that continues to this day. That performance was all about business for the band. For John, it was a place where he could bring together the structure of the music industry (Saturn) with the process of his own music (Jupiter). Miami was a powerful place for him (and for the band) to take a position in the global music market, and it was certainly a good place for boosting his career.

The Beatles later visited the Maharishi in Rishikesh, India. Although eventually disillusioned by this teacher, they embraced Hinduism, and later invited Srila Prabhupada to visit in England. Rishikesh is in northern India, near the borders of Nepal and China.

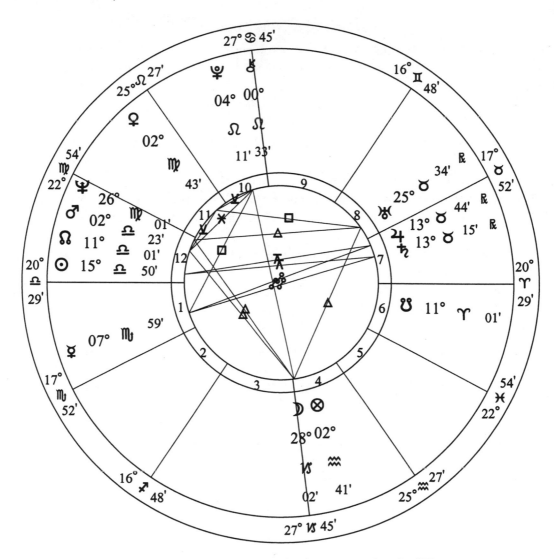

October 9, 1940 / Liverpool, England / 7:00 A.M. Standard Time
Koch Houses

Figure 8: Birth Chart for John Lennon in Liverpool, England

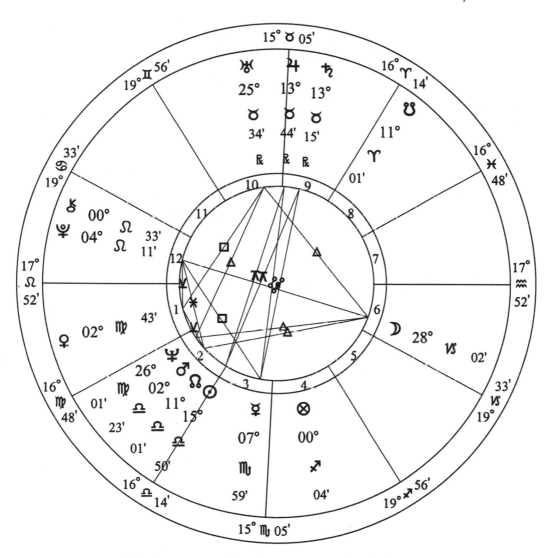

October 9, 1940 / Miami, FL / 7:00 A.M. Standard Time
Koch Houses

Figure 9: Relocated Birth Chart for John Lennon in Miami, Florida

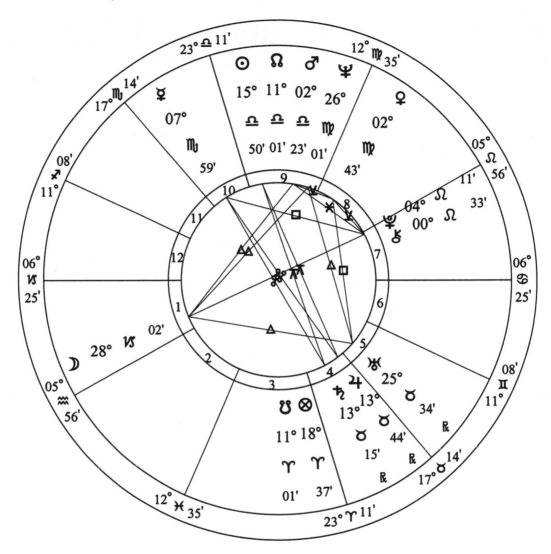

October 9, 1940 / Rishikesh, India / 7:00 A.M. Standard Time
Koch Houses

Figure 10 : Relocated Birth Chart for John Lennon in Rishikesh, India

When John Lennon's chart is relocated to Rishikesh, there are no planets close to the angles (First, Fourth, Seventh, and Tenth House cusps). This is completely consistent with astrological expectations. Lennon was not in India for ego-centered reasons, but to pursue the study of Hinduism. Therefore, the lack of planets on the angles may have actually been a benefit to him at that time, as he would have been able to focus on his religious practices more easily.

Astrological Mapping Techniques

Astrological computer programs allow you to create maps to show the geographic directions of the planets in your birth chart, and to show locations on the earth's surface where each planet will be conjunct an angle in your chart. Using these maps reduces the time needed to determine where the planets will be at your new location. You can also create a new chart for any location to get a complete picture of your birth potential in that location.

HELIOCENTRIC ASTROLOGY

The geocentric birth chart, which is the subject of most of this book, has provided an excellent description of birth potential and the unfolding of life's processes. The heliocentric chart, in contrast, reveals a strikingly different view of the cosmos at the birth hour.

The geocentric and heliocentric charts are not independent of each other. The planets are in the same astronomical positions they hold in the earth-centered chart. Three differences occur:

- In the heliocentric chart, there is no Sun, but there is an earth. From the heliocentric point of view, there is no Sun to be seen, but the earth and its Moon are visible. These are always found in the opposite zodiacal degree from where the Sun is found in the geocentric chart. By using the time of year and the time of day in the geocentric chart, we locate the Sun; in the heliocentric chart we will have located the earth, but in the opposite sign.

- The second difference has already been suggested: the earth's Moon in the heliocentric chart will be quite close to the earth. The difference is so small that the heliocentric chart will not indicate the Moon's position at all.

- The third difference is that there are no houses in a heliocentric chart. This is because an individual's birth time is of relatively little significance from the heliocentric perspective. Hundreds or thousands of people are being born each day, and they are all represented by the same degree of the earth in the chart.

A striking similarity is the general positions of the stars. The zodiacal configurations will have changed very little—the Sun is within the earth's orbit, and therefore the perspective of the Sun is well within the range of what is seen from the earth throughout the year. Because the stars are so far away from us, they appear nearly the same from the earth and the Sun, and both charts use the zodiacal divisions as a reference. The heliocentric chart is generally displayed with 0 degrees of Aries in the position of the Ascendant on the left side of the chart. For the purpose of comparison, the heliocentric chart positions can also be arranged around the earth-centered chart, in which case the earth will be found opposite the birth Sun.

The addition of the rest of the planets provides some interesting differences. The planets do not fall in the same positions in both charts. There are several reasons for the differences:

- As already mentioned, the Moon is so close to the earth that it effectively has the same position. This is comparable to the way we see the outer planets—we need a telescope to see their moons and rings.

- There are no retrogrades in the heliocentric chart because all the planets orbit the Sun. This is comparable to the Moon, which always pursues forward motion around the earth, and is therefore always direct in motion in the geocentric chart.

- Mercury and Venus in the earth-entered chart are always close to the Sun. In fact, Mercury and Venus are never more than 76 degrees from each other. In the heliocentric chart, they can be in any position relative to each other and to the earth. This means that Mercury and Venus can be on opposite sides of the heliocentric chart.

- The outer planets will always be relatively close to the same position in both charts. Mars can vary by as much as 47 degrees. The farther away from the Sun a planet is, the less difference there will be in its position between the two charts.

- In the heliocentric chart, a conjunction means that the two planets are on the same side of the Sun, and an opposition means that they are on opposite sides. In an earth-centered chart, Mercury and Venus can be conjunct, but they may not be exactly conjunct or opposite from the heliocentric perspective. They are simply aligned with each other from our point of view on earth.

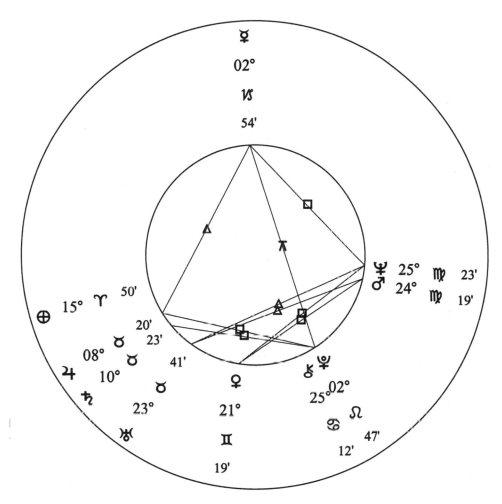

October 9, 1940 / Liverpool, England / 7:00 A.M. Standard Time
Koch Houses

Figure 11: John Lennon's Heliocentric Natal Chart

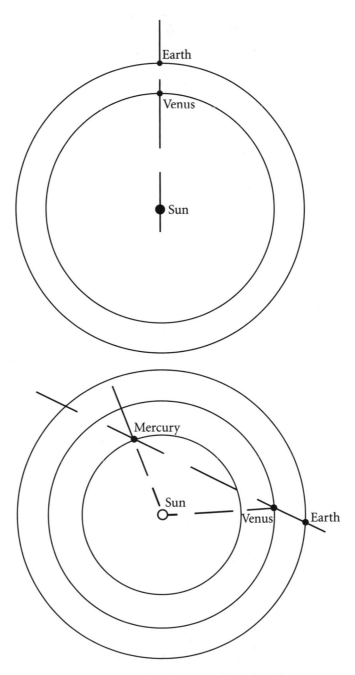

Figure 12: Heliocentric and Geocentric Conjunctions Illustrated:
Heliocentric View of Venus Conjunct the Earth (top)
and Geocentric View of Venus Conjunct Mercury (bottom)

- Declination is not a factor in a heliocentric chart. Declination is a phenomenon of the earth-centered system. It is a measurement north or south of the equator. From our point of view, the Sun's apparent path takes to a northern declination in the summer and a southern declination in the winter. This means that in the heliocentric chart, parallels are not a factor.

- Latitude is a measure from the ecliptic, or the plane of the earth's orbit around the Sun. In the heliocentric chart, we can measure latitude. The plane of 0 degrees latitude must be established, and we can use the plane of the earth's orbit as a standard.

- The Nodes of the Moon are not considered in a heliocentric chart. However, the Nodes of the planets may take on greater significance in the heliocentric chart, as will the aphelion and perihelion of each planet, or their maximum and minimum distances from the Sun.

- There are no eclipses in the heliocentric chart. However, there may be occultations. An occultation occurs when two objects in the sky are at the same exact longitude, and also at the same latitude.

What is the significance to an individual of the many differences between the geocentric and heliocentric charts? There is no Sun or Moon, and therefore two of the most powerful indicators of individuality are missing. In their place is the earth, indicative of all beings born close to the same time anywhere on the planet. The heliocentric chart provides a picture for all those individuals, but from the Sun's point of view. Thus it provides a map that all people born on a given day can share. Abraham Lincoln and Charles Darwin were born on the same day, within hours of each other. Their lives were quite different, yet they also shared many things in common, including their drive for significance, their interest in nature, and the timing of many of the major events in their lives.

Setting individual personalities aside, and using the heliocentric chart, the planets indicate the same energies in the heliocentric chart as they do in the geocentric chart, but from an impersonal, or transpersonal, perspective. That is, there is no personal ego involved. The chart shows what a person might experience if ego were not a factor.

Planets in the Heliocentric Chart

- Mercury: This planet indicates the fullest range of possibilities for skillful communication. Because Mercury is always close to the Sun in the geocentric chart, communication potential is always tied to the expression of the individual. When the full 360 degree range of communication is possible, the particular location of Mercury is strongly indicative of the expression of all persons born with Mercury in that degree. It indicates the means for mediation—conflict resolution—for those individuals.

- Venus: The geocentric Venus indicates social relationships. By their nature, relationships are interdependent, and they can become codependent. From the heliocentric perspective, relatedness can exist without dependence. The heliocentric Venus thus reveals the potential for knowledge and relatedness on a social, global, or cosmic level.

- Earth: The position of the earth in the heliocentric chart indicates the natural direction of intelligent activity for all individuals born at that time.
- Mars: In the geocentric chart, Mars is a focal point for action and energy. By contrast, the heliocentric Mars provides a picture of the direction of devotion—desire unencumbered by ego.
- Jupiter: Heliocentric Jupiter indicates how individuals come to understand the interaction between love and wisdom. The synthesis of these two capacities is sought through religion, philosophy, and higher law.
- Saturn: In the heliocentric chart, Saturn indicates the point of evolution where choice becomes reality. It shows a more accurate picture of the nature of karma in the individual's life. Because the positions of geocentric and heliocentric Saturn will be quite close, the personal experience of karma and its truth are quite similar.
- Uranus: This planet indicates how to gather skills, talents, and energy into a skillful package, directed by intuition. The more centered the person, the greater the person's potential for maintaining equilibrium where Uranus is involved.
- Neptune: This planet indicates the potential path for psychic abilities. It also indicates the nature of sensitivity, higher vision, and compassion.
- Pluto: This planet indicates the potential to feel, see, and hear beyond ordinary human limits. It indicates the capacity to exert power and will. The heliocentric and geocentric positions are nearly identical, suggesting that the potential is there, to be used through the ego or through selfless expression of will.

CHIRON AND THE MAJOR ASTEROIDS

In addition to the planets in our solar system, many astrologers include five additional objects: Chiron, Ceres, Juno, Vesta, and Pallas. Chiron has been described as a planet orbiting between Saturn and Uranus, and also as a comet. Its orbit is more irregular than that of the any of the planets. The orbital period is about 49 to 50 years. The other four objects are asteroids, numbered one through four, as they were the first four to be discovered and identified. They are located in orbits between Mars and Jupiter. The asteroid belt occupies an area of space where Bode's Law predicts there should be a planet. Some astronomers theorize that the asteroids are actually part of a planet that has disintegrated. They are not spherical, like planets. Most are small, although Ceres is about 620 miles in diameter, and is roughly spherical, as is Vesta, just over half the diameter of Ceres. The four asteroids were discovered between 1801 and 1807. Chiron was discovered in 1977, although its existence was predicted by astrologer Charles Jayne in 1975.

⚷ *Chiron*

Chiron, the Wounded Healer, is related to shamanism and healing traditions. In mythology, Chiron is part human, part horse, incorporating human qualities into a form that utilizes primal instinctual energy and sheer physical power. The position of Chiron in the birth chart indicates a degree to watch where issues of wounding and healing are concerned. The tradition of the shaman includes the metaphorical, and also sometimes very literal transformation that comes through a death or near-death experience. The shaman can heal others because he or she knows what it means to be right at the critical point, and to return.

Part man and part horse, Chiron is also living on the edge of some very wild energies. Sometimes physician, sometimes musician, sometimes prophet, Chiron reflects the eccentric orbit of the planet in its very nature. Chiron indicates a place where we can react wildly to our own wounding, slipping into an obsessive, or worse, unconscious behavior pattern, based on a somewhat mistaken view of what has occurred. At the same time, this is the place where we can find the deepest personal healing, and where we can in turn heal others.

The sign and house Chiron occupies in a chart provide indicators about where the individual feels blocked. The placement may show where obstacles arise to prevent the flow of healing energy. It also shows how the individual can be of service in the healing of others, aiding them in responding to their own creative urges. Aspects to Chiron may indicate places where we will not or cannot see things clearly. In order to change such a pattern, the individual must be willing to take a hard look at the issues of wounding. This means not trying to fix what is wrong, but simply examining it. Masking symptoms does not work. Healing can occur best when we understand the problem.

The Asteroids

The four asteroids described here represent four feminine roles: Mother, Wife, Warrior, and Sister. By considering their placement in the chart, the student can develop a fuller picture of the feminine that is traditionally associated with Venus, who is often depicted as the Lover.

⚵ Ceres (Demeter)

Ceres, the goddess of fertility, is also viewed as the Mother. Her mythic struggle to reclaim her daughter Persephone from the realm of Hades is reflected in the astrological chart as the capacity for dealing with mother issues. These include such things as dependency, attachment, and loss. It also includes issues of self-esteem, separation, and rejection. There is a relationship to the reproductive cycle in women, from menstruation to pregnancy and breastfeeding, to menopause and beyond.

The relationship to food is part of Ceres' domain, as she is the goddess of fertility, grains, general nutrition, and diet. The position of this asteroid can reveal how an individual relates to any or all of these issues, and aspects show how these issues are tied in to the rest of the chart—and one's life.

⚵ Juno (Hera)

Juno, wife of Jupiter (Hera and Zeus are the Greek counterparts), was both the queen of the heavens, and an archetypal expression of the wife. In both depictions, she could be jealous of her husband's lovers, and caused great problems for those who fell from her favor. She valued loyalty, monogamy, and faithfulness. This asteroid may indicate areas where intimate partnering is a focus.

On the less constructive side, Juno also indicates where issues of disloyalty and infidelity may arise. In addition, divorce, abuse, and any marital conflict come under her rulership. The associated anger and jealousy, or lack of these emotions, may be seen in the aspects she makes to planets and angles in a chart.

♀ Pallas Athene (Minerva)

Pallas Athene was born fully grown, from the brow of Jupiter. She is a warrior, and also is the goddess of wisdom. Although a virgin, Athene did not avoid men, but instead relished her contact with them. Pallas Athene was the patron goddess of Athens. The wise owl is her symbol.

This goddess finds expression in women from various eras. All heroines may fall within the scope of this asteroid. Joan of Arc led the French army to victory, and Xena graces television programming each day. She also is an indicator of skill in sports—and she demands that we play by the rules.

On the less positive side, Pallas Athene may indicate any connections to incest and sexual abuse. Mythology includes a story of Athene avoiding rape by disappearing miraculously. Unfortunately, this is what many victims attempt to do by withdrawing emotionally, or simply repressing all memory of incidents of abuse.

Aspects to Pallas Athene indicate how people handle the above issues.

⚶ Vesta (Hestia)

Vesta is the goddess associated with home and hearth. She reflects the feminine role of Sister. In addition to her role as guardian of the hearth, Vesta was also guardian of the sacred flame. The vestal virgins conducted ceremonies in her honor, and took vows of chastity while in her service.

Women who strongly reflect Vesta in their personalities are often dedicated to helping others. They may become profoundly dedicated to their work, so much so that they cannot imagine life without the work. They accept their sexual role, but as a matter of choice, not a matter of responsibility, or of weakness. The relationship of Vesta to Mars in the chart may indicate how the various roles of independence, sexuality, and vocation develop throughout one's life.

It is easier to think of the asteroids, and perhaps Chiron, in the chart of a female. However, males have all these qualities to some degree. To be balanced individuals, we all must consider roles that were once reserved for the opposite sex. Stay-at-home or work-from-home fathers embody many of the best characteristics of the asteroids, and women who are employed outside the home do so as well.

Because the four asteroids each reflect specific feminine qualities, there may be some logic in considering them together in a chart. For example, if Vesta conjoins the Sun by solar arc, and Ceres forms a sextile to the Moon by transit, it probably makes good sense to see what the other two asteroids are doing in the way of aspects. When considered as a whole, along with Venus, they can provide a picture of how the ebb and flow of feminine energy is working at a given time in one's life. If one is not aspected in any way, that will suggest that that feminine principle is not in the forefront of daily activities. If one is heavily aspected, that indicates the direction feminine energy *is* taking.

TRANSNEPTUNIANS

Unlike Chiron and the asteroids, the Transneptunians are hypothetical points. They represent potential planets far beyond the orbit of Pluto, and are used by the Hamburg School and other astrologers in delineation of natal and other charts. The foundation for interpretation is mythological literature. The Transneptunians are expressions of cultural archetypes, and thus are not personal points in the chart, but rather indications of much broader cultural influences. Astrology programs often include these points.

⚶ *Cupido*

Cupid is generally the depiction of love, and Cupido reflects this archetype in its broader communal sense. Note that the symbol is a combination of Jupiter and Venus. The energy is of happiness, love, and harmonious companionship. Devotion to others is also a factor with Cupido.

⚴ *Hades*

God of the Underworld, the name Hades has become synonymous with the underworld itself. The symbol is the crescent Moon with a cross. There is both emotional and spiritual energy involved with this point. The metaphysical aspect of life is reflected here, and Hades may aid in understanding death, grief, and even fear.

⚵ *Zeus*

Zeus is the Greek counterpart of Jupiter. Through the actions of his mother, Rhea, Zeus escaped being killed by his father and went on to overthrow him. The *X* is actually open triangles, and the upward arrow represents ascending to a higher level. Zeus reflects the energy of creativity on the mental level, rising from the physical creative capacity of sexuality, through the emotional creative capacity of the individual.

♈ *Kronos*

Kronos (or Cronos) was a titan who killed his father, and was then fated to be slain by his own son. The symbol is the cross beneath an inverted crescent. The archetypal energy is that of rising above ordinary circumstances. Kronos in connection with one's planets indicates where the transpersonal perspective may best be expressed.

♃ *Apollon*

Son of Zeus and twin brother of Artemis, Apollon (Apollo) later became associated with wisdom and also with healing. The symbol is that of Jupiter, with a second vertical line to emphasize the cross. The archetype of wisdom is expressive of the demand for conscious interaction of the less conscious with transcendent consciousness. Such wisdom leads to inner peace.

☿ *Admetos*

Admetos was a king to whom the Fates granted a boon—he would not die if he could find someone to take his place. His wife, Alcestis, did this, and was then given back to him. Here the symbol for Mercury has been altered—the cross has moved partially inside the circle. Admetos therefore is inclusive of the mental strength of Mercury, but may be slowed down so that consideration may be broadened and deepened.

⟁ *Vulkanus*

Vulkanus (Vulcan) was a god with a physical flaw—he was lame. He had great skill in creating metal objects, including a throne for his mother and a net to capture his wife, Aphrodite, in an act of infidelity. The symbol of the upright triangle and the upward-directed arrow reflects tremendous potential coupled with great enthusiasm. Because Vulcan (Hephaestus) worked deep underground, there is a focus on the Collective Unconscious in this point.

♓ *Poseidon*

Poseidon and his brothers Zeus and Hades divided the world among themselves after Zeus overthrew Cronos. Poseidon's portion was the sea. He was known to stir the sea with his trident, causing fierce waves and storms that endangered ships. The Greeks attempted to soothe his anger to ensure safer travel. The symbol includes an upward crescent of spirituality and a downward crescent of the Collective Unconscious, connected by a vertical line. This suggests a connection between the two. The balance of these two influences indicates where we may gain greater objectivity.

Planet	Distance from Sun (Earth =1 AU)	Motion (10 years)
Cupido	41	13° 51'
Hades	50.5	10° 07'
Zeus	59	8° 02'
Kronos	65	7° 02'
Apollon	70	6° 35'
Admetos	73.5	5° 50'
Vulkanus	77	5° 25'
Poseidon	83.5	4° 51'

Table 11: Data for the Transneptunian Orbits

Summary

Because these points move so slowly through the Zodiac, they represent consistent energies that affect entire generations as they move through one sign. Therefore, they cannot be used as timers for prediction in the same way that faster-moving planets function. Instead, they offer an anchor to the collective, archetypal expressions of human experience. When prominent in a birth chart, they indicate archetypes that are felt deeply in that individual's life.

COSMOBIOLOGY: SOLAR ARCS, MIDPOINTS, THE 90° DIAL

The Hamburg School in Germany originated many of the techniques used today in the branch of astrology known as *cosmobiology*. The subject was formally introduced in the United States with the *Combination of Stellar Influences*, written by Reinhold Ebertin and translated into English in 1972. The school of astrology known as cosmobiology uses rather different techniques to achieve their natal and forecasting results. The principal methods are midpoints, the 90° dial, solar arc directions, and the graphic ephemeris.

The 90° Dial

The typical birth chart is depicted in a circle of 360 degrees. In this chart, each zodiacal sign is shown in order around the chart. The 90° dial uses the same planetary positions, but arranges them differently. The 360 degree circle is divided into four equal parts, beginning at 0° Aries, rather like cutting a pie into four equal sections. These four sections of the astrological chart are then stacked upon each other so that 0° of Aries, 0° Cancer, 0° Libra, and 0° Capricorn align at a single point in the dial. Then the 90° of each section are stretched around the circle so that each degree now occupies four times as much space.

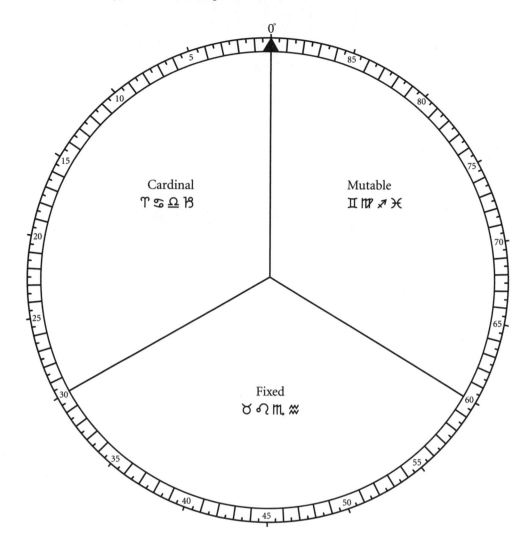

Figure 13: The 90° Dial

There are three advantages to the 90° dial. The first is that each degree is much easier to see on the circle because it is wider. The second is that the conjunction, square, and opposition aspects all line up on top of each other. For example, a Mars at 6° Aries and Mercury at 6° Libra will be together on the 90° dial. If Venus is at 21° Taurus, forming a semisquare to Mars and a sesquiquadrate to Mercury, it will be on the opposite side of the 90° dial. The third advantage is in the use of solar arc directions. When using the dial and solar arcs, the entire wheel is turned the amount of the solar arc.

Generally, the aspects used in cosmobiology include the conjunction, square, opposition, semisquare and sesquiquadrate. These aspects indicate events that can be perceived in the material world and the associated tension and agitation individuals feel internally when under the influence of events outside themselves. By using the 90° dial, the astrologer can easily see all of these aspects to each planet. The sextile, trine, and other aspects are not used.

In earlier sections of this book, the cardinal, fixed, and mutable signs were discussed. In cosmobiology, the cardinal signs occupy the first third of the dial, the fixed signs the second third, and the mutable signs the third section.

Midpoints

A midpoint is the degree of longitude halfway between two planets. By convention, the midpoint is placed between the planets on the segment of the Zodiac that represents the shorter distance between them.

Example

The Sun is at 22° Taurus and Jupiter is at 18° Virgo. The distance from 22° Taurus to 18° Virgo is shorter than the distance from 18° Virgo to 22° Taurus. Therefore the midpoint is located at 20° Cancer.

The midpoint is thought to be a sensitive point in one's chart. When a natal planet forms an aspect to the midpoint, it will stimulate a relationship with the two planets forming the midpoint, *even if they are not forming a significant aspect by themselves.*

Example

Mars is at 10° Aries and Mercury is at 22° Gemini. The midpoint is 16° Taurus, halfway between Mars and Mercury on the shorter segment of the zodiac. If the Moon is at 16° Taurus, it is directly in the midpoint. This is written as ☽ = ☿/♂. Thus the Moon is involved in an energetic relationship with Mercury and Mars.

If the Moon were at 16° Scorpio, this is called the indirect midpoint, because the path to the midpoint takes the longer (indirect) route.

Using keywords for the planets—the same keywords used elsewhere in this book—the midpoint can be delineated like this:

- The Moon reflects emotions.
- Mercury reflects communication.
- Mars reflects energy.

Therefore an individual with the Moon in the midpoint of Mercury and Mars, ☽=☿/♂, is likely to experience emotional communications, or may have a vibrant, emotional communication style.

In the practice of cosmobiology, the planets are arranged in a 90° dial. Some of the midpoints in this dial actually line up as conjunctions.

Example

The Sun is at 14° Aries, Jupiter at 15° Libra, and Saturn at 16° Capricorn. On the 90° dial, the three planets are together, about ⅙ of the way around the circle, starting at the 0° point of the chart and moving in a counterclockwise direction.

Midpoints are not limited to planets that make standard aspects. Every chart has a midpoint between each pair of planets, the North Node, Ascendant, and Midheaven. Thus each chart has seventy-eight midpoints. Some of these midpoints are activated in the birth chart by having a planet at the midpoint, while others are not. The midpoints are arranged in "trees" to show where the focal points in the chart may be found.

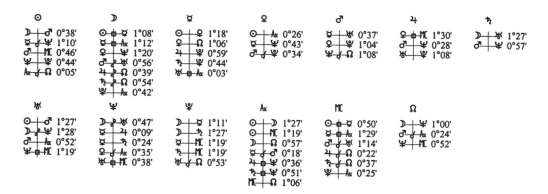

Figure 14: Midpoint Structure Patterns (Trees)

Solar Arc Directions

Solar arc directions (or progressions) are based on the daily movement of the Sun. The solar arc Sun is the same as the secondary progressed Sun, as both are calculated from the movement of the Sun at the rate of one day for each year. "Direction" means directing all the planets to move forward through the Zodiac at the same rate as the Sun. Using solar arcs, all the planets are directed forward. All the planets stay in the same relationship in the solar arc chart.

Solar arc planets can be added to the typical astrological chart, just as progressions and transits are added. The aspects from solar arc planets to natal planets are calculated in the same way as well. Because the planets in the solar arc chart all move forward at the same rate, one does not need to consider aspects between solar arc planets, because these aspects will always be identical to those in the natal chart.

In cosmobiology, the 90° dial is the tool used to work with solar arc planets. The dial's name comes from the tool that was developed before the advent of computer charts. The astrologer would prepare two dials, one slightly smaller than the other. The smaller dial was cut out and placed on top of the original dial. They were then attached to a background board by placing a pin through the centers. The smaller top dial could then be turned in a counterclockwise direction. The distance it was turned was equal to the solar arc. Thus, to direct the chart to age ten, the dial was turned by the distance the Sun had moved in ten days after the individual was born (approximately 10 degrees), moving all the planets forward. In contemporary practice, using computerized charts, the directed chart is on the outside circle, similar to the way secondary progressed charts are prepared. The center portion of the computer chart sometimes shows the planets in a 360° Zodiac. In this way, one can show the actual birth chart (without house cusps), the 90° dial, and the directed chart on one page.

Example

Using the chart for September 11, 2001, the solar arc has been calculated for the date designated as the end of the current Mayan calendar, December 21, 2012. Looking at the ephemeris, we find that the Sun has moved from 18♍20 to 29♍3. The difference is 10°43'. Roughly three months more have passed (from September 11 to December 21), so we will add ¼ of the daily motion of the Sun (15'). The result is 10°58'. This estimate is very close to the exact solar arc of 11°.

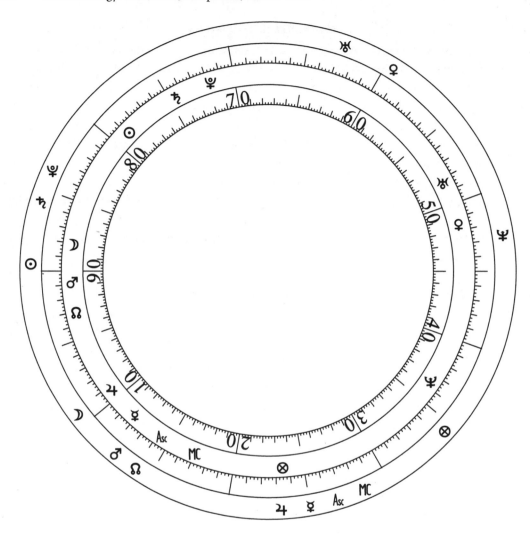

Inner Wheel:
90° Dial Natal Chart—World Trade Center
September 11, 2001 / New York, NY / 8:46 A.M. EST

Outer Wheel:
90° Dial Solar Arc Direction for December 21, 2012 at 12:00 A.M. GMT

Figure 15: Natal Chart with Solar Arc Dial

Note that the Sun has moved from a point just short of 79° to a point just short of 0° in the dial. The Sun in the outer circle is midway between Mars and the Moon on the inner circle. Thus the Sun is in the midpoint (written as s☉=n☽/n♂). Generally an orb of only 1° is allowed when considering midpoints, either in the birth chart or by solar arc or transit.

With a direct midpoint like this one, delineation is similar to progressions:

- The Sun—individuality.
- Mars—energy.
- The Moon—emotions.

We can forecast that on December 21, 2012, and actually for about a year beforehand, considering the 1° orb allowed, there will be intensified focus on the events of September 11, 2001. This focus will be both energetic and emotional. Consideration of other midpoint combinations would further reveal the kinds of events to be expected. With the Moon involved, there could be celebrations for the people who were lost at that time, and the people who were immediately affected by the events. With Mars, there could be a show of strength. With the Sun, there could be monuments or other memorials.

The decision to use secondary progressions or solar arc directions often depends on the reason for casting the chart. Both systems have been proven to work well. The reader may want to try both systems to see which provides more consistent, precise results.

COMPOSITE AND RELATIONSHIP CHARTS

While we think of relationships as romantic, there are numerous other types of relationships that can be delineated through astrology. Some of them include parent-child, employer-employee, business partnerships, lawyer-client, physician-patient, and just friends. There can be male-female or same-sex relationships. All of these and more are worth examination by the astrologer.

There are also several ways to approach the subject of relationships:

- How does an individual tend to relate with other people? What are the main pathways for forming relationships? These considerations come from the individual natal chart.

- How does one individual's astrological chart "fit" with another? This kind of comparison is called *synastry*.

- How do two people, who have formed a significant relationship, tend to function as a unit in the world? The *composite chart* is used to evaluate this kind of relationship.

- How do the two partners view each other within the relationship? This can be defined through the *Davison relationship chart.*

- What is the significance of the time for formalizing a relationship, either through marriage, a business contract, or other means? This kind of question is read through a new chart set for the time of the marriage or contract.

- Finally, how are relationships affected by the movements of progressions or transits?

Some relationship charts—those based on actual birth times—can be progressed. Others, like the composite chart, cannot.

Individual Capacity for Relationships

Throughout this book, the personal potential for relationships has been considered. The Seventh House focuses on marriage and business partnerships—those partnerships that involve formal, legal contracts. In addition to these, each person has the potential for relationships with siblings, friends, children, and other family members, teachers, and business people encountered in daily activities. Depending on the signs in the related houses, and the planets there, one can make a clear statement about relationship potential.

Here we will discuss the potential for marriage. By following the principles involved, and applying them to any house in the chart, the astrologer can evaluate other types of relationships.

Marriage Potential

There are four factors to consider for the success of a marriage:

- Partnership: The Seventh House sign, its ruling planet, and planets in the Seventh House all are indicators of the potential for partnership. Aspects to the Seventh House cusp and to the associated planets show the ways in which the partner will affect the individual's life. More prominent planets and more exact aspects will indicate more involvement with partners. The nature of the aspects indicates the quality of partnership interactions.

  Generally, Uranus and Neptune tend to disrupt the smooth flow of relationships, and frequently lead to the dissolution of partnerships. The Sun and Uranus in a woman's chart tend to indicate unusual partnerships. The Moon and Uranus in a man's chart indicate the same. The Sun and Neptune in a woman's chart (or Moon and Neptune in a man's) tend to indicate idealism where partners are concerned, and sometimes a lack of objectivity leads to disappointment.

- When dealing with members of the opposite sex, the Sun afflicted in a woman's chart indicates misfortune through male partners. For a man, the Moon afflicted can cause the same problem. Because relationships require a balancing of the magnetic contact between the partners, some relationships that seem ideal on the surface do not work well, while other very unusual partnerships are totally successful.

- Affection for the partner is separate from either magnetism or sexuality. When Venus is prominent in one's chart, affection is a key issue. The aspects Venus forms are indicative of the satisfaction or lack of it on the emotional side of a relationship.

- In love affairs, and in all sexual matters, there are several astrological concerns. With Mars in the Fifth House, one can expect strife or, at the very least, high levels of physical energy. With Saturn in the Fifth, there may be a coolness or aloofness in intimate relationships. With the Moon there, one can experience inconstancy of feelings.

Opportunities to Marry

One of the most frequent questions asked of astrologers concerns when marriage may occur. In the birth chart, there are indicators of the likelihood of marriage. Progressions and transits suggest the likely timing of marriages. In our contemporary world, many relationships never result in marriage. However, when a firm commitment is made to the other person, one can see strong indications in the charts of both partners. Those indicators include applying aspects of the progressed (and transiting) Moon in a man's chart, and similar aspects from the Sun in a woman's chart. Each of these represents an opportunity, in the order of perfection (the order in which the aspects become exact). All aspects, up to the point where the Sun or Moon change signs, may be considered. This naturally means that a Sun or Moon in early degrees of a sign in the birth chart may have more opportunities to form partnerships, although this is not necessarily the case.

Whom to Marry

Another frequently asked question concerns the type of partner one should seek. There are many factors to consider:

- Physical harmony: For physical harmony, there should be connections between the Sun, Moon, Mercury, and Ascendant, both in the individual birth charts and between the two charts. Harmonious aspects indicate a freer flow of magnetism between two charts. Generally, connections of fire and air signs to each other, or earth and water signs, are desirable.

- Mental harmony: Before even considering the charts, one must examine factors that are largely provided by the environment. These factors include evolutionary (genetic) conditions, the environment in which the individual lives, conditioning by family, peers, and other associates, and inherited position. Mental harmony within each individual is indicated astrologically first by the dominant planet. The strongest planet in the chart indicates where one's energy will naturally go if nothing occurs to change its flow. This potential is explained in the chapters dealing with the planets in natal and progressed or transiting charts.

- Personality can be seen in the Ascendant and aspects to it and to its planetary ruler. Also consider the decanate of the Ascendant. Many fundamentally unchanging personality traits can be seen through careful examination of the Ascendant.

- Mentality: The mind of the individual is a private area. However, the chart reveals the mechanisms that govern its operation. The Moon sign and decanate, along with aspects, indicate the basic mental traits of individuals.

- Individuality: Individuality is seen in the Sun sign and decanate. They show who and what a person is on the core level. Aspects of the Sun indicate core character traits that are unlikely to change over time.

Given that many of these traits are unlikely to change throughout one's life, it is good to understand them before making a lifelong commitment to a partner. That way, undertaking a marriage or business partnership is done from a position of informed awareness.

A final consideration is mental ability. While many relationships survive on the basis of sexual attraction and friendship, mental compatibility is also very important. The sign occupied by Mercury indicates the direction in which intellectual thought will go. The decanate indicates loftier ideas, and can show where a person seeks to be noticed. Mercury aspects indicate the smooth or rough flow of expression. For example, a hard aspect of the Moon to Mercury may indicate obstacles to clear expression. All of these considerations tell a story about the individual and his or her personal attitudes. Because what you see is not always what you get (for example, with Mercury and the Sun in the Twelfth House in a mutable sign), it is wise to gather information astrologically wherever possible.

Synastry

When comparing two charts, remember that one chart is actually a transit to the other, and vice versa. Thus the instructions for considering transits will apply to chart comparison. Some combinations are obviously more favorable than others for harmonious and/or long-term relationships. One key is to observe if there are numerous, strong contacts. If there are very few contacts between two charts, the individuals may come together for a single purpose and then go their separate ways. The following are indicators of strong, harmonious connections between the charts of partners:

- The Sun in harmonious aspect to the Moon is a strong indicator of physical attraction, particularly the Sun in one chart relating to the Moon in the other.
- Moon-Jupiter contacts may be good for financial aspects of the relationship, but can lead to marital differences, especially with less harmonious aspects. Part of the reason is that this combination often indicates religious or legal differences.
- Venus-Mars connections are good for physical attraction, even difficult aspects.
- Venus in harmonious aspect to Uranus can stimulate a long-lived romantic relationship.
- Venus-Pluto aspects indicate a karmic tie between the partners. The same is true of Venus-Saturn contacts. The nature of the aspect addresses the nature and quality of the karmic tie.
- Physical harmony: Look for harmonious connections to the Ascendants in both charts. These can involve the Ascendant or the planets. The same consideration should be made for the Descendant (usually, if the Ascendant is aspected, the Descendant is also aspected).
- The Sun, Moon, Venus, or Mars aspecting the planetary ruler of the Ascendant is good for personal connections between partners.

- The Moon and Venus in a man's chart indicate his sexual drive. The Sun and Mars indicate this in a woman's chart. From this, one can see that same-sex relationships can have friction, as each person has their own style where sexual function is concerned, and yet may be seeking the same sorts of satisfaction.
- Mars, Uranus, and Neptune in one's Seventh House, or in the partner's Seventh House, can cause problems. Neptune indicates idealism that will be difficult to live up to; Mars and Uranus indicate an unfortunate union (often the first partnership fails, but the individual learns something and manages better in later relationships).

To summarize, look for the greatest harmony when the Sun, Moon, Venus, and Mars form compatible aspects between charts. Look for the greatest excitement when Uranus is involved. Look for longevity when Saturn is well aspected between the charts. Wider orbs can be allowed for the Sun, Moon, and Ascendant. Generally, look for aspects of only a 1° orb. As the relationship matures, aspects of wider orb will come into play, just as they do in the individual birth chart.

The Composite Chart

A composite chart is a chart derived by computing the midpoints between the same planets in each chart. For example, if the Sun in one chart is at 14 degrees Aries and the Sun in the other chart is at 12 degrees Gemini, the midpoint is 13 degrees Taurus. The midpoints are calculated for each planetary pair. The midpoint between the Midheavens is calculated in the same way. Then the Ascendant and other house cusps are derived the same way one would calculate them for a natal chart, using the latitude where the partners are living.

A composite chart can be set up for any kind of relationship, for two persons, a person and his horse, or an individual and her car (assuming you know when the car was built or the exact time of purchase). The chart is read according to the nature of the relationship. The chart indicates how the relationship functions in the world. This may have something to do with the individual intentions; however, the main purpose for this kind of chart is to see how the relationship itself will function.

- *Sun:* The Sun's house placement tells what the basic purpose of the relationship is and what major issues will arise. The aspects tell the kinds of behavior that will be most important for the relationship. For example, a weak Sun, by sign, house, or aspects, could indicate that the basic energy of the relationship is not handled well and thus can damage the partnership, while a strong Sun provides promise of long-term success of the relationship.
- *Moon:* The house position of the Moon shows the area where the partners feel they have the most in common. Badly placed, it shows the area of the greatest emotional stress. Well placed, the partners will feel they understand each other better than most couples. The action of the relationship is shown by the Moon's placement as well. When they are seen in the world, they are seen as coming from the nature of the house and sign occupied by the Moon.
- *Mercury:* The quality of communication between the partners is reflected in their communication with the world. If Mercury is well placed and aspected, then the couple is effective in the

world. The nature of the sign describes the best approach to communication. If badly placed, Mercury will reveal where difficulties lie in the path of effective action between the partners and in the world at large.

- *Venus:* The house position of Venus indicates how far this relationship will allow the partners to express themselves through love. A well-placed Venus indicates a strong attraction, but may not make up for other incompatibilities. Badly placed, the relationship may last, but be basically devoid of love. The impact of these possibilities has a dramatic effect on the social interactions the couple may have with others.

- *Mars:* The need for energetic expression is seen in the Mars placement in the composite chart. Both partners need to have freedom to express their desires and needs if the partnership is to be effective. A weak placement can lead to destructive conflicts, within the relationship and in public. A strong Mars provides the energy for a successful sexual relationship. With a strong Venus, the sense of values blends with the physical energy to bring this success. A weak Mars can affect the partners' ability to get along together or in the world.

- *Jupiter:* The process of growth within the relationship, as well as the growth of the relationship vis-à-vis the world, is seen through Jupiter's placement. A strong Jupiter reflects the benefit to both partners in the relationship. A weak Jupiter may indicate a lack of benefit, or a tendency toward excess in relationship matters.

- *Saturn:* The structure of the partnership is reflected by Saturn. If there are insecurities, Saturn shows them as well. Thus a strong Saturn bolsters the relationship and helps the partners be active forces in their environment, while a weaker Saturn, or one with hard aspects, can indicate an unendurable pain when the partners must interact with each other, or in social situations. This is because the confines of Saturn's structure can become oppressive. Therefore, the partners will want to develop and maintain a secure yet flexible structure in their dealings together.

- *Uranus:* Uranus is where the spark of intuition is found between the partners. It is also where ritual plays a powerful role in creating and maintaining a strong partnership. The capacity to move between alternating views of reality will help any relationship—there are always at least two realities to be considered, one for each partner. Ritual skill also helps the couple respond to the needs of the larger world. A flexible Uranus is a great benefit to the growth and maintenance of a good relationship. The partnership suffers when a weak Uranus fails to provide intuitive insight.

- *Neptune:* Neptune indicates where the partners idealize their own relationship, as well as how they appear to the world. Some idealism is a good thing, but too much can detract from normal social skills. Too much illusion also prevents the partners from deepening their spiritual connection. All relationships require work to become and to remain successful. A little idealism helps this process along. Too much makes it seem like everything is fine, when it isn't.

- *Pluto:* Here is where the power of transformation is found. Most relationships undergo change due to major life events that demand attention from one or both partners. Where we find powerful forces for change, we also find powerful forces for conflict. Pluto indicates where, if the partners fail to pay attention, conflict can arise. Strong Pluto aspects provide the energy to change in a positive direction. Weak aspects leave an atmosphere of inattention or disempowerment, which destroys the values within the relationship.

- *The Nodes:* The Nodes indicate the types of associations the couple can form with each other and with the world around them. Aspects to the Nodes are not as strong as interplanetary aspects. So these aspects are supportive, but perhaps not as critical as other aspects in the composite chart.

- *Ascendant:* The Ascendant in a composite chart can be the midpoint between the two Ascendants, or it can be derived in the same way that the Ascendant in a birth chart is calculated, based on the position of the Midheaven. Because the midpoint can produce results that are impossible in the order of zodiacal signs, the derived method is more generally used. Aspects to the Ascendant increase the importance of the planets involved, as they indicate how the energy of the relationship creates its own persona, and affects the individual partners in different ways, based on their birth chart. A strong Ascendant can make the partnership much more than the sum of the individuals, while a weak Ascendant can diminish the individuals.

- *Midheaven:* The Midheaven is a calculated midpoint between the two charts. It represents the locus of self-awareness of the partnership. Because it is generally in a different sign from either of the partners, awareness within the relationship is quite different from the individual's sense of self. A strong Midheaven carries the relationship toward greater understanding of the world and of each other.

The Davison Relationship Chart

The Davison relationship chart is named for its creator. It is calculated for the midpoint in time between the births of the partners, and the midpoint in longitude and latitude. This can result in birth places in the middle of the ocean. The location is not as important as the fact that the chart is an actual calculated chart, unlike the composite chart.

The Davison chart is about the relationship itself, and not about how the relationship functions in the environment. It indicates how the partners interact with each other. It is read just like an individual birth chart, but the entity under consideration is the relationship. The houses relate to the usual areas of life, and the planets reflect the same kinds of energy. The aspects indicate the areas where the relationship itself works well, and where it is weak.

Progressions and Transits in Relationships

Because the composite chart is derived, it is questionable whether it can be progressed. However, transits to composite charts appear to work as one would expect. The student may want to experiment with solar arc directions.

Synastry charts, being birth charts, can be progressed as usual. The Davison relationship chart is also a regular chart, and thus can be progressed. Direction and transits to both kinds of charts can be used to forecast high and low points in relationships, and to plan ahead for contingencies. Progressions and transits can be read much like those for any birth chart. They may then be compared to the active elements in the individual charts of the partners, in order to determine the best way to handle the energies being reflected in the aspects.

Students will do well to investigate partnership charts for people they know before undertaking analysis for acquaintances or clients. This field is very important to astrology, as it has the potential to help partnerships grow and weather difficult periods. At the same time, there is potential to misread charts, causing damage to relationships that otherwise might come through tough stretches. Relationship analysis deserves equal consideration to working with the charts of individuals.

CHART PATTERNS

Chart patterns are arrangements of planets that dominate the chart and affect all areas of life, even those not directly included in the patterns. There are two kinds of patterns:

- Those composed of planets forming aspects within a particular harmonic (squares or trines, for example)
- Those in which the planets are arranged in describable patterns (bundle or bowl, for example)

The descriptions of each type of pattern indicate that the features of one type are included in the other; for example, the defining features of a bowl are the "surface," an opposition, and the "container," either squares or trines and sextiles.

Chart patterns are significant because they define relationships among the planets. When planets are closely related by aspects or by forms, they tend to reflect consistent, predictable behavior on the part of the individual. Through understanding the main astrological patterns, the student is able to grasp the principal tendencies within the personality. This method considers the chart as a whole first, and then considers the individual planets and aspects. There are many patterns worth consideration. The patterns included here are primarily defined by the aspects that make up the twelfth harmonic—conjunction, semisextile, sextile, square, trine, quincunx, and opposition. These patterns are often prominent in the second type of pattern, defined by the overall appearance of the chart.

To begin, let us consider the most open and diffuse of the patterns. The Splash pattern is just as it sounds—the planets are spaced fairly evenly around the chart. Patterns, by definition, involve only the planets, and not the angles or the Nodes. Some astrologers also include Chiron and the four major asteroids in the consideration of patterns. The Splash does not have any gaps between planets that are larger than 60 degrees, and ideally there is one planet in each of the ten houses. The positions of specific planets are not important to the definition of this or other patterns, but should be considered in interpretation.

The Splash personality is one that has multiple interests and no single focus. While this could indicate a scattering of energies, it also may indicate a personality that uses the breadth of interests to form the life in a conscious way, guided by the will. In children, this can be seen in willful behavior. In thoughtful adults, this can indicate a rich diversity of interests and goals.

As the planets group more closely together, the remaining patterns emerge. The second pattern is the Splay. The Splay is defined by close groupings of planets. These groupings that may not define patterns based on the aspects formed among the planets. These individuals have very intense personalities, but do not fit in with the rest of the "pack." They have determination and certainty in their actions, but the internal logic is their own, and no one else's.

Grand Trine

The Grand Trine is a pattern composed of three or more planets that form trine aspects. Typically, the planets occupy three signs of the same element. If you were to draw lines between the planets, you would have a nearly equilateral triangle. The Grand Trine might be found within the Splash or Splay chart, but is not necessarily found there. It is often found within two other patterns: the Locomotive and the Bucket. The Locomotive is a chart where there is an open third—four signs/houses where there are no planets. Ideally the planets are evenly distributed within the remaining two thirds of the chart. Two of the Grand Trine planets are on the ends of the Locomotive, and the third is midway in the pattern. The Grand Trine also can be found within the Bucket pattern. The Bucket is defined as a chart with all the planets within one half of the chart, except for a single planet that forms a "handle." Ideally, the planets are evenly spaced within the full ("bowl") half of the chart.

The Grand Trine usually involves planets in each of the signs of one element. There is a great deal of ease within this pattern—perhaps too much—which allows the individual to relax and take life as it comes. The problem can be that the person expects life to deliver on a regular basis, and becomes frustrated when this does not happen, due to a lack of progressed and transiting influences. The strength of this pattern is maximized when the individual sets goals and pursues them in ways compatible with the element in which the pattern occurs. Fire trines are constantly active, trying new things. Earth trines capitalize on a method, working with it to get the biggest and best results. The air trine pursues ideas to the ultimate limit, while water trines do the same with feelings.

Grand Square

The Grand Square, in contrast to the Grand Trine, has its planets in the same mode. Four or more planets are approximately 90° apart. Connecting lines will form a square. In addition to the planets being in the same mode—cardinal, fixed, or mutable—they are usually in like houses—angular, succedent, or cadent. Depending on the latitude of birth, the latter may not be true, but generally the former is true.

This is a relatively rare pattern. It indicates a life in which there are many challenges, and a strong awareness of one's place in the world. If there are problems, little can be done to change them, and the difficulty is that there are four problems at one time. As the individual moves through life, awareness can be helpful in forecasting periods of difficulty, and then using past experience to manage situations that arise. One way to use the energy is to funnel it into a planet that forms a good aspect to one or more of the planets in the Grand Square. For example, a planet that trines and sextiles two of the planets can provide easier conditions to fall back on, as well as opportunities to use the abundant energy of the squares. Such a planet may also be forming a semisextile or quincunx to the remaining planets in the square, providing two additional outlets.

The picture patterns often associated with the Grand Square are the Seesaw and the Bucket (which we already mentioned). In the Seesaw pattern, the planets are grouped on opposite sides of the chart, with two 90° sections empty. The energy of this pattern is that of a seesaw—maintaining balance becomes very difficult. When the individual has moved into the center, closer to the fulcrum of the Seesaw, shifts continue to occur, but they are not as dramatic nor as devastating.

The Bucket pattern is formed when all but one of the planets are in one half of the chart, and a single planet is near the middle of the empty hemisphere. The Bucket is a relatively contained pattern. The individual gathers energy and then directs it toward the planet in the handle. The container portion of the bucket may also be defined by having all the planets in one hemisphere, but this is not a necessary part of its definition. The closer the handle is to the midpoint of the empty sector, the more forceful the expression of energy. The Grand Cross is the ultimate expression of the focused energy of the bucket pattern.

Grand Sextile

This is an extremely rare pattern. It requires that six of the Splash or Splay planets be even spaced at 60° intervals. Typically, the Grand Sextile pattern will be composed of planets in either fire and air signs, or earth and water signs. The expressive possibilities of such a pattern are tremendous, as opportunities are constantly arising to use the energy of the two elements involved.

It is more common that individuals who have many sextiles in their chart will have progressions or transits that complete this pattern. When this occurs, the individual is at a peak of expressive potential, and many seem to work magic in all areas of life. It also occurs that one's partner may fill in the empty angles, forming a union of two individuals who can direct the energy of their partnership very powerfully.

T-Square

The T-Square is a fairly common pattern in charts. It is defined by an opposition between two planets, with a third planet forming a square to both. The focus is on the planet forming the squares. Whatever the awareness of conflicting relationships, indicated by the opposition, the third planet is the source of the potential solution. If the energies are obstructed, then problems develop for the individual, over and over, until the behavior pattern is clearly understood. Then the individual can achieve a life of accomplishment, as there is abundant energy for effective action, as well as destructive action.

Picture patterns containing a T-Square are numerous. The most obvious is the Bowl. The Bowl configuration is defined by the opposition, with the planets spaced evenly on one side of it. There will be a third planet at the "bottom" of the bowl. When the T-Square is also a Bowl, the individual is quite self-contained most of the time. If the Bowl is in the Northern Hemisphere, this self-containment is nearly total. However, if the Bowl is tilted, or even upside down in the chart (occupying the Southern Hemisphere), then the individual finds that personal energies are collected and contained, only to spill out periodically.

Other patterns that may contain a T-Square are the Locomotive, Splash, Splay, and Seesaw. Each of these will express both the fundamental nature of the T-Square and the nature of the picture pattern.

Yod

The Yod is made up of two planets that form a sextile, and also form a quincunx to a third planet. The very focused nature of the triangle formed suggests the nature of the pattern. There are opportunities for action, but they are restricted by the fact that adjustments are constantly being made to one's plans. The planets are generally in incompatible signs, either by element or mode, and thus do not naturally work together easily.

There is an element of destiny in such a pattern. The individual must adapt to the energies or experience great pain, or even destruction. The quincunx aspect is often involved in health questions, so the individual may strain the health to the breaking point if the energy is not managed well. Another possibility is that, through no apparent personal effort, the person is given (inherits) exactly what is needed to make further progress. Usually something in the middle occurs. The individual comes to a fork in the road, evaluates the possibilities, and chooses one direction over the other. Actually this choice is not between new possibilities, but is based on potentials that have been developing, and now need to be refined, one way or the other.

The Yod can appear within any pattern that includes more than 210 degrees of the chart—the Bucket, Seesaw, Locomotive, Splash, or Splay.

The Bundle

The only picture pattern remaining is the Bundle. This pattern is the opposite of the Locomotive. In this case there are two empty trines, and all the planets are grouped within 120 degrees of the Zodiac. This pattern can only occur when the outer planets are close together in the sky, and then must await the movement of Mars into the trine. Then the inner planets move into the trine in due season, followed by the Moon. Interesting patterns may occur, but none of the major aspect patterns will be formed.

The Bundle is very concentrated, both literally and figuratively. This pattern indicates an individual who resists influences from outside the self, and is very focused in terms of goals and emotions. The person tends to be somewhat inhibited, as the potential directions of energy are so limited. Yet great deeds may be accomplished through the sheer concentration of will. There will very likely be numerous opportunities—the planets so close together tend to form sextile aspects—and there may also be great challenges represented by squares within the Bundle.

Major changes for the Bundle type occur when planets, by progression or transit, occupy the open areas of the chart. The progressed Moon, for example, will form all the possible aspects by the age of thirty, and again by the age of sixty, providing multiple glimpses into the broadest possible experience.

Lack of a Pattern

Occasionally, the astrologer sees a chart that defies any of these definitions of pattern. In such a case, the individual must cultivate the potential energy of each planet, and then combine them through an effort of will. This individual will feel like a free agent to family and friends who have more typical styles of expression.

SOLAR, LUNAR, PLANETARY, AND PHASE ANGLE RETURNS

The exact time when a planet returns to the position it held in the birth chart is its *Return*. Solar Returns occur annually, and Lunar Returns occur monthly. The table below shows the average planetary periods.

Planet	Orbital Period
Mercury	87.907 days
Venus	224.70 days
Mars	686.98 days
Jupiter	11.86 years
Saturn	29.46 years
Uranus	84.01 years
Neptune	164.79 years
Pluto	247.69 years

Table 12: Average Planetary Periods

Solar Return

The time when the Sun returns to the zodiacal position it occupied in the birth chart under consideration is called the Solar Return. The Solar Return is thought to mark a significant point, and the Solar

Return chart is used to forecast events for the following year. Because the Solar Return is timed very precisely, the house positions in the Return chart are the key indicators, whereas the signs are not as important.

The house placement of the Sun in the Solar Return indicates the personal focus for the year. This is the area of life where the individual's energy will be concentrated, and where events and conditions will have the greatest impact. The house placement of the Moon indicates what kind of action will occur during the following year. The Solar Return chart can be interpreted in very much the same way as the birth chart, keeping in mind that it depends on the birth chart, just as other transits do, and that it is valid for the year in question.

Some astrologers say the year of the Solar Return chart begins three months before the birth date, and will wane toward the end of the following year, around the time the next Solar Return begins to take effect. In other words, we are able to experience the nature of the coming year before it actually begins.

Another technique suggests dividing the houses in the Solar Return chart into twelve segments, each of which represents one month in the following year. If a planet falls in a particular segment, that month will be an active one with regard to the particular planet.

Lunar Returns

Where the Solar Return provides a picture of the coming year, the Lunar Return captures the sense of the energy available during each lunar month. It deals with the less conscious side of your nature—the inner "tides" that shift with the position of the Moon. The Solar Return provides a game plan for the year, and the Lunar Return indicates thirteen specific plays that will work out best throughout the year. These plays are based on your internal understanding of yourself and how you respond to the world at large.

The value of the Lunar Return chart is in its expression of the feeling tone of a time period. It indicates when to forge ahead and when to hold back, within the larger effort of the annual cycle.

Planetary Returns

The rest of the planets have cycles of one year or longer. Each of these returns indicates the nature of the following cycle, based upon the birth chart. For example, the Saturn Return is familiar to many people. It represents a transition from the developmental cycles of childhood and young adulthood to the productive cycles that dominate the middle third of life. The second Saturn Return indicates what lies ahead for the final third of the potential lifespan.

The longer cycles resist analysis, as they cover too much time to be meaningful to most people. Yet they offer insights into those stretches of life that seem to defy any sort of ordinary logic. The square and opposition points provide insights into developmental processes at any age. Reading these charts often reveals the core issues of the planet to be dealt with during the coming cycle.

Phase Angle Returns

Modern astrology, with the advent of computers, can easily track the relationships of any planetary pairs. The phase angles between any pair of planets are significant. However, the most evident of these is the Sun-Moon phase angle.

The relationship between the Sun and Moon was probably the first astronomical observation of ancient people. The significance of these two bodies cannot be overestimated, as the Sun provides the light and energy to sustain life, and the Moon controls the tides of the oceans and within the human body. The Sun and Moon also provide timing mechanisms for the year and the month. Ancient people used these two to determine when to move camp, when to plant, and when to celebrate rituals. The importance of these relationships in the birth chart becomes apparent by examining the Sun-Moon phase angle, or the distance between the Sun and Moon in the birth chart.

Native American and Eastern Indian cultures both made use of this phase angle to determine the best times for conception. The Internet is full of articles on the phase angle, from both the astronomical and astrological perspectives. Many of these articles focus on two potential fertility cycles—the biological cycle and the Sun-Moon cycle. In the simplest terms, a woman is most likely to conceive when the biological and the astronomical Sun-Moon cycles are aligned. In other words, conception is more likely when the Sun and Moon are in the same phase as they were at the time of birth.

Research has confirmed the astrological premise that women are far more likely to become pregnant when the Sun and Moon form the same angle they held in the birth chart, and the signs matter a good deal less than the angle itself. Of course, some signs are more compatible than others, and some are more fruitful than others. Still, it is the angle that is important. The physical fertility cycle provides an apt metaphor for the broader importance of the phase angle in individual lives. The Sun-Moon phase angle represents the time each month when personal power is at its peak. This is a time to conceive new plans, develop ideas, explore solutions to problems, and evaluate goals. It may be a peak point in the dreaming cycle as well. The Sun-Moon phase cycle marks the moments each month when individuals may gain deeper understanding of their personal process.

This personal cycle is a reflection of the larger planetary cycle. Many religious calendars are tied to the Sun-Moon cycles. Easter, for example, occurs on the first Sunday after the first Full Moon after the spring equinox. This is a celebration of the return of life and the beginning of new growth. Passover is also a variable holiday, but is linked to Rosh Hashanah, the Jewish New Year celebrated at the New Moon closest to the autumn equinox. This could be before or after the equinox, depending on the calendar. The Tibetan and Chinese New Years are linked to the lunar cycle as well.

The phase angle between other planetary, asteroid, and angular combinations is also significant. Each pairing of objects and angles in the birth chart represents the relationship between two distinct energies, and the angle represents the quality of that relationship. When the same relationship is repeated, the birth potential is highlighted. The individual has an opportunity to focus on the talent and skills indicated by the combination in the natal chart. Just as the Sun-Moon angle indicates a good time for conception in the female chart, the relationship between any two planets indicates a good time to conceive or begin activities associated with those planets.

Keep in mind that the phase angle does not have to be in the same degree and sign as in the birth chart. It can occur in any sign. The relationship under consideration is the angle between the two planets.

How to Use Phase Angle Returns

Throughout the book you have encountered the concept of aspects—the angle between two points in the chart. Wherever there is a significant aspect, delineation of the character and life is possible. The concepts of progressions and transits have been added to this mix, with the positions of the planets in progressed, solar arc, transit, and other charts providing information about current trends in one's life.

The phase angle is another way of looking at aspects. The angle in the birth chart, whether or not it forms a recognized aspect, remains significant throughout a person's life. When that angle is repeated, energy very compatible with the birth chart is available to the individual. The simplest example is the Sun and Moon. Suppose the individual has the Sun conjunct the Moon at birth. Each New Moon will have special significance, greater than the other twenty-six or twenty-seven days of each month. The individual is a "New Moon" type.

The Moon cycle is very regular and relatively short. The angle between Mars and Saturn occurs much less frequently—about every two years, with occasional irregularities due to the retrograde patterns of both planets. Because Mars and Saturn are closely related to career progress, the times when these angles return can be powerful indicators of career developments. The same can be said for any phase angle. The association in the birth chart between any two planets, asteroids, or Transneptunian points will be reinforced when the same angle occurs by transit.

Without the aid of a computer, calculation of the phase angles would be tedious work, paging through an ephemeris to find the appropriate dates. Several of the more powerful astrological computer programs on the market have the capacity to search for the phase angle returns and provide the dates and times they occur.

It is important to remember that the phase angle is what is significant, not the signs or houses in which it occurs. Thus, if the Sun and Moon are conjunct, they may be anywhere in the Zodiac, not just the degree and sign they occupy in the birth chart. This may seem odd at first. One is quite comfortable with one's own Sun in its own degree. However, the particular angle between them also is very significant to human life, independent of the signs involved.

How to Use the Phase Angle Technique

A few simple steps are involved in the use of this technique.

- Decide which two planets you wish to work with in the birth chart. Calculate the exact number of degrees between these two planets.

- Estimate how much time passes before the phase angle will occur again (see the following table).
- In the ephemeris, turn to the appropriate date and search for positions of the two planets that repeat the natal angular relationship. Remember that the angle between the planets must be the same as in the birth chart, but the signs and degrees may be different.

Or:

- Using a computer program, employ the phase angle calculator, entering the planets you are working with.
- Make a list of the dates when the phase angles are the same as in the birth chart.
- Consider the energies or events promised in the birth chart, based on the two planets. Then reflect on dates in the past, or plan for dates in the future. The same energy will be evident in some way on each return date.

Planet	Second Planet	Estimated Phase Angle Return Time
Moon	Any	27 days
Mercury	Any	1 year
Venus	Any	1 year
Sun	Any	1 year: the Solar Return produces the same Sun phase angle to every planet
Mars	Jupiter	26 months
	Saturn and outer planets	24 months
Jupiter	Saturn	20 years
	Uranus and outer planets	13 to 14 years
Saturn	Uranus	43 to 48 years
	Neptune and Pluto	36 years
Uranus	Neptune and Pluto	170 years
Neptune	Pluto	Can be as frequent as twice a year, due to slow orbits

Table 13: Estimated Phase Angle Returns

ESOTERIC AND PSYCHOLOGICAL ASTROLOGY

Two significant developments in modern astrology have grown out of the developing field of psychology. One branch takes the Freudian/Jungian approach, examining the astrological chart in terms of the psychological tendencies of the planets and signs. The other takes a spiritual approach, relating the signs to the path of spiritual development laid out by Theosophists and Alice Bailey. Both are grounded in traditional Western astrology, and neither is totally exclusive of the other.

Psychological Astrology

Psychological astrology uses the symbolic language of astrology to describe the workings of the human mind. Parallels between psychological theories and astrological language are remarkably refined. For example, the traditional four elements of Western astrology parallel the personality types of Jungian psychology:

- Fire: Intuition
- Earth: Sensation
- Air: Thinking
- Water: Feeling

One's Sun sign very often reflects one's personality type.

The astrological houses rule areas of one's life, parts of the body, and also parts of one's mental activity.

- First House: The persona—the face one shows to the world; childhood developmental experiences.
- Second House: Self-esteem; the capacity for endurance; sense of form.
- Third House: Relationships with persons in the immediate environment; versatility, adaptability.
- Fourth House: Hereditary traits, capacity for feeling, receptivity.
- Fifth House: Sex drives, self-confidence, creative capacity.
- Sixth House: Critical faculty, capacity to conform.
- Seventh House: Sense of obligation, capacity for social interaction, partnership.
- Eighth House: Survival instinct, passion and its expression; understanding of mortality.
- Ninth House: Spiritual tendencies, transcendent values.
- Tenth House: Self-awareness, seriousness, capacity for patience.
- Eleventh House: Hopes and dreams, capacity to plan, capacity to observe, willingness to help others.
- Twelfth House: Emotional and intellectual reserve, receptivity to influences of all kinds, capacity for serenity.

Taken together with the planets, the houses provide an elegant map of consciousness that has grater depth than many contemporary psychological theories. The advantage of astrology is that it also indicates, through progressions and transits, the developmental movement of the individual through time.

From the psychological perspective, the planets express motivations. These motivations have been delineated throughout the book, but a short statement here may help gather the psychological data together for the reader. More constructive facets are mentioned first; the less constructive side follows.

- Sun: The capacity to make decisions; the will to live; indecision, lack of vitality.
- Moon: The capacity to nurture, changeability; moodiness, impressionability.
- Mercury: Critical ability, capacity for judgment; weak intellect, lack of understanding.
- Venus: Capacity for a positive outlook, capacity for feeling; lack of discrimination.
- Mars: Courage, determination, urge to take action; impulsiveness, lack of energy.
- Jupiter: Capacity for expansion, optimism, moral or religious consideration; amoral thought and action, greed, materialistic attitude.
- Saturn: Capacity to learn from experience, concentration; inhibition, lack of adaptability.
- Uranus: Capacity to act independently, intuition, strong perception; rebelliousness, impulsiveness, emotional tension.
- Neptune: Capacity for imagination and fantasy, contemplation; vagueness, confusion, inability to plan.
- Pluto: Will to power, unconscious forces; fanaticism, agitation.

Example

An individual has the Sun in Gemini in the Tenth House. Gemini is an air sign, so the primary mental style is Thinking. This means that, presented with a problem, the individual will tend to think it through. Depending on the complexity of the problem, this may take some time. This could look like a period of indecision to others. In the Tenth House, the Sun is capable of patience and self-awareness. The individual therefore is probably quite aware of the fact that he or she requires time to think through a situation and make a decision. Beneath any apparent indecisiveness, seriousness of nature may be found.

Esoteric Astrology

Esoteric astrology goes beyond the psychology of the individual. It seeks to explore the realm of the universe, Universal Mind, or Unity. It examines the development of the human race against this larger background. From this transpersonal perspective, the individual is then considered. The emphasis remains, throughout esoteric astrology, on the larger, more inclusive sphere, seeking to understand how information from that sphere, in the form of intuition or other forces, enters the individual's experience.

In the system of esoteric astrology, the earth itself is said to radiate energy. The earth's Moon is thought to be inert, veiling the energy of other planets. The principal considerations in esoteric astrology are as follows:

- Planetary influences reflect circumstances outside oneself.
- The Sun sign reflects the nature of the individual on the physical, mental, and spiritual levels. The object of understanding the Sun sign is to support the soul's purpose.
- The rising sign, or Ascendant, indicates more remote spiritual goals to be pursued in the current incarnation, as well as the future.
- The Moon indicates one's past, and therefore the limitations of the present, due to experience in previous incarnations.

While we think of the astrological signs as moving forward through the Zodiac as the seasons do, in esoteric astrology the reverse is true. Over the longer cycle of birth and rebirth, one traverses the signs from Pisces, to Aries via Aquarius, etc.

Esoteric astrology also concerns energies thought to come from the great constellations. These energies enter our local system, and thus our awareness, through the planets. Individuals respond to these energies differently, depending on their level of physical, intellectual, and spiritual development. Esoteric astrology is a complex system that expresses the profound spiritual possibilities available to us, should we decide to pursue them. This system cannot be proven by ordinary scientific means, and is generally apprehended through meditation and study of the solar system as a whole. The bulk of esoteric astrology relates to the signs of the Zodiac and the universal energies that express through them.

HORARY AND MUNDANE ASTROLOGY

Besides using astrology to delineate the charts of individuals, astrologers have been considering the charts of nation and corporations for many years. In addition, astrology can be used to answer the kinds of questions we have about our personal lives, and about the future, by delineating the chart for the question, or for the times. The branch of astrology associated with answering questions is called *horary,* and it uses a chart for the time of the question. Charts used to make forecasts for the world in general, or specific areas of the world, are based on the time the Sun moves into the cardinal signs: Aries, Cancer, Libra, and Capricorn. These are called *ingress* charts, and can be used to forecast the weather, politics, economics, and other mundane matters.

All these charts follow basically the same rules as natal charts. The planetary dignities, the aspects, and the houses retain basically the same meanings, only modified to consider the type of chart involved.

Charts for Nations

Charts for nations are treated very much like birth charts for individuals. Some nations survive intact far longer than people do, so the cycles of the outer planets come into play in ways that are not possible in individual birth charts. Still, these charts have an organic quality that parallels the birth chart for a person.

The following table lists the houses in the national chart, and their meanings. Keep in mind that all these people and things relate to the nation as a whole.

House	Meaning in the Chart of a Nation
1	The people, their disposition and personal affairs, national traits, majority party (among registered voters).
2	Wealth, coined money, personal property, national treasury, banks, bonds and securities, places where money is handled, wages, prices, fluctuation of currency, stock exchange activities.
3	Transportation of all kinds, railroads, highways, telegraph, telephone, mail, printing, newspapers, magazines, thoughts of the people, reading habits of the public, traffic lights, post office.
4	Land, homes, buildings, weather, agriculture, crops, mining, political party that is out of power, territories, real estate, patriotic inclinations of the people, buried treasure.
5	Entertainment, birth rate, speculation, stock market and exchanges, foreign ambassadors to the U.S., children, schools, gambling.
6	Illness, food, labor and laborers, employees, armed forces, stored grain and harvest, restaurants, drug stores, small animals, police, public health agencies, bureaucracy, uniformed workers, juries and their deliberations, court records.
7	Foreign nations, war, marriage and divorce rates, opposition in an election, the judiciary system, social gatherings.
8	Death rate, debts owed to the nation, taxes, tariffs, insurance, the president's cabinet or similar group, mortality and suicide rates, surgeons, medical discoveries.
9	Interstate and international commerce, navy, foreign shipping, foreign communication, the Internet, law, the Supreme Court, religion, teachers, publishing, advertising, books, lectures, courts, judges, philanthropic institutions, grants.
10	The administration, president, king, dictator, etc.; credit of the nation, business of the nation, famous persons, employers, political party presently in power, national integrity.
11	Legislature, aldermen, congress, ambassadors to foreign nations, humanitarian aims, stock exchange as an organization.
12	Prisons, hospitals, charities, crime, detectives, secret societies, spies, secret enemies of the people, large animals, pests, smugglers, sabotage, kidnapping, slavery, the occult.

Table 14: Houses in National Charts

There are also specific meanings for the planets in national charts, listed in the following table. Note that these meanings, like the house meanings, are similar to the meanings in individual charts.

Planet	Thought	Business	Politics	Miscellaneous
Sun	Politics	Administration, executive work	Bosses, rulers, classes	The person in power, pilot
Moon	Family, home	Groceries, commodities	Women, common people	Many people involved, passengers
Mercury	Science	Literary work	The press	Controversy and much talk
Venus	Beautiful things	Art	"Society"	Women
Mars	Mechanics	Manufacturing, military profession	Militarism	Strife, violence, accidents, liquor
Jupiter	Religion, philosophy	Finance, commerce	Capitalism	Expansion, higher prices, spending
Saturn	Orthodoxy	Land, basic utilities, business	Conservatism, farmer, miner	Labor, contraction, loss, lower prices
Uranus	Ultraprogressive, occult	Invention, disruption, unusual methods	Radicals	Change, unexpected events
Neptune	Mystical, psychic	Promotion, marketing, inflation, stock brokers	The ideal, exaggerated hopes	Aviation, motion picture industry
Pluto	Spirituality, inversion, influence of invisible intelligences	Group activity (either selfish or for universal good)	Compulsory cooperation	Necessary cooperation, rival factions

Table 15: Planets in National Charts

Charts for Corporations

The charts of corporations and other businesses are read in a similar way to those of nations. The houses and planets take into consideration the functioning parts of the company.

House	Corporate or Company Meaning
1	The organization, morale, personnel, attitude toward competitors, stockholders
2	Liquid assets, ownership, expenditures
3	Communication with the public, interoffice communications
4	Home office, board of directors, manager, real-estate holdings
5	Speculation, educational functions, executive personnel
6	Employees, services, health conditions of employees, beginning of strikes or other labor problems
7	Relationship to other organizations, legal matters, competitors
8	Frozen assets, interest rates, social security benefits, outcome of speculation, company treasurer, competitor's financial condition
9	Proxy or emissary, advertising department, results of mail-order business, consultants, publicity
10	Governing authority, president, chairman of the board
11	Vice president, friendly affiliations, associates outside the company
12	Unknown competitors or enemies, labor unions, information-gathering operations

Table 16: Houses in Corporate Charts

The planets in corporate charts are strongest in angular houses, similar to the natal charts of individuals. Planets in succedent houses are capable of sustained activity, while cadent planets are generally in weakened positions, unless they are in a house they rule.

Planet	Role in Corporate Chart	Transiting Planet
Sun	Establishes affairs, gives authority	Vitalizes activity
Moon	Reorganizes	Temporary activity by transit
Mercury	Minor involvements, details	Makes the news
Venus	Protects, company looks good in this area	Protects
Mars	Area of disruption and energy	Rash action, violence, danger
Jupiter	Publishing, marketing, visionary thinking; work flow	Urges growth, expansion, and speculation; sheer luck
Saturn	Deliberate activities, sustained thriftiness	Delays action, limits scope
Uranus	Unexpected activities or people	Disorganizes, disrupts, breaks existing structure or ties
Neptune	Work behind the scenes, visionary efforts, utopian ideas	Tricks, produces illusion
Pluto	Charismatic persons, persons who exert unusual control	Slow or late action, compounds trouble in the house

Table 17: Planets in Corporate Charts

Horary Charts

The horary chart is a chart cast for the time a question is first seriously asked. The querent (the person asking the question), and his or her location, are used to cast the chart. Horary astrologers have develop a list of considerations of the chart itself, regardless of the question.

- If the Ascendant is in the first 3 degrees or the last 3 degrees of a sign, then it is too soon or too late to do anything, or to answer the question. The exception to this rule is when the Ascendant is in the degree of a natal planet in the querent's chart. This placement increases the likelihood of a favorable answer or outcome.

- If the Moon is in the Via Combusta (15 degrees Libra to 15 degrees Scorpio), events take a sudden, unexpected turn.

- If Saturn is in the Seventh House, the astrologer's judgment is clouded, or the chart has been cast inaccurately.

- The aspects of the Moon as it transits to the end of the sign it occupies are indications of how the action or question unfolds. If a planet (usually the Sun or Mercury) leaves its sign before the Moon can make an aspect, then the action of that planet is impeded.

- Retrograde planets are said to be less constructive because their energy is a more passive force.

- A peregrine planet (a planet that has no dignity in the chart) is nearly powerless to act. It may indicate idle curiosity or a lack of cooperation.
- The question may only be asked once.
- The aspects in horary charts, and the aspects the Moon forms as it moves forward, indicate the nature of the event, or the answer to a question.
- Opposition: Pulling apart, separation.
- Conjunction: Cooperation, bringing together.
- Sextile: Effort is needed to manifest the opportunity (if one planet is retrograde, the opportunity may be overlooked).
- Square: Obstacles, losses, the need to make a major effort.
- Trine: Success is easier than one might normally expect. May also indicate the nature of the reward.
- Parallel (of declination): The thing is as good as done now.
- Quincunx: The querent must support another person in some way.
- In an event chart, the event is of the nature of the house where the Sun is found, based on the house where Leo is found.
- In an event chart, the Moon indicates the activity to be expected, based on the house where Cancer is found.
- The querent (person asking the question) is indicated by the First House and its ruler.
- The question is identified by the house in the chart that governs that kind of question.

House   Indications in Horary Charts

House	Indications in Horary Charts
1	The querent (person asking the question).
2	Movable possessions (but usually not vehicles), money, the future, tomorrow.
3	Letters, messages, siblings, vehicles, short trips (according to the querent's definition of short).
4	Home, real estate, the end of the matter (how the question or matter will turn out), circumstances surrounding the outcome.
5	Children, speculation, gambling, participation sports, parks, bedrooms, love given.
6	Health or ill health, co-workers and work environment, office or study at home, computers, calculators, everyday activity, eating places.
7	Close relationships, other people, the lawyer, the "opposition," close friends.
8	Taxes, insurance, welfare, unemployment benefits, death, crisis, restitution in a lawsuit.
9	Spectator sports, ceremony, ritual, courts and legal matters, long-distance travel.

10   Authority, reputation, public life, fate of the matter, police officers, career.

11   Hopes and wishes, organizations, circumstances beyond the querent's control, acquaintances, love received.

12   Yesterday, the past, worries, secrets, confinement; may show the reason for what is now occurring.

Table 18: Houses in Horary Charts

Ingress Charts

Ingress means "the act of entering." Astrologically, an ingress chart is cast for the moment the Sun enters a cardinal sign (Aries, Cancer, Libra, or Capricorn). These are the moments for the beginning of the four seasons (spring, summer, autumn, and winter).

The ingress chart can be cast for any location on the planet, and all resulting charts will have the planets in the same degree and sign, and will also form the same aspects. The houses will be different for different locations. For some locations the Sun will be above the horizon (daytime charts) and for some it will be below (nighttime charts).

The ingress chart is effective for the three months following the ingress. It can be used to forecast weather and economic cycles, predict political upheavals, and generally evaluate conditions for cities, nations, or regions of the world. The Moon's phases (relationship to the Sun) throughout the three-month period indicate an additional set of energies. The Moon can indicate the severity of weather, for example. Each lunar phase lasts for approximately one week. The lunar phase chart modifies what is promised in the ingress chart itself. As in natal astrology, the transits can act as timers for specific events.

Generally, the planets in angular houses, or actually conjunct the angles (Midheaven, Ascendant, *Imum Coeli*, or Descendant), are the most active in ingress charts.

CHINESE, TIBETAN, VEDIC, MAYAN, AND CELTIC ASTROLOGY

The Western astrology taught in this volume is not the only system of astrology in use today. Other systems include Chinese astrology, based on twelve signs and five elements; the Vedic system, which has twelve signs and also a strong lunar component; the Tibetan system, which is a combination of concepts from the Vedic and Chinese systems; Mayan astrology, based on the ancient Mayan calendar system, and focused on the planet Venus; and the Celtic system, composed of thirteen signs connected to the lunar cycle and to different trees.

Chinese and Tibetan Astrology

We are quite familiar with the animal signs of the Chinese zodiac. We find little bits of information about them each time we go to a Chinese restaurant. The animals are not the same as the Western zodiac, nor do they represent months of the year. Instead, each animal is given a year in its turn. In addition, the five elements of the Chinese energy system are included. Thus there is a cycle of sixty years, one for each animal in each of the elements. The animals and the element cycles are essentially the same in Tibetan and Chinese astrology. Both systems are far more complex than the material presented here.

The order of the animals through the years is as follows: Horse (the year of the Water Horse is 2002), Sheep, Monkey, Bird (Rooster), Dog, Pig, Mouse, Ox, Tiger, Hare, Dragon, Snake. The order of the elements is as follows: Iron (Metal), Water, Wood, Fire, Earth. The next year of the Water Horse will be 2062.

The elements modify the meaning of the animal signs. Iron is strong, cutting, and direct. Water is soft, fluid, and clear-seeing. Wood is long-lived, beautiful, and good. Fire is strong, instant, and warm. Earth is stable, strong, and grounded.

Vedic Astrology

The astrology of India is grounded in very old texts—the Vedas. The use of astrology is prevalent in India, being used to arrange marriages, manage businesses, and for any area of concern. Vedic astrology uses a system of twenty-eight lunar "mansions." This system is also used in Chinese and Middle Eastern astrology, but rarely used in Western astrology.

Vedic astrology also uses the constellations. In Western astrology, 0° Aries (♈) is defined as the first day of spring. In the Vedic system, the sign of Aries is closer to the position of the constellation, about 23° earlier in the Zodiac. The Vedic system, like the Chinese and Tibetan systems, is far more complex that this simple discussion would indicate.

Mayan Astrology

The Maya did not have an integrated system of astrology per se. However, the Mayan methods of calculating the positions of the planets were quite refined. The root of their concerns was probably human fertility, a very basic survival consideration. Their calculations were based on the Sun cycle, in concert with the planets. Venus held a position of major significance in Mayan cosmology.

The Mayan calendar was probably developed some time before the birth of Jesus. The beginning of the long count calendar is dated about 3114 B.C., but the development of the calendar probably occurred much later. Some of the major timing mechanisms are tied to the solstices rather than the equinoxes. The significance of the first day of winter as a turning point is essential to understanding the Mayan concept of calendar and time. The end date, and thus the beginning date, for the larger cycles is December 21, 2012. On this date the Mayan calendar comes to a date written as 13.0.0.0.0. The Mayans believe the world will be reborn on this date. The date coincides with a significant galactic alignment.

Celtic Lunar Astrology

The Druids had a Zodiac containing thirteen signs. Each of these signs is associated with a tree and an animal. The year is divided evenly into thirteen lunar months. These lunar months can be overlaid with the twelve signs for the Tropical Zodiac, producing unique interpretations of the birth chart. One system of interpretation considers decans (10° divisions) of the Tropical Zodiac, and adds information about the particular lunar month. Because of the constant overlapping of solar (Tropical) and lunar (Celtic) signs, the decans at the end of each lunar sign overlap with the next lunar sign. In essence, the two systems provide a continuous energy flow, as there is no point in the system where both systems end on the same day.

The subtle interplay of the Sun and Moon cycles provides a depth of interpretation for Celtic astrology. It honors the solar cycle of growth, death, decay, and rebirth, and it also honors the lunar developmental cycle—a more feminine expression of consciousness. The system also includes one day each year that is not part of a lunar sign. This "nameless day" marks the end of the time when the Sun has sunk to its lowest point and is now returning northward. December 23 is not associated with any of the trees that rule the thirteen lunar signs, but instead with mistletoe, the symbol of life through death.

The different astrological systems each reflect the concerns of their cultures, as well as the precision of calculation methods. Contemporary astrology benefits from the wealth of perspectives, as well as from the incredible precision and speed of calculation offered by astrology software. Both enrich the possibilities for today's astrologer.

HOUSE SYSTEMS

Placidus

This system is in widespread use. The Ascendant and Midheaven are calculated the same way for Placidus, Koch, Porphyry, Whole Sign, and Equal House systems. For the Placidus house system, the intermediate cusps are determined by dividing the length of time the Ascending degree takes to reach the Midheaven (this time is called the *semidiurnal arc,* meaning half-day arc) into three equal parts. A similar method is used to divide the arc between the MC and the Descendant. The opposite cusps share the same degree in their respective signs. Because some signs rise faster than others, the three segments in any quarter of the chart will generally not be the same number of degrees of longitude.

Koch

The Koch house system begins by dividing the diurnal semi-arc of the Midheaven (the longitudinal distance between the Midheaven and Ascendant). It then rotates the Midheaven to the horizon. The MC is advanced to the point that is one-third of the distance between the original Ascendant and Midheaven. With the Midheaven on the 12th House cusp, the new Ascendant is designated as the 11th House cusp. The process is repeated, moving the MC to two-thirds of the original distance. The new Ascendant then becomes the 12th House cusp.

Porphyry

In the Porphyry house system, the Midheaven and Ascendant are calculated the same way as for Placidus. Then the intermediate cusps are calculated by dividing the degrees of longitude between the Ascendant and Midheaven, or the Midheaven and Descendant, into equal units. This mathematically elegant system results in the fact that houses 11, 3, 5, and 9 share the same degree and minute, while houses 12, 2, 6, and 8 share another degree and minute, of their respective signs.

Equal House

The degree on the Ascendant (some astrologers use the Midheaven) is used for the other houses. Thus all the houses are equal in size, and have the same degree on the cusp, with consecutive signs arranged around the chart. The Equal House system usually places the Midheaven on the 9th or 10th House. However, at higher latitudes the MC could be in the 11th or 8th House, and possibly even the 12th or 7th. A similar relocation of the Ascendant occurs when the degree of the MC is used on the cusps. An advantage of this system is that it indicates the true distance between Ascendant and Midheaven, and thus provides a distinct delineation of these angles, separate from the house cusps.

Whole House

This system traditionally places 0 degrees of the sign of the Ascendant on the cusp of the First House, and all other houses are 0 degrees of their respective signs. Therefore the Ascendant is always in the First House. The Midheaven can fall in any of the houses above the horizon, depending on the birth time and the birth latitude.

Other House Systems

Other house systems include Campanus, Regiomontanus, and Alcabitius.

Fixed Stars

From the perspective of the earth, all stars are fixed, except for our Sun. The fixed stars actually do move very small amounts, from our perspective, and we know that they are moving very quickly through the sky. Yet they are so distant that the motion seems very slow.

Astrologers have identified a few of these stars, primarily very bright stars in the Northern Hemisphere, as important points. When the planets conjoin these stars, the nature of the star affects the planet. The list of fixed stars is quite long, and only a few examples are included here. These are some of the stars identified by William Lilly, an Elizabethan astrologer, for the year 2000.

Star	Longitude	Meaning
Caput Algol	26° ♉ 10'	Very unfortunate—Saturn/Jupiter
Alcyone	0° ♊ 00'	Neutral—Moon/Jupiter
Aldebaran	9° ♊ 47'	Unfortunate—Mars
Betelgeuse	28° ♊ 45'	Unfortunate—Mars/Mercury

Star	Longitude	Meaning
Sirius	14° ♋ 05'	Fortunate—Jupiter/Mars
Canopus	14° ♋ 58'	Unfortunate—Saturn/Jupiter
Procyon	25° ♋ 47'	Unfortunate—Mars/Mercury
Regulus	29° ♌ 50'	Fortunate—Mars/Jupiter/Uranus
Denebola	21° ♍ 37'	Neutral—Saturn/Venus
Spica	23° ♎ 50'	Very Fortunate—Venus/Mars
Arcturus	24° ♎ 14'	Very Fortunate—Jupiter/Mars
Alphecca	12° ♏ 18'	Fortunate—Venus/Mercury
Antares	9° ♐ 46'	Fortunate—Mars/Jupiter/Mercury
Vega	15° ♑ 19'	Fortunate—Venus/Mercury
Altair	1° ♒ 47'	Neutral—Mars/Jupiter
Fomalhaut	3° ♓ 52'	Neutral—Venus/Mercury/Neptune
Markab	23° ♓ 29'	Unfortunate—Mars/Mercury/Venus

MYTHOLOGY OF THE PLANETS

The names for the planets and signs, and even the names for the moons of most of the planets, have come to us through mythology. The details of myths often provide insight into the nature of each planet in the astrological chart. The following are brief glimpses into the rich lore of mythologies from around the world.

The Sun and Moon

The Sun (Roman Sol, Greek Helios) ruled the day and was thought to travel under the world by sailing across the ocean in a bowl. Ra was the Egyptian counterpart of Sol. Ra was thought to enter the underworld each evening, to be born again each morning. Ra created order out of chaos, and the Sun's travel through the year provides order to the seasons.

Cybele, Diana, and other goddesses embodied the powers of birth, nurture, and sometimes death and regeneration. They also were emotional goddesses, reflecting the emotional tides represented by the Moon in astrology. The three goddesses Diana, Selene, and Hecate, all aspects of the Moon, reflect three aspects of the feminine as well: Virgin, Mother, and Crone.

While many Moon deities are goddesses, Sin, the Sumerian-Babylonian Moon god, is masculine. He was the father of the sun god Shamash, as well as other deities. Sin sailed across the heavens in his crescent-shaped boat. The Full Moon was his crown. Sin's wisdom was reflected in the fact that his phases provided a way to mark the passage of time.

The interaction of the Sun and Moon in astrology reflects the basic realities of life. Whether they are masculine or feminine is secondary to the fact that they represent the energy necessary for life, and the unfolding of life's processes. The Sun maps the growth cycle as an annual passage, while the Moon maps the monthly cycle associated with female menses. Together, these two provide the information necessary for planting, harvesting, and storing food. They also reveal the two sides of human nature—conscious and unconscious—in all their potential variety.

Mercury

As the messenger of the gods, the Roman Mercury (Greek Hermes) reflects his communication role in the speed of the planet's orbit. He is depicted with wings on his feet, which aid him in the swift performance of his duties. In other cultures, Mercury-like gods also share other qualities that astrology gives to Mercury in the chart. Mummu was an emissary of Apsu. Odin (or Woden) breathed life into people, reflecting the roles of respiration and inspiration of Mercury in the chart. Woden also worked magic, and the Magician of the Tarot is associated with the planet Mercury. The creative intelligence of this planet is anchored in the Bible—both testaments begin with passages concerning the power of words with regard to creation. Two of the names for this god are used in different languages for Mercury's day of the week—Woden for Wednesday (*Mercredi* or *Miercoles* in French and Spanish).

Mercury's mythology is laden with various aspects of magic, communication, and mediation between or among different factions (planets). As the messenger in the astrological chart, Mercury is androgynous—it carries the nature of the planet it aspects.

Venus

Venus, Aphrodite, Inanna, Isis—these four goddesses, and many others, share the fundamental qualities associated with Venus in the astrological chart. These goddesses share beauty as a fundamental attribute. Sometimes the goddess embodies sexual attraction and uses her beauty as a weapon to control both men and gods. However, she also has other traits that astrologers associate with this planet.

Inanna, a younger Sumerian goddess, had ambitions. She wanted to be more than a beautiful queen. She sought to charm her uncle Enki, and got him drunk enough to reveal magical formulae that would help develop human civilization. She learned about government, religious functions, weapons, writing, woodworking, the creation of musical instruments, and yes, about prostitution.

Isis, in contract to Inanna, was the devoted wife of Osiris and the mother of Horus. It was through these associations that she became a more important Egyptian goddess. The social role Venus plays in the astrological chart takes its expression partly from Isis, and partly from Inanna, who also was reputed to be the source of many social customs and skills needed to form strong communities.

Venus also plays an active role in associations that are not sexually based. The role of companion, for example, involves the social contact and intelligence of this goddess. Venus also embodies the less conscious feminine aspect for men. The muse, for example, is often understood to be the ideal woman who encourages the man to his best work. The anima, as she is known, has a counterpart for women (the animus). These two Jungian energies provide a richness of experience in social, partnering, and sexual relationships.

Mars

The Roman Mars (Greek Ares) was primarily a god of agriculture. This is logical, as Mars is associated with the sign Aries, which begins the spring season in the tropical system. Yet, in the *Iliad,* Zeus finds the god Ares uncontrollable, and decries his constant involvement in arguments, strife, and wars. The Roman god eventually took on the warlike qualities of his Greek counterpart. Where the goddess Venus strove to build connections between herself and others, Mars sought to break those connections. Any alliances he formed were for the purpose of furthering independence.

Contemporary astrologers recognize the importance of independence on the one hand, and the potentially destructive energy of ambition and aggression on the other. It is wise to keep both expressions of this god in mind when considering Mars in the astrological chart. The agricultural capacity makes human beings more independent—they are no longer limited to hunting as a means of finding food, but can produce their own food from the earth. The angrier, more warlike side of human nature is another reflection of the desire to be independent. It is easy to see how Mars earned its title as "malefic." The balance between stability and independence can easily be shifted when Mars energy is used for personal gain.

Jupiter

Jupiter (Zeus in the Greek tradition) was chief among the gods. He was presumably empowered with the wisdom and clarity necessary to manage the wide range of personalities found among the gods and goddesses of Rome (or Greece). Counterparts in other traditions include Thor, Marduk, and Taranis, a Celtic sky god. All of these share qualities of great power. Not all of their actions measure up to the contemporary astrological view of Jupiter as a "benefic" planet. They all had harsh tempers when provoked, a quality associated with the father in many cultures. Zeus tried to solve disagreements amicably, but sometimes resorted to punishment and even torture when his will was ignored. Thor is renowned in stories for his brutal battles. Marduk, in the act of creating the world and the sky, battled Tiamat, sometimes depicted as the primordial dragon of chaos. Taranis was associated with the thunderbolt, as was Thor.

In astrology, Jupiter is the "greater benefic," bestowing confidence, opportunity, and luck. The name "Jove" is the root for the term "jovial," certainly unlike many of the mythological expressions of the god and associated deities. Yet Jupiter retains the qualities of expansiveness and even overconfidence. This planet can indicate extravagance, fanaticism, and pompous display. As with each of the planets, Jupiter has its downside. Well managed, the energy of this planet can express as honor, tolerance, and generosity.

Saturn

Saturn is often compared to Cronos, a Greek Titan/god who slew his father, Ouranus, and was later overthrown by his own son Jupiter (Zeus). Associated with corn, Saturn does not seem harsh enough to earn the title of "greater malefic." Cronos was father to Poseidon (Neptune). After he was overthrown, his three sons divided up the world. Zeus got the sky, Poseidon the oceans, and Hades the underworld. His three daughters had governance over the earth: Hestia (Vesta) ruled the hearth, Demeter (Ceres) was the goddess of vegetation, and Hera (Juno) was the earth goddess.

In astrology, Saturn is associated with structure. This includes the concept of time, the organization of the world, and the skin, bones, and hair of the body. Structure can be experienced as fiercely limiting conditions, much as Cronos was experienced before he was overthrown. Structure may also be experienced as the structure of the home, agricultural pursuits, and the earth in general, as well as the oceans, the sky, and the underworld. We are able to accomplish tasks because of the structures around us. Saturn indicates both the potential for action and the results of that action.

Uranus

Astrologically, Uranus is the planet that governs change. This change can be in the direction of improvement, although it is often experienced as disruptive. The Greek god Ouranus was overthrown by his son Cronos, who was overthrown in his turn. This is the essence of change.

The Hindu god Varuna offers a more fully developed picture of the qualities of Uranus. Varuna was the god who maintained order and morality. One of eight offspring of Aditi, the Hindu mother goddess, he is also said to be manifested from the belly of Avalokiteshvara, a Buddhist Bodhisattva. The belly is the center of gravity for the human body, and this point is variously called "one point" in Aikido, "tan tien" in Tai Ch'i, or simply "center." Uranus, in its role of change, provides events, people, and even intuitive insights into how we may maintain our individual center more successfully.

Neptune

Neptune (Poseidon in Greek) was the ruler of the oceans. He was said to be responsible for earthquakes, and his worship was widespread among the Greeks, as they were a maritime nation. He carried a trident, and the modern glyph for Neptune reflects this form. Neptune played a lesser role in Roman mythology, as an ancient water god. Neptune did intercede to help Aeneas when Hera sent a violent storm in the path of his fleet.

As the god Neptune rules the oceans, the planet Neptune rules the kinds of sensitivity that move within us very much as the waters of the ocean move. There is little about this planet that is solid. Its effects are subtle, psychic, and imaginative. Thus the modern rulership of the film industry is well suited to Neptune.

Pluto

Hades, the Greek counterpart of Pluto, ruled the underworld. He chose Persephone as his wife, and she sealed her fate by eating pomegranate seeds while in the underworld. Only after a complex bargain was struck could Persephone return to her mother, Demeter, for part of the year. The story of Orpheus and Eurydice involves a bargain wherein Orpheus and Eurydice could leave the underworld, but only if Orpheus would not look back to see her until they were in the land of the living. This Orpheus failed to do, and Eurydice turned back into a ghost. Hades later became a name synonymous with Hell, or the underworld.

Hel, a Nordic god, was represented as a monster who was the essence of destruction and darkness. Hel is also the name of the land of the dead in Nordic mythology. Odin's magical ring was rescued from Hel, and represented the promise of growth after the winter season, similar to the return of Persephone.

The stories of Persephone and Eurydice reflect the transformational capacity attributed to the planet Pluto in astrology. These stories also evoke the power of Hades, which is also attributed to the planet Pluto. Kidnapping is ruled by Pluto, along with gangsters and racketeering, which reflect the coercive nature of the god of the underworld. Yet the emergence of Persephone in the spring should be remembered. No death, whether it be physical, emotional, mental, or spiritual, is without its eventual rebirth.

HEALTH CONSIDERATIONS

The brief comments here concerning astrology and health cannot take the place of a physician's care or medical treatment. They are intended as guidelines for understanding the most basic associations between astrology, the body, and health. Cell salts, herbs, vitamins, and minerals, when assimilated properly, can strengthen the constitution and the immune system, thereby providing a strong body/mind connection. The reader is advised to consult with a physician before using the herbs or remedies associated with each sign, as some of these are contraindicated for pregnant women and persons already taking prescribed medications.

Planet or Sign	Physical Associations
Sun	Cells, the body in general, heart and circulatory system
Moon	All body fluids, lymph system, fertility, mucous membranes
Mercury	Nervous system, speech and hearing organs; health throughout youth
Venus	Hormones, glandular system, kidneys, veins
Mars	Muscles, sexual functions; middle age
Jupiter	Liver, organic systems, blood
Saturn	Skin, bones, teeth, hair; old age, hardening of tissues
Uranus	Pulse, breathing patterns, peristalsis, all functions that depend on rhythm
Neptune	Weakness, paralysis, pineal gland, solar plexus
Pluto	Regenerative capacity, rectum

Planet or Sign	Physical Associations
Aries	Skull, face, brain
Taurus	Lower jaw, ears, throat, larynx, pharynx
Gemini	Shoulders, collarbones, arms, lungs, hands
Cancer	Stomach, esophagus, breasts, sternum, diaphragm, chest cavity
Leo	Heart, back, spine, heat of the body
Virgo	Abdomen, health or illness in general, regularity (constipation)
Libra	Buttocks, kidneys, ureters, veins in general
Scorpio	Pelvis, adenoids, sexual organs, organs of elimination
Sagittarius	Thighs, hips, liver, sciatic nerve
Capricorn	Knees, bones in general, skin
Aquarius	Calves, ankles, circulation in general, action of the heart
Pisces	Feet, toes, water in the body

Table 19: Physical Associations

Sign	Herbs	Cell Salts
Aries	Gentian, cayenne, garlic, honeysuckle, blessed thistle	Potassium phosphate (lettuce, cauliflower, olives, cucumbers, spinach, radishes, cabbage, onions, pumpkin, walnuts, apples)
Taurus	Thyme, plantain, coltsfoot, sage, bearberry (uva ursi)	Sulphate of soda (beets, spinach, horseradish, cauliflower, cabbage, radish, cucumber, onion, pumpkin)
Gemini	Lily of the valley, flax, parsley, caraway, lavender	Potassium chloride (asparagus, green beans, beets, sprouts, carrots, spinach, tomato, sweet celery, oranges, peaches, pineapple, apricot, pear, plum)
Cancer	Waterlily, chickweed, lettuce, honeysuckle	Flouride of lime (milk, eggs, cabbage, lettuce, watercress, pumpkin)

Sign	Herbs	Cell Salts
Leo	Wake robin, eyebright, mistletoe, marigold, St. John's Wort, walnuts	Phosphate of magnesia (barley, whole wheat, rye, almonds, lettuce, apples, figs, asparagus, eggs, cabbage, cucumber, coconut, walnut, blueberry, onion)
Virgo	Skullcap, fennel, mandrake (use sparingly), endive, dill	Potassium sulphate (endive, chicory, carrot, whole wheat, oats, rye, salad vegetables)
Libra	Violet, pennyroyal, feverfew, catmint, burdock, silverweed	Sodium phosphate (celery, carrots, spinach, asparagus, apple, fig, strawberry, blueberry, raisins, almonds, fresh coconut, oatmeal, unpolished rice)
Scorpio	Horehound, blackberry leaves, blessed thistle, leek, horseradish, toad-flax, wormwood, sarsaparilla	Sulphate of lime (onion, asparagus, kale, garlic, mustard, cress, turnips, figs, cauliflower, radishes, leeks, prunes, black cherries, gooseberries, blueberry, coconut)
Sagittarius	Agrimony, burdock, chicory, red clover, dandelion, oak (generally not ingested)	Silica (skin of fruits, outer covering of grains, figs, prunes, strawberries)
Capricorn	Comfrey, horse tail, shepherd's purse, slippery elm, knot grass	Calcium phosphate (strawberries, plums, blueberries, figs, spinach, asparagus, lettuce, cucumber, almonds, coconut, lentils, brown beans, whole wheat, rye, barley, sea fish, cow's milk)
Aquarius	Valerian, lady's slipper, sage, snakeroot (spotted plantain)	Sodium chloride (strawberries, apples, figs, spinach, cabbage, radish, asparagus, carrots, cucumber, lettuce, chestnuts, coconut, lentils)
Pisces	Irish moss, gentian, ginger	Phosphate of iron (lettuce, strawberries, radishes, horseradish, spinach, lentils, cabbage)

Table 20: Herbs and Cell Salts

Planet	Vitamin	Minerals
Sun	A, D, PABA	Oxygen, iodine, magnesium, manganese
Moon	B_2 (riboflavin)	Water, fluorine, potassium
Mercury	B_1 (thiamin), B complex in general, thyroxin	
Venus	E, niacin, vitamin P	Copper, molybdenum, chromium
Mars	B_{12}, F	Cobalt, iron, phosphorus
Jupiter	B_6 (pyridoxine), F, K, choline, inositol, lecithin, biotin (H)	Sulfur, selenium
Saturn	C, folic acid	Calcium
Uranus		Zinc
Neptune	Pantothenic acid (a B vitamin)	All toxins, poisons, alcohol, heavy metals
Pluto	enzymes	

Table 21: Vitamins and Minerals

Because the planets and signs are not found in isolation in the birth chart, but in combination, careful attention to the house placement of planets and their aspects is needed. The Ascendant and the Sixth/Twelfth House axis are the areas closely associated with health and illness. The Eighth House should be explored in cases where surgery is indicated. Some basic considerations when working with health issues are as follows:

- The sign on the Ascendant and its ruling planet (constitution in general)
- Planets in the First House and their aspects
- The sign on the Sixth House cusp and its ruling planet (health and illness in general)
- Planets in the Sixth House and their aspects
- The sign on the Twelfth House and its ruling planet (confinement due to health issues)
- Planets in the Twelfth House and their aspects
- The sign on the Eighth House and its ruler (surgery, medical intervention)
- Planets in the Eighth House and their aspects

Health issues are only one of the possible considerations for these houses, their rulers, and the planets in these houses. Not every aspect poses an immediate, or even a long-term, health problem when placed in these positions. However, these positions, taken as a group, often indicate the central health conditions for the individual whose chart is being considered.

Hard aspects (square, opposition, semisquare, and sesquiquadrate) indicate potential areas of stress or difficulty. By the same token, they indicate where the individual can actively make the best use of physical attributes. Soft aspects (trine, sextile, semisextile) indicate areas where conditions may exist or develop without effort, and thus where disease may develop if proper care is not taken. The conjunction and quincunx indicate areas where health or illness will be evident, and where adjustments in nutrition and activities, and possible surgery, will be necessary to regain a state of wellness.

As in any area of life, proper attention to the needs of the physical body can heal, relieve, or make manageable many health conditions. Where there is a weakness in the birth chart, proper care may prevent most or all of the promised health problems. Strong health indications can be maximized through a healthy diet and exercise, and they may help support weaker areas.

There is no substitute for medical care from a doctor or other qualified healthcare professional. Astrology can provide insight into whatever health issues arise, and can provide the structure of personal efforts to maintain wellness and aid the healing process.

Appendix One

ASTROLOGICAL CALCULATIONS

This section is included for the student who wishes to learn how to calculate an astrological chart. Computer technology reduced the need for hand calculation, but it is advantageous to study the theory behind the chart. By understanding how a chart is constructed, the student gains an understanding and appreciation for the movement of the planets, as well as the movement of the earth around the Sun.

The first part deals with calculating the birth chart: finding the true sidereal birth time, calculating the house cusps, calculating the exact positions of the Sun, Moon, and planets, and listing the aspects. The second part includes the mathematics needed to calculate progressions.

Parallels of declination have been included. While it is true that many modern ephemerides do not include declinations, the older ones do. This very important part of delineation should be understood, as it makes precise delineation and prediction possible.

Many students will skip this section entirely. You may wish to return to it at some point in the future, as your astrological studies progress.

Birth Chart Calculations

In order to calculate a chart using standardized tables, there are several things we need to consider. We need to find out the exact birth time, stated in terms of sidereal time (star time) instead of standard time. Using that information, we need to calculate the exact house cusps in the chart. Finally, we need to calculate the exact positions of the Moon and planets, as they have moved since the previous midnight

Greenwich Mean Time (GMT) as listed in the ephemeris. To make these calculations, you will need these references:

- An ephemeris for the birth date. The ephemeris contains the sidereal time that corresponds to midnight GMT, and also the positions of the planets in the Zodiac.
- A Tables of Houses for the house system you plan to use.
- A Table of Logarithms to aid in calculations. If you own a calculator that computes degrees, minutes, and seconds, you can use that, following the instructions supplied with the calculator.

The ephemeris, or standard table of planetary data, is calculated for midnight in Greenwich, England (the zero hour point on the planet, where longitude is defined as zero degrees). This means that we must first determine, from the individual's birth time, what time it is in Greenwich. The second problem relates to the actual time difference between Greenwich and the birthplace.

Note: You will find four forms for calculating the birth chart on the following pages (tables 22, 23, 24, and 25). You may want to make copies of these forms, or prepare similar forms to use in calculations.

Note: For all calculations, the result has to fall between the values drawn from the Tables of Houses or the ephemeris. You can estimate the positions of house cusps by guessing the fraction of a day that has passed at the birth time (a sidereal time of 15:35 is over half a day, but not three-quarters), so the cusp is over half a degree but less than 45'. A latitude of 38°N42' is just about three-fourths of the way between latitudes. Thus the resulting house cusp must be both over half the distance between the two columns and three-fourths of the distance between the latitudes. For an Equivalent Greenwich Mean Time Interval of 7 hours 22 minutes, the interval is more than one-fourth of a day, and less than one-third. Thus the planetary position will be about one-third of the distance the planet travels that day, plus the value from the previous day.

Standard Time

Very few locations are exactly on the time meridians. Some are in the eastern part of a time zone, and some are in the west. Even though we agree to a standard time within a time zone, the true (actual) local time is as much as half an hour earlier or later, and more in some cases. Sometimes we experience this difference in our lives. For example, a person living in El Paso, Texas, has the clocks set to Mountain Standard Time. El Paso is close to the same prime meridian as Denver, Colorado. In both places the Sun will be at its highest point at noon or close to it. Drive across the Rio Grande to Cuidad Juarez, and you are magically in the Central Standard Time zone. It is one hour later on the clock. Yet the Sun is still at its highest point in the sky.

Why does this happen? It occurs because we use standard time to make our lives more convenient. In El Paso it is convenient to be on the same clock time as Denver, Santa Fe, and other U.S. cities. In

Sidereal Birth Time Calculations

Name _____

Birth Date _____

Birthplace _____

Longitude_____ Latitude _____

Hours to Greenwich _____

		Hours	Minutes	Seconds
Birth Time (use a 24-hour clock)				
Daylight Time (subtract one hour from birth time)	−			
Daylight Birth Time	=			
Add Hours to Greenwich	+			
Greenwich Mean Time				
Add Correction for the Interval (always less than four minutes)	+			
Result	=			
Add Sidereal Time for Previous Midnight	+			
Result is Sidereal Birth Time in Greenwich	=			
Subtract Longitude Equivalent	−			
Result	=			
Subtract 24 hours, if necessary	−			
Result is TRUE SIDEREAL BIRTH TIME	=			

Table 22: Form for Calculation of True Sidereal Birth Time

Calculation of Precise House Cusps Using Logarithms

True Sidereal Birth Time   _____

Subtract Previous Sidereal Time
    from Tables of Houses   − _____

Excess Sidereal Time   _____

Later Sidereal Time
    from Tables of Houses   _____

Subtract Previous Sidereal Time
    from Tables of Houses   − _____

Difference   _____

Log of Excess Time   _____

Subtract Log of Difference   − _____

Result is the Constant Factor for
    Sidereal Time (CFST)   _____

Birth Latitude   _____

Subtract Lower Latitude   − _____

Result is Excess Latitude   _____

Log of Excess Latitude   _____

Subtract Log of 1° of Latitude   − _____

Result is the Constant Factor
    For Latitude   _____

Table 23: Form for Calculation of Logarithms for House Cusp Calculation

	MC	11th	12th	Asc	2nd	3rd
Cusps at Later Sidereal Time	_____	_____	_____	_____	_____	_____
Earlier Cusps	_____	_____	_____	_____	_____	_____
Difference	_____	_____	_____	_____	_____	_____
Log of Difference	_____	_____	_____	_____	_____	_____
Constant Factor Log	_____	_____	_____	_____	_____	_____
Add (the sum equals correction log)	_____	_____	_____	_____	_____	_____
Sidereal Time Correction	_____	_____	_____	_____	_____	_____
Cusps at Higher Latitude		_____	_____	_____	_____	_____
Cusps at Lower Latitude		_____	_____	_____	_____	_____
Difference		_____	_____	_____	_____	_____
Log of Difference		_____	_____	_____	_____	_____
Constant Factor for Latitude		_____	_____	_____	_____	_____
Add (the sum equals correction log)		_____	_____	_____	_____	_____
Correction		_____	_____	_____	_____	_____
Previous Cusp, Lower Latitude		_____	_____	_____	_____	_____
Sidereal Time Correction		_____	_____	_____	_____	_____
Latitude Correction			_____	_____	_____	_____
Precise House Cusps	_____	_____	_____	_____	_____	_____

Table 24: Form for Calculation of Exact House Cusps

Calculating Exact Planetary Positions

Name _____ EGMTI _____ Log of EGMTI _____

Sun	Moon	Mercury	Venus	Mars	Jupiter	Saturn	
_____	_____	_____	_____	_____	_____	_____	1) Later Date Position
_____	_____	_____	_____	_____	_____	_____	2) Subtract Earlier Date Position
_____	**_____**	**_____**	**_____**	**_____**	**_____**	**_____**	3) **Difference (Daily Planetary Motion)**
_____	_____	_____	_____	_____	_____	_____	4) Constant Log
_____	_____	_____	_____	_____	_____	_____	5) Add Log of Planetary Motion
_____	**_____**	**_____**	**_____**	**_____**	**_____**	**_____**	6) **Log of Motion for Birth Time**
_____	_____	_____	_____	_____	_____	_____	7) Earlier Date Position
_____	_____	_____	_____	_____	_____	_____	8) Add Motion (calculated from Log of Motion, step 6). Subtract if planet is retrograde.
_____	**_____**	**_____**	**_____**	**_____**	**_____**	**_____**	9) **Exact Birth Position of Planet**

Uranus_____ Neptune _____ Pluto _____ North Node _____

The same procedure is used to calculate declination, if you have that information in your ephemeris. The declination for each planet will be indicated as North or South instead of having a zodiacal sign.

Table 25: Form for Calculating Exact Planetary Positions

Juarez, it is more convenient to be on the same clock time as Ciudad, Mexico, the seat of the Mexican government. Standard time was created for our convenience. In fact, it was created so that railroad schedules could be printed more easily. As people began to travel faster across longer distances, the constant change of Local Mean Time, measured by the Sun, became unwieldy. Standard units of twenty-four approximately equal segments of the earth provide an easier way to set the clocks of the world.

There are some places where the time is set on the half hour, and this is, again, for local convenience. For many years, all of China has shared the same time zone, even though this country spans the width of nearly four standard hours. Most of Europe and a large part of Africa share a clock time that is one hour later than Greenwich, England, even though some regions are separated by more than two hours of clock time. All this is for political and economic convenience.

Regardless of how a time zone is organized, the standard time, as measured from Greenwich, is the significant factor we need to cast an accurate horoscope. We will address the distance factor in the second part of our calculation.

Step One: Calculate the Greenwich Mean Time of Birth

1. Begin with the standard time of birth. Express this time in terms of a 24-hour clock. For example, the birth time of a person born at 5:30 p.m. (post meridian, or past the highest point in the sky; after noon) would be expressed as 17:30 (after the previous midnight).

2. Make any corrections for Daylight Time (or War Time for those born in many places during World War II). This correction usually involves subtracting one hour.

3. If the birth place is west of Greenwich, add one hour for each time zone the standard time is from Greenwich. If west of Greenwich, this addition may result in a total of more than twenty-four hours, or a Greenwich time in the next day. If east of Greenwich, subtract this amount. For birth places east of Greenwich, you may need to "borrow" the twenty-four hours from the previous day, and consider the previous date in the ephemeris for your calculations.

Example: Denver, Colorado is in the Mountain Time Zone, or seven hours from Greenwich. You would add seven hours to the birth time because it is seven hours later in Greenwich. A birth time of 10:00 p.m. (22:00) plus seven hours equals twenty-nine hours, or 5:00 a.m. the next day.

Example: Beijing is eight hours from Greenwich, standard time. You would subtract eight hours because it is eight hours earlier in Greenwich. A birth time of 7:00 a.m. minus eight hours equals 11:00 p.m. (23:00) the previous day.

The result of this calculation is the GMT (Greenwich Mean Time of Birth). Using these two examples, notice that a person born at 8:00 p.m. in Beijing and a person born at 5:00 a.m. in Denver share the same noon Greenwich birth time.

If the total is more than twenty-four hours, subtract twenty-four, and consider that your calculations will be based on the next day in the ephemeris. The Greenwich Mean Time Interval is the time you will use to calculate the positions of the planets in the ephemeris.

Step Two: Calculate the Solar-Sidereal Correction for the Time Interval from Midnight, Greenwich.

There is a small time correction necessary for all cases where the Greenwich Mean Time is not exactly midnight. This is due to the fact that the sidereal day is 3 minutes and 56 seconds different from the standard 24-hour day. This small time interval is sometimes called the "acceleration correction." The correction is very close to 10 seconds per hour. Simply multiply the number of hours by 10 and divide by 60 to get the correction. Consider the minutes in the birth time as a fraction of an hour.

Example: The Greenwich Mean Time of birth is 7:33 A.M. Thirty-three minutes is .55 hours. Multiply 7.55 hours x 10 seconds. The result is 75.5 seconds. Divide by 60 to find the number of minutes. 75.5 divided by 60 is 1.258 minutes, or 1 minute 15 seconds. The correction for the interval is one minute 15 seconds.

Step Three: Determine the Local Sidereal Time of Birth.

Just what is the sidereal birth time? This time is defined as the amount of time that has passed since zero degrees of Aries (the spring equinox) was at the Midheaven. The amount of time cannot be more than twenty-four hours.

1. To determine the local sidereal birth time, we first need to calculate the birth time at Greenwich. To do this, simply add the Greenwich Mean Time of Birth to the Sidereal Time from the ephemeris, using the midnight before the Greenwich birth time. Remember that you could have gone into the next day for birth places west of Greenwich, or into the previous day for birth times east of Greenwich. However, in both cases you add the Sidereal Time from the ephemeris. If the total goes over 24 hours, simply subtract 24.

2. Then add the Correction for the Interval. This adjusts for the difference in length of standard and sidereal days.

3. Then we need to determine what the actual time difference is from Greenwich to the birthplace. In essence, this is a geography problem, where the first problem was a problem involving time. The goal is to determine the real time interval between Greenwich and the birthplace (called the Equivalent Greenwich Mean Time Interval). The following table lists the equivalent unit of time for units of longitude.

September 2001

Longitude

Day		Sid. Time	☉	☽	True ☊	☿	♀	♂	♃	♄	♅	♆	♇
		h m s	° ' "	° ' "	° '	° '	° '	° '	° '	° '	° '	° '	° '
1	Sa	22 40 53	8♍ 37 50	17♒ 52 59	4♋R 26.5	29♍ 57.6	5♌ 44.8	26✗ 14.2	9♋ 56.7	14♊ 21.6	22♒R 13.0	6♒R 33.5	12✗R 33.4
2	Su	22 44 50	9 35 53	29♒ 43 37	4 16.8	1♎ 26.0	6 56.5	26 42.1	10 6.6	14 24.3	22 10.7	6 32.2	12 33.7
3	M	22 48 47	10 33 57	11♓ 35 49	4 5.2	2 53.0	8 8.3	27 10.3	10 16.4	14 26.9	22 8.5	6 30.9	12 34.0
4	Tu	22 52 43	11 32 4	23 31 9	3 52.5	4 18.6	9 20.2	27 39.0	10 26.1	14 29.4	22 6.3	6 29.7	12 34.4
5	W	22 56 40	12 30 11	5♈ 31 0	3 39.9	5 42.9	10 32.1	28 8.0	10 35.7	14 31.9	22 4.1	6 28.4	12 34.8
6	Th	23 0 36	13 28 21	17 36 48	3 28.3	7 5.8	11 44.2	28 37.4	10 45.1	14 34.2	22 1.9	6 27.2	12 35.2
7	F	23 4 33	14 26 33	29 50 20	3 18.9	8 27.2	12 56.3	29 7.2	10 54.5	14 36.4	21 59.7	6 26.0	12 35.6
8	Sa	23 8 29	15 24 46	12♉ 13 49	3 12.1	9 47.2	14 8.5	29 37.3	11 3.7	14 38.5	21 57.6	6 24.8	12 36.1
9	Su	23 12 26	16 23 2	24 50 2	3 8.0	11 5.6	15 20.7	0♑ 7.8	11 12.8	14 40.5	21 55.5	6 23.6	12 36.6
10	M	23 16 22	17 21 19	7♊ 42 14	3D 6.4	12 22.5	16 33.1	0 38.6	11 21.8	14 42.4	21 53.4	6 22.5	12 37.2
11	Tu	23 20 19	18 19 39	20 53 53	3R 6.2	13 37.8	17 45.5	1 9.8	11 30.7	14 44.2	21 51.3	6 21.4	12 37.8
12	W	23 24 15	19 18 1	4♋ 28 11	3 6.5	14 51.4	18 58.0	1 41.3	11 39.4	14 45.8	21 49.2	6 20.3	12 38.4
13	Th	23 28 12	20 16 25	18 27 22	3 5.7	16 3.3	20 10.5	2 13.1	11 48.1	14 47.4	21 47.2	6 19.2	12 39.1
14	F	23 32 9	21 14 51	2♌ 51 50	3 3.0	17 13.3	21 23.1	2 45.3	11 56.6	14 48.9	21 45.2	6 18.2	12 39.7
15	Sa	23 36 5	22 13 19	17 39 14	2 57.7	18 21.4	22 35.8	3 17.7	12 4.9	14 50.3	21 43.3	6 17.2	12 40.5
16	Su	23 40 2	23 11 49	2♍ 43 58	2 49.7	19 27.4	23 48.6	3 50.5	12 13.2	14 51.5	21 41.3	6 16.2	12 41.2
17	M	23 43 58	24 10 21	17 57 19	2 39.6	20 31.3	25 1.4	4 23.6	12 21.3	14 52.7	21 39.4	6 15.2	12 42.0
18	Tu	23 47 55	25 8 55	3♎ 8 35	2 28.5	21 32.8	26 14.3	4 57.0	12 29.3	14 53.7	21 37.5	6 14.3	12 42.8
19	W	23 51 51	26 7 31	18 6 58	2 17.7	22 31.8	27 27.3	5 30.6	12 37.1	14 54.6	21 35.7	6 13.3	12 43.6
20	Th	23 55 48	27 6 9	2♏ 43 30	2 8.2	23 28.2	28 40.3	6 4.6	12 44.8	14 55.5	21 33.9	6 12.5	12 44.5
21	F	23 59 44	28 4 48	16 52 27	2 1.1	24 21.7	29 53.4	6 38.8	12 52.4	14 56.2	21 32.1	6 11.6	12 45.4
22	Sa	0 3 41	29 3 29	0♐ 31 36	1 56.7	25 12.2	1♍ 6.5	7 13.3	12 59.8	14 56.8	21 30.4	6 10.8	12 46.4
23	Su	0 7 38	0♎ 2 12	13 41 56	1 54.6	25 59.3	2 19.7	7 48.1	13 7.1	14 57.3	21 28.6	6 10.0	12 47.3
24	M	0 11 34	1 0 57	26 26 41	1 54.1	26 42.8	3 32.9	8 23.1	13 14.2	14 57.7	21 27.0	6 9.2	12 48.3
25	Tu	0 15 31	1 59 43	8♑ 50 26	1 54.1	27 22.5	4 45.3	8 58.4	13 21.2	14 57.9	21 25.3	6 8.4	12 49.4
26	W	0 19 27	2 58 31	20 58 22	1 53.4	27 57.9	5 59.6	9 33.9	13 28.0	14 58.1	21 23.7	6 7.7	12 50.4
27	Th	0 23 24	3 57 21	2♒ 55 43	1 50.9	28 28.8	7 13.0	10 9.7	13 34.7	14 58.1	21 22.1	6 7.0	12 51.5
28	F	0 27 20	4 56 13	14 47 15	1 45.9	28 54.7	8 26.5	10 45.7	13 41.2	14R 58.1	21 20.6	6 6.4	12 52.7
29	Sa	0 31 17	5 55 6	26 37 8	1 38.0	29 15.4	9 40.0	11 21.9	13 47.6	14 57.9	21 19.1	6 5.8	12 53.8
30	Su	0 35 13	6♎ 54 1	8♓ 28 45	1♋ 27.4	29♎ 30.2	10♍ 53.6	11♑ 58.4	13♋ 53.8	14♊ 57.7	21♒ 17.7	6♒ 5.2	12✗ 55.0

Table 26: Sample Ephemeris Page from the *American Ephemeris* for September, 2001.

Longitude Units (degrees, minutes)	Time units (hours, minutes, seconds)
15 degrees	One hour
1 degree	Four minutes
15 minutes	One minute
1 minute	4 seconds

Table 27: Longitude/Time Equivalents

Example: Denver, Colorado. The longitude for Denver, Colorado is +104°W59'.[1] We can estimate using 105°, or seven hours. We know the final answer will be very close to seven hours because 105° divided by 15° per hour gives us exactly seven hours. To be precise, we calculate:

104° long. x 4 minutes time = 416 minutes divided by 60 = 6 hours 56 minutes.

59' long. x 4 seconds = 236 seconds divided by 60 = 3 minutes 56 seconds.

6 hours 56 minutes + 3 minutes 56 seconds = 6 hours 59 minutes 56 seconds. Our result is indeed very close to an even seven hours.

Example: Beijing, China. The longitude for Beijing is 116°E25'. 116° long. x 4 minutes time = 464 minutes, divided by 60 = 7 hours 44 minutes. 25 minutes long. x 4 seconds = 100 seconds divided by 60 = 1 minute 40 seconds.

 7 hours 44 minutes + 1 minute 40 seconds = 7 hours 45 minutes 40 seconds.

    4. Because the sidereal day is not exactly 24 hours, a small amount must be subtracted for births west of Greenwich, and added for births east of Greenwich. This is called the "acceleration correction," and it is always an amount less than four minutes. The acceleration correction is ten seconds per hour.

Example: Denver, Colorado. The time difference in Denver is 6 hours 59 minutes 56 seconds. This is so close to seven hours that we can take the acceleration correction for seven hours, which is 70 seconds. This is subtracted from the Greenwich Mean Time of Birth.

Example: Beijing, China. The time difference in Beijing is 7 hours 45 minutes 40 seconds. The acceleration correction for seven hours is 70 seconds. The correction for 45 minutes 40 seconds is about ¾ of 10, or 7 seconds. 70 + 7 = 77 seconds, or 1 minute 17 seconds. This amount is added to the Greenwich Mean Time of Birth.

    5. For a birth place west of Greenwich, subtract the longitude time equivalent. You subtract because the birth time is earlier than the time in Greenwich. For a birthplace east of Greenwich, add this amount. Here you add because the birth time is later than the time in Greenwich.

---

1. Information for longitude and latitude can be found in reference books such as the *ACS Atlas*.

The result of this calculation is the Sidereal Birth Time. This is the time you will use to calculate the house cusps in the chart.

Step Four: Find the Midheaven, Ascendant, and House Cusps

Using the sidereal time you have calculated, you will now look at the Tables of Houses.

The illustration uses the *AFA Tables of Houses: Koch System*, published by the American Federation of Astrologers. At the top of each column, there is some information. The first number is given in hours. This is the Sidereal Time in hours. The center number is the longitude of the Midheaven at that time. The third number is the arc of Right Ascension. You will note that the arc of Right Ascension and the Sidereal Time are given in even numbers. This is because Right Ascension is a measurement in degrees that is exactly equivalent to the Sidereal Time. The longitude is a measure along the ecliptic, and varies because some signs rise to the Midheaven faster than others. This is the result of the apparently elliptical shape of the ecliptic. In *Daltons' Tables of Houses*, the reverse is true: the longitude of the Midheaven is always an even degree, while the Sidereal Time and arc of Right Ascension vary.

In the Tables of Houses, the exact Sidereal Birth Time will fall between two of the columns. Find those two columns, and use them to calculate the Midheaven and the other house cusps. You will also need a logarithm table. This table allows you to perform simple addition and subtraction of decimal numbers, instead of multiplying and dividing, using quantities stated in degrees, minutes, and seconds.

Now calculate the exact house cusps.

1. Record the Sidereal Birth Time.
2. Find and record the previous Sidereal Time from the Tables of Houses.
3. Subtract the previous time. The result is the excess Sidereal Time.
4. The difference between the later and previous Sidereal Times is four minutes. If you use *Daltons' Tables of Houses,* you need to calculate the difference between the two Sidereal Times.
5. In the Logarithm Table, find the column and row that corresponds to the excess time you calculated in step 3. Enter this number on the form.
6. In the Logarithm Table, find the column and row that corresponds to the Difference between the columns you are using. In the AFA Table, the difference is always four minutes. The log for four minutes is .7781. Record it on your calculation form.

		0	1	2	3	4	5	6	7	8	9	10	11
M	0	INFINITE	1.38021	1.07918	.90309	.77815	.68124	.60206	.53511	.47712	.42597	.38021	.33882
I	1	3.15836	1.37303	1.07558	.90068	.77635	.67980	.60086	.53408	.47622	.42517	.37949	.33816
N	2	2.85733	1.36597	1.07200	.89829	.77455	.67836	.59965	.53305	.47532	.42436	.37877	.33750
U	3	2.68124	1.35902	1.06846	.89591	.77276	.67692	.59846	.53202	.47442	.42356	.37805	.33685
T	4	2.55630	1.35218	1.06494	.89354	.77097	.67549	.59726	.53100	.47352	.42276	.37733	.33619
E	5	2.45939	1.34545	1.06145	.89119	.76920	.67406	.59607	.52997	.47262	.42197	.37661	.33554
S	6	2.38021	1.33882	1.05799	.88885	.76743	.67264	.59488	.52895	.47173	.42117	.37589	.33489
	7	2.31326	1.33229	1.05456	.88652	.76567	.67122	.59370	.52793	.47083	.42038	.37517	.33424
O	8	2.25527	1.32585	1.05115	.88420	.76391	.66981	.59251	.52692	.46994	.41958	.37446	.33359
F	9	2.20412	1.31951	1.04777	.88190	.76216	.66840	.59134	.52591	.46905	.41879	.37375	.33294
	10	2.15836	1.31326	1.04442	.87961	.76042	.66700	.59016	.52489	.46817	.41800	.37303	.33229
T	11	2.11697	1.30710	1.04109	.87733	.75869	.66560	.58899	.52389	.46728	.41721	.37232	.33164
I	12	2.07918	1.30103	1.03779	.87506	.75696	.66421	.58782	.52288	.46640	.41642	.37161	.33099
M	13	2.04442	1.29504	1.03451	.87281	.75524	.66282	.58665	.52187	.46552	.41564	.37090	.33035
E	14	2.01223	1.28913	1.03126	.87056	.75353	.66143	.58549	.52087	.46464	.41485	.37019	.32970
	15	1.98227	1.28330	1.02803	.86833	.75182	.66005	.58433	.51987	.46376	.41407	.36949	.32906
O	16	1.95424	1.27755	1.02482	.86611	.75012	.65868	.58317	.51888	.46288	.41329	.36878	.32842
R	17	1.92791	1.27187	1.02164	.86390	.74843	.65730	.58202	.51788	.46201	.41251	.36808	.32777
	18	1.90309	1.26627	1.01848	.86170	.74674	.65594	.58087	.51689	.46113	.41173	.36737	.32713
A	19	1.87961	1.26074	1.01535	.85951	.74506	.65457	.57972	.51590	.46026	.41095	.36667	.32649
R	20	1.85733	1.25527	1.01223	.85733	.74339	.65321	.57858	.51491	.45939	.41017	.36597	.32585
C	21	1.83614	1.24988	1.00914	.85517	.74172	.65186	.57744	.51392	.45852	.40940	.36527	.32522
	22	1.81594	1.24455	1.00607	.85301	.74006	.65051	.57630	.51294	.45766	.40863	.36457	.32458
	23	1.79663	1.23928	1.00303	.85087	.73841	.64916	.57516	.51196	.45679	.40785	.36387	.32394
	24	1.44515	1.23408	1.00000	.84873	.73676	.64782	.57403	.51098	.45593	.40708	.36318	.32331
	25	1.76042	1.22894	0.99699	.84661	.73512	.64648	.57290	.51000	.45507	.40631	.36248	.32267
	26	1.74339	1.22386	0.99401	.84450	.73348	.64514	.57178	.50903	.45421	.40555	.36179	.32204
	27	1.72700	1.21884	0.99105	.84239	.73185	.64381	.57065	.50805	.45335	.40478	.36109	.32141
	28	1.71120	1.21388	0.98810	.84030	.73023	.64249	.56953	.50708	.45250	.40401	.36040	.32077
	29	1.69596	1.20897	0.98518	.83822	.72861	.64117	.56841	.50612	.45164	.40325	.35971	.32014
	30	1.68124	1.20412	0.98227	.83614	.72700	.63985	.56730	.50515	.45079	.40249	.35902	.31951
	31	1.66700	1.19932	0.97939	.83408	.72539	.63853	.56619	.50419	.44994	.40173	.35833	.31888
	32	1.65321	1.19457	0.97652	.83203	.72379	.63722	.56508	.50322	.44909	.40097	.35765	.31826
	33	1.63985	1.18988	0.97367	.82998	.72220	.63592	.56397	.50226	.44825	.40021	.35696	.31763
	34	1.62688	1.18523	0.97084	.82795	.72061	.63462	.56287	.50131	.44740	.39945	.35627	.31700
	35	1.61429	1.18064	0.96803	.82592	.71903	.63332	.56177	.50035	.44656	.39869	.35559	.31638
	36	1.60206	1.17609	0.96524	.82391	.71745	.63202	.56067	.49940	.44571	.39794	.35491	.31575
	37	1.59016	1.17159	0.96246	.82190	.71588	.63073	.55957	.49845	.44487	.39719	.35422	.31513
	38	1.57858	1.16714	0.95971	.81991	.71432	.62945	.55848	.49750	.44403	.39643	.35354	.31451
	39	1.56730	1.16273	0.95697	.81792	.71276	.62816	.55739	.49655	.44320	.39568	.35286	.31389
	40	1.55630	1.15836	0.95424	.81594	.71120	.62688	.55630	.49560	.44236	.39493	.35218	.31326
	41	1.54558	1.15404	0.95154	.81397	.70966	.62561	.55522	.49466	.44152	.39419	.35150	.31264
	42	1.53511	1.14976	.094885	.81201	.70811	.62434	.55414	.49372	.44069	.39344	.85083	.31203
	43	1.52489	1.14553	0.94617	.81006	.70658	.62307	.55306	.49278	.43986	.39269	.35015	.31141
	44	1.51491	1.14133	0.94352	.80811	.70504	.62180	.55199	.49184	.43903	.39195	.34948	.31079
	45	1.50515	1.13717	0.94088	.80618	.70352	.62054	.55091	.49091	.43820	.39121	.34880	.31017
	46	1.49560	1.13306	0.93825	.80425	.70200	.61929	.54984	.48998	.43738	.39046	.34813	.30956
	47	1.48626	1.12898	0.93565	.80234	.70048	.61803	.54877	.48905	.43655	.38972	.34746	.30894
	48	1.47712	1.12494	0.93305	.80043	.69897	.61678	.54770	.48812	.43573	.38899	.34679	.30833
	49	1.46817	1.12094	0.93048	.79853	.69746	.61554	.54664	.48719	.43491	.38825	.34612	.30772
	50	1.45939	1.11697	0.92791	.79663	.69596	.61429	.54558	.48626	.43409	.38751	.34545	.30710
	51	1.45079	1.11304	0.92537	.79475	.69447	.61306	.54452	.48534	.43327	.38678	.34478	.30649
	52	1.44236	1.10914	0.92283	.79287	.69298	.61182	.54347	.48442	.43245	.38604	.34411	.30588
	53	1.43409	1.10528	0.92032	.79101	.69149	.61059	.54241	.48350	.43164	.38531	.34345	.30527
	54	1.42597	1.10146	0.91781	.78915	.69002	.60936	.54136	.48258	.43082	.38458	.34278	.30466
	55	1.41800	1.09766	0.91532	.78729	.68854	.60813	.54031	.48167	.43001	.38385	.34212	.30406
	56	1.41017	1.09390	0.91285	.78545	.68707	.60691	.53927	.48076	.42920	.38312	.34146	.30345
	57	1.40249	1.09018	0.91039	.78361	.68561	.60569	.53823	.47984	.42839	.38239	.34080	.30284
	58	1.39493	1.08648	0.90794	.78179	.68415	.60448	.53719	.47893	.42758	.38166	.34014	.30224
	59	1.38751	1.08282	0.90551	.77996	.68269	.60327	.53618	.47803	.42677	.38094	.33948	.30163
	60	1.38021	1.07918	0.90309	.77815	.68124	.60206	.53511	.47712	.42597	.38021	.33882	.30103

HOURS OR DEGREES

12	13	14	15	16	17	18	19	20	21	22	23	
.30103	.26627	.23408	.20412	.17609	.14976	.12494	.10146	.07918	.05799	.03779	.01848	0
.30043	.26571	.23357	.20364	.17564	.14934	.12454	.10108	.07882	.05765	.03746	.01817	1
.29983	.26516	.23303	.20316	.17519	.14891	.12414	.10070	.07846	.05730	.03713	.01785	2
.29922	.26460	.23253	.20267	.17474	.14849	.12373	.10032	.07810	.05696	.03680	.01754	3
.29862	.26405	.23202	.20219	.17429	.14806	.12333	.09994	.07774	.05662	.03647	.01723	4
.29802	.26349	.23151	.20171	.17384	.14764	.12293	.09956	.07738	.05627	.03615	.01691	5
.29743	.26294	.23099	.20123	.17339	.14722	.12253	.09918	.07702	.05593	.03582	.01660	6
.29683	.26239	.23048	.20076	.17294	.14679	.12213	.09880	.07666	.05559	.03549	.01629	7
.29623	.26184	.22997	.20028	.17249	.14637	.12173	.09842	.07630	.05524	.03516	.01597	8
.29563	.26129	.22945	.19980	.17204	.14595	.12133	.09804	.07594	.05490	.03484	.01566	9
.29504	.26074	.22894	.19932	.17159	.14553	.12094	.09766	.07558	.05456	.03451	.01535	10
.29445	.26019	.22843	.19884	.17114	.14510	.12054	.09729	.07522	.05422	.03418	.01504	11
.29385	.25964	.22792	.19837	.17070	.14468	.12014	.09691	.07486	.05388	.03386	.01472	12
.29326	.25909	.22741	.19789	.17025	.14426	.11974	.09653	.07450	.05353	.03353	.01441	13
.29267	.25854	.22690	.19742	.16980	.14384	.11935	.09616	.07414	.05319	.03321	.01410	14
.29208	.25800	.22640	.19694	.16936	.14342	.11895	.09578	.07379	.05285	.03288	.01379	15
.29148	.25745	.22589	.19647	.16891	.14300	.11855	.09540	.087343	.05251	.03256	.01348	16
.29090	.25690	.22538	.19599	.16847	.14258	.11816	.09503	.07307	.05217	.03223	.01317	17
.29031	.25636	.22488	.19552	.16802	.14217	.11776	.09465	.07272	.05183	.03191	.01286	18
.28972	.25582	.22437	.19505	.16758	.14175	.11736	.09428	.07236	.05149	.03158	.01254	19
.28913	.25527	.22386	.19457	.16714	.14133	.11697	.09390	.07200	.05115	.03126	.01223	20
.28854	.25473	.22336	.19410	.16669	.14091	.11658	.09353	.07165	.05081	.03093	.01192	21
.28796	.25419	.22286	.19363	.16625	.14049	.11618	.09316	.07129	.05047	.03061	.01161	22
.28737	.25365	.22235	.19316	.16581	.14008	.11579	.09278	.07094	.05014	.03029	.01130	23
.28679	.25311	.22185	.19269	.16537	.13966	.11539	.09241	.07058	.04980	.02996	.01100	24
.28621	.25257	.22135	.19222	.16493	.13925	.11500	.09204	.07023	.04946	.02964	.01069	25
.28562	.25203	.22084	.19175	.16449	.13883	.11461	.09166	.06987	.04912	.02932	.01038	26
.28504	.25149	.22034	.19128	.16405	.13842	.11421	.09129	.06952	.04878	.02899	.01007	27
.28446	.25095	.21984	.19081	.16361	.13800	.11382	.09092	.06916	.04845	.02867	.00976	28
.28388	.25041	.21934	.19035	.16317	.13759	.11343	.09055	.06881	.04811	.02835	.00945	29
.28330	.24988	.21884	.18988	.16273	.13717	.11304	.09018	.06846	.04777	.02803	.00914	30
.28272	.24934	.21834	.18941	.16229	.13676	.11265	.08981	.06810	.04744	.02771	.00884	31
.28214	.24881	.21785	.18895	.16185	.13635	.11226	.08943	.06775	.04710	.02739	.00853	32
.28157	.24827	.21735	.18848	.16141	.13593	.11187	.08906	.06740	.04676	.02706	.00822	33
.28099	.24774	.21685	.18802	.16098	.13552	.11148	.08869	.06705	.04643	.02674	.00791	34
.28042	.24720	.21635	.18755	.16054	.13511	.11109	.08832	.06670	.04609	.02642	.00761	35
.27984	.24667	.21586	.18709	.16010	.13470	.11070	.08796	.06634	.04576	.02610	.00730	36
.27927	.24614	.21536	.18662	.15967	.13429	.11031	.08759	.06599	.04542	.02578	.00699	37
.27869	.24561	.21487	.18616	.15923	.13388	.10992	.08722	.06564	.04509	.02546	.00669	38
.27812	.24508	.21437	.18570	.15880	.13347	.10953	.08685	.06529	.04475	.02514	.00638	39
.27755	.24455	.21388	.18523	.15836	.13306	.10914	.08648	.06494	.04442	.02482	.00607	40
.27698	.24402	.21339	.18477	.15793	.13265	.10876	.08611	.06459	.04409	.02450	.00577	41
.27641	.24349	.21289	.18431	.15749	.13224	.10837	.08575	.06424	.04375	.02419	.00546	42
.27584	.24296	.21240	.18385	.15706	.13183	.10798	.08538	.06389	.04342	.02387	.00516	43
.27527	.24244	.21191	.18339	.15663	.13142	.10760	.08501	.06354	.04308	.02355	.00485	44
.27470	.24191	.21142	.18293	.15620	.13101	.10721	.08464	.06319	.04275	.02323	.00455	45
.27413	.24138	.21093	.18247	.15576	.13061	.10682	.08428	.06284	.04242	.02291	.00424	46
.27357	.24086	.21044	.18201	.15533	.13020	.10644	.08391	.06250	.04209	.02259	.00394	47
.27300	.24033	.20995	.18155	.15490	.12979	.10605	.08355	.06215	.04175	.02228	.00363	48
.27244	.23981	.20946	.18110	.15447	.12938	.10567	.08318	.06180	.04142	.02196	.00333	49
.27187	.23928	.20897	.18064	.15404	.12898	.10528	.08282	.06145	.04109	.02164	.00303	50
.27131	.23876	.20848	.18018	.15361	.12857	.10490	.08245	.06111	.04076	.02133	.00272	51
.27075	.23824	.20800	.17973	.15318	.12817	.10452	.08209	.06076	.04043	.02101	.00242	52
.27018	.23772	.20751	.17927	.15275	.12776	.10413	.08172	.06041	.04010	.02069	.00212	53
.26962	.23720	.20702	.17881	.15232	.12736	.10375	.08136	.06006	.03977	.02038	.00181	54
.26906	.23668	.20654	.17836	.15190	.12695	.10337	.08099	.05972	.03944	.02006	.00151	55
.26850	.23616	.20605	.17790	.15147	.12655	.10298	.08063	.05937	.03911	.01974	.00121	56
.26794	.23564	.20557	.17745	.15104	.12615	.10260	.08027	.05903	.03878	.01943	.00091	57
.26738	.23512	.20509	.17700	.15061	.12574	.10222	.07991	.05868	.03845	.01911	.00060	58
.26683	.23460	.20460	.17654	.15019	.12534	.10184	.07954	.05834	.03812	.01880	.00030	59
.26627	.23408	.20412	.17609	.14976	.12494	.10146	.07918	.05799	.03779	.01848	.00000	60

MINUTES OF TIME OR ARC

Table 28: Table of Logarithms

| 7h 12m 0s | | MC | 108° 0' 0" | | N LAT | 7h 16m 0s | | MC | 109° 0' 0" | |
| | | ♋ 16° 35' 58" | | | | | | ♋ 17° 31' 54" | | |
11	12	Ascendant	2	3		11	12	Ascendant	2	3
♌15 32.3	♍16 57.4	♎19 30.1	♏20 26.4	♐18 57.9	0	♌16 32.7	♍18 2.3	♎20 34.3	♏21 25.6	♐19 53.3
15 36.7	16 42.5	18 48.4	19 32.8	18 16.8	5	16 35.9	17 45.3	19 50.5	20 30.5	19 11.3
15 41.0	16 28.4	18 8.9	18 41.0	17 35.6	10	16 39.0	17 29.3	19 8.9	19 37.0	18 29.3
15 45.0	16 14.8	17 30.9	17 50.1	16 53.8	15	16 41.9	17 13.8	18 28.9	18 44.6	17 46.5
15 45.8	16 12.1	17 23.4	17 40.0	16 45.3	16	16 42.5	17 10.7	18 21.0	18 34.1	17 37.8
15 46.5	16 9.4	17 16.0	17 29.8	16 36.7	17	16 43.1	17 7.6	18 13.2	18 23.7	17 29.0
15 47.3	16 6.7	17 8.6	17 19.7	16 28.1	18	16 43.6	17 4.6	18 5.3	18 13.2	17 20.2
15 48.1	16 4.0	17 1.2	17 9.6	16 19.4	19	16 44.1	17 1.5	17 57.5	18 2.7	17 11.2
15 48.8	16 1.3	16 53.8	16 59.4	16 10.6	20	16 44.6	16 58.5	17 49.7	17 52.2	17 2.2
15 49.6	15 58.6	16 46.4	16 49.2	16 1.7	21	16 45.2	16 55.4	17 42.0	17 41.7	16 53.2
15 50.3	15 55.9	16 39.0	16 39.0	15 52.8	22	16 45.7	16 52.3	17 34.2	17 31.2	16 44.0
15 51.0	15 53.2	16 31.6	16 28.8	15 43.7	23	16 46.2	16 49.2	17 26.4	17 20.6	16 34.7
15 51.7	15 50.5	16 24.2	16 18.5	15 34.6	24	16 46.6	16 46.1	17 18.6	17 10.0	16 25.3
15 52.4	15 47.7	16 16.9	16 8.2	15 25.3	25	16 47.1	16 43.0	17 10.9	16 59.4	16 15.8
15 53.1	15 45.0	16 9.5	15 57.9	15 16.0	26	16 47.5	16 39.9	17 3.1	16 48.6	16 6.2
15 53.7	15 42.2	16 2.0	15 47.5	15 6.4	27	16 48.0	16 36.7	16 55.2	16 37.9	15 56.4
15 54.4	15 39.3	15 54.6	15 37.0	14 56.8	28	16 48.4	16 33.6	16 47.4	16 27.0	15 46.5
15 55.0	15 36.5	15 47.1	15 26.4	14 47.0	29	16 48.8	16 30.4	16 39.5	16 16.1	15 36.4
15 55.6	15 33.6	15 39.7	15 15.8	14 37.1	30	16 49.2	16 27.1	16 31.7	16 5.2	15 26.2
15 56.2	15 30.7	15 32.1	15 5.2	14 27.0	31	16 49.5	16 23.8	16 23.7	15 54.1	15 15.8
15 56.8	15 27.8	15 24.6	14 54.4	14 16.7	32	16 49.9	16 20.5	16 15.8	15 42.9	15 5.2
15 57.4	15 24.8	15 17.0	14 43.5	14 6.2	33	16 50.2	16 17.2	16 7.7	15 31.7	14 54.5
15 57.9	15 21.7	15 9.3	14 32.6	13 55.6	34	16 50.4	16 13.7	15 59.7	15 20.3	14 43.5
15 58.4	15 18.6	15 1.6	14 21.5	13 44.7	35	16 50.7	16 10.3	15 51.5	15 8.9	14 32.3
15 58.8	15 15.5	14 53.8	14 10.3	13 33.6	36	16 50.9	16 6.8	15 43.3	14 57.3	14 20.9
15 59.3	15 12.3	14 46.0	13 59.0	13 22.3	37	16 51.1	16 3.2	15 35.1	14 45.6	14 9.2
15 59.6	15 9.0	14 38.1	13 47.6	13 10.7	38	16 51.2	15 59.5	15 26.7	14 33.8	13 57.2
16 0.0	15 5.6	14 30.1	13 36.1	12 58.9	39	16 51.3	15 55.8	15 18.3	14 21.8	13 45.0
16 0.3	15 2.2	14 22.1	13 24.4	12 46.7	40	16 51.3	15 51.9	15 9.8	14 9.7	13 32.5
16 0.5	14 58.7	14 13.9	13 12.6	12 34.3	41	16 51.3	15 48.0	15 1.2	13 57.4	13 19.7
16 0.7	14 55.0	14 5.7	13 0.6	12 21.6	42	16 51.2	15 44.0	14 52.5	13 44.9	13 6.5
16 0.8	14 51.3	13 57.3	12 48.5	12 8.5	43	16 51.0	15 39.8	14 43.7	13 32.3	12 53.0
16 0.8	14 47.4	13 48.9	12 36.2	11 55.1	44	16 50.7	15 35.5	14 34.8	13 19.6	12 39.1
16 0.7	14 43.4	13 40.3	12 23.8	11 41.3	45	16 50.3	15 31.1	14 25.8	13 6.6	12 24.8
16 0.5	14 39.2	13 31.6	12 11.2	11 27.1	46	16 49.8	15 26.6	14 16.6	12 53.5	12 10.1
16 0.1	14 34.9	13 22.8	11 58.4	11 12.4	47	16 49.2	15 21.8	14 7.3	12 40.1	11 54.9
15 59.6	14 30.4	13 13.8	11 45.4	10 57.4	48	16 48.7	15 16.9	13 57.8	12 26.6	11 39.2
15 59.0	14 26.7	13 4.7	11 32.2	10 41.8	49	16 47.4	15 11.7	13 48.2	12 12.9	11 23.1
15 58.1	14 20.7	12 55.4	11 18.9	10 25.7	50	16 46.3	15 6.4	13 38.4	11 58.9	11 6.3
15 57.0	14 15.5	12 46.0	11 5.4	10 9.1	51	16 44.9	15 0.7	13 28.5	11 44.8	10 49.0
15 55.7	14 9.9	12 36.4	10 51.7	9 51.9	52	16 43.2	14 54.7	13 18.3	11 30.5	10 31.1
15 53.9	14 4.0	12 26.6	10 37.8	9 34.1	53	16 41.1	14 48.4	13 8.0	11 15.9	10 12.5
15 51.8	13 57.8	12 16.6	10 23.8	9 15.6	54	16 38.7	14 41.7	12 57.4	11 1.2	9 53.2
15 49.2	13 51.0	12 6.4	10 9.7	8 56.5	55	16 35.8	14 34.5	12 46.6	10 46.4	9 33.2
15 46.1	13 43.7	11 55.9	9 55.4	8 36.7	56	16 32.3	14 26.7	12 35.6	10 31.4	9 12.4
15 42.2	13 35.8	11 45.2	9 41.2	8 16.1	57	16 28.0	14 18.4	12 24.3	10 16.4	8 50.7
15 37.4	13 27.1	11 34.3	9 27.0	7 54.7	58	16 22.9	14 9.2	12 12.8	10 1.3	8 28.2
15 31.5	13 17.4	11 23.1	9 12.9	7 32.6	59	16 16.7	13 59.1	12 1.0	9 46.3	8 4.8
15 24.1	13 6.5	11 11.6	8 59.1	7 9.8	60	16 9.1	13 47.9	11 48.8	9 31.6	7 40.5
15 14.9	12 54.2	10 59.8	8 45.8	6 46.3	61	15 59.6	13 35.2	11 36.4	9 17.3	7 15.4
15 3.0	12 39.9	10 47.7	8 33.4	6 22.2	62	15 47.6	13 20.6	11 23.6	9 3.7	6 49.5
14 47.5	12 23.0	10 35.2	8 22.5	5 58.1	63	15 32.0	13 3.4	11 10.4	8 51.4	6 23.1
14 26.7	12 2.4	10 22.4	8 13.8	5 34.4	64	15 11.3	12 42.6	10 56.8	8 41.3	5 56.8
13 57.1	11 35.9	10 9.1	8 9.4	5 13.0	65	14 42.5	12 16.3	10 42.9	8 35.0	5 31.9
13 11.5	10 59.1	9 55.5	8 13.1	4 57.9	66	13 58.8	11 40.5	10 28.5	8 36.0	5 11.8
5	6	Descendant	8	9	S LAT	5	6	Descendant	8	9
		♑ 16° 35' 58"						♑ 17° 31' 54"		
19h 12m 0s		MC	288° 0' 0"			19h 16m 0s		MC	289° 0' 0"	

Table 29: Page from *AFA Tables of Houses:* Koch System

7. Subtract the Log for the Difference from the Log for the Excess Time. **The result is the Constant Factor for Sidereal Time.** You will use this to calculate the Midheaven and other house cusps.

8. Enter the birth latitude onto the form, using degrees and minutes. Now look down the columns until you find the latitude that is just lower than the birth latitude, and enter it onto the form.

9. Subtract the lower latitude from the birth latitude. Find the log for the result, using the log table. Note in the log table that degrees and hours are read across, and minutes are read down. You will be using the first column in the table to find your log.

10. Enter the log for 1° (1.3802) and subtract this from the Log of Excess Latitude. **The result is the Constant Factor for Latitude.** You will use this number to calculate all of the cusps except for the Midheaven.

You now have all the information you need to calculate the exact house cusps.

Now calculate six house cusps. Keep in mind that the opposite cusps will be in the same degree and minute, but in opposite signs.

1. On the top line of the form, enter the cusps at the later sidereal time. You will find the Midheaven at the top of the column, and the five remaining cusps at the latitude just higher than the birth latitude.

2. On the second line, enter these values from the preceding column for the earlier sidereal time.

3. Subtract. Then find the Log of the Difference for each cusp.

4. Record the Constant Factor Log. Add the two logs. **The sum is the Correction Log for this step.**

5. For these log values, read up to the top of the column, and across to the side of the row. Record the number at the top in degrees (should be zero) and record the number at the side in minutes.

6. For the Midheaven, you will skip the next few steps. For the other cusps, list the cusps for the higher latitude, and below them the cusps for the lower latitude. Find these cusps in the column for the sidereal time previous to the birth time, and for the latitude that is lower than the birth latitude.

7. Subtract. Find the log for each resulting difference. In the Log Table, find the log for each difference.

8. Enter the constant factor for Latitude for each cusp. Add the two logs. **The result is the Correction Log for this step.**

9. Using the log table, and reading across the row, find the number of minutes and record it for each cusp (the degree will be zero because the result has to be less than one full degree).

10. Reenter the cusps from the lower latitude from step 6. In the case of the Midheaven, reenter the cusp from the earlier sidereal time.

11. Enter the sidereal Time Correction for each cusp.

12. Enter the Latitude Corrections for each cusp.

13. Add the three values (two in the case of the Midheaven). **The results are the precise house cusps for the chart.**

Step Five: Calculate the Exact Planetary Positions

If an individual were born at exactly midnight GMT, there would be no need to calculate the planets' positions, as they would be exact in the ephemeris. For everyone else, we need to figure the exact positions of the planets. This step in the process allows you to determine how far a planet has traveled from its midnight Greenwich Mean Time (GMT) position at the actual birth time. For the outer planets, you will discover from the ephemeris that the motion each day is quite small and can be easily estimated. However, for the inner planets, and especially for the Moon, this estimation is more difficult.

The method for calculating the exact planetary positions is the same as the method used for calculating house cusps. For the planets, the positions in the ephemeris are listed in degrees and seconds, and the logs work the same here as for degrees and minutes of latitude, or the hours and minutes of time. It is a matter of finding the information in the ephemeris, listing it, and adding the resulting log to the log for the Equivalent Greenwich Mean Time Interval. This value was found in step 1 of the process of calculating the True Sidereal Birth Time.

1. From the Sidereal Birth Time Calculations, find the Equivalent Greenwich Mean Time Interval. Enter this time (up to 24 hours) in the Form for Calculating Planetary Positions.

2. From the Table of Logarithms, find the log for the time interval. Use the numbers across the top to find the hour, and the numbers down the side to find the minutes. Then, reading down the appropriate column and across the appropriate row, find the log. Record this number on the form. This is the Constant Log for planetary motion.

3. For the Moon and each planet, record the positions for the midnight after the birth time, and for the midnight before the birth time.

4. Subtract these positions. **The result is the daily planetary motion for each planet.**

Note: For retrograde planets, the resulting motion is a negative number. This means that your final calculated motion will be subtracted from the position on the previous day, instead of added.

5. From the Table of Logarithms, find the log corresponding to the planetary motion for each planet. Record these numbers for each planet.

Note: For most of the planets, the values will come from the first column, and in some cases the second column, as the daily motions will be less than one degree, or just a bit over one degree in the case of the Sun, Mercury, and Venus. For the Moon, the values will come from somewhere near the middle of the table.

6. Add the two logs for each planet. **The result is the log of motion for the birth chart.**

7. Using the resulting logs, find the corresponding number of degrees and minutes. Remember that most of your answers should be coming form the first column of the log table. Record the result. **This is the actual motion of the planet since the previous midnight**. The value should be less than the total motion between the previous and following midnights.

8. Add the actual motion to the planet's position at the previous midnight. Remember to subtract the actual motion if the planet is retrograde. **The result is the actual planetary position for the birth chart.**

You now have all the information you need to put the birth chart together. Using the blank chart form in figure 16, enter the chart information. Because the ephemeris may not contain information about declination, you may not be able to calculate the parallels. If you have the declination information, the method used to calculate planetary positions is used to calculate the parallels, as they are also measured in degrees and minutes. Remember to note whether the planet is moving from south to north or north to south, and record the results.

1. Write the Midheaven at the top of the chart, and the Ascendant at the left side. Enter the intermediate cusps for the Eleventh, Twelfth, Second, and Third Houses. Write the degree, the glyph for the sign, and the minutes.

2. Using the same degrees and minutes, enter the opposite house cusps, using the appropriate signs. For the Fourth House, for example, the degree and minute of the Midheaven is used, with the sign opposite the Midheaven. Thus, for a 5°♎32' Midheaven, you would write 5°♈32' at the cusp of the Fourth House.

3. For each planet, determine which house it occupies. This will be the house that has a lower degree of the Zodiac on the cusp, and a higher degree of the Zodiac on the following cusp. Then write the glyph for the planet, the degree, the glyph for the sign, and the minutes.

Note: You will want to develop a consistent method for recording this information. For example, you may choose the method used in this book, which is to record the planet on the outside of the wheel, then the degree, the sign, and the minutes, moving toward the center of the chart.

Calculating Aspects

Now that you have the birth chart calculated and drawn, you will want to identify the aspects in the chart. There are some tricks that you can use to calculate aspects quickly.

1. Planets at or near the same degree of any sign are in aspect to each other. Count the number of signs between them to determine the aspect.

   1 sign = semisextile

   2 signs = sextile

   3 signs = square

   4 signs = trine

   5 signs = quincunx

   6 signs = opposition

Example: The Sun is at 12°ß34', and the Moon is at 14°♋21'. They are close to the same degree, and they are six signs apart. Therefore they form an opposition (♂) aspect.

2. To find semisquare and sesquiquadrate aspects, from the position of the planet, add one sign and add fifteen degrees. The *element* of the resulting sign is where both aspects will be found, and the degree tells you the degree to look for.

Example: Venus is at 13°♐25'. Adding one sign equals 13°ß25'. Adding fifteen degrees equals 28°ß25'. Any planets close to 28° of a cardinal sign form semisquares or sesquiquadrates to Venus. Suppose that Uranus is at 27°♋11', and that Jupiter is at 29°♎49'. Uranus is more than 90° from Venus, so it forms a sesquiquadrate to Venus. Jupiter is less than 90° away, so it forms a semisquare.

3. As you look for aspects, record them in a list or in the aspect grid on the chart form.

When you have calculated the aspects, you are ready to begin the delineation of the chart. See the appropriate chapters in this book for delineation of the birth chart.

Calculating the Part of Fortune

The Part of Fortune shares the same relationship to the Ascendant that the Moon has to the Sun. For example, if the Sun and Moon are conjunct, then the Part of Fortune will be conjunct the Ascendant.

Convert the sign for the Sun, Moon, and Ascendant to a number. For example, Scorpio is the eighth sign.

Add the longitude of the Ascendant to the longitude of the Moon.

Then subtract the longitude of the Sun. The remainder will be the place of the Part of Fortune.

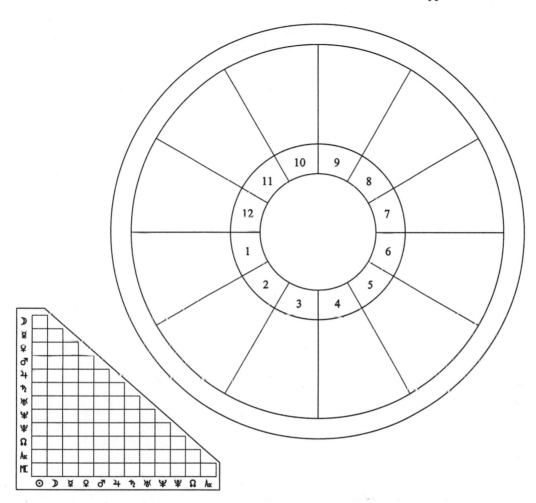

Figure 16: Blank Chart Form with Aspect Grid

Example

Ascendant   12°♌43'   5S 12° 43'

Because the Ascendant degrees and minutes are less than the Moon's, "borrow" 60' from the degrees, and "borrow" 30 degrees from the signs.

                                                     4S 41° 103'
              Moon   + 22°♈5'   1S 22° 45'
                                                     3S 19° 58'

Because the result of the above addition has fewer signs than the Sun, add twelve to the signs.

                                                     15S 19° 58'
              Sun   − 7°♐11'   09S 07° 11'
                                                     6S 12° 47'

The Part of Fortune is located at 6°♍12'47", or 6°♍13'.

A to Z Progressions Math

Having learned to make the natal chart correctly, students will find it easy to erect the progressed chart. The rule simply stated is: count forward in the birth year ephemeris, beginning with the day *after* the birth day, one day for each year to the year of age required. Call the date thus found *the progressed birth date* and from it make a chart in the usual way, using the same birth time (hour and minute) and the same Tables of Houses used for erecting the natal chart. The complete rule, with examples, and the various details associated with the making of a progressed horoscope, are given further on in this lesson. However, before proceeding with the calculations required in a progressed chart, let us first discuss some of its salient features. The insight and understanding thereby acquired will not only simplify the necessary final efforts, but also considerably increase our appreciation of the value of the various features embraced in the work. The student who undertakes this progressed horoscope lesson will very likely find it necessary to read and reread it a number of times in order to form a general idea of the process, its purpose and application to life.

    The horoscope of birth and the progressed chart may be likened to a book of information: the index shows what the volume contains and the chapters give the details. The birth chart is like an index and the progressed chart like a chapter, and as the book contains only what is indexed, so from a progressed chart must be read *only* that which is indicated at birth.

Constructing the Progressed Chart

Finding the Progressed Birth Date

To erect a progressed chart, refer to an ephemeris for the date and year of birth and count each day after birth as one year in life, i.e., a chart made for the first day after birth would show (by planets, positions, aspects, etc.) the conditions that operate between one year and two years old. A chart cast for the second day after birth would show the conditions for the twelve months following the second birthday, etc.

Examples

Throughout this lesson, the example chart used to illustrate the calculations is for September 11, 2001, 8:46 A.M., Manhattan, New York.

If a progressed chart is to be erected for the year 2012, the birth year is subtracted from 2012, giving the remainder of 11. This is equivalent to 11 days after birth. Eleven is then added to the birth date, September 11, giving the progressed birth date of September 22, 2001. Thus, a chart erected for 8:46 A.M., September 22, 2001, corrected for the longitude and latitude of Manhattan, New York, will represent the year September 11, 2012, to September 11, 2013.

2012 (year for which chart is desired)
−2001 (birth year)
      11

September 11, 2001 (birth date)
      + 11
September 22, 2001 (progressed birth date for 2012)

The Table of Days on the following pages is very handy for finding the date representing the progressed year. For the previous example, September 11 is day number 254. To find the date to use from the ephemeris, add 11. We get day number 265, or September 22. If the dates involved include February 29 in a leap year, remember to subtract one for the leap year.

Calculating the Progressed Horoscope

After finding the progressed birth date, we proceed with the calculations just as for the birth chart, using the same birth time, latitude, and longitude. Refer back to the previous section on calculating the birth chart for instructions. Some astrologers choose to use the latitude of the residence on the date of the progressed horoscope. This will make a difference in the Ascendant and intermediate house cusps.

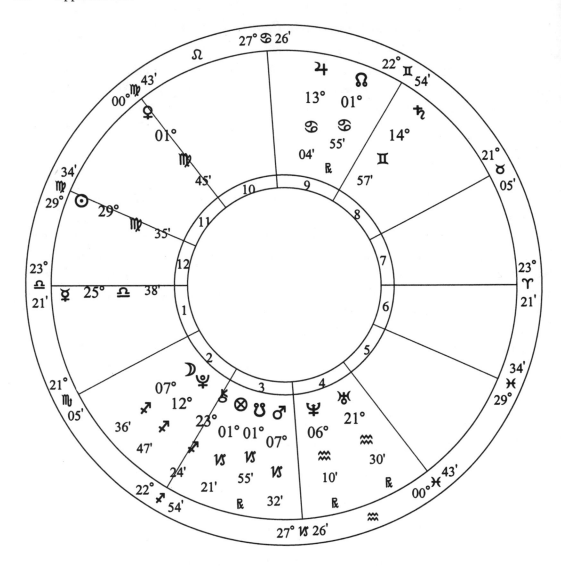

World Trade Center
September 11, 2001 / New York, NY / 8:46 A.M. EST
Chart progressed to September 11, 2012
Placidus Houses

Figure 17: Progressed Chart: September 11, 2012

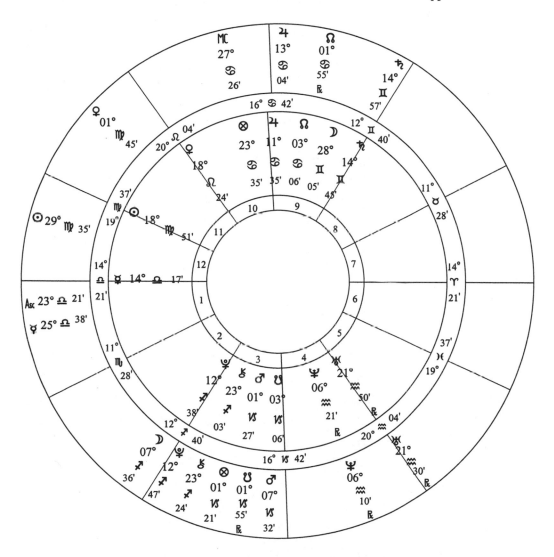

Inner Wheel: World Trade Center Natal Chart
September 11, 2001 / New York, NY / 8:46 A.M. EST
Placidus Houses

Outer Wheel: Progressed Chart for September 11, 2012
Placidus Houses

Figure 18: Chart for September 11, 2001, Natal and Progressed

D/M	j	f	m	a	m	j	j	a	s	o	n	d
1	1	32	60	91	121	152	182	213	244	274	305	335
2	2	33	61	92	122	153	183	214	245	275	306	336
3	3	34	62	93	123	154	184	215	246	276	307	337
4	4	35	63	94	124	155	185	216	247	277	308	338
5	5	36	64	95	125	156	186	217	248	278	309	339
6	6	37	65	96	126	157	187	218	249	279	310	340
7	7	38	66	97	127	158	188	219	250	280	311	341
8	8	39	67	98	128	159	189	220	251	281	312	342
9	9	40	68	99	129	160	190	221	252	282	313	343
10	10	41	69	100	130	161	191	222	253	283	314	344
11	11	42	70	101	131	162	192	223	254	284	315	345
12	12	43	71	102	132	163	193	224	255	285	316	346
13	13	44	72	103	133	164	194	225	256	286	317	347
14	14	45	73	104	134	165	195	226	257	287	318	348
15	15	46	74	105	135	166	196	227	258	288	319	349
16	16	47	75	106	136	167	197	228	259	289	320	350
17	17	48	76	107	137	168	198	229	260	290	321	351
18	18	49	77	018	138	169	199	230	261	291	322	352
19	19	50	78	109	139	170	200	231	262	292	323	353
20	20	51	79	110	140	171	201	232	263	293	324	354
21	21	52	80	111	141	172	202	233	264	294	325	355
22	22	53	81	112	142	173	203	234	265	295	326	356
23	23	54	82	113	143	174	204	235	266	296	327	357
24	24	55	83	114	144	175	205	236	267	297	328	358
25	25	56	84	115	145	176	206	237	268	298	329	359
26	26	57	85	116	146	177	207	238	269	299	330	360
27	27	58	86	117	147	178	208	239	270	300	331	361
28	28	59	87	118	148	179	209	240	271	301	332	362
29	29		88	119	149	180	210	241	272	302	333	363
30	30		89	120	150	181	211	242	273	303	334	364
31	31		90		151		212	243		304		365

Table 30: Table of Days Between Two Dates for All Twelve Months

D/M	j	f	m	a	m	j	j	a	s	o	n	d
1	366	397	425	456	486	517	547	578	609	639	670	700
2	367	398	426	457	487	518	548	579	610	640	671	701
3	368	399	427	458	488	519	549	580	611	641	672	702
4	369	400	428	459	489	520	550	581	612	642	673	703
5	370	401	429	460	490	521	551	582	613	643	674	704
6	371	402	430	461	491	522	552	583	614	644	675	705
7	372	403	431	462	492	523	553	584	615	645	676	706
8	373	404	432	463	493	524	554	585	616	646	677	707
9	374	405	433	464	494	525	555	586	617	647	678	708
10	375	406	434	465	495	526	556	587	618	648	679	709
11	376	407	435	466	496	527	557	588	619	649	680	710
12	377	408	436	467	497	528	558	589	620	650	681	711
13	378	409	437	468	798	529	559	590	621	651	682	712
14	378	410	438	469	499	530	560	591	622	652	683	713
15	380	411	439	470	500	531	561	592	623	653	684	714
16	381	412	440	471	501	532	562	593	624	654	685	715
17	382	413	441	472	502	533	563	594	625	655	686	716
18	383	414	442	473	503	534	564	595	626	656	687	717
19	384	415	443	474	504	535	565	596	627	657	688	718
20	385	416	444	475	505	536	566	597	628	658	689	719
21	386	417	445	476	506	537	567	598	629	659	690	720
22	387	418	446	477	507	538	568	599	630	660	691	721
23	388	419	447	478	508	539	569	600	631	661	692	722
24	389	420	448	479	509	540	570	601	632	662	693	723
25	390	421	449	480	510	541	571	602	633	663	694	724
26	391	422	450	481	511	542	572	603	634	664	695	725
27	392	423	451	482	512	542	573	604	635	665	696	726
28	393	424	452	483	513	544	574	605	636	666	697	727
29	394		453	484	514	545	575	606	637	667	698	728
30	395		454	485	515	546	576	607	638	668	699	729
31	396		455		516		577	608		669		730

Table 30: Table of Days Between Two Dates for All Twelve Months

Positioning the Planets

The positions of the planets at the time of birth on the progressed birth date are found in the same way as for a natal chart. We first find the constant log, then calculate the daily motion of the planets, and finally figure their positions at birth. The positions of the planets are calculated from the ephemeris for the progressed birth date.

Entering the Planets in the Chart

Only the Sun, Moon, Mercury, Venus, and Mars move fast enough to make figuring their precise positions practical. The noon positions of the other planets are copied from the ephemeris onto the chart blank. All the planets are drawn in the progressed chart exactly the same as in a natal chart.

The Moon's Nodes

The motion of the Moon's Nodes is retrograde at the rate of about three minutes of longitude per day. The Nodes are of some value in natal astrology and are useful in the horary branch. They can be copied from the ephemeris and entered in the chart.

The Part of Fortune

The position of the Part of Fortune depends partly on the location of the Moon. As the Moon in the progressed chart is constantly moving forward and travels about 13 degrees during the year, it follows that the place of the Part of Fortune in the progressed chart would likewise be constantly changing. Due to this, there is a likelihood of error in placing it, so it may be omitted, if preferred. In fact, like the Moon's Nodes, many astrologers do not use the Part of Fortune at all, except in horary astrology. We mention these points in order to aid those who desire to do practical research into the matter. In Llewellyn George's own experience, he found these factors important and deserving of serious attention.

The Declination of the Sun and Moon

As in the natal chart, the declinations of the Sun and Moon must be interpolated to the exact birth time. This is done in the same manner as finding the birth-time positions of the faster-moving planets. The daily motion is found, its log is added to the constant log, and the product added (if declination is increasing) or subtracted (if declination is decreasing) to the progressed birth-date declination.

The Progressed Aspects

When interpreting the progressed horoscope, there are six basic considerations:

1. Aspects between the progressed Moon and both natal and progressed planets and cusps, which will be discussed separately in this lesson.
2. Directions from progressed planets or cusps to progressed planets or cusps.
3. Directions from progressed planets or cusps to natal planets or cusps.

4. Parallel Aspects.

5. Transits over progressed aspects to natal.

6. Transits over progressed mutual aspects.

Unless systematic tabulation of aspects is made, some important aspects may be overlooked. The student is advised to lay out six columns for these six categories and to figure the aspects in groups.

A very good plan is to make a chart of the progressed horoscope, and then to enter the progressed planets into the birth chart, with colored ink for distinction. Note aspects from progressed planets to the planets as they were at birth, allowing a 2° orb to make an aspect. Only the aspects that are forming are to be tabulated for delineation.

When using a computer program, the progressed planets can be included in a separate circle, arranged to suit personal preference. Some programs also include a third or even fourth circle, to include transiting positions and/or planets for an additional method of calculation.

The Progressed Moon

The motion of the Moon is approximately 13° per day (per year by progression), consequently it will require about 2½ years to progress through a sign of the Zodiac. In approximately twenty-eight years, it will progress completely around the circle and return to the place it originally held at birth.

The Moon's aspects formed as it progresses from house to house through both the natal and progressed charts are very important and indicate most of the conditions and events encountered in life. This will be appreciated by noting its various influences as indicated by the houses it traverses, all of which are accentuated in accordance with the aspects that the Moon may form. In fact, in the course of its apparent twenty-eight-year circle of the signs and houses, it will form every possible aspect in the natal chart and almost every possible aspect in the progressed chart. One of the main features connected with progressed horoscope work is to record the monthly place of the progressing Moon and tabulate the month and year of the various aspects that it will form.

Calculating the Motion of the Progressed Moon

To find the motion of the Moon on the progressed birth date, count the number of degrees and minutes of longitude it will travel between its given place on the progressed birthday and its given place on the next day. Then change this amount of the Moon's motion from degrees and minutes to all minutes by multiplying the degrees by 60 and adding the minutes to this product. Then divide the total by 12 to determine the rate the Moon will move forward in the Zodiac through the chart in each of the twelve months during the progressed year. By adding this amount of the Moon's monthly motion twelve times to the place of the Moon at the birth hour on the progressed birth date, it will show in what degrees the Moon will be each month during the coming twelve months.

The average motion of the Moon is about 13° (varying from 12° to 15°), which is equal to 1°05' of longitude per month by progression. The Moon's motion is calculated using the progressed birth date (noon positions in the ephemeris are adequate). Use the following steps.

1. The Moon's position in the ephemeris on the progressed birth date is subtracted from its position on the next day to find its daily motion. This motion is converted to all minutes by multiplying the degrees by 60 and adding the minutes to the product. The result represents the Moon's progressed motion during the year. This is then divided by 12 to get the progressed motion during any one month.

2. Add the monthly motion to the earlier position of the Moon. Continue doing this twelve times. The results are the monthly positions of the progressed Moon.

Position of Moon by progression, January 22, 1978

(actual position, March 4, 1936, birth): 10°♌15'00"
+1°01'25"
——————

February 22, 1978: 11°♌16'25"
+1°01'25"
——————

March 22, 1978: 12°♌17'50"
+1°01'25"
——————

April 22, 1978: 13°♌19'15"
+1°01'25"
——————

May 22, 1978: 14°♌20'40"
+1°01'25"
——————

June 22,1978: 15°♌22'05"
+1°01'25"
——————

July 22, 1978: 16°♌23'30"
+1°01'25"
——————

August 22, 1978: 17°♌24'55"
+1°01'25"
——————

September 22, 1978: 18°♌26'20"
+1°01'25"
——————

October 22, 1978: 19°♌27'45"
+1°01'25"
——————

November 22, 1978: 20°♌29'10"
+1°01'25"
——————

December 22, 1978: 21°♌30'35"
+1°01'25"
——————

January 22, 1979: 22°♌32'00"

Many astrology software programs include a search feature. Using this feature, one may prepare a chronological list of aspects for six months, a year, or longer. This list covers progressed planets to natal, progressed to progressed, solar arc to natal, transits to progressed, solar arc, or natal, etc., depending on personal preferences. This list eliminates the need to compile lists of aspects.

Lunar Progressed Aspects

After compiling a table of the Moon's position each month throughout the progressed year, you are ready to record the aspects made by the Moon in its monthly motion. These are termed *lunar aspects* and are very important. By working in the foregoing manner, you may readily see in which month during the year an aspect will become complete and thus prepare to improve or offset its effects according to its nature, whether good or adverse.

Remember that an aspect by this progressive direction has an orb of only 2° for the major aspects and an orb of 1° for the minor aspects. All aspects whether major or minor should be recorded, but their influence is to be judged relative to their power and their indications in the natal chart. For instance, if the progressed Moon forms an adverse aspect with Venus, do not predict something adverse unless they were in adverse aspect at birth, although it would not be a good month to press matters relating to courtship and marriage or other things governed by Venus.

The other planets move so slowly by direction that it is not necessary to find their monthly motion, as with the Moon.

The lunar progressed aspects require the closest attention because they refer to whatever the Moon signifies by the house it then occupies and the house it rules in the progressed chart, as well as the house it occupies and rules in the natal chart. In addition, one will consider the house the Moon may be working through in the natal chart when placed in it from the progressed chart.

Calculating the Time a Lunar Progressed Aspect Becomes Partile

In connection with aspects between the progressed Moon and natal planets, the following example illustrates a method of calculating the date and time when the influence reaches its maximum or peak, or in other words, the date and time the aspect becomes partile.

Note: The resultant time of day derived through the use of the following methods must be approximate and not exact, due to various technical factors involving slight irregularity in motion of the planets, etc., which for the sake of simplicity are omitted. However, the variation is slight and so will rarely cause your answer to vary more than a few minutes in time. Therefore, for practical purposes these calculations may be considered correct.

Example: Person born October 11, 1937, 4:00 A.M., Los Angeles, California.

Progressed birth date: November 10, 1937, representing the native's thirtieth year, October 11, 1967, to October 11, 1968.

Question: When will the progressed Moon reach an exact trine to the natal Sun?

Datum:
Progressed Moon (November 10, 1937, 4:00 A.M.) 7°♒27'16".
Natal Sun (October 11, 1937, 4:00 A.M.) 17°♎45'09".
Progressed lunar motion—12°24'40" per day, representing one year.

1. Calculate the Distance the Planet Must Travel to Partile.

The progressed Moon will make an exact trine to the natal Sun when it reaches 17°45'09", a distance of 10°17'53".

   17°45'09" (position of exact aspect)
 − 7°27'16" (position on progressed birth date)
   10°17'53" (distance needed to travel)

2. Calculate the Time Needed to Cover that Distance.

Since the position of the natal Sun is fixed, we need only calculate the time needed for the Moon to move the needed distance. This is done by using logarithms to find out what portion of the Moon's daily motion is needed to bring it to the proper place.

   .3674 (log of distance 10°17'53")
 −.2862 (log of daily motion 12°24'40")
   .0812 (log of proportional distance)
   .0812 = 19h 55m (time needed to cover the distance)

3. Calculate the Equivalent Time in the Current Calendar.

The Moon must travel 19h 55m after the progressed birth date (November 10, 1937, 4:00 A.M.) for the aspect to become exact. This must be translated into time in the current calendar—the amount of time past the current birth date (October 11, 1967, 4:00 A.M.)—with the aid of the following table.

24 hours, 1 day = 1 year by progression
2 hours motion = 1 month by progression (30 days)
1 hour motion = ½ month by progression (15 days)
4 minutes motion = 1 day by progression (24 hours)
1 minute motion = 6 hours by progression (¼ day)
10 seconds motion = 1 hour by progression
1 second motion = 6 minutes by progression

Table 31: Time Key

19 hours = 9½ months by progression (9 months 15 days)

55 minutes = 13¾ days by progression (13 days 18 hours)

October 11, 1967, 4:00 a.m. + 9 months 28 days 18 hours = August 8, 1968, 10:00 p.m.

The progressed Moon will form an exact trine to the natal Sun on August 8, 1968, at 10:00 p.m.

Progressed Aspects

Progressed Mutual Aspects

Upon completion of the progressed chart, the aspects are calculated and tabulated exactly as in the natal chart. These are entered under column 2, *Progressed Mutual Aspects.*

Progressed Aspects to the Natal Chart

After all the aspects have been noted between the planets in the progressed chart, insert the progressed planets in the birth chart with colored ink or pencil for distinction, and note if they form any aspects with the natal planets. Pay particular attention to the aspects that may be formed by the Moon and Sun. *Solar aspects are very important.*

It makes no difference in the nature of an aspect whether it is found in the natal or progressed chart; the square will always be adverse, the sextile always good, etc.

A progressed or directional aspect is technically due to operate when the aspect is exactly complete, but the transit of a planet over the place of a directional aspect that is still forming (within a degree or so) may excite it into action prematurely. Enter these aspects in column 3, *Progressed Aspects to the Natal Chart.*

Aspects to House Cusps

When the exact time of birth was used, the aspects formed by any of the planets to the degree of a house are important. If only an approximate birth time was used, the degrees on house cusps would be only approximately correct, and consequently it would be uncertain when a planet would reach conjunction with the actual degree ruling the cusp.

Jupiter or Venus conjunct, trine, or sextile the Midheaven (sign and degree of the Tenth House cusp) is a very fortunate indication for business affairs, honors, etc.; but the amount of good they will bring depends upon their power for good in the natal chart. If either planet is heavily afflicted in the natal chart, is cadent, or in debility, its power for good by direction is correspondingly weakened.

The influences of minor aspects to house cusps are hard to detect. Of the major aspects, the conjunction is the most important. The orb of influence is but 2° for a planet or a cusp by progression. If the time of birth is not accurately known and the chart is erected for an approximate time of birth, the house cusp degrees may not be correct. Consequently, in such cases it is useless to figure aspects of planets to cusps. However, a few hours of difference (exact birth time unknown) would not appreciably affect the aspects of planets one with another, except the Moon.

Any of the planets coming to a conjunction, parallel, opposition, trine, square, sextile, etc., with the sign and degree on the cusp of a house will bring an influence to bear according to the nature of the house and in proportion to the planet's powers in the natal chart by essential dignity, aspect, location, and position. The conjunction, however, is of the most importance.

For instance, when Mars by its progressive motion comes to a conjunction with the cusp of the Fourth House in either the natal or progressed chart, it would bring trouble, controversy, loss, and difficulty with regard to property, father, and domestic affairs. If Mars were also much afflicted at birth, it would make the problem that much worse; whereas if it had been well aspected and dignified at birth, the problem would be much lessened; and so on in like manner with the other planets and the other cusps. The conjunction of a planet to a cusp is more important than other aspects to it, i.e., the sextile, square, trine, etc. The more a planet is afflicted in the natal chart, the more adverse is the nature that it carries with it by progression. The same rule holds both ways. The more a planet is dignified and well aspected in the natal chart, the more beneficent is the nature that it carries with it by progression. The influence of minor aspects to cusps is almost imperceptible. Aspects to cusps should be within 2°, forming. Separating aspects do not count; the conditions they represent have already passed, so they are not to be tabulated.

Aspects to cusps of houses either natal or progressed need not be considered unless the birth time is known to be correct, or corrected by a system of rectification, as a difference of every four minutes changes the cusps 1°, while a difference of every four minutes or so does not perceptibly change the planets' locations in the Zodiac; therefore pay most attention to aspects involving planets.

Calculating the Time a Progressed Mutual Aspect Becomes Partile

In connection with progressed mutual aspects, the following example illustrates a method of calculating the time when the aspect becomes exact. The same method may be used for calculating the time an aspect between two transiting planets becomes partile.

Example: Person born October 11, 1937, 4:00 A.M., Los Angeles, California.

Progressed birth date: November 28, 1937, representing the native's forty-eighth year, October 11, 1985, to October 11, 1986.

Question: When will the progressed Moon reach an exact sextile to the progressed Mercury?
Datum:
Progressed Moon (November 28, 1937, 4:00 A.M.)—16°55'16".
Progressed Mercury (November 28, 1937, 4:00 A.M.)—22°09'.
Progressed lunar motion—12°11'15" per day, representing one year.
Progressed motion of Mercury—1°28' per day, representing one year.

1. Calculate the Distance the Planet Must Travel to Partile.

The progressed Moon will be sextile progressed Mercury when it reaches 22°09', a distance of 5°13'44".

    22°09'00" (position of exact aspect)

   −16°55'16" (position of progressed birth date)

    5°13'44" (distance needed to travel)

2. Calculate the Time Needed to Cover that Distance.

Since both the Moon and Mercury are moving, the Moon's relative motion is first calculated. Then logarithms are used to find out what portion of the Moon's daily motion is needed to bring it to the proper place.

    12°11'15" (Moon's daily motion)

   − 1°28'00" (Mercury's daily motion)

    10°43'15" (Moon's motion relative to Mercury)

    .6614 (log of distance 5°13'44)

  −.3501 (log of relative lunar motion 10°43'15")

    .3113 (log of proportional distance)

   .3113 = 11 h 43 m (time needed to cover the distance)

3. Calculate the Equivalent Time in the Current Calendar.

The Moon must travel 11 h 43 m after the progressed birth date (November 28, 1937, 4:00 A.M.) for the aspect to become exact. This must translated into time in the current calendar—the amount of time past the current birth date (October 11, 1985, 4:00 A.M.)—with the aid of the Table of Days.

   11 hours = 5½ months by progression (5 months 15 days)

   43 minutes = 10¼ days by progression (10 days 18 hours)

   October 11, 1984, 4:00 A.M. + 5 months 25 days 18 hours = April 7, 1986, 9:00 A.M.

   The progressed Moon will form an exact sextile to the progressed Mercury on April 7, 1986, at 9:00 A.M.

Effects of Aspects by Direction

Lunar aspects are very important as they show many of the common events of minor importance and at the same time many serious events, especially when one directional aspect is followed closely by another. Often a series of evil lunar directions cause severe or even fatal sickness if they occur at the same time as a bad transit or an adverse solar direction. Generally, a lunar direction has its full effect within two weeks of the time when the aspect is complete, but under some of the favorable aspects affecting business affairs, the native will have from six weeks to two months of good conditions while the aspect is forming and separating.

The following delineations have reference to all aspects, whether formed in the natal chart, in the progressed chart, or between one planet in the natal chart and the other in the progressed chart. The interpretations are general indications only and subject to modification according to the strength of the aspect; that is, whether major or minor, position of planets in chart, whether angular, succedent, or cadent, and the strength by dignity or weakness by debility according to the sign occupied and also according to the planet's power and influence in the birth chart.

Planets in the Houses

The meaning of the houses in the progressed chart is the same as in the natal chart.

When a planet is in the First House, or is the ruler of the First House (natal or progressed), the aspects formed by direction refer to health and personal affairs.

When a planet is in the Second House, or is the ruler of the Second House (natal or progressed), the aspects formed by direction refer to money matters.

When a planet is in the Third House, or is the ruler of the Third House (natal or progressed), the aspects formed by direction refer to brethren, neighbors, short journeys, writings.

When a planet is in the Fourth House, or is the ruler of the Fourth House (natal or progressed), the aspects formed by direction refer to parents, property, domestic affairs, the father.

When a planet is in the Fifth House, or is the ruler of the Fifth House (natal or progressed), the aspects formed by direction refer to speculation, pleasure, love affairs, children.

When a planet is in the Sixth House, or is the ruler of the Sixth House (natal or progressed), the aspects formed by direction refer to sickness, employees and employment, small animals, food, medicines, clothing.

When a planet is in the Seventh House, or is the ruler of the Seventh House (natal or progressed), the aspects formed by direction refer to marriage, partners, opponents, opposition, lawsuits.

When a planet is in the Eighth House, or is the ruler of the Eighth House (natal or progressed), the aspects formed by direction refer to deaths, legacy, gain through money of others.

When a planet is in the Ninth House, or is the ruler of the Ninth House (natal or progressed), the aspects formed by direction refer to long journeys, voyages, visions, dreams, psychic experiences.

When a planet is in the Tenth House, or is the ruler of the Tenth House (natal or progressed), the aspects formed by direction refer to business affairs, occupation, profession, or the mother.

When a planet is in the Eleventh House, or is the ruler of the Eleventh House (natal or progressed), the aspects formed by direction refer to friends.

When a planet is in the Twelfth House, or is the ruler of the Twelfth House (natal or progressed), the aspects formed by direction refer to restraint, limitations, difficulty, sorrow.

Progressed Parallels

The next step is to work up the declinations to find whether any parallels are formed during this progressed year. Two planets or cusps are parallel when they are equally distant from the celestial equator, north or south; or one north and the other south.

Some modern ephemerides do not give the declination and latitude. Most astrology computer programs give this information and much more. The declinations for the planet are given on the right hand pages of the *Rosicrucian Ephemeris*. The ten-year compilations of the *American Ephemeris* give this information in the section at the middle of each page. When using an ephemeris that only gives the declinations every other day, or every third day, interpolate. Beginners need not try to reduce the declination of the planets (except the Sun and Moon) to the hour and minute of birth, as it is sufficient to record it for the day only.

To find out whether or not any of the planets are parallel, compare their declinations. If you find any planet within 1 degree of another, they are parallel. Whether north or south or one north and the other south is immaterial, for if they are equidistant from the celestial equator, they are parallel. Some astrologers denote a contraparallel when one planet is north and one south.

Parallels may be found not only between planets as they were located at birth, but also as they may progress and come to the degree of another planet's declination in the natal or progressed chart.

Lunar Declination

As the Moon is likely to move several degrees in declination any day (equal to a year in progression), it is liable to form several parallels in the course of such a period. The influence of a parallel is likely to begin when within 1 degree of being complete, but is most apt to operate when the parallel is exact.

The calculation and tabulation of declinations for the progressed chart are identical in method to those of the natal chart, but we go one step further when the Moon is concerned. The Moon's declination is treated similarly to its progress in longitude month by month in order to ascertain whether it will come into parallel with the declination of any planet in either the natal or progressed chart during that year. When it does come into a parallel, the effects are similar to a conjunction between the same planets and should be delineated in the same terms as a conjunction.

Calculating the Monthly Lunar Progressed Declination

To find the Moon's declination each month in the progressed year, proceed as follows. Count the number of degrees and minutes the Moon's declination will travel between its given place on the progressed birth date and its given place on the next day. Using the method for calculating the longitude of the progressed Moon, change this amount of the Moon's declination motion from degrees and minutes to all minutes by multiplying the degrees by 60 and adding the minutes to this product. Then divide the total by 12 to determine the rate the Moon will move in declination in each of the twelve months during the progressed year. By adding this amount of the Moon's monthly motion twelve times to the declination of the Moon on the progressed birth date at time of birth when the declination is increasing, but subtracting when the declination is decreasing, we will find in what degree of declination the Moon will be each month during the coming twelve months.

> **Note:** When the motion of the Moon in declination is less than 1 degree for any year (as will sometimes be the case), multiply the given minutes by 60, thus reducing the motion to seconds. Divide the seconds by 12 to get the number of seconds of declination the Moon moves per month. Divide the seconds by 60 to transform the figure to minutes and seconds of motion in declination, and then add or subtract this amount from the Moon's declination on the progressed birth date, according to whether the Moon is increasing or decreasing in declination.

Example 1. Person born January 22, 1936, 10:20 P.M., Sillersvllle, PA—progressed birth date March 4, 1936. The Moon's declination on the day after the progressed birth date (13°N44') is subtracted from its declination on the progressed birth date (17°N49') to find its daily motion. This motion is converted to all minutes by multiplying the degrees by 60 and adding the minutes to the product. The result of 245' represents the Moon's progressed motion of declination during the year January 22, 1978, to January 22, 1979. This is then divided by 12 to get the progressed motion of declination during any one month.

$$17°N49' \text{ (declination progressed birth date)}$$
$$-\underline{13°N44'} \text{ (declination day after progressed birth date)}$$
$$04° 05' \text{ (daily motion)}$$

$$4°05' = 245' \text{ (number of minutes in daily motion)}$$

$$245 \div 12 = 20' \tfrac{5}{12}" = 20'25" \text{ (progressed monthly motion of declination)}$$

Add the monthly motion twelve times to the Moon's declination on the progressed birth date at the time of birth when the declination is *increasing; subtract* the monthly motion twelve times from the Moon's declination on the progressed birth date when the declination is *decreasing*.

> **Note:** When the ephemeris shows that the declinations will change from north to south, or from south to north, between the two dates, add (instead of subtracting) to find the daily motion. Then from its place on the progressed birth date, subtract the monthly motion until it is reduced as small as possible, after which add the monthly motion for the remainder of the year.

Declinations of the Planets

The declinations of the planets are found in the progressed chart in exactly the same way as in the natal chart. The declinations are copied from the ephemeris for the year in which the chart was erected. When the declinations are given every other day and the necessary day falls between the two days, find the *motion for two days* by subtracting the smaller number from the larger. Half of the motion for two days is *added* to the earlier date if the declination is *increasing,* or *subtracted* if the declination is *decreasing*.

Example 1. Person born January 22, 1936, 10:20 P.M., Sillersville, PA—progressed birth date March 4, 1936. The declinations of the Sun and Moon were interpolated to get their exact progressed birth time declinations. The declinations for the other planets are copied from the ephemeris.

Moon: 16°N21' Moon parallel Mercury and Venus

Sun: 6°S14' Sun parallel Neptune

Mercury: 16°S34' Mercury parallel Venus

Venus: 17°S06'

Mars: 3°N01'

Jupiter: 22°S37' Jupiter parallel Pluto

Saturn: 8°S18'

Uranus: 11°N59'

Neptune: 6°N41'

Pluto: 23°N12' (March 1 position)

Declinations of House Cusps

The cusp of a house (sign and degree) has the same declination as the Sun when in that sign and degree. Using the ephemeris for the same year for which the chart was erected or, in the case of the progressed chart, the year the chart represents, find when the Sun is in the same sign and degree as the house cusp in question and note its declination. This will be the approximate declination of the house cusp.

The declinations for the cusps of the First House (Ascendant), Second House, and Third House, and for the Tenth House (Midheaven), Eleventh House, and Twelfth House, are looked up in this manner. The opposite houses have the opposite declination; that is, the same number of degrees and minutes but north instead of south, or south instead of north.

Note: The declinations of the cusps are not to be used except when the time of birth is known to be absolutely correct or proved so by a reliable system of rectification. Every four minutes of time changes the cusps 1 degree in longitude, and consequently the declination changes also.

Example 1. Person born January 22, 1936, 10:20 P.M., Sillersville, PA—progressed birth date March 4, 1936. Looking up the Sun's position in a 1936 ephemeris, note when it has the same sign and degree as the cusps of the birth chart houses. Use the Sun's declination for the declination of the house cusps.

It will be noticed, that the declination of one cusp is the same as on the opposite cusp. Therefore, when a planet comes to a parallel of one cusp, it is also parallel with the opposite cusp. It affects that house more that is on the same side of the equator as itself by north or south declination.

Unless the Tables of Houses for the exact latitude of birthplace were used in erecting the chart and the birth time is known to be exact, it is useless and perhaps misleading to attempt to use cusp declinations. For this reason, it is extremely difficult to get the declinations absolutely exact and hence to state just when an event would occur, indicated by an oncoming parallel, except to state it in terms of a certain month or year.

However, a parallel usually takes about a year to complete (excepting those of the Moon), and while the parallel is on, it influences matters connected with that house. For example, Saturn parallel the cusp of the Second House (ħ∥2nd Hs) would depress finances and prevent the native from accumulating an oversupply of money that year at least. If other directions for financial reserves were shown, this parallel would indicate heavy financial stringency when the aspect was on, or when a planet in transit came to a parallel with, this afflicted cusp.

Comparisons and Considerations

Lunar Declination

After having made the column of figures showing the Moon's degree of declination each month, compare its declination each month with the degrees of declination of the other planets in both the natal and progressed charts to ascertain in which months the parallel aspects will be formed that year. It is quite possible that in some years there will be no parallels in operation.

The most important parallels are those which may be formed by the Moon in its monthly motion or place in progress. Parallels among the other planets bear an influence upon the whole year.

Declinations of the Planets and House Cusps

When you have found all the declinations, arrange them in two columns: one for the natal chart and the other for the progressed chart, on one sheet of paper for convenience in comparing them for checking off parallels. Do not compare declinations of house cusps with each other. Compare planet's declinations with the declinations of cusps to find parallels.

Remember that when a planet is parallel with a cusp, it is also parallel with the opposite cusp, but its influence is on the house that is in the same direction (north or south) of declination as the planet.

Four types of comparisons are made:

1. Compare the progressed planets' declination with those of the natal chart, but do not compare a major planet's progressed declination with its natal declination.
2. Compare the progressed planets' declinations with each other.
3. Compare the progressed planets' declinations with the house cusp declinations in both the natal and progressed charts.
4. Compare the Moon's declination each month with the declinations of the natal and progressed planets and cusps, as described in the above paragraph.

A planet is in influence of parallel with another planet as soon as it is within 1 degree, regardless of whether both are north or south, or one north and the other south.

When a planet appears to be within parallel of another or with a cusp, examine the ephemeris and your figures carefully to see whether the parallel is forming, or has already been formed and is separating or past. In the latter case, we do not tabulate it. Record only those that are applying or forming. Observe whether a planet's declination is increasing or decreasing in order to determine if it is approaching or separating from a parallel.

Some near parallels are never actually completed, or not for many years, because of the slow motion in declination. Take, for instance, the case of a progressed Neptune at 16°N52', parallel a natal Venus at 17°N13' (p♆ ∥ n♀). The difference between them is only 21' of declination, but reference to the ephemeris for several years in advance reveals the fact that Neptune will never reach the exact declination of Venus in this native's lifetime. However, as there is always an orb of parallel between them, the effect of the parallel will be active when some planet by transit comes to a point between these two declinations and by *translation* unites Neptune and Venus by parallel of declination. The parallel of these two planets is not particularly important. We deal with it here only as an illustration.

It is not absolutely necessary to work out exactly on what day or date the parallel falls due, because its influence extends over an uncertain period, varying according to its motion in declination, and it may begin to exert a perceptible effect several weeks before the birth date to several weeks after. Some declinations change so slowly that when a parallel begins, by orb, it may be many days (years by progression) before it becomes partile and therefore shows up in as many years' progressed charts.

Parallels seem to affect conditions that the native will find it necessary to meet, and these conditions are accompanied by events, more or less radical, according to the native's plane of progress or state of consciousness.

For instance, the Moon parallel Mars (☽ ∥ ♂) would produce a feverish, passionate, rash disposition in an undeveloped type living on the purely physical plane, which would lead to accidents and quarrels. For an advanced, refined being, this same parallel would produce added energy resulting in constructive activity. In the one case the influence is apparently evil, but in the other the effects are good, the difference being not in the planets but in the state of understanding of the being through which the influences operate. In other words, the sort of reactions that an individual makes to an aspect largely determines the results of the influence. Some people make a bad aspect worse by the way they think and act. Others greatly modify an adverse aspect by their intelligent response to planetary influences.

Date	Progressed ☽	P ☽ to P or R	P planets to P	P planets to R	T to P	T to R
11/11/ 2012	9°♐48'	p☽∥p♄ p☽∠☿p			t♃☌p☽ t♄✶p♂	
12/11/ 2012	10°♐54'			p☽⊼n♃	t♅SD 4°♈37' t♃⊼p♂	t♅∥n♆
01/11/ 2013	12°♐00'	p☽⬍pMc p☽☌n♇ p☽n3rd			t♃SD 6°♊20'	t♃△n♆

Figure 19: Forecasting Tabulation Example

Date	Progressed ☽	P ☽ to P or R	P planets to P	P planets to R	T to P	T to R

Figure 20: Forecasting Tabulation Form

Appendix Two

COUNTRIES, CITIES, AND STATES

The following is a list of countries, cities, and states showing their sign rulerships. Note that some of the listings have more than one ruling sign. This information is useful in connection with ingresses, eclipses, and New Moons in relation to mundane events, helping determine where the influences will be operative. It is also helpful in determining the best locality for an individual.

Suppose, for example, that an individual suffering severe afflictions was told to go away for his health. That person could be correctly advised to go some place that was under the benign influence of Jupiter, whereas otherwise he might go to a place under the influence of Mars or Saturn, and become worse off than before.

Aries

Countries: Denmark, England, Faroe Islands, Germany, Iceland, Lebanon, Lithuania, Peru, Poland, Syria.

Cities: Birmingham (England), Brunswick, Capua, Cracow, Dallas, Florence, Leicester, Marseilles, Naples, Saragossa, Utrecht, Verona.

Taurus

Countries: Australia, Austria, Cyprus, Greenland, Holland, Ireland, New Guinea, Iran, Poland, Tasmania, Israel.

Cities: Dublin, Leipzig, Palermo, Parma, Rhodes, St. Louis.
States: Florida, Georgia, Louisiana, Maryland, Minnesota.

Gemini

Countries: Armenia, Belgium, Colombia, Ecuador, Egypt, Sardinia, Saudi Arabia, United Arab Republic, Venezuela, South Vietnam, Wales.
Cities: Bruges, London, Melbourne, Metz, Nuremburg, Plymouth (England), Rio de Janeiro, San Francisco, Tripoli, Versailles.
States: Arkansas, Kentucky, Rhode Island, South Carolina, Tennessee, West Virginia, Wisconsin.

Cancer

Countries: Canada, Holland, Iraq, New Zealand, Paraguay, Scotland, United States.
Cities: Algiers, Amsterdam, Berne, Cadiz, Genoa, Istanbul, Manchester, Milan, New York City, Pittsburgh, Stockholm, Tunis, Venice, York.
States: Idaho, New Hampshire, New York, Wyoming.

Leo

Countries: France, Italy, Madagascar, Sicily, the Vatican, Zanzibar.
Cities: Bath, Berlin, Bombay, Bristol, Chicago, Damascus, Detroit, Miami, Oklahoma City, Philadelphia, Portsmouth, Prague, Ravenna, Rome.
States: Alaska, California, Colorado, Hawaii, Missouri, Oregon, Washington.

Virgo

Countries: Assyria, Brazil, Crete, Croatia, Greece, Rhodesia, Switzerland, Turkey, Uruguay, North Vietnam, Virgin Islands, West Indies.
Cities: Baghdad, Basel, Boston, Corinth, Heidelberg, Jerusalem, Los Angeles, Lyons, Moscow, Norwich, Padua, Toulouse.
States: Alaska, California, Hawaii, Virginia.

Libra

Countries: Argentina, Burma, China, Egypt, Japan, Siberia, Tibet.
Cities: Antwerp, Charleston, Copenhagen, Frankfurt-am-Main, Johannesburg, Leeds, Lisbon, Vienna.

Scorpio

Countries: Algeria, East Indies, Korea, Morocco, Norway, Paraguay, Philippines, Syria, Turkey, Soviet Union.
Cities: Baltimore, Cincinnati, Cleveland, Dover, Fez, Halifax, Hull, Liverpool, Milwaukee, New Orleans, Newcastle, Portland (Oregon), Tokyo, Washington D.C.

States: Montana, Nevada, North Carolina, North Dakota, Oklahoma, South Dakota.

Sagittarius

Countries: Australia, Bolivia, Borneo, Chile, Czechoslovakia, Hungary, Madagascar, Pakistan, Spain, Yugoslavia.

Cities: Avignon, Budapest, Cologne, Naples, Nottingham, Province, Seattle, Sheffield, Singapore, Toledo, Toronto.

States: Alabama, Delaware, Illinois, Indiana, Mississippi, New Jersey, Ohio, Pennsylvania.

Capricorn

Countries: Afghanistan, Albania, Bulgaria, Greece, India, Lithuania, Mexico.

Cities: Brandenburg, Brussels, Port Said.

States: Connecticut, Iowa, New Mexico, Texas, Utah.

Aquarius

Countries: Arabia, Abyssinia, Cyprus, Iran, Lithuania, Poland, Prussia, Russia, Sweden, Syria.

Cities: Bremen, Brighton, Detroit, Hamburg, Salzburg, Wichita.

States: Arizona, Kansas, Massachusetts, Michigan, Oregon.

Pisces

Countries: Polynesia, Portugal, Samoa.

Cities: Alexandria (Egypt), Bournemouth, Lancaster, Seville, Worms.

States: Florida, Kansas, Maine, Nebraska, Vermont.

Appendix Three

ASTROLOGICAL DICTIONARY

Accidental Dignity: See *Dignity.*

Affliction: Unfavorably aspected. A debility. A planet is said to be afflicted when in square, conjunction, opposition, or quincunx to other planets or angular house cusps, or when in any aspect to Mars, Saturn, Uranus, or Pluto. An afflicted planet is said to be *impedited,* or *impeded.*

Air Signs: See *Elements.*

Anareta: Destroyer. Traditionally, the planet that is believed to correspond with the termination of life. Usually an afflicted malefic planet, in conjunction or adverse aspect to the Hyleg.

Angles: The four points of the chart dividing it into quadrants. The angles are sensitive areas that lend emphasis to planets situated near them.

> *The Ascendant:* Eastern horizon, cusp of the First House, or Oriens.
>
> *The Midheaven:* South Vertical, Zenith, cusp of the Tenth House, Meridian, or *Medium Coeli* (MC).
>
> *The Descendant:* Western horizon, cusp of the Seventh House, or Occidens.
>
> *The North Vertical:* Cusp of the Fourth House, or *Imum Coeli* (IC). Popularly called the *Nadir,* with which it sometimes corresponds.

Angular Houses: See *Houses.*

Animoder of Tetrabiblos: A method of birth time rectification presented by Ptolemy, now obsolete. Sometimes referred to as the *Sunrise indicator.*

Antipathy: Inharmonious relations between planets, which rule or are exalted in opposite signs. Also, conflict between the natal horoscopes of two people corresponding with the aversion they feel for each other.

Antiscia: See *Parallel.*

Aphelion: See *Elongation.*

Apheta: See *Hyleg.*

Apogee: That place in a planet's orbit that is farthest from the earth. Opposite of *Perigee.*

Apparent Motion: Motion of the planets as seen from the earth, geocentrically measured, as opposed to the actual movement of the planets in their heliocentric, or Sun-centered, orbits.

Application: The approach of one planet to another planet, house, cusp, or exact aspect. The faster-moving planet *applies* to the aspect with the slower-moving planet. An applying aspect is considered stronger than a separating aspect. Opposite of *separation.*

Arabian Parts: Points that are usually the arithmetic combination of two planets and the Ascendant, sometimes involving eclipses and house cusps. The most commonly used of the Arabian Parts is the *Part of Fortune,* although the other parts provide additional interesting information as well.

Arc: Distance measured along a circle. In astrology this refers to zodiacal longitude.

Ascendant: Rising Sign. Cusp of the First House. The degree of the Zodiac on the eastern horizon at the time and place for which the horoscope is calculated. Each sign takes approximately two hours to rise above the horizon. Opposite of *Descendant.*

> *An ascending planet, or rising planet:* is one that is between 12° above and 20° below the Ascendant. A planet is strengthened by this position. More generally, any planet in the Eastern Hemisphere, between the Tenth House and Fourth House.
>
> *The ruling planet:* is the planet that rules the sign on the Ascendant.
>
> *Ascension:* Due to the obliquity of the ecliptic, signs of long ascension require more time to rise above the horizon than do signs of short ascension.
>
> *Signs of long ascension in the Northern Hemisphere:* Cancer, Leo, Virgo, Libra, Scorpio, Sagittarius.
>
> *Signs of short ascension in the Northern Hemisphere:* Capricorn, Aquarius, Pisces, Aries, Taurus, Gemini. These are the signs most often intercepted in a horoscope.

Aspect: The angular relationship between planets, sensitive points, or house cusps in the horoscope. Lines drawn between the two points and the center of the chart, representing the earth, form the angle of the aspect, which is equivalent to the number of degrees of arc between the two points. Parallels and conjunctions are also termed aspects, though no angles are formed.

Major aspects: *conjunction,* 0°, a neutral aspect, its effect determined by the natures of the planets involved; *sextile,* 60°, a favorable aspect; *square,* quadrate, quartile, or tetragonous aspect, 90°, an adverse aspect; *trine,* 120°, a favorable aspect; and *opposition,* 180°, a neutral aspect, its effects determined by the natures of the planets involved.

Minor aspects: *semisextile,* 30°; *semisquare,* or semiquadrate, 45°; *sesquiquadrate,* 135°; *quincunx,* inconjunct, disjunct, or quadrasextile, 150°.

Seldom used aspects: *vigintile,* or semidecile, 18°; *quindecile,* 24°; *decile,* or semiquintile, 36°; *quintile,* 72°; *tredecile,* 108°; and *biquintile,* 144°.

Asteroid: Planetoid. Numerous small celestial bodies whose orbits lie between those of Mars and Jupiter. The asteroids are not normally used in astrology; yet, some attention is being paid to four of them: Ceres, Pallas, Juno, and Vesta. Another asteroid, Lilith, is used by some astrologers and its zodiacal longitude is recorded in an ephemeris.

Astro-twins: Two people with the same Sun sign, Moon sign, and Ascendant.

Average Daily Motion: See *Mean Motion.*

Ayanamsa: See *Precession of the Equinoxes.*

Barren Signs: See *Fertility.*

Benefics: Fortunes. Beneficial planets. Jupiter is traditionally called the *Greater Benefic,* while Venus is considered the *Lesser Benefic.*

Birth Time: The exact moment of the first in-drawn breath of a baby.

Cadent Houses: See *Houses.*

Celestial Equator: The extension of the earth's equator out into space, perpendicular to the earth's axis of rotation. Distance measured along the celestial equator, eastward from the point of the vernal equinox, is called *Right Ascension* (RA), which corresponds to terrestrial longitude. Right Ascension is measured in hours, 24 hours to the circle of 360°, 4 minutes of Right Ascension for each degree of arc. The distance of a planet north or south of the celestial equator is measured in *Declination,* which corresponds to terrestrial latitude. The maximum declination of the Sun is 23°28' North at 0° Cancer, and 23°28' South at 0° Capricorn. A planet situated on the celestial equator has no declination. Measurement along the celestial equator between any point and the meridian (the line perpendicular to the equator passing through the Midheaven and Nadir) is called the *meridian distance,* expressed in hours and minutes.

Collection of Light: A planet in aspect to two others that are not in themselves in aspect to each other. The *collector of light* acts as an intermediary. Used in horary astrology.

Comets: Small, luminous celestial bodies that circle the Sun on eccentric orbits. Comets often develop long, fuzzy tails that point away from the Sun. Traditionally, comets presage history-making events. The most famous comet is *Halley's Comet,* which appears every 76 years.

Combust: Within 8°30' of zodiacal longitude of the Sun. The nature of the combust planet is combined with that of the Sun; a weakening configuration. Mercury and Venus are the planets most often combust. *An inferior conjunction* between Mercury or Venus and the Sun occurs when the planet comes between the earth and the Sun. A *superior conjunction* between Mercury or Venus and the Sun occurs when the planet is on the opposite side of the Sun from the earth. *Under the Sun's beams* is a traditional term used to indicate a planet that is within 17° of the Sun. Its influence is weakened, but not as much as if combust.

Composite Chart: See *Midpoint.*

Conjunction: See *Aspect.*

Constellation: Asterism. A group of stars named after a figure or pattern it is said to represent. Twelve constellations have the same names, but are no longer located in the same places, as the signs of the Zodiac. This group of twelve constellations is called the *Sidereal Zodiac,* Fixed Zodiac, or the Zodiac of the Constellations.

Converse Directions: A system of directions that employs the symbolic reverse motion of the planets, movement contrary to the natural course of the planets.

Co-significator: See *Significator.*

Cosmobiology: That branch of contemporary astrology that uses midpoints, the 90° dial, solar arc directions, and the graphic ephemeris as basic tools for delineation of natal charts, and for forecasting.

Critical Degrees: Mansions of the Moon. The subdivision of the Zodiac into 28 parts of 12 and %° each, representing the Moon's average daily motion, beginning with 0° Aries, divided by sensitive points, the critical degrees, in the various signs. Critical degrees of the cardinal signs, Aries, Cancer, Libra, and Capricorn: 0°, 13°, 26°. Critical degrees of the fixed signs, Taurus, Leo, Scorpio, and Aquarius: 9°, 21°. Critical degrees of the mutable signs, Gemini, Virgo, Sagittarius, and Pisces: 4°, 17°.

Culmination: The arrival of a planet at the Midheaven, by progression, direction, or transit. Also, the completion of an aspect.

Cusp: See *Houses.*

Cycle: See *Revolution.*

Daylight Saving Time: DST. Summer Time. An artificial adjustment of clock time, one hour ahead. One hour must be subtracted from birth times recorded in Zone Standard when Daylight Saving Time is in effect, before the horoscope can be calculated. During World War I (3/31–10/27, 1918, and 3/30–10/26, 1919) and World War II (2/9, 1942–9/30, 1945), Daylight Saving Time was in effect and was called *War Time.*

Debility: Positions and aspects that weaken the nature of the planets. A planet is debilitated when adversely aspected, in a cadent house, or in the sign of its detriment or fall. Opposite of *dignity.*

Decan: Decanate. Divisions of each of the signs into three equal segments of 10° each.

Declination: See *Celestial Equator.*

Decreasing in Light: Waning. Third and Fourth Quarters of the Moon. A planet, particularly the Moon, during the half of its cycle from opposition with the Sun to the next conjunction with the Sun. Opposite *of increasing in Light.*

Degree: Degree of arc. One of 360 divisions of a circle. The circle of the Zodiac is divided into 12 signs of 30° each. Each degree is made up of 60' (minutes), and each minute is made up of 60" (seconds) of zodiacal longitude.

Descendant: Cusp of the Seventh House. The degree of the Zodiac on the western horizon at the time and place for which the horoscope is calculated. Opposite of *Ascendant.* A *descending planet* is one that is generally between the Tenth House and the Fourth House in the Western Hemisphere.

Detriment: The sign in which a planet is unfavorably placed; the opposite sign of its own sign: The Sun in Aquarius; the Moon in Capricorn; Mercury in Sagittarius and Pisces; Venus in Aries and Scorpio; Mars in Libra and, traditionally, Taurus; Jupiter in Gemini and, traditionally, Virgo; Saturn in Cancer and, traditionally, Leo; Uranus in Leo; Neptune in Virgo; Pluto in Taurus.

Dexter Aspect: An aspect in which the faster-moving planet is ahead of, or has greater zodiacal longitude than, the aspected planet. This occurs when the aspecting planet is moving away from the slower-moving planet by direct motion, or toward it by retrograde motion. Also, loosely, a separating aspect. Opposite of *sinister aspect.*

Dignity: Positions and aspects that strengthen the nature of the planet. Opposite of *debility. Accidental dignity* refers to the planet's position by house, aspect, or motion. A planet is accidentally dignified when it is near the Midheaven, in an angular house, in its natural house, favorably aspected, swift in motion, direct in motion, or increasing in light. The most important accidental dignity occurs when a planet is near the Ascendant or Midheaven.

    Essential dignity: Refers to the planet's position by sign. A planet is essentially dignified when it is in the sign it rules, or in the sign of its exaltation.

    Domal dignity: Occurs when a planet is in its own sign.

    Joy: is an obsolete term for a favorable position for a planet, though not technically a position of dignity.

Direct Motion: Proper Motion. Proceeding in the order of the signs, from Aries toward Taurus, etc. Denoted in the ephemeris by a "D". Opposite of *retrograde motion.*

Directions: The aspects between planets or house cusps in a progressed horoscope and those in the natal horoscope, or between transiting and natal planets or house cusps. Also, loosely, progressions.

Primary directions: are aspects formed in a system of progressions that calculates one degree of forward movement for each of the planets in the natal horoscope, for each year of life.

Dispositor: The planet ruling the sign in which another planet is posited. A planet in its own sign has no dispositor. Used in horary astrology, and sometimes in progressed work.

Diurnal: Belonging to the day. Above the horizon, between the Ascendant and Descendant in the Southern Hemisphere of the chart. Opposite of *nocturnal.*

Diurnal arc: Refers to the portion of a planet's daily travel in which it is above the horizon. Opposite of *nocturnal arc.*

Domal Dignity: See *Dignity, Planetary Rulership.*

Dragon's Head: See *Nodes.*

Dragon's Tail: See *Nodes.*

Dwadasamsa: A subdivision of each sign into twelve equal parts of 2½° each. Used in Hindu astrology.

Earth: Terra. The planet on which we live, represented by the center of the horoscope. The daily axial rotation of the earth from west to east, its diurnal movement, produces the appearance of the Sun, Moon, and planets rising in the east and setting in the west. The earth's annual revolution around the Sun produces the appearance of the Sun transiting through the signs. The earth appears to be in the opposite sign of the Sun.

The terrestial equator: is a belt around the earth, halfway between the North and South Poles.

Geographical longitude: is a measurement east or west along the earth's equator beginning with the prime meridian at Greenwich, England, designated 0°, and proceeding east and west to 180° on the opposite side of the earth. Lines of longitude form circles perpendicular to the equator.

Geographical latitude: is a measurement north or south of the earth's equator beginning with the equator itself, which is designated 0°, and proceeding north and south to 90°. Lines of latitude form circles parallel with the equator.

Earth Signs: See *Elements.*

Eclipse: A phenomenon that involves the Sun, Moon, and the earth or occasionally other planets. There are usually two to six eclipses a year. The sign and degree of an eclipse is important, particularly in mundane astrology.

A solar eclipse: is produced by the Moon passing between the Sun and the earth, cutting off the light of the Sun. This occurs when a New Moon, the conjunction of the Sun and Moon, takes place near a lunar Node.

A lunar eclipse: is produced by the earth passing between the Sun and Moon, casting its shadow on the Moon. This occurs when a Full Moon, the opposition of the Sun and Moon, takes place near a lunar Node.

An occultation: is an eclipse of a planet by the Moon.

Immersion: is the beginning of an eclipse or occultation. Emersion is the ending when the planet comes out from under the Sun's rays.

Ecliptic: Via Solis. The Sun's apparent path around the earth, which is in actuality the earth's orbit extended out into space. So named because it is the path along which eclipses occur. The ecliptic forms the center of the Zodiac.

The obliquity of the ecliptic: is the angle between the plane of the ecliptic and the plane of the celestial equator, which varies according to the season.

Electional Astrology: The branch of astrology dealing with the selection of an auspicious time for a particular purpose. Sometimes considered a branch of horary astrology.

Elements: Triplicities. Trigons. Four groups of three signs each symbolized by the four elements of the ancients: fire, earth, air, water.

Fire Signs: are active and enthusiastic: Aries, Leo, Sagittarius.

Earth Signs: are practical and cautious: Taurus, Virgo, Capricorn.

Air Signs: are intellectual and sociable: Gemini, Libra, Aquarius.

Water Signs: are emotional and sensitive: Cancer, Scorpio, Pisces.

Elevation: Altitude. The distance of a planet above the horizon. The most elevated position in a horoscope is at the cusp of the Tenth House. The higher the elevation, the more powerful the planet.

Elongation: The distance of a planet from the Sun, as viewed from the earth. The maximum elongation of the inferior planets is 28° for Mercury and 48° for Venus. Mercury can therefore only form a conjunction and semisextile to the Sun; while Venus can only form a conjunction, semisextile, or semisquare to the Sun.

Aphelion: is the maximum elongation of a planet; the point in its orbit in which it is farthest from the Sun.

Perihelion: is the minimum elongation of a planet; the point in its orbit in which it is closest to the Sun.

Ephemeris: A listing of the Sun, Moon, and planets' places and related information for astrological purposes.

Equator: See *Celestial Equator, Earth.*

Equinox: Equal night. The point in the earth's orbit around the Sun at which the day and night are equal in length.

The Vernal Equinox: occurs annually around March 21, when the Sun enters Aries, and marks the beginning of the Zodiac. The ecliptic crosses the equator from south to north at the vernal equinox.

The Autumnal Equinox: occurs annually around September 21, when the Sun enters Libra. The ecliptic crosses the equator from north to south at the autumnal equinox.

Essential Dignity: See *Dignity.*

Esoteric Astrology: Spiritual astrology. The branch of astrology dealing with the spiritual nature of the individual.

Exaltation: A sign in which a planet is favorably posited: the Sun in Aries; the Moon in Taurus; Mercury in Virgo; Venus in Pisces; Mars in Capricorn; Jupiter in Cancer; Saturn in Libra; Uranus in Scorpio; Neptune in Cancer; and Pluto in Pisces. Opposite of *fall.*

Excitation: The influence of a transiting planetary aspect bringing into effect a progressed aspect of similar nature.

Extra-Saturnian Planets: Modern planets. Outer planets. The three planets not visible to the naked eye, which lie outside the orbit of Saturn, and were discovered in recent times: Uranus, discovered in 1781; Neptune, discovered in 1846; Pluto, discovered in 1930. Each of the extra-Saturnian planets is considered to be a *higher octave* of another planet: Uranus is a higher octave of Mercury; Neptune is a higher octave of Venus; Pluto is a higher octave of Mars.

Face: Divisions of each of the signs into six equal segments of 5° each. Not used by modern astrologers.

Fall: The sign in which a planet is unfavorably placed; the sign opposite of its exaltation: the Sun in Libra; the Moon in Scorpio; Mercury in Pisces; Venus in Virgo; Mars in Cancer; Jupiter in Capricorn; Saturn in Aries; Uranus in Taurus; Neptune in Capricorn; Pluto in Virgo.

Familiarity: Any kind of aspect or reception between the planets.

Fertile Signs: See *Fertility.*

Fertility: Classification of sign according to productivity.

> *Fertile or fruitful signs:* Cancer, Scorpio, Pisces. The fertile signs are good for planting when occupied by the Moon, and are indicators of offspring when occupying the cusps of the Fifth or Eleventh Houses.

> *Semifruitful or moderately fruitful signs:* Taurus, Libra, Capricorn.

> *Barren or sterile signs:* Aries, Gemini, Leo, Virgo, Sagittarius, Aquarius. The barren signs are good for cultivation when occupied by the Moon, and are indicators of not having children when occupying the cusps of the Fifth or Eleventh Houses.

Fire Signs: See *Elements.*

Fixed Signs: See *Modes.*

Fixed Stars: The visible, seemingly immovable stars as opposed to the Sun, Moon, and planets, which are traditionally called the wandering stars. Major visible stars in the Northern Hemisphere are sometimes taken into account in astrological work.

Focal Point: A planet or aspect formation that is of primary importance within a horoscope.

Fortunes: Beneficial planets. Jupiter and Venus are always called the fortunes. The Sun and Moon, if favorably placed and aspected, are also considered fortunate. Mercury and Neptune, being neutral, are fortunate when favorably placed and in favorable aspect to Venus or Jupiter.

Frustration: A term used in horary astrology when one planet is applying to an aspect of another, but before the aspect culminates, a third planet, by its swifter motion, interposes by completing an aspect of its own, thus deflecting the influence of the slower-moving planet.

Genethliacal Astrology: Natal astrology. The branch of astrology dealing with the individual. The horoscope cast for the birth time of the individual, showing his or her life potential, is called a *natal horoscope,* geniture, radix, or nativity. The individual under consideration is called the *native.*

Geocentric: Earth-centered.

Great Circle: Any circle, the plane of which passes through the center of the earth, such as the celestial equator, the meridian, the ecliptic, and the lines of terrestrial longitude.

Greenwich Mean Time: GMT. Universal Time. The time at the prime meridian of 0° longitude. The standard for navigation, astronomy, international communications, and astrology. Ephemerides are usually calculated for either noon or midnight Greenwich Mean Time.

Heavy Planets: The slower-moving planets whose influence is considered more serious than the other planets: Jupiter, Saturn, Uranus, Neptune, Pluto.

Heliocentric: Sun-centered.

Hemisphere: Half-circle. The division of the celestial vault into halves by the horizon and prime vertical. Also, the division of the horoscope into overlapping halves:

> *The Eastern Hemisphere:* from the Midheaven through the Ascendant to the IC: the Tenth through Third Houses.

> *The Northern Hemisphere:* from the Ascendant through the IC to the Descendant; the First through Sixth Houses.

> *The Western Hemisphere:* from the IC through the Descendant to the Midheaven; the Fourth through Ninth Houses.

> *The Southern Hemisphere:* from the Descendant through the Midheaven to the Ascendant; the Seventh through Twelfth Houses.

Horary Astrology: The branch of astrology in which a chart is calculated for the time a question is asked in order to ascertain the answer to that question.

Horizon: The circle that separates the visible and invisible world.

> *The rational or true horizon:* is the great circle that surrounds the observer passing through the cardinal points. The poles of the rational horizon are defined by the Zenith overhead and the

Nadir directly underneath the observer. A line between the Zenith and the Nadir would be perpendicular to the plane of the rational horizon.

The celestial horizon: is the rational horizon extended infinitely out into space. The intersection of the eastern horizon and the ecliptic determines the Ascendant. This is the eastern point of the chart. The intersection of the western horizon and the ecliptic determines the Descendant at the west point of the chart.

The visible or apparent horizon: is the small amount of earth visible with the naked eye. It is parallel to the rational horizon.

Horoscope: Map. Chart. Figure. A diagram of the positions of the planets, including the Sun and Moon, calculated for a specific time and place.

A natural chart: is a horoscope with Aries on the Ascendant and no intersected signs.

A solar chart: is a horoscope in which the planets' positions are calculated for noon Greenwich (taken from a noon ephemeris), but with the Sun's longitude on the Ascendant. Used when the birth time is unknown.

Houses: Mundane houses. Division of the horoscope into twelve segments beginning with the Ascendant. The dividing lines between the houses are called *house cusps.* Each house corresponds to certain aspects of daily living or earthly affairs. The houses are divided into three groups:

Angular Houses: are the strongest houses, corresponding to the cardinal signs: First, Fourth, Seventh, and Tenth Houses.

Succedent Houses: are neutral houses, corresponding to the fixed signs: Second, Fifth, Eighth, and Eleventh Houses.

Cadent Houses: are the weakest houses, corresponding to the mutable signs: Third, Sixth, Ninth, and Twelfth Houses.

Day Houses: Houses above the horizon in the horoscope, the Seventh through Twelfth Houses, are called the *day houses.* The First House through the Sixth House, below the horizon, are called the *night houses.*

Hyleg: Giver of Life. Particular zones in the horoscope concerned with longevity: 5° above to 25° below the Ascendant; 5° below to 25° above the Descendant; 5° below the Ninth House cusp to 25° past the Eleventh House cusp. A planet that is hyleg is called the *Apheta* or the *Prorogator.*

Imum Coeli: IC. Bottom of the Heavens. Cusp of the Fourth House. The lowest point on the ecliptic at which it intersects the meridian below the horizon. The northern point of the horoscope. Opposite the Midheaven. Also, loosely called the *Nadir,* which is opposite the Zenith.

Increasing in Light: Waxing. First and Second Quarters of the Moon. A planet, particularly the Moon, during the half of its cycle from conjunction to opposition with the Sun. Opposite of *decreasing in light.*

Inferior Conjunction: See *Combust.*

Inferior Planets: Those whose orbits are between the earth and the Sun: Mercury and Venus.

Infortunes: Malefic planets. Mars, Saturn, and Uranus are always called the infortunes. Mercury and Neptune, being neutral, are infortunate when afflicted by position or aspect. Pluto is sometimes considered an Unfortunate planet.

Ingress: The entrance of any planet into any sign. Also, loosely applied to the Sun's entrance into the four cardinal signs at the solstices and equinoxes.

Inner Planets: The swifter-moving planets most active in the horoscope: Sun, Moon, Mercury, Venus, Mars.

Intercepted: A sign that is contained wholly within a house; it does not appear on any house cusp. Intercepted signs appear only in horoscopes; there are never any intercepted signs in the Zodiac.

Latitude: See *Zodiac, Earth.*

Lights: See *Luminaries.*

Lilith: See *Asteroids.*

Local Space: An astrological method that uses a compass or map to plot the geographical directions in which the planets lie in a birth chart.

Local Time: Sun Time. True Local Time. Solar Time. The actual time at a location within a time zone, adjusted to compensate for the standardization of time throughout the zone. Noon local time is always when the Sun transits the meridian of that place.

Logarithms: Proportional logarithms. Tables of representational numbers that simplify the processes of multiplication and division into addition and subtraction. Used in horoscope calculation.

Longitude: See *Zodiac, Earth.*

Luminaries: Lights. The Sun and Moon, as distinguished from the planets. The Sun is the *Greater Light,* or *Greater Luminary;* the Moon is the *Lesser Light,* or *Lesser Luminary.*

Lunar Phase: The Moon's cycle from New Moon to New Moon is divided into four phases, each lasting about seven days.

> ***First Quarter:*** From the conjunction (New Moon) to the square of the Sun and Moon. During the first half of this phase, when the Moon is between 0° and 45° ahead of the Sun, it is called the *Crescent Moon.* A waxing phase.

Second Quarter: From the square to the opposition (Full Moon) of the Sun and Moon. During the second half of this phase, when the Moon is between 135° and 180° ahead of the Sun, it is called the *Gibbous Moon.* A waxing phase.

Third Quarter: From the opposition (Full Moon) to the square of the Sun and Moon. During the last half of this phase, the Moon is between 135° and 90° behind the Sun, it is called the *Disseminating Moon.* A waning phase.

Fourth Quarter: From the square to the conjunction (New Moon) of the Sun and Moon. During the last half of this phase, when the Moon is between 45° and 0° behind the Sun, it is called the *Balsamic Moon.* A waning phase.

Lunation: Lunar period. New Moon. Synodical lunation. The period from one New Moon, the conjunction of the Sun and Moon, until the next New Moon; 29 days, 12 hours, 44 minutes. Also, a chart drawn up for the time of the New Moon, used in mundane astrology. Also, loosely, the occurrence of the New Moon itself. *Neomenium* is a traditional term for the New Moon, especially near the vernal equinox. An *embolismic lunation* occurs each month when the Moon and Sun are in the same angular relationship, or lunar phase, as they were in the natal horoscope. The embolismic lunation coincides with a woman's fertile period and is the basis of astrological birth control.

Malefics: Evil planets. Saturn is traditionally called the *Greater Malefic,* while Mars is considered the *Lesser Malefic.*

Mansions of the Moon: See *Critical Degrees.*

Matutine: Stars or planets that rise before the Sun in the morning, particularly the Moon (Fourth Quarter), Mercury, or Venus (oriental) when they appear in the morning. Opposite of *vespertine.*

Mean Motion: Average Daily Motion. Rate of motion. The average motion of any planet during a 24-hour period: The Sun, 59'08"; the Moon, 13 10'36"; Mercury, 1°23'; Venus, 1°12'; Mars, 33'28"; Jupiter, 4'59"; Saturn, 2'01"; Uranus, 42"; Neptune, 24"; Pluto, 15". When traveling less than the average daily motion, a planet is *slow in motion,* or *slow in course;* when traveling more, it is *swift in motion.* When a planet is moving faster than on the day previous, it is *increasing in motion;* when moving slower, it is *decreasing in motion.*

Mean Time: Mean Solar Time. Civil Time. The average day of 24 hours as measured by our clocks. Due to the uneven rotation of the earth, the day from noon to noon is slightly unequal depending on the season. Mean time refers to the agreed-upon average in standard use.

Meridian: The North-South Great Circle. A great circle that passes through the south point of the horizon, through the Zenith directly overhead, and through the north point of the horizon, and under the earth, through the Nadir. The Sun crosses the meridian at midday. The meridian corresponds to geographical longitude, and is at right angles to the prime vertical. Every point on earth has its own meridian. Also, in a horoscope, the line from the IC (see *Nadir*) to the Midheaven.

Meridian Distance: See *Celestial Equator.*

Metonic Cycle: A cycle of 19 years at the end of which the conjunctions of the Sun and Moon (New Moons) begin to occur successively in the same places in the Zodiac as during the previous cycle.

Midheaven: *Medium Coeli.* MC. Middle of the Heavens. Meridian. Cusp of the Tenth House. The highest point on the ecliptic at which it intersects the meridian, which passes directly overhead of the place for which the horoscope is cast. The southern point of the horoscope. Opposite the *Imum Coeli.*

Midnight Mark: The mean local time at any place that is equivalent to midnight in Greenwich, England.

Midpoint: Half-sum. A point equally distant to two planets or house cusps. In the horoscope, there are actually two midpoints for each pair of planets: one on the shorter arc, usually used in astrology, and one on the longer arc, its opposite.
    A composite chart: is a chart using the midpoints between pairs of planets in two or more natal horoscopes, interpreted as an indication of the relationship between the people involved.

Modes: Quadruplicities. Qualities. Three groups of four signs, one of each element.
    Cardinal Signs: are active and powerful: Aries, Cancer Libra, Capricorn.

    Fixed Signs: are organized and resistant to change: Taurus, Leo, Scorpio, Aquarius.

    Mutable Signs: are adaptable and resourceful: Gemini, Virgo, Sagittarius, Pisces.

Mundane Astrology: Political astrology. Judicial astrology. State astrology. The branch of astrology dealing with affairs of the world and collective activities of people.

Mundane Parallel: See *Parallel.*

Mutable Signs: See *Modes.*

Mutual Reception: See *Reception.*

Nadir: A point opposite the Zenith. Often incorrectly applied to the *Imum Coeli.* The IC, being on the ecliptic, is the point opposite the Midheaven.

Natal Astrology: See *Genethliacal Astrology.*

Nativity: See *Genethliacal Astrology.*

Navamsas: A subdivision of each sign into nine equal parts of $3^1/3°$ each. Used in Hindu astrology.

Nocturnal: Belonging to the night. Below the horizon, between the Descendant and Ascendant in the Northern Hemisphere of the chart. Opposite of *diurnal.*
    Nocturnal arc: Refers to the portion of a planet's daily travel in which it is below the horizon. Opposite of *diurnal arc.*

Nodes: The points at which the orbit of the Moon or other planet crosses the ecliptic. The Sun has no Nodes and its orbit defines the ecliptic. The planets' Nodes change very slightly in a century. The Moon's Nodes, however, retrograde along the ecliptic about 3' per day. The *ascending Node,* or

North Node, occurs when the planet passes through the ecliptic from south to north latitude. The *Descending Node,* or South Node, occurs when the latitude changes from north to south.

> **Dragon's Head:** Caput Draconis. Moon's North Node. The point at which the orbit of the Moon crosses the ecliptic from south to north latitude. A beneficial point. Opposite the Dragon's Tail.

> **Dragon's Tail:** Cauda Draconis. Moon's South Node. The point opposite the Moon's North Node. An unfavorable point.

Nonagesimal: The point 90° from the ascending point; the highest point on the ecliptic above the horizon.

Noon Mark: The mean local time at any place that is equivalent to noon at Greenwich, England.

Occidental: Western. A planet that rises and sets after the Sun. Also, the Western Hemisphere of the chart, from the Tenth House cusp through the Descendant to the Fourth House cusp. Opposite of *oriental.* Mercury is occidental during its *Epimethean Cycle,* beginning with its superior conjunction with the Sun, moving direct until its maximum distance from the Sun, 28°, then moving retrograde until it reaches its inferior conjunction with the Sun. Venus is occidental when it is *Hesperus,* the *Evening Star,* beginning with its superior conjunction with the Sun, moving direct until its maximum distance from the Sun, 48°, then moving retrograde until it reaches its inferior conjunction with the Sun.

Occultation: See *Eclipse.*

Opposition: See *Aspect.*

Orb: The range of zodiacal longitude within which the influence of a planet or aspect operates, varying in size according to the specific planet and aspect. An aspect that is exact (has no orb) is called an exact aspect, or *partile aspect.* It has the strongest influence. An aspect that is not exact, yet still within the orb of influence, is called a wide aspect, or *platic aspect.* Its influence is weakened.

Oriental: Eastern. A planet that rises and sets before the Sun. Also, the Eastern Hemisphere of the chart, from the Fourth House cusp through the Ascendant to the Tenth House Cusp. Opposite of occidental. Mercury is oriental during its *Promethean Cycle* beginning with its inferior conjunction with the Sun, moving retrograde until its maximum distance from the Sun, 28°, then moving direct until it reaches its superior conjunction with the Sun. Venus is oriental when it is *Lucifer,* the *Morning Star,* beginning with its inferior conjunction with the Sun, moving retrograde until its maximum distance from the Sun, 48°, then moving direct until it reaches its superior conjunction with the Sun.

Parallel: Two planets that are equally distant from the celestial equator, having the same declination, either both north or both south, or one north and the other south. Similar in meaning to a conjunction.

*A **mundane parallel:*** occurs when two planets are equally distant from any angle in the horoscope. The planets are then *antiscia.*

*A **rapt parallel:*** occurs when two planets are equally distant from the meridian, at the point of the Midheaven.

Part of Fortune: Pars Fortuna. A point that is equally distant from the Ascendant as the Moon is from the Sun in longitude. An indicator of the lunar phase. The Part of Fortune is found by adding the longitude of the Moon to the longitude of the Ascendant and subtracting from the sum the longitude of the Sun. A mildly favorable point. The only commonly used of the many Arabian Parts. If the Part of Fortune is conjunct the Ascendant, the native was born under a New Moon; if the Part of Fortune is conjunct the IC, the Moon was just beginning the Second Quarter. If the Part of Fortune is opposite the Ascendant, the native was born under the Full Moon; if the Part of Fortune is conjunct the Midheaven, the Moon was just beginning the Fourth Quarter.

Perigee: The place in a planet's orbit that is closest to the earth. Opposite *of Apogee.*

Peregrine: Foreign. The position of a planet in a sign in which it is neither dignified nor debilitated. No planet is peregrine if it is in mutual reception with another. Used in horary astrology.

Perihelion: See *Elongation.*

Planet: In astrology, this commonly refers to the Sun, the star at the center of our solar system, the Moon, the earth's satellite, and the eight planets excluding the earth: Sun, Moon, Mercury, Venus, Mars, Jupiter, Saturn, Uranus, Neptune, Pluto.

Planetary Hours: A system in which the various hours of the day are ruled by the seven visible planets, beginning at sunrise with the planet that rules that day of the week: Sunday, the Sun; Monday, the Moon; Tuesday, Mars; Wednesday, Mercury; Thursday, Jupiter; Friday, Venus; Saturday, Saturn. The time between sunrise and sunset is divided into twelve equal segments. Since these times vary with the season, the length of a "planetary hour" is different from that of a normal hour.

Planetary Rulership: The sign in which a planet is most harmoniously placed: the Sun in Leo; the Moon in Cancer; Mercury in Gemini and Virgo; Venus in Taurus and Libra; Mars in Aries and, traditionally, Scorpio; Jupiter in Sagittarius and, traditionally, Pisces; Saturn in Capricorn and, traditionally, Aquarius; Uranus in Aquarius; Neptune in Pisces; and Pluto in Scorpio.

Planetoid: See *Asteroid.*

Polarity: The division of the signs and planets into positive, masculine, creative, dry, and yang, and its opposite, negative, feminine, receptive, moist, yin.

*The **positive signs:*** are the fire and air signs: Aries, Gemini, Leo, Libra, Sagittarius, Aquarius. The *positive planets* are the Sun, Mars, Jupiter, Saturn, Uranus, and Pluto.

The negative signs: are the earth and water signs: Taurus, Cancer, Virgo, Scorpio, Capricorn, Pisces. The *negative planets* are the Moon and Venus. Mercury and Neptune are *neutral* or *convertible planets,* positive or negative depending on whether they are located in positive or negative signs.

Gender emphasis: refers to the predominance of masculine or feminine elements in the horoscope.

Political Astrology: *See Mundane Astrology.*

Ponderous Planets: See *Superior Planets.*

Precession of the Equinoxes: The gradual movement of the Vernal Equinox Point, 0° Aries, which marks the beginning of the Tropical Zodiac, backward in relation to the constellations that define the Sidereal Zodiac, at the rate of approximately 50" per year, or one sign every 2,150 years, determining the *Astrological Ages,* or the *Great Months.* The Equinox Point regressed into Pisces at the birth of Christ, the beginning of the Age of Pisces. The *Age of Aquarius* would then begin around 2150 A.D. The gap between the Tropical Zodiac and the Sidereal Zodiac is called the *Ayanamsa,* and was approximately 24°25' in 1975.

Prenatal Epoch: The astrological moment of conception, about nine months before birth, but not necessarily coinciding with the actual time of biological conception. Used in rectification work.

Primary Directions: See *Directions.*

Prime Vertical: The East-West Great Circle. A great circle that passes through the east point of the horizon, through the Zenith overhead, through the west point of the horizon, and under the earth through the Nadir. It is perpendicular to the meridian.

Progressions: The symbolic movement of the planets after birth representing the future of the native. Usually refers to *secondary progressions.* Secondary progressions is the most popular system of progressions in which each day after birth represents the corresponding year in the life of the native.

Promittor: Promissor. A planet or configuration that signifies certain events. Used in horary astrology.

Prorogator: See *Hyleg.*

Proper Motion: See *Direct Motion.*

Quadrants: The four quarters of the chart. Also the four seasons of the year.

Quadrature: The Moon's dichotomes: changes, phases, or quarters. Also, a square aspect to the Sun, as occurs when the Moon is at the beginning of the Second Quarter or the beginning of the Fourth Quarter.

Quadruplicities: See *Modes.*

Qualities: See *Modes.*

Rapt Motion: The apparent diurnal motion of the Zodiac and planets from east to west caused by the earth's rotation in the opposite direction.

Rate of Motion: See *Mean Motion.*

Reception: A planet is received by the dispositor of the sign it occupies. Also, a planet receives an aspect by a faster-moving planet.

>   *Mutual reception:* occurs when two planets occupy each other's signs, or more loosely, the signs of each other's exaltation.

Rectification: The process of correcting the given birth time by reference to known events or characteristics pertaining to the native.

Refranation: A situation in which one of two planets applying to an aspect turns retrograde before the aspect is complete. The retrograde planet is said to *refrain,* signifying that the effect indicated by the approaching aspect will not materialize. Used in horary astrology.

Relocation Chart: Locality chart. A horoscope cast for a change of residence by putting the natal positions of the planets into houses calculated for the new location.

Retrograde Motion: Apparent backward motion of a planet in the reverse order of the signs, from Aries toward Pisces, etc. Denoted in the ephemeris by a "℞". Retrograde motion is an infusion caused by the relative motion of the earth and the other planets in their elliptical orbits. The Sun and Moon are never retrograde. Opposite of *direct motion.* Mercury has a 20–24 days retrograde period; Venus, 40–43 days; Mars, 58–81 days; Jupiter, 120 days; Saturn, 140 days; Uranus, 155 days; Neptune, 157 days; Pluto, 160 days.

Revolution: Return. The return of the Sun, Moon, or another planet to its natal place. Also, a chart erected for such an event. Used in progressed work. Also, loosely, any orbit or movement describing a circle. The revolutions of the planets are measured in the time taken to circle the Zodiac: the Sun, 1 year; the Moon, 28 days; Mercury, 1 year; Venus, 1 year; Mars, 2 years; Jupiter, 12 years; Saturn, 28–30 years; Uranus, 84 years; Neptune, 165 years; Pluto, 250 years.

Right Ascension: See *Celestial Equator.*

Rising Sign: See *Ascendant.*

Ruling Planet: See *Ascendant, Significator.*

Satellite: A planet or moon that revolves around another. The Moon is a satellite of the earth. Mercury and Venus have no moons; Mars has 2 moons; Jupiter has 12 moons; Saturn has 9 moons; Uranus has 5 moons; Neptune has 2 moons.

Satellitium: Stellium. A cluster or group of three or more planets in one sign or house. Often the focal point of the horoscope.

Secondary Progressions: See *Progressions.*

Separation: The movement of a planet away from another planet, house cusp, or exact aspect. The faster-moving planet *separates* from the aspect with the slower-moving planet and is called the *separator.* A separating aspect is considered weaker than an applying aspect. In horary astrology, a separating aspect corresponds to events just past. It is the opposite of *application,* where a faster-moving planet *applies* to the aspect with a slower-moving planet. See also *application.*

Sextile: See *Aspect.*

Sidereal Time: Time based on the interval between two successive transits of 0° Aries over the upper meridian. One *Sidereal Day* equals 23 hours 56 minutes 4.09 seconds; which is divided into 24 sidereal hours of 60 sidereal minutes each. Sidereal time for noon or midnight for each day is given in the ephemeris and is four minutes later than the previous day.

Sidereal Zodiac: See *Constellations.*

Significator: Ruling planet. Lord. The planet that rules the Ascendant. Also, the planet that rules the horoscope, section of a horoscope, mundane event, area of life, or question in horary astrology. Also, the planet that rules a sign.

> ***The co-significator, or co-ruler:*** is a secondary or equal significator of a horoscope, section of a horoscope, mundane event, or area of life. Also, the traditional rulers of the signs now ruled by the extra-Saturnian planets: Mars is co-ruler of Scorpio together with Pluto; Jupiter is co-ruler of Pisces together with Neptune; Saturn is co-ruler of Aquarius together with Uranus.

Signs: The twelve 30° divisions of the Zodiac, beginning with the position of the Sun at the vernal equinox around March 21, 0° Aries: Aries, Taurus, Gemini, Cancer, Leo, Virgo, Libra, Scorpio, Sagittarius, Capricorn, Aquarius, Pisces.

Singleton: A planet standing alone in a quadrant or hemisphere of the horoscope. A singleton planet often acts as the focal point of the chart.

Sinister Aspect: An aspect in which the faster-moving planet is behind, or has lesser zodiacal longitude than, the aspected planet. This occurs when the aspecting planet is moving toward the slower-moving planet in direct motion, or moving away from it in retrograde motion. Also, loosely, an applying aspect. Opposite of a *dexter aspect.*

Solar System: The Sun with the group of celestial bodies that revolve around it. This group comprises nine planets, attended by 31 satellites, about 1,200 asteroids that revolve in an orbit between that of Mars and Jupiter, and also comets and meteors. In order of increasing distance from the Sun: Mercury, Venus, the earth and Moon, Mars and 2 moons, asteroids, Jupiter and 12 moons, Saturn and 9 moons, Uranus and 5 moons, Neptune and 2 moons, and Pluto.

Solar Tune: See *Local Time.*

Solstice: Standing still. The point in the earth's orbit around the Sun in which the ecliptic reaches its maximum obliquity.

The Summer Solstice: occurs annually around June 22, when the Sun enters Cancer at $23^1/_2°$ N declination, highest overhead in the Northern Hemisphere. The longest day of the year.

The Winter Solstice: occurs annually around December 22, when the Sun enters Capricorn at $23^1/_2°$ S declination, its lowest point in the Northern Hemisphere. The shortest day of the year.

Speculum: A table appended to a horoscope, containing the principal data concerning the horoscope, such as longitude, latitude, declination, right ascension, meridian distance, semi-arc, and ascensional difference of the planets. Used in Primary Directions. A *speculum of aspects* is a table made to show every degree in a horoscope that may be in aspect to the natal planetary positions. Used in transit work.

Square: See *Aspect.*

Standard Time: Clock Time. Zone Time. Agreed upon clock time consistent through the time zone. The *Standard Time Zones* are areas comprising 15° geographical longitude, 1 hour apart.

Stationary: A period in which a planet appears to be motionless just before turning retrograde or direct in motion. When the planet is in its *station.* The Sun and Moon are never stationary. Mercury is stationary for 1 day before and after its retrograde periods; Venus for 2 days; Mars for 3 days; Jupiter for 5 days; Saturn for 5 days; Uranus for 6 days; Neptune for 7 days; Pluto for 7 days.

Stellium: See *Satellitium.*

Succedent Houses: See *Houses.*

Sun Sign: The sign of the Zodiac in which the Sun is located at any given time. The Sun sign can be determined by knowing the day of the year, and is the basis for popular or newspaper astrology.

Superior Conjunction: See *Combust.*

Superior Planets: Ponderous planets. Those whose orbits are on the other side of the earth from the Sun: Mars, Jupiter, Saturn, Uranus, Neptune, and Pluto.

Synastry: The process of comparing two or more horoscopes interpreted in reference to the relationship between the people involved.

Synodic: The period between two successive conjunctions of two planets.

Synodical Lunation: See *Lunation.*

Synthesis: The art of combining the various and often contradictory influences seen in the horoscope, in order to give a balanced interpretation of the whole chart.

Szygy: Yoking together. Three planets in a straight line, such as occurs between the Sun, Moon, and earth during the New Moon and Full Moon. Also, loosely, conjunctions and oppositions.

Tables of Houses: Tables giving the signs and degree for the cusps of houses in a horoscope appropriate to the latitude of birth, according to the Sidereal Time of Birth.

Tables of Diurnal Planetary Motion: Tables that give the distance a planet travels in a given period of time with reference to its daily motion.

Tenancy: The location of a planet in a sign or house.

Terms: Traditional subdivisions of the signs into five sections ruled by different planets, now largely in disuse.

Testimony: Indications seen in a horoscope. The synthesis of several testimonies or arguments constitutes a *judgment*.

Transit: The ephemeral, or ongoing, movement of the planets. The movement of a planet over or in aspect to a sensitive point, planet, or house cusp in a horoscope.

Translation of Light: A situation in which one planet, separating but still within orb of aspect to another planet, applies to an aspect to a third planet, forming a chain in which the influence of the first aspected planet is passed on to the third planet.

Trine: See *Aspect.*

Triplicity: See *Elements.*

Unknown Planets: Hypothetical planets. Eight symbolic indicators in Uranian astrology: Cupido, Hades, Zeus, Kronos, Appolon, Admetos, Vulkanus, and Poseidon. Also, possible actual undiscovered planets, some of which have been hypothesized as Trans-Pluto, Persephone, Lilith, Vulcan, and Arcturus or Psyche.

Vespertine: Stars or planets that set in the evening after the Sun, particularly the Moon (Third Quarter), Mercury, or Venus (occidental) when they appear in the evening. Opposite *of matutine.*

Void of Course: A situation in which a planet will form no more major aspects before leaving the sign in which it is tenanted. Most often applied to the Moon in horary astrology.

War Time: See *Daylight Saving Time.*

Water Signs: See *Elements.*

Zenith: The point directly overhead. A line from any place to its Zenith would always be perpendicular to the plane of its horizon. Often incorrectly applied to the Midheaven. The Midheaven, being on the ecliptic, is south of the Zenith in the Northern Hemisphere. Opposite of *Nadir.*

Zodiac: Tropical Zodiac. Moving Zodiac. Circle of Animals. The circle or band following the path of the ecliptic, extending about 9° on either side of it. Distance along the Zodiac is measured in terms of *zodiacal longitude,* divided into 12 signs of 30° each beginning with the Vernal Equinox Point at 0° Aries. Distance perpendicular to the center of the Zodiac, the ecliptic, is measured in terms of *elliptical* or *celestial latitude,* in degrees north or south of the ecliptic. The Sun has no latitude as its path defines the ecliptic.

Appendix Four

STUDY GUIDE

Part 1: Basic Principles of Astrology

The first section of *Llewellyn's New A to Z Horoscope Maker and Interpreter* is designed to present all the basic building blocks you need to begin working with astrological charts. This section on basic principles is only sixteen pages long, but it is essential to read and study these pages in order to recall the many factors under consideration. The lessons therefore may be repeated, and the basic material should be memorized.

Signs of the Zodiac

- Practice writing the glyphs (symbols for the zodiacal signs and the planets).
- Memorize the order of the signs in the Zodiac.
- How quickly does the degree on the Ascendant change throughout the day?
- Approximately how many different astrological types exist?
- What is the role of free will in astrology?
- Which signs fall in the fire element? Earth? Air? Water? What are the characteristics of each element?
- List the signs in each mode: cardinal, fixed, and mutable. What are the characteristics of each mode?

• List the signs and the glyphs. Next to each, list the sign and glyph for the first, second, and third decanate of the sign.

The Planets

Using the blank chart in appendix 1:

• Enter the house numbers in the innermost circle.

• Enter the signs in order, beginning with Aries on the Ascendant.

• In the inner house segment of the chart, write the glyphs for the sign ruler; also write the glyph for the planet that is exalted in that sign, if any. Make a note of the exalted planet (E) next to it.

• In the outer segment of each house, write the glyphs for planets that are in detriment and fall. Write (D) and (F) next to each.

• Write a brief definition for domicile, detriment, exaltation, and fall.

• Note on the chart the areas of the "hyleg." Shade them in a different color.

• Write a brief statement of how you will determine the strength of the planets in the chart. (Hint: You should have at least five considerations.)

The Houses

In another blank chart, or in a simple list, make notes about the houses:

• Note which houses are angular, succedent, and cadent. List one or two words about what each of these terms means.

• List the parts of the body related to each house.

• List the areas of life related to each house.

You may want to keep notes in a loose-leaf notebook as you study each chapter.

The Aspects

The relationships among the planets form the key to accurate chart interpretation. These relationships are called aspects.

• List the basic aspects, and the number of degrees for each.

• From what point in the chart are the angular relationships (aspects) measured?

• List the quality of each aspect. What is each aspect's nature?

• How do the signs, houses, planets, and aspects work together? (Hint: The answer to this question can only be found through an extended study. However, you should be able, at this early point in your studies, to write a basic statement of how the parts of the astrological chart are related to each other. The definition you write here will no doubt change as you learn more about astrology.)

Part 2: Interpreting the Horoscope

This section of the book contains the essentials of delineation of the birth chart. Regardless of anything else you may do with astrology, the birth chart will always be the key. Thus, understanding the many concepts presented in these chapters will provide a solid foundation for delineation of any kind.

You may find it useful to calculate or to obtain charts for a number of individuals you know well, or for famous individuals. Family members and close friends are good to study because you know a great deal about them, and can confirm astrological indicators more readily. You may wish to use the following study guides as you work with each chart, refining your knowledge and understanding of the numerous astrological indicators you find.

To obtain birth charts, you may wish to find an Internet site that provides them. Many New Age bookstores have a computer chart service that you can use. If you have a computer, you can download freeware or shareware to produce charts. One excellent free program can be obtained from Cosmic Patterns from their website. You can also order astrological charts or software directly from Llewellyn (see the contact information in the front of this book, or in the information at the back of the book).

You can take each lesson, one step at a time, considering several charts. An alternative is to follow one chart through all the chapters in this section, finding and recording significant information as you go. Then you can take a second chart, and a third chart, and explore them in the same manner. The first method has the advantage of deepening your understanding of one factor at a time. The second has the advantage of assuaging your curiosity about your own chart, or that of an important family member, associate, or celebrity. Either way, you will learn best by using concrete examples.

Introduction to Horoscope Interpretation

This chapter outlines one approach to chart delineation.

1. Using your study birth charts, examine the Sun, Ascendant, Moon, and Mercury, and Significator in each chart. Make notes:

   • The sign each occupies.
   • Exaltation, detriment, or fall.
   • Aspects to or from other planets and angles.
   • The house placement of each planet.

Then consider the remaining planets in the same way. You can look ahead to find specific delineations as you work with each chart. Following the outline in this chapter will always be helpful in exploring a chart fully. Make notes about your conclusions about each planet.

2. Now consider the list of features of the horoscope. Evaluate each feature according to the rules given. Make notes to summarize your findings. Especially note areas that you can strongly confirm through knowledge of the subject, or areas that you cannot confirm, or that you feel are inaccurate.

3. Consider your conclusions. Can you explain why some things fit the individual whose chart you are examining, and why some do not?

The Signs

To study and learn the material in this chapter, organized notes are important. For each sign, designate a page in a loose-leaf notebook. As you read, and as you study each chart, make notes for the different things associated with each sign. These may include parts of the body, stars, constellations, locations, associations, desirable characteristics, undesirable characteristics, etc.

You may also want to include notes about individuals whose charts have planets in each sign, and qualities that you associate strongly with those people. Some of the items you note will come to make more sense to you, while others may not fit with what you know. Don't accept every word as gospel. Instead, make intelligent judgments about what you read, in this or any other astrology book. Compile information from a variety of sources, keeping in mind that you will evaluate what writers say, and determine whether it fits with your understanding of the signs (or other astrological factors).

The Ascendants and the Midheavens

It is suggested that the student consider the Ascendants and the Midheavens together because the angles of the chart are part of one system. The location of the Midheaven determines, for the most part, the location of the Ascendant, and vice versa. The only variations occur because of the latitude of the birth place.

- In your study of birth charts, consider the Ascendant and its indications of personality, physical appearance, and mental tendencies.
- Consider the Midheaven and its indications for career and self-awareness.
- Consider how the particular Ascendant and Midheaven work together, based on whether the Midheaven is inclined toward or away from the Ascendant.
- Add this information to what you already know about the individual. Does it change your earlier assessment in any way?

The Planets

This chapter includes rich material about those things related to each planet. The student will want to read and reread this chapter, and may choose to memorize part or all of the lists.

- In your loose-leaf notebook, on pages prepared for the planets, make notes of those concepts that seem particularly meaningful to you.
- If you think of categories other than the three provided, create new ones that will help you understand the main expressions of each planet's energy.

This material should become part of your memory, so you can look at each chart from the broadest possible perspective.

The Planets in the Signs

Here you begin the serious work of integrating various chart factors. The planets are the actors, and the signs are the stage upon which they act. The fieriest planet will fizzle on a wet, rainy stage, and the most grounded energy will float away in an airy atmosphere. The signs definitely color the action of the planets.

- As you read this chapter, take note of the placements of planets that make the most sense to you. Also note areas where the combinations seem strange or unworkable.
- Using your study charts, make notes of the combinations of planet and sign in each chart. Which combinations seem likely to produce strong, positive results? Which planets seem weak? Does this information correspond with what you know of each person? Why or why not?
- How does a planet act differently in its sign of detriment? In its fall?
- Is the exaltation planet of a sign always a good thing?
- Looking at the planets in the signs, try to determine which single planet is the strongest in each chart, and which is the weakest.

The Planets in the Houses

Llewellyn George makes the point that the student cannot actually interpret the planets in the houses without also considering the sign it occupies and the aspects it makes. This point cannot be overemphasized. However, in the process of learning, it is helpful to gain an understanding of the roles of the planets in each house, without being concerned about signs and aspects.

- Using your study charts, consider the Sun in the houses. How will the Sun seem different in each chart? Consider each of the planets in the houses in the same way.
- In your loose-leaf notebook, in the pages for planets, make notes about the planets in each house, as you find them in your study charts.
- In your loose-leaf notebook, in the pages for the houses, make notes about each planet you encounter in your study charts.

Eventually, when you have examined a number of charts, you will have a nearly complete set of notes for the planets in each house.

Interpreting the Aspects

Aspects provide the backbone for all interpretation and forecasting. Learning how to identify aspects in charts, and how to interpret them, will be a large part of the student's work.

- Which aspects are considered good, beneficial?
- Which aspects are considered bad, adverse?

- What is the true nature of the aspects? The individual's response to them?
- What does "platic" mean?
- What does "partile" mean?
- Describe "applying" and "separating" aspects.
- What do the words "sinister" and "dexter" mean? How are they related to aspects?
- What is the significance of the house placement of planets that aspect each other?
- What are the two most important questions concerning aspects?
- In general, which aspect is the most significant? Why?

Planetary House Rulers

- How do you determine the planetary house ruler?
- What is the difference between the planetary house ruler and a planet occupying the house? Which is more significant in interpretation? Why?
- Where does a planet express itself best, in terms of house?
- What branch of astrology uses planetary house rulerships the most?

The Part of Fortune and the Moon's Nodes

- What is the Part of Fortune? How do you find it in the chart?
- Describe the general significance of the house placement of the Part of Fortune.
- What are the Moon's Nodes?
- What is the house significance of the Nodes?

Part 3: Advanced Techniques

The Progressed Chart

This chapter describes the theory of secondary progressions and discusses the effect of a change of residence on the progressed chart. The questions listed here are designed to help the student assimilate the concepts involved.

- Why are the positions of the planets at birth a permanent picture of the possibilities of the individual?
- What is the basic reason for using secondary (day-for-a-year) progressions?
- Describe the movement of the birth planets through the progressed chart.
- Describe the movement of the progressed planets through the birth chart.
- Why don't we relocate the progressed chart?

Transits

The consideration of transits is integral to forecasting. Transits indicate the moments in time when potentials in the birth chart are released. Secondary progressions indicate periods of time when this release is most likely, but transits act to trigger events.

- What orb of influence is recommended for transiting planets?
- What is the approximate speed of each planet as it transits through a chart?
- Describe the difference between a transit of Neptune (or any outer planet) and Mercury (or any inner planet).
- Describe the effect of a transiting conjunction, as compared to other aspects.
- What is the advantage of knowing the declinations of natal, progressed, or transiting planets?
- What is the effect of a planet when it retrogrades to form an aspect the second time?
- Try the recommended method for tracking aspects given in appendix 1. Prepare your list of degrees for each natal planet in a chart, considering the five basic aspects: the conjunction (this one is obvious), opposition, sextile, square, and trine. Then examine the ephemeris page for September, 2001, given in appendix 1. See if there were any aspects to planets in your study chart.
- Using an astrological calendar or datebook, or the current ephemeris, track the movement of the Moon for several months. Note its aspects to planets in your own chart, and keep a journal of notes concerning any effects you notice concerning daily activities, emotional shifts, etc.
- What is the scientific evidence for an effect of an apparently retrograde planet?

Example Progressed Horoscope

The techniques used to interpret secondary progressions and transits are basically the same. One difference is the duration of each aspect. Progressed aspects may be within 1 degree of orb for many years, while transits are much faster. The complicated part is the consideration of the many relationships formed by progression and transit.

Interpreting Progressed Aspects

Using the example from the previous lesson, and using the information in this chapter, make notes concerning the natal chart for September 11, 2001, and the potential events for September 11, 2012. You will find the birth chart and progressed chart in appendix 1.

Do the same exercise with your other study charts, selecting the current date, or a date of your choice. It could be the date of an event that occurred in the past.

- What differences in interpretation do you find between the natal chart and progressions?
- What is the time limit on an aspect in the birth chart? The progressed chart? A transit?
- What is the prerequisite for significance for a progressed aspect?

Interpreting Transits

Fine-tuning the delineation of progressions and transits is one key to understanding astrology at the deepest level. Practice is the only way to reach this understanding. The more charts you consider, and the more dates you use for progressions and transits, the better your delineations will be. The previous lesson concerning transits provided the outline for their study.

- What is the most significant difference in the calculation of progressions and transits?
- What is the meaning of transiting aspects to transiting planets? Do these transiting aspects have an effect on the individual? How does the individual experience such a transit?
- What is the effect on you personally if a transiting planet aspects planets in the chart of a family member or acquaintance?
- Explain why there must be indications in the birth horoscope, the progressions, *and* the transits in order for an event to occur.

Part 4: Contemporary Developments in Astrology

Part 4 of *Llewellyn's New A to Z Horoscope Maker and Interpreter* takes you beyond traditional astrological charting of the natal chart. It encompasses other branches of astrology, as well as techniques to enhance your work with birth charts.

Rectification

- What does the term "rectification" mean?
- When is it necessary to adjust the birth time?
- What approach might you take if no birth time is known?
- Why is the progressed Moon a good tool to use in rectification?
- How do you use the progressed Moon to narrow down the birth time?
- What is the role of the Ascendant and Midheaven in rectification?
- What part of the birth chart is most affected by changing the birth time?
- Using the chart of an individual who is unsure of the birth time, and using the instructions in this chapter, cast several charts for possible birth times, and calculate the progressed Moon in each.
- With a list of events that have occurred in the life, determine which birth time gives the more appropriate and exact progressed lunar aspects.
- Recalculate the birth chart using this time, and progress the chart for several dates of events.
- Identify progressed aspects involving the Midheaven and Ascendant. This may include progressed Midheaven and Ascendant aspects to the birth chart.

- Also calculate transits for each date.
- Do your results seem valid? That is, does the new birth time reflect appropriate aspects of the progressed Moon, as well as natal and progressed Midheaven and Ascendant, for the time of each event?
- Go back as needed to adjust the time.

The Locality Chart

People are always moving from one place to another, whether it be across town or across the country. Careful examination of the locality chart can help smooth the way for such moves. Mapping techniques make locality work much simpler. However, there are basic charting techniques that can be implemented without the use of maps.

As a reminder, when you calculated the birth chart, you arrived at a value called the Sidereal Birth Time in Greenwich. Using this time, you can add or subtract the longitude equivalent for any location on earth, thereby arriving at the True Sidereal Birth Time for that location. This is the time to use to calculate house cusps for that location.

- Recalculate your chart for the place where you are presently living, if it is different from the place where you were born. Or select a place where you would consider living, and recalculate your chart for that location.
- Notice which planets change house position.
- Delineate these changes in house position. What differences in emphasis do you find? Which areas of life are more influential? Less influential?
- Keeping in mind that the birth chart is still the most important chart, consider the differences you found, or might find, in living at the new location.

Heliocentric Astrology

The Sun-centered chart (heliocentric chart) provides you with a picture of your birth time, from the perspective of the Sun.

- How do the planets change position in your heliocentric chart?
- What is the relationship between Mercury and Venus?
- How does the heliocentric chart change your thinking about your relationship to all other beings born at the same time as yourself?
- Does the heliocentric chart give you any thoughts about how you may pursue your life differently?

Chiron and the Major Asteroids

These five additional objects are worthy of study. The material presented here is only the briefest introduction to their qualities.

- Where are Chiron and the asteroids located in your chart?
- Study the glyphs and their meanings.
- Do these objects form significant aspects or aspect patterns in your chart?
- How do the asteroids expand your understanding of your conscious or unconscious feminine nature?
- What are the four feminine roles associated with each asteroid? How are they different from each other?
- How does Chiron amplify your understanding of any personal wounding?

Transneptunians

Follow the same outline for Chiron and the asteroids for study of the Transneptunians. In addition, consider the transpersonal values associated with these points.

- What higher values do the Transneptunians represent?
- Which of these points is significant in your chart? In your study charts?
- The Transneptunians move very slowly. How will that affect delineation?

Cosmobiology

Cosmobiology is an entire system for delineation, and can be used separately from traditional astrological techniques. Some of the techniques can also be used in conjunction with traditional astrology.

- What is a midpoint?
- What is the value of the 90° dial?
- How do solar arc directions work? What is a solar arc?
- How do graphs help you understand the motion of the planets through the Zodiac?
- Why are some of the lines on the graph not straight?
- What is the significance of a sloping line that slopes upward instead of downward?
- Compare the midpoints in a tree (structure pattern) with aspects. Are different planets emphasized?

The study of cosmobiology, like many of the techniques in part 4 of this book, can take months or years to complete. You will want to find books that explore the techniques in much greater depth, if these areas of astrology are of particular interest.

Composite and Relationship Charts

Chart comparison is one of the biggest interest areas in astrology. Compatibility questions are central to relationship counseling, perhaps the largest single topic on astrological counseling.

- What is synastry?
- Why is one individual's chart actually a transit to another person's chart?
- Name a few of the main considerations in chart comparison.
- Name and explain two other ways of comparing the charts of individuals.
- Which method feels "right" to you? Do you know why?
- Practice comparing charts. Use very narrow orbs—1 degree at first.
- Why do you use such narrow orbs? (Hint: One chart is a transit to the other.)

Chart Patterns

This section briefly introduces the topic of patterns. Through study, you will identify which patterns work in your chart and your study charts.

- How do the names of the "picture" patterns describe the energy of charts that have each pattern?
- Describe two differences between the Grand Trine and the Grand Square. How do these differences reflect the nature of each pattern?
- The patterns considered here each focus on a specific harmonic (the aspects divide the 360° circle harmonically). How do the aspects themselves reflect the nature of the harmonic? (Hint: A square, 90°, is one-fourth of a circle, while a trine is one-third, and a sextile is one-sixth.)
- Do you find other patterns in your chart that seem important? Do they follow a harmonic pattern, or are they irregular shapes? Do your other study charts include similar patterns?

Return Charts

Many people have heard about the Saturn Return, which occurs around age twenty-eight to thirty. We observe the Solar Return each year at the time of our birthday. We also observe the Lunar Return, even if we don't know anything about astrology, because of lunar phases.

- How does the return of each planet mark a point in time with regard to that planet's energy?
- Which planets move too slowly for us to experience an actual return?
- What is the phase angle between any two planets? That is, how do you find the phase angle between two planets?
- What is the significance of the phase angle between the Sun and Moon?

- What other phase angles are important? Why?

Esoteric and Psychological Astrology

- What is the potential value of considering esoteric astrology?
- What chart factors are used most often in esoteric astrology?
- What is the value of the psychological approach to astrology? Is this an approach you might use often? Never?

Horary and Mundane Astrology

These studies take us away from the realm of natal astrology. They use charts to answer questions, or to forecast events on the larger social, political, and geophysical levels. Astrologers are often called upon to answer specific questions. We also are often curious about the weather, the economy, or other cycles occurring outside ourselves.

- How is a horary chart cast? Is it different from a birth chart?
- What dates are usually used in casting mundane charts?
- What chart factor is used to identify the part of the chart related to a specific question?
- Where in the horary chart do you find the person asking the question?
- Do the houses take on different significance in the horary chart? A mundane chart?
- What is the significance of the movement of the Moon in horary charts?
- What is the significance of lunar phases in mundane charts?

Other Branches of Astrology

Astrology developed in many areas of the world. Cultural differences are reflected in the different styles of astrology.

- What is the astronomical focus of each of the different astrologies discussed in this chapter?
- Which of these systems resonates with you personally?

Declination and Declination Graphs

The declination graph is a visual aid to understanding the relationships of planets that is different from longitude. Parallel aspects are calculated using declination.

- Why are all declination graphs essentially the same shape, even though the planets are in different places? (Hint: Think about the definition of right ascension, which is one of the coordinates on the graph.)
- How close do planets need to be to be considered parallel?

- What does the term "out of bounds" mean?

House Systems

There are many ways of looking at the heavens, and of dividing them into houses. Each system has a specific rationale.

- Why does one's birthplace perspective matter in astrology?
- Does one system seem more pleasing to you mathematically?
- What is the importance of intermediate house cusps in delineation?
- Cosmobiology does not use intermediate cusps. This means the system does not use houses. Does this approach to astrology make sense to you? Why or why not?

Fixed Stars

As the background of the heavens, including the Zodiac, the fixed stars are markers used to determine the seasons, and one's location on the planet. For example "dog days" is a term used to describe the period of summer when the Dog Star, Sirius, rises with the Sun.

- Are any of the fixed stars listed here conjunct your natal planets?
- If so, does the nature of the fixed star seem consistent with how you experience yourself?
- Is there a star or constellation that feels more meaningful to you?
- Can you identify constellations in the sky at night? You may want to get an astronomy book and learn about them.

Mythology of Planets

- Do the myths of each planet add to your understanding of their energies?
- You may want to read more about mythology and relate it to what you are learning about astrology. The art of storytelling is one of the astrologer's counseling skills, and myths provide easily recognizable stories about each planet, reflecting its energy vividly.
- Considering one aspect in your chart, create a mythical story involving the gods and goddesses of the two planets. Allow your characters to act out their personalities, as described in the myths.

Health Considerations

This book is in no way a substitute for appropriate medical care. Consult with your physician or other healthcare provider before using the herbs and other remedies listed here.

- In the birth chart, how do planetary placements relate to health?

- Which houses are most significant when considering health questions?
- How do the signs relate to health?

Final Exercise: Calculating and Interpreting a Birth Chart

Take plenty of time on this study. Work out one point at a time and do it thoroughly and completely. When delineating your own chart, do not read it simply from what you know of yourself, but hold fast to the principles and procedures already outlined.

- Make a horoscope for a person you know, following the directions given in appendix 1.
- Using the blank chart form and grid given in appendix 1, list the aspects in the natal chart. If necessary, reread the instructions on how to identify aspects quickly and easily.
- Practice finding aspects on your own for your study charts, and compare your results with computer printouts. Did you find/miss any aspects?
- Practice reading the aspects in printouts. (Note: Each astrology program prints the aspects slightly differently, so you will need to familiarize yourself with a new form.)
- Use a systematic approach to be sure you find all the aspects. One such method is to do each planet in order on the form you are using. Another approach is to consider the planets in order in the particular chart, beginning at the Ascendant.
- As you find the aspects, you will begin to see which aspects are occurring more frequently. This will suggest the general nature of the individual's approach to life.
- Work through the details of aspect interpretation.
- Consider the mathematical techniques for astrological calculations. For some of these you can obtain the necessary charts on the Internet, or your local New Age or metaphysical bookstore may have a computer program. You may want to consider purchasing an astrology program to handle these calculations.

In the preceding chapters and lessons, you acquired information about the various elements constituting a horoscope. You learned of the tendencies bestowed by the signs, how the planets stir those tendencies into characteristic action, and how their indications are modified according to the house occupied, by dignity or debility and especially their aspects. You learned what matters are embraced in each of the twelve houses of a chart; how the zodiacal signs add their special influence to the house and planet. Throughout the book, you have been guided concerning how to correlate these elements in delineating a chart.

If you find it difficult to compile the notes, turn back to the preceding chapters and study everything related to the influences and indications employed in horoscope reading, as already mentioned.

No instructor or book can give the student the ability to synthesize a chart, but the proper procedure can be outlined to develop this needed faculty. The art of synthesis is like good judgment or intuition: it cannot be handed from one to another; it is *a growth within the person,* an expansion of knowledge, as a result of careful study of authentic texts, assimilation of the information thus acquired, and application of the principles thus learned.

INDEX

For readers of

Llewellyn's New A to Z Horoscope Maker and Interpreter

only

FREE Birth Chart Offer

Thank you for purchasing *Llewellyn's New A to Z Horoscope Maker and Interpreter*. There are a number of ways to construct a chart wheel. The easiest way, of course, is by computer, and that's why we are giving you this one-time offer of a free birth chart. This extremely accurate chart will provide you with a great deal of information about yourself. Once you receive a chart from us, *Llewellyn's New A to Z Horoscope Maker and Interpreter* will provide everything you need to know to interpret your chart.

Also, by ordering your free chart, you will be enrolled in Llewellyn's Birthday Club! From now on, you can get any of Llewellyn's astrology reports for 25% off when you order within one month of your birthday! Just write "Birthday Club" on your order form or mention it when ordering by phone. As if that wasn't enough, we will mail you a FREE copy of our fresh new book *What Astrology Can Do for You!* Go for it!

Complete this form with your accurate birth data and mail it to us today. Enjoy your adventure in self-discovery through astrology!

Do not photocopy this form. Only this original will be accepted.

Please Print

Full Name:_____

Mailing Address:_____

City, State, Zip:_____

Birth time:_____ A.M. P.M. (please circle)

Month:_____ Day:_____ Year:_____

Birthplace (city, county, state, country):

_____

_____

Check your birth certificate for the most accurate information.

**Complete and mail this form to: Llewellyn Publications, Special Chart Offer,
P.O. Box 64383, 0-7387-0322-2, St. Paul, MN 55164.**

Allow 4–6 weeks for delivery.

Mapping Your Birthchart
Understanding Your Needs & Potential

STEPHANIE JEAN CLEMENT, PH.D.

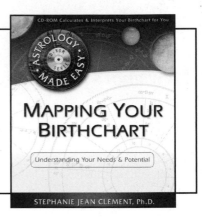

CD-ROM calculates & interprets your birthchart for you

Become your own astrologer.

You know your "sign," but that's just the tip of the astrological iceberg. You've got a Moon sign, a rising sign, and loads of other factors in your astrological makeup. Together they form the complete picture of you as an individual: your desires, talents, emotions . . . and your public persona and your private needs.

Mapping Your Birthchart removes the mystery from astrology so you can look at any chart and get a basic understanding of the person behind it. Learn the importance of the planets, the different signs of the zodiac, and how they relate to your everyday life. A free CD-ROM is included in the book so you can print out astrological reports and charts for yourself, your family, and friends.

- Includes a CD-ROM that calculates and interprets your birthchart for you
- Introduces the basics of the astrology chart
- Devotes a chapter to each planet, with information about signs, houses, and aspects
- Provides simple explanations of astrological and psychological factors
- Includes examples from the charts of well-known people including Tiger Woods, Celine Dion, and George W. Bush

0-7387-0202-1, 240 pp., 7½ x 9⅛   **$19.95**
index, glossary and appendix

To order, call 1-877-NEW-WRLD
Prices subject to change without notice